COMMERCE Made Simple

The Made Simple series
has been created
primarily for self-education
but can equally well
be used as
an aid to group study.
However complex the subject,
the reader is taken
step by step,
clearly and methodically,
through the course. Each volume
has been prepared by
experts,
using throughout the
Made Simple technique of teaching.
Consequently the gaining
of knowledge now becomes
an experience to be enjoyed.

COMMERCE Made Simple

G. M. Whitehead, B.Sc. (Econ.)

Made Simple Books
W. H. ALLEN London
A Howard & Wyndham Company

© W. H. Allen & Co. Ltd., 1969

Made and printed in Great Britain
by Richard Clay (The Chaucer Press), Ltd, Bungay, Suffolk
for the publishers W. H. Allen & Company Ltd,
44 Hill Street, London, W1X 8LB

First edition May, 1969
Reprinted February, 1971
Second (revised) edition March, 1972
Third (revised) edition January, 1973
Fourth (revised) edition February, 1974
Reprinted January, 1975
Fifth (revised) edition October, 1975
Sixth (revised) edition October, 1976

ISBN 0 491 01890 8 paperback

Preface

This book covers all the basic commercial activities in modern free-enterprise societies. It explains simply and clearly the activities performed by wholesalers, retailers, importers and exporters in the distribution and exchange of goods. The activities of bankers, insurance companies and transport organizations are fully described, and the important aspects of communications are discussed.

Although principally designed for self-study, the book is of equal value to schools and colleges. Teachers and lecturers will find that it meets their requirements for the Ordinary Level Examinations of the University Examination Boards, the Certificate of Secondary Education, the Certificate in Office Studies, the commercial aspects of the first-year Economics syllabuses of the Ordinary National Certificate and Ordinary National Diploma in Business Studies of the Department of Education and Science.

The frequency with which new editions of this book have been required has enabled the text to be revised to take account of the many developments in commerce. In this 1976 revision the chapter on Export Trade has been up-dated, and documentation which takes account of changes in V.A.T. has been included. The 1971 Census of Distribution figures are now available and the chapters on Retail Trade have been accordingly revised.

In revising and up-dating this book I have received much help from firms, institutions and individuals. I must thank them most sincerely for their unfailing co-operation. A full list of their names appears on the next page, but I should particularly like to mention the helpful advice of Mr. Leslie Basford and Mr. Alfred Marr whose detailed comments on the typescript were invaluable.

GEOFFREY WHITEHEAD

Acknowledgments

The assistance of the following individuals, firms and institutions is most gratefully acknowledged:

The Bank of England
Mr. E. N. Hanley of Allen, Harvey and Ross Ltd.
Barclays Bank Ltd.
The Council of the London Stock Exchange
The Corporation of Lloyds
The Council of the Baltic Exchange
The Accepting Houses Committee
The British Insurance Association
The Board of Trade
The London Commodity Exchange Co. Ltd.
The Department of Trade and Industry
The Co-operative Union
Olivetti Ltd.
F. W. Woolworth and Co. Ltd.
Lamson Paragon Ltd.
Wallwork Gears Ltd.
The Port of London Authority
G-Plan Ltd.
Cerebos Foods Ltd.
The Bankers' Clearing House
Willik Bros. Ltd.
National Cash Register Co. Ltd.
Mr. G. Jenkins, Thurrock Technical College
The Museum of Natural History, Paris
The University of London
The Royal Society of Arts
The Associated Examining Board
The East Anglian Examination Board

The views expressed and statements made in this book are entirely my own responsibility and do not represent the views of any official body, or any individual named above.

G. W.

Table of Contents

CHAPTER ONE

COMMERCE IN THE FRAMEWORK OF PRODUCTION

(1) Introduction

There are 3,000 million people in the world today, and we can say with certainty that they want things, from the cradle to the grave. It doesn't make any difference whether you were born an Englishman or an Eskimo, a Mexican or a Russian, you were crying for milk before many hours had gone by. All your life you will be wanting things: drinks when you are thirsty, food when you are hungry, clothes when you are cold and shelter in bad weather.

Different races all over the world have learned how to satisfy their wants in different ways. Some men are hunters, some raise crops, some fish, some breed cattle; the most developed races have discovered complex methods of doing all these things so that output rises and they become more wealthy. Today we plough fields with giant tractors and sow seeds with supplies of artificial fertilizer alongside to increase the yield of the crops. We harvest with combine harvesters and use the crops to feed cattle, poultry, and pigs. We then use the wide variety of foods we have produced to make an even greater variety of prepared foods. Similarly we produce a huge range of natural and synthetic fibres for clothing, while a vast array of sophisticated technical products satisfies our wants in other ways.

(2) The Basic Wants of Mankind

The six elementary wants of mankind are food, water, clothing, shelter, land, and medical care. Most of these are obvious, but the inclusion of land is worth a moment's discussion. As we are earth-bound creatures, everyone must have somewhere to live, some geographical spot that can be called home.

Nothing reduces a people to a condition of poverty more rapidly than to be driven off their land by some natural or man-made disaster. Conversely history is full of examples of the sudden expansions of particular races at the expense of their neighbours, because of some technological advance which enabled them to overrun the land of others. The hordes of Gengis Khan are a famous example.

If he has the six essentials, man prospers and raises a family; if he is unable to secure them, family life is abandoned. It is not only unfortunate primitive people who behave in this way: even highly civilized

1

people, faced with a change in their circumstances, abandon the moral
and ethical codes of civilization.

One author, describing an early wagon train bound for California in
1846, speaks of the accelerating pace of the collapse of the emigrants'
moral code. When the first man died they waited a full day in reverent
respect, burying him in a well-made coffin. When the next one died they
just dug a hole and put a board over the body. Later, they left the dead
unburied. Later still they abandoned the living who could not keep up.
Trapped in the mountains, men fought each other for food for their
families. Strong men pushed on to get help; strong women left their
children behind them to try to get through to California. Those left behind turned to cannabalism, eating Red Indians first, then dead white
people.

If we are to understand commerce we must see it as part of man's
natural drive to provide himself with his basic wants.

(3) The Sophisticated Wants of an Advanced Society

Professor Galbraith, an American lecturer in economics, has called
our type of society 'The Affluent Society'. Affluence is wealth, and there
can be little doubt that Western civilization today is wealthier than any
previous civilization. We have more material things, more useful goods,
than any civilization before us; yet we can still think of things we wish
we had.

Some of us want to be trend-setters in fashion, others want washing
machines, colour TV, transistor radios, tape-recorders, and record
players. The very rich want swimming-pools or tennis courts in their
gardens; they want to water-ski or to own two or three cars as status
symbols.

In fact human wants never decrease even among the wealthiest people
or nations. It has been truthfully said that 'appetite grows with feeding'.

(4) Goods and Services

All the wants of mankind can be classified under the headings of
either 'goods' or 'services'. Goods are tangible things such as clothes,
motor vehicles, furniture, etc. Services are intangible things such as
education and entertainment. If we are to have our wants satisfied as
fully as possible, we must provide for ourselves both the material goods
that we need to lead a happy and contented life, and the less tangible,
but equally important, services. The provision of goods and services is
called **production.**

(5) Satisfying Human Wants—Methods of Production

There are two methods of production: direct and indirect production. Direct production occurs where man satisfies his wants entirely

unaided by other people. Indirect production occurs when we co-operate with other people in the production of the goods and services we need.

(6) Direct Production—Satisfying our Wants Entirely Unaided by Other People

Robinson Crusoe was a versatile character. Cast away on a desert island, forced to do everything for himself, he succeeded in building a house, taming a flock of goats, hunting, fishing, and farming to supply his daily needs, and making a friend of Man Friday.

Many people have pointed out how unlikely it would be for a cast-away to find so many useful articles saved from the wreck of his vessel. Crusoe had not only a gun, powder and shot, sails and needles, but also a box of tools, some chickens, pigs, and a cat as a companion. Robinson Crusoe's method of satisfying his wants is an example of **direct production**. Direct production is the name economists give to production entirely unaided by other people—although Robinson Crusoe did cheat by starting off with a useful supply of things others had made for him.

Some years ago an American student attempted to improve upon Robinson Crusoe's efforts, by trying to support himself by his own efforts for one year in the woods. He entered the woods wearing only a pair of shorts, and emerged one year later more dead than alive.

He had found by a whole year of ceaseless struggle just how difficult it is for a man to satisfy his wants entirely unaided by other people. Three days after entering the wood he secured his first meal—by braining a rabbit with a club he had torn from a tree. He had been forced to sit for hours by a rabbit hole in the hopes that a meal would emerge. He had found it difficult, because of his preoccupation with food, to obtain shelter and clothing. He had been taken ill and barely survived. His efforts at producing directly for himself had been singularly unsuccessful, yet he was one of the more intelligent members of his year, and he had the experience of civilized man to draw upon.

This production of goods entirely unaided by other people is a very inefficient form of production, for the producer has to leave one task to perform another urgent one before he has really mastered the first.

People who do satisfy their wants entirely by their own efforts, e.g. the Eskimos of northern Canada and the Fuegians of Tierra del Fuego, are nearly always very poor. They are chiefly preoccupied with finding food; their shelter is quickly contrived from what Nature has provided —a cave or snow hut. They are liable to be killed off by the slightest piece of hard luck, such as a blizzard that prevents them hunting, or a sudden thaw that traps them on a lonely ice floe. Darwin found that the Fuegians, in hard times, killed off and ate the old women. They had dogs, but these were more valuable than the old women, who were forced to accept this useful end to their lives.

Fig. 1 shows a typical Fuegian as Darwin described him in his book *The Voyage of H.M.S. Beagle*. Tierra del Fuego, the tip of Cape Horn, has one of the most bitter climates in the world. The mantle of seal skin is this man's only protection against the weather.

Such primitive races have no commerce, because they have nothing to trade with other tribes.

Direct production is practised hardly anywhere in the world today.

Fig. 1. A typical Fuegian with primitive seal-skin mantle

The quantity of goods that can be obtained in this way is so small that direct producers are always poor.

(7) Indirect Production—Producing by Specialization

We have seen that direct production generally results in poverty. Man quickly finds that working together gives better results, chiefly because people can specialize. The best hunters go hunting, the best anglers fish, the best potter makes pots for the whole village, and so on. The fruits of their labour are then shared so that all are satisfied, and all enjoy a higher standard of living.

Commerce really begins with such simple societies, for any surplus left over after all the tribe has been supplied can be exchanged with 'foreigners' from other tribes. This extra output achieved by specialization results in extra wealth. The tribesmen are no longer producing directly for themselves: they are producing indirectly.

Modern Advanced Societies

All the advanced nations have highly complex social organizations which enable people to live together in a secure atmosphere, helping one another. In these societies, people do not build their own houses, grow their own food, make their own clothes, or defend themselves against law-breakers. Experts are appointed to do certain jobs and work exclusively in them. The most gifted people become scientists, research workers, administrators or university professors. Their knowledge becomes so highly specialized that few ordinary people can understand what they are talking about.

Below this range of gifted people the types of task performed grade off into less and less skilled work. The least able people still find useful work to perform, for the range of human wants is endless. The humble worker who keeps the factory clean, for example, is performing useful work even though he has no special gifts.

A great British economist, Adam Smith, investigated the way in which nations become wealthy. In his famous book, *The Wealth of Nations*, his inquiries led him to conclude that wealth came from specialization. Smith studied the methods of production used in the pin trade and said:

A man not educated to this business could scarcely perhaps with his utmost industry make one pin a day, and certainly could not make twenty . . . . But in the way this trade is carried on it is divided into a number of branches, of which the greater part are likewise peculiar trades. One man draws out the wire, another straights it, a third cuts it, a fourth points it, a fifth grinds it at the top (for receiving of the head). To make the head requires two or three distinct operations. To put it on is a peculiar business, to whiten the pins is another. It is even a trade by itself to put them into the paper, and the important business of making a pin is divided in this way into eighteen different processes, which in some manufactories are all performed by distinct hands.

I have seen a small manufactory of this kind where ten men only were employed, and where some of them consequently performed two or three distinct operations. But although they were very poor, and therefore but indifferently accommodated with the necessary machinery they could, when they exerted themselves, make among them twelve pounds of pins a day. There are in a pound upwards of 4,000 pins of a middling size. Each person, therefore, could make one-tenth of 48,000 pins in a day. But if they had wrought separately, without having been educated to this peculiar business, they certainly could not have each made twenty, and possibly not even one.

Britain is still a leader in the manufacture of pins, but the processes have been largely mechanized. A modern pin-making machine heads, cuts and points the wire automatically. It makes about 500–600 pins per minute and about 250–300 tons are made every year in about 20 different sizes. To market this enormous output of about 2½ billion pins, the manufacturers need a world-wide market, and pins are exported by Britain to many countries, including the United States of America, which buys about one-fifth of the total.

Adam Smith found the advantages of specialization to be those shown below.

(8) The Advantages of Specialization

The five main advantages of specialization which lead to the production of increased wealth are:

(*a*) People choose the work they like.
(*b*) They save time by using the same equipment all day.
(*c*) The specialist becomes more skilled because of repetition.
(*d*) He invents special tools.
(*e*) These tools can be mechanized, and speeded up.

Some explanation of these points is desirable.

(*a*) *People choose the work they like.* Everyone has some sort of natural inclination; one man likes to lead, to assume responsibility, another likes routine work. If people are allowed to choose freely they will generally find work that appeals to them; they will take steps to master the necessary skills and work hard. This hard work makes the country wealthy.

(*b*) *If a man specializes he saves a great deal of time with tools and equipment.* The man who does not specialize has to do more than one job in his working day. This will involve him in putting away one set of tools and materials and getting out the next set. The man who does the same job all day uses the same tools and thus saves time. Extra time means extra output, so more wealth is created.

(*c*) *The specialist becomes more skilled because of repetition.* A fairly difficult task will occupy even a skilled worker for some considerable time. If he then does it again he will do it more quickly. When he has done it 20 times he will have overcome most of the difficulties and will almost be able to do it blindfolded. This means greater output and greater wealth.

(*d*) *The specialist invents special tools.* Every specialist sooner or later comes up with a bright idea that may save time or materials. Possibly it is a new tool, or a different layout, or a change in material. These improvements in efficiency mean more output and greater wealth.

(*e*) *Tools can be mechanized—and machines can be speeded up.* A machine can nearly always be made to work faster than a human being. For instance, an electric drill can be rotated more quickly than a hand drill. With the latest electronic computers an addition sum can be performed in seven-tenths of a microsecond, i.e. well over a million additions can be made in one second. Such fantastic speeds reduce the time spent on complex calculations. The output of scientists, design engineers, and accountants increases, and the world gets richer.

(9) Specialization and the Growth of Surplus Output

The primitive producer, searching for food in the jungle or on the sea shore, may find enough food to keep himself alive for the day, or he may find enough to leave him a small surplus which he can exchange with other tribesmen.

In civilized societies every producer must provide much more than for his own needs: he must produce a large surplus. This is because in civilized societies many people do not produce goods at all, but depend entirely on the output of others. The schoolteacher, the doctor, the nurse, the lawyer, the typist and many other people do not produce goods at all, but give their services to others. The surpluses achieved by skilful work on farms, in factories, in mines and in the fishing industry grow larger every year as more thought is given to the problems of production. Special studies are made by scientists and research workers into the processes of manufacture and production, and experiments are carried out to discover which methods will yield the largest output.

The term **mass production** is used to describe any system which aims at producing, with the fewest workers, the greatest output of goods. In nearly every industry today techniques have been developed which allow manufacturing processes to be carried on continuously, often day and night. The work flows through the factory in an endless stream, and operators at various stages perform individual operations with specially designed machinery.

Henry Ford in America developed the motor-car industry from a system whereby one man built a car completely, to a system where hundreds of men, each performing one operation repeatedly, produce an endless stream of cars. At one time a car was rolling off the production lines every ten seconds. Henry Ford's definition of mass production was: 'It is the focusing upon a manufacturing project of the principles of power, accuracy, economy, system, continuity, speed and repetition.'

Two other factors have been found to affect greatly the volume of production. They are **simplification** and **standardization**. Together with

specialization they are the source of wealth in our affluent society. These three methods, simplification, standardization, and specialization, are sometimes called **the three S's.**

Simplification is the process of making a manufactured article as simple and functional as possible. Our Victorian ancestors took great delight in embellishing their furniture and their homes with decorative knobs and patterns. We have done away with these adornments, and our furniture, kitchen equipment, houses and cars have clean, sweeping, functional surfaces—because this is the easy way to make them. This trend can be seen in the contrast between the Houses of Parliament, which are richly decorated with ornate carvings, points, and windows, and some modern buildings in concrete such as the Royal Festival Hall or Castrol House, which have smooth clean lines, and perhaps a single piece of sculpture for decoration.

When an article is designed to be produced in the simplest possible way, the job for which it is intended is borne in mind, and quite often the article is not allowed to be more efficient than is really required. Hence a happy compromise is reached between cheapness and ability to do the job.

The famous Sten gun invented during the Second World War was efficient enough to do the job for which it was intended, i.e. to fire bullets rapidly; but it was so cheap that if a soldier was tired and had used up all his ammunition, he could throw the gun away to save carrying it. A more modern example is a ball-point pen, which is discarded when used. If you simplify an article you make it cheaper and it becomes easy to afford a new one when its working life is over.

Standardization is the process of making things in standard parts, which can be used in many similar articles. For instance, a valve in one television set is very much like the valve in another set. These valves are standard parts. We can choose from perhaps 50 different makes of television set, but they will all use the same valves, resistors, transformers and picture tubes. Naturally design costs are heavy for these technical products, but the production runs of the finished article are very long and the design costs are spread over the greater volume of output.

Fig. 2 shows standard spiral bevel gear-boxes for transmitting drive from one shaft to another. The gear-boxes are so designed that the driving shaft can enter the box from any of six different positions. It then drives either one, two or three shafts, which can emerge from the gear-box in ten different ways. This gives a total of 60 possible shaft positions. It is difficult to imagine a more versatile component.

Many examples of standardization can be seen in the motor-car industry. A company or group of companies can economize by using the same standard parts on several different vehicles. For instance, the Mini, the Mini Clubman, the Mini Cooper and the Minivan all have very similar outlines. By using the same standard parts for all these cars, economies can be achieved which drastically reduce the price of all of them and help the manufacturers secure a larger share of the car market. In one recent year British Leyland made 858,775 vehicles, most of which had standard parts.

Automation in Industry

When products are made of standard parts with a high degree of specialization, it becomes possible for more and more of the work to be done automatically by machines.

The invention of electronic devices and tape recorders has had a profound influence on industry. Instructions can be inserted into tapes and

PINION SHAFT CAN BE IN ANY ONE OF SIX DIFFERENT POSITIONS:

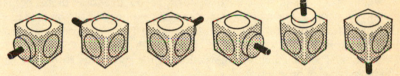

AND WITH ANY OF THESE POSITIONS, ONE, TWO OR THREE DRIVEN SHAFTS CAN BE TAKEN OFF IN TEN DIFFERENT ARRANGEMENTS:

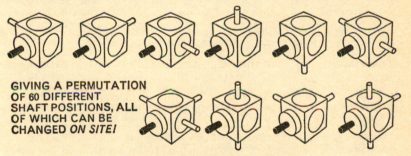

GIVING A PERMUTATION OF 60 DIFFERENT SHAFT POSITIONS, ALL OF WHICH CAN BE CHANGED *ON SITE!*

Fig. 2. Standard spiral bevel gear-boxes

run through a machine as an endless belt. This instruction will be obeyed countless times as the tape repeats its journey. Such automatic devices operate much faster than human beings; they are not temperamental, and do not need holidays or days off.

Today output in the factories and fields of the advanced nations is greater than ever seemed possible in the wildest dreams of our forefathers. We have reached such a stage of productivity that it is possible for the vast majority of people in these nations to be well fed, well clothed, well housed, and well cared for.

(10) Surplus Goods and the Provision of Services

The surplus output of highly specialized producers in the fields and factories of advanced nations sets some people free to concentrate on providing services—education, entertainment, health and dental services, legal advice, etc.

They are still 'producers', however; to the economist the only people who are not producers are those who actually withdraw from economic activities and become tramps, beatniks or 'drop-outs' as the Americans call them. Such people can truly be said to be unproductive; they have deliberately chosen to live on the fringes of society. Naturally they do not enjoy the highest standard of living and their numbers tend to decrease in colder climates where the struggle for survival is hardest.

(11) The Three Types of Production

We all specialize in some sort of work, producing some useful commodity or service, but to study production we must try to sort out the different classes of producers. The three main types of production are known as **Primary Production, Secondary Production,** and **Tertiary Production.** The table below names some of the specialists who work in the three types of production.

Table 1. Types of Production

Primary Production	Secondary Production	Tertiary Production	
(The production of goods made available by Nature. Man's inheritance of natural wealth)	(The production of more sophisticated products which are derived from the natural primary products)	(The production of services)	
		Commercial Services	*Personal Services*
Coal miner	Engineer	Wholesaler	Doctor
Gold miner	Electronic Engineer	Retailer	Dentist
Tin miner	Builder	Banker	Nurse
Lead miner	Decorator	Insurance agent	Teacher
Oil driller	Cabinet maker	Stockbroker	Lecturer
Lumberjack	Carpenter	Importer	Policeman
Farmer	Plastics engineer	Exporter	Detective
Fisherman	Refinery technologist	Transport driver	Entertainer
Whaler	Stillman	Merchant	Vocalist
Pearl diver	Potter	Navy	TV Personality
Herdsman	Tailor	Captain	Clergyman
Fur trapper	Steelworker	Ship's crew	Undertaker
etc.	Shipbuilder	Communications engineer	Editor
	Aeronautical engineer		Author
			Psychologist

The enormous range of production activities is only hinted at above, for the intricate pattern of civilized life is made up of countless specialist employments which contribute directly or indirectly to the wealth of the nations. There are scientists who do nothing but measure the chemical composition of the water we drink; farmers who raise nothing but edible snails; mathematicians who devote their lives to predicting statistical probabilities in insurance. Every one of them is doing something to provide the goods and services we need in the most economical way.

(12) Commerce—Impersonal Tertiary Services

Commerce is the distribution and exchange of all the surplus goods produced in the fields, mines, seas, forests, and factories of the earth so that they reach the final consumer in the right place, and the right condition, at the right time, in the right quantity, and at the right price.

The following points are important in this definition:

(*a*) It is only the surplus goods that commerce deals with; goods consumed by the producer do not enter the commercial network at all.

(*b*) The goods have to reach the final consumer. This involves bridging the geographical gap that separates the producer from his market.

(*c*) The goods have to arrive in the condition in which the customer requires them. This means bridging the time gap between production and consumption so that the goods are still in perfect condition when required.

(*d*) Production is usually mass production these days, but consumption is in tiny quantities. Somewhere along the line the bulk has to be broken down to the right quantity for one family or even one individual.

(*e*) The whole process must be so efficient that the price is still reasonable.

The Expansion of Commerce

We have already seen that it is only the producers' **surplus** goods that are available to be distributed to other people. The larger the surpluses, the more commerce will be needed because of the increased distribution and exchange that has to take place before the goods can reach the consumer. If a firm needs the whole world for its market the chain of distribution will be long. As the goods are passed from one person to another changes of ownership will occur. The most significant development in the modern world is the growth of commerce as mass production has made larger surpluses available.

Some of the advantages of mass production are inevitably lost in providing the expensive commercial services that are needed to dispose of the surpluses. One well-known manufacturer recently said of his product 'It is not just a question of how to make ten million stainless-steel razor blades. There is a commercial problem too . . .'. That problem is to distribute and sell them to other people willing to give **money** in exchange for them. Money is the medium through which exchange takes place. It represents all the other goods we can buy with it, and a sale of surplus razor blades for money is really an exchange of this commodity for a variety of other goods which the seller is free to select in the way that gives him maximum satisfaction of his wants.

Commerce at Work Even Before Production Begins

Even before the goods are produced, commercial firms will have been at work ensuring the proper financial backing for the enterprise. Once this has been secured the necessary orders will be placed for the capital assets required by the enterprise, and for the employment of expert, skilled or semi-skilled labour as required. These capital assets and personnel will be summoned through the communications network and transported by the commercial transport systems to the area where production is to be started. On the way the assets will be insured against loss and accidental damage so that the enterprise shall not founder because of some unfortunate event.

The **branches of commerce** that perform these varied functions are **banking** and **finance**, **insurance**, **transport** and **communications.**

Once the assets and personnel of the business have been assembled and put to work the output of goods begins. Because of specialization this output will be greater than the actual producers need for their own use, and there will be a surplus for commerce to deal with.

Commerce at Work Disposing of Surplus Output

One way to dispose of a surplus is to move it to some area where there is a shortage. If we alter the geographical position of goods we can usually find a market for them. This important function of commerce is carried on by wholesalers, importers, and exporters. They must have a transport system, while communications, finance, and insurance are also important.

The other way to dispose of goods is to transport them not from one place to another but from one time period to another. If no one wants the strawberries a grower picks this week, because strawberries are plentiful, he may be able to get a reasonable price for them next winter when strawberries are scarce. If he is able to bottle them, can them, or deep-freeze them he may be able to make a profit after all. Since these are specialist occupations we usually find that a market gardener prefers to hand on the strawberries to a cannery, or jam manufacturer. This involves a change of ownership, so that a commercial exchange has taken place. This is called **trade.**

Trade is divided into four branches: **wholesale**, **retail**, **import**, and **export.**

All these branches of trade have as part of their functions the bridging of the time gap between production and consumption. It is the trader's function to hold goods until they are required, and to take such measures as are needed to bridge the time gap successfully: goods must be safely delivered over the time gap as well as the geographical gap.

This time gap presents many problems. Bread goes stale; ice-cream melts; meat goes bad; strawberries rot; woodworm attacks timber; iron rusts; silver tarnishes; clothing becomes unfashionable or moth-eaten. Commercial firms must take the necessary action to prevent the ravages of time and bring the product to the consumer in perfect condition. This may mean refrigerating perishable goods, providing insect-proof storage or merely taking precautions against theft and misappropriation.

The Complexity of Commerce

The intricate pattern of commercial firms has arisen because of the need for specialization. In a free-enterprise society people may do anything they like that is not actually criminal to earn their living. If a man sees an opportunity to offer a better service at a profit to himself he will do it, and make the profit as his reward for his efforts. This rapidly develops into a complicated network of specialist firms able to offer goods or services to the producer or consumer. This book is about that intricate network.

Commerce, like all other human activities, is not *static*, but *dynamic*. It is always on the move, always changing, always developing. It is because of its dynamic nature that commerce improves from year to year. New methods, new ideas, new materials can revolutionize commerce. What is efficient and reasonable today will be old-fashioned and expensive tomorrow compared with the new techniques that science and business research have produced.

The world commercial scene is a very complicated picture. Everyone is busy either producing, transporting or expediting the movement of goods. The producers of all this wealth are specializing in their own trades, but in return they expect to be able to purchase a selection of the goods created by other producers. The organization required to supply us with our fair share of other people's products is complex but necessary.

Only a few people can be left out of the productive system. A few tramps, hobos, or beatniks elect to live on the fringes of life, unproductive and careless of whether they get a reasonable share of the goods produced. A few fortunate rich people do not produce, although with taxes and death duties as high as they are the unproductive rich get fewer year by year. The rest of us play our part in creating wealth and in consuming it. Living in a social organization of one type or another, civilized people make laws and regulations to preserve their society.

Civilized life brings the advantages that co-operation gives to all who join in and help. If we are sick the doctor will do his best to cure us. If we need shelter a builder will erect a house. If we are cold a tailor will make a suit. If we like fast travel the engineer will make us a motor cycle, the chemical engineer will provide petrol, the rubber planter will

14   *Commerce Made Simple*

supply the material for tyres and the glass-maker will help us to see our way with headlamps. Each of these undertakings is a skilled process and requires expert knowledge which only civilized men can discover. Uncivilized men have to learn the arts of self-protection and of self-preservation. They have no time to learn skills other than personal immediate skills such as hunting and self-defence. The world of commerce is a civilized world.

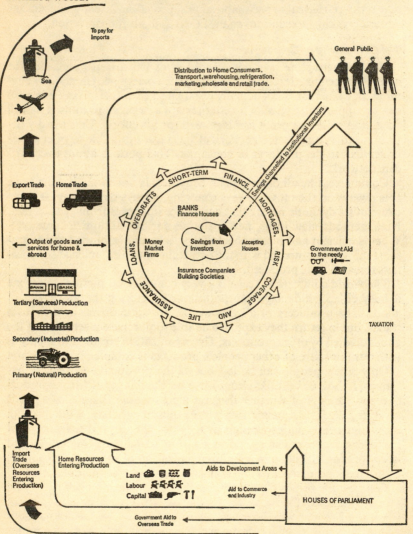

Fig. 3. Commerce in the framework of production

(13) A Page to Test You on the Framework of Production

Cover the page with a sheet of paper, then read a question at a time.

Answers	Questions
—	1. What are the basic wants of mankind?
1. Food, water, clothing, shelter, land, and medical care.	2. Is man satisfied when he has these basic needs?
2. No, he develops more sophisticated wants.	3. How would you classify these wants?
3. Into either goods or services.	4. What are the two methods of production?
4. Direct production and indirect production.	5. What is direct production?
5. Producing directly for your own use.	6. What is indirect production?
6. Producing by specialization in one particular trade or profession.	7. What are the advantages of specialization?
7. (a) People choose a job they like. (b) They save time by using the same equipment all day. (c) They get more skilled by repetition. (d) They invent cunning devices and new methods of work. (e) These devices can be mechanized and even automated. (f) As a result surpluses are produced which can be exchanged for other goods.	8. What are the three S's?
8. Simplification, standardization and specialization.	9. What part does commerce play in production?
9. (a) It helps find the capital so that production can be planned. (b) It helps transfer men and materials to the site so that production can begin. (c) It transports the goods geographically to the market. (d) It carries the goods through time so that present production is available for future consumption.	10. As mass production increases the supply of goods, what happens to commerce?
10. It expands, because there are more surplus goods to distribute, bigger geographical gaps to cover and longer time gaps to overcome before goods reach the final consumer.	11. How many did you answer correctly? Go over the list again.

Exercises Set 1

(14) Commerce in the Framework of Production

1. Man provides the goods and services he needs by a system of specialized production. Explain.

2. Choose one primary product and make a detailed study of it. You will have to use reference books from the library, and may have to write to firms that handle the product chosen. Suitable topics are: cotton, wool, tea, coffee, cocoa, softwood timber, jungle hardwoods, palm oil, copra, diamonds, coal, chalk, oil, opals, rubies, emeralds, iron, gold, silver, uranium, aluminium, sulphur, brazil nuts, beef, mutton, eggs, butter, milk, oranges and lemons, tomatoes, sugar, copper.

3. What do you understand by secondary production? Illustrate your answer by referring in detail to a Canadian red cedar which reaches your house as a prefabricated fence made up into 2 metre panels.

4. 'Manufacturing is productive, but so is transport.' Justify this statement.

5. Drilling for oil is primary production, cracking oil is secondary production and selling oil is tertiary production. Explain these statements and give your views as to which of the three processes named is the most vital to an advanced industrial nation.

6. How do simplification, standardization and specialization benefit humanity? Refer in your answer to the motor-car industry.

7. Discuss the journey, either geographically or in time, made by one of the following goods from the point of production to the point of final consumption: (*a*) a teak tree, cut down in the Burmese jungle 30 miles north of Mandalay, and eventually made into a sideboard; (*b*) a nugget of silver, mined by an Indian slave at the Potosi silver mines in Peru, in 1548. Sent to Spain, it was sunk in the West Indies by a British privateer, recovered from the wreckage in 1963 by an American skin-diver and sold by him to an antique dealer who sold it to the Museum of New York; (*c*) a cod, caught off the Newfoundland Grand Banks by an Icelandic trawler, sold to a Scottish frozen-food company and eaten in a factory canteen, 18 months later.

8. Write an essay entitled 'The distribution of goods is just as important as the production of them'.

9. What is meant by *mass production* methods? Why are they often used in the manufacture of bicycles, but not in their repair?

(*University of London*)

10. Describe the commercial activities which make supplies of a commodity produced overseas (e.g. tea) available to consumers in Britain.

(*R.S.A.*)

11. Set out carefully the principal divisions and subdivisions of commerce and give an idea of the relative importance of each.

(*R.S.A.*)

12. Describe briefly, in your own words, what you consider to be the purposes of commerce, and indicate how (*a*) an accounts clerk in a wholesale warehouse, (*b*) a butcher's boy, (*c*) a cinema attendant, help in the attainment of these purposes.

(*R.S.A.*)

13. Discuss the view that commercial activities are as important as the manufacturing industries in the economic life of Britain?

(Associated Examining Board)

14. To what extent do you consider that efficiency in different branches of commerce affects the standard of living in Britain?

(Associated Examining Board)

15. What are the functions of the commercial occupations in the working of the British economy?

(University of London)

CHAPTER TWO

TYPES OF BUSINESS UNIT IN PRODUCTION AND COMMERCE

(1) Starting a Business

Whenever a man sets up in business it is because he feels he can produce some useful commodity or service which will be needed by his fellow men. In return he expects to be able to earn a profit on his business, which will be a reward for his efforts. Most businesses require certain equipment, premises, machinery, furniture, etc., which must be contributed by the proprietor. Such items are known as **assets,** and the money to buy them which is contributed by the owner of the business is called his **capital.** The first task of any person wishing to start a business is to accumulate capital, and in former times the only method of obtaining it was to save it up by self-denial and the postponement of present consumption to a future date. Economists said

$$\frac{\text{Capital available}}{\text{for investment}} = \text{Savings} = \frac{\text{Consumption}}{\text{Postponed}}$$

Today there are other ways of obtaining capital. For instance, we can borrow it from someone who has capital to spare. But if we do so we must usually pay interest on it and this means that some of the profits earned will be creamed off to reward the owner of the capital.

Building up a business is a slow process. As the capital grows, so the business expands, and once it is clear that a successful enterprise has been built up it becomes easier to obtain further capital. Penniless inventors search the world for sponsors to back their ideas, while prosperous companies are deluged with millions of pounds of further capital whenever they ask the public for funds with which to expand.

The types of business unit therefore show a progression from small scale to large scale, the size of the enterprise reflecting the amount of capital invested. Differences between the various units reflect (*a*) the ownership of the capital concerned, (*b*) the control of the conduct of the enterprise, (*c*) the accountability of the controllers to the investors, in so far as they are different people, (*d*) the division of the profits.

(2) Types of Business Unit

Business units may be divided into three main groups: **private enterprises, non-profitmaking units,** and **public enterprises.** A full list includes:

18

Us only to what they have put into the business

Private Enterprises

(*a*) Sole Traders ①
(*b*) Partnerships 2 - 20. (except solicitors + accountants)
(*c*) Limited Partnerships
(*d*) Private Limited Companies
(*e*) Public Limited Companies
(*f*) Holding Companies (a more advanced type of Public Company)

Non-Profitmaking Units

(*a*) Clubs of many sorts
(*b*) Co-operative Societies

Public Enterprises

(*a*) Municipal undertakings
(*b*) Nationalized undertakings

Ownership is the key to the difference between these three types of undertaking. In the case of the first group, private enterprises are owned and operated by certain clearly identified people, who are also entitled to the reward of the enterprise. In the case of non-profitmaking groups, the society exists in order to confer benefits on the members which are outside the commercial activities of the unit. Profit is a mere incidental, but any surplus is shared between the membership. With public-enterprise units, the enterprise is socially owned and operated, possibly on a commercial basis but with the intention of supplying goods and services at reasonable prices for the benefit of the whole community.

(3) **Sole-Trader Enterprises**

A sole trader is a person who enters business on his own account, contributing the capital to start the enterprise, labouring in it with or without the assistance of employees, and receiving as his reward the proceeds of the venture. The advantages are as follows:

(*a*) No formal procedures are required to set up in business. A licence must be obtained for certain classes of business, and the name of the business must be registered under the Registration of Business Names Act, 1916, if it is anything other than the true name of the proprietor.

(*b*) Independence is a chief feature of these businesses. Having no one to consult, the sole trader can put his plans into effect quickly.

(*c*) Personal supervision ensures effective operation at all times; customers are known to the proprietor who can cater for their tastes and avoid bad debts by a personal assessment of credit worthiness; employees are under personal supervision; waste is avoided. - seek economies

(*d*) Expansion need only be pressed to the point where the market is adequately supplied. In isolated areas this makes the sole trader the effective business unit.

(*e*) He is accountable only to himself and (apart from income tax) need reveal the state of his business to no one. ~~Business kept private Das not have to make public disclosure of profit.~~

The <u>disadvantages include</u>:

(*a*) <u>Long working hours</u> and little time off for vacations.

(*b*) <u>Sickness</u> may mean the business gets into difficulties.

(*c*) The proprietor has '<u>unlimited liability</u>', which means that he is per- <u>sonally liable</u> to the <u>full extent of his private wealth</u> for the debts of the business. <u>Insolvency</u> may mean the sale of his house and home to pay the creditors.

(*d*) <u>Expansion</u> is usually <u>only possible</u> by <u>ploughing back</u> the <u>profits of a business as further capital</u>. He may be able to borrow from a bank, or privately, but he is <u>not allowed to borrow from the public.</u> He may take <u>a partner</u>, but this means a <u>loss of independence.</u> He can keep this inde- pendence if he takes a limited partner, but these are not easy to find in present conditions of high taxation. ~~Borrow from bank not easy does not have large security co has~~

(*e*) The <u>business is</u> part of the <u>estate of the proprietor</u> at his death, and it may be <u>necessary to sell</u> the business in order to <u>pay death duties</u>.

(*f*) Like most small-scale enterprises it will be a high-cost enterprise because the degree of specialization will be small.

~~g) No legal entity. h) cannot get economies of scale.~~

Vulnerability of the Sole Trader

In recent years there has been a decline in the number of sole-trader enterprises, as the advantages of large-scale enterprises have become more noticeable. Every improvement in transport and communications exposes the local shop and the local factory to a blast of competition from larger and more efficient enterprises. The general raising of social standards of hygiene, sanitation, working conditions, and safety has made it more and more difficult for the small man to compete. One small factory owner complained that when trade is booming he cannot find the raw materials at a price that pays him to manufacture, and when trade is bad he cannot find a customer for his product.

In seeking to achieve a larger scale he may well decide to take a partner.

(4) Partnerships   ~~2 types : General. LTD.~~

Why take a Partner?

There are several reasons why sole traders combine together to form partnerships. The chief advantages are:

(*a*) <u>Increased capital</u>, permitting the business to expand more rapidly than is possible by the 'ploughing back' of profits earned.

(*b*) The <u>responsibility of control</u> no longer rests with one person. This makes possible holidays and free week-ends, and reduces the worry the sole trader experiences in times of ill health.

(*c*) Wider experience is brought to the firm and some degree of speciali-zation is possible: this is particularly true of professional partnerships. A physician and a surgeon may form a partnership; or lawyers with experience in different fields—divorce, criminal law, commercial law—may combine to offer a more comprehensive service to the public.

(*d*) Very often a young man teams up with an older man. The young man has his health and strength; his partner has the capital and the experience. Together they make a satisfactory team.

(*e*) The affairs of the business are still private.

The Partnership Act of 1890

The possibility always exists that, even if the partners agree now, they will disagree later. This has led to a very complicated and ancient case law on partnership matters which was finally codified by the Partner-ship Act of 1890. This Act is very short, containing only 50 sections, but it is a very good example of an Act of Parliament. Any British reader who is not familiar with the layout of an Act of Parliament is strongly advised to study a copy of this one.

Disadvantages of a Partnership

(*a*) The partners still have unlimited liability for the debts of the business.

(*b*) Each partner must consult the other and consider his views every time a decision has to be made.

(*c*) The partnership is adversely affected by the death of a partner whose share may be withdrawn to pay the beneficiaries. It is therefore desir-able for each partner to take out life assurance on his partner, to provide a lump-sum benefit in the event of his death.

The partnership is particularly suitable for professional people such as doctors, lawyers, and accountants. It is also suitable for small-scale enterprises of all sorts, in retail trade, manufacturing, agriculture and horticulture, road haulage, and local wholesaling.

(5) Limited Partnerships

A modification to Partnership Law was enacted in 1907 with the Limited Partnership Act. This Act permits a partnership to be formed between an active partner or partners and one or more sleeping part-ners who are accorded the privilege of Limited Liability.

The Privilege of Limited Liability

Where a person has funds to contribute which can be used by others for the promotion of business activity, but does not wish himself to take any part in the conduct of the business or the management of the firm, it seems unfair to require him to carry the burden of unlimited liability which attaches to sole traders or partners. The principle of limited liability holds that such a person should be liable to the extent of the capital he has contributed, but no further than this. The limitation of liability in this way unlocks savings which would otherwise merely be hoarded by their owners, and releases them to play a productive part in the industrial and commercial fields.

In the early days of the Industrial Revolution people who contributed capital to industrial firms were held to be full partners, and many lost their homes when speculative projects collapsed and the partners were required to contribute to pay the debts of the firms concerned. Only in 1855, when the increasing demands for capital met resistance from savers who had already seen others suffer hardship through no fault of their own, did Parliament sanction limited liability for shareholders.

The 1907 Act sanctioned limited liability for partners with capital to contribute, provided that there was at least one partner, the **general partner,** who did assume unlimited liability for the affairs of the business, and provided that the limited partner took no part in the management of the firm. This Act also helped solve the problem of a retiring partner. Retirement, like death, required a partner's share of the business to be repaid; this time without the benefit of life assurance. If the retiring partner agreed to leave his capital in the business as a limited partner, he could receive a share of the profits in return, and enjoy the privilege of limited liability.

(6) **The Private Limited Company and the Public Limited Company**

These two types of business unit are very closely connected since they are controlled by the Companies Acts of 1948 and 1967. Since 1967 they have been brought even closer together by the removal of the exemption clauses which had previously made the exempt private company so attractive a form of business organization. Before considering these points let us look at the formation of such a company.

Floating a Company

The promoter of a company must find either one more (in the case of a private company) or six more (in the case of a public company) persons prepared to join with him as **members** in signing a **Memorandum of Association**. This document governs the relationship of the company with the external world. Its six main clauses are as follows:

(*a*) The name of the company with the word 'Limited' as the last word. This word is a warning to all people who do business with the company that the shareholders have limited liability. It is a warning to them not to deal with the company unless they are quite sure they can afford the risk. Many people think a company is more reliable to deal with than a sole trader or partnership, but this is not necessarily so.

(*b*) The address of its registered office.

(*c*) The objects of the company. This states what the company will do when it is established, and forms the legal basis for its activities. It will have to keep its activities within the fields specified, or the Courts may rule them *ultra vires* (beyond the powers). This is a protection to the shareholders. Suppose that I invested £500 in a company that was to develop a revolutionary type of aero engine, which I believed had a great future. I suddenly discover that the directors are using my money to buy sugar which happens to be rising on world markets. I would naturally feel that this was not the purpose for which I had subscribed my capital, and would be able to obtain an injunction restraining them from using my money in an *ultra vires* way.

(*d*) A statement that the liability of the members is limited.

(*e*) The amount of share capital to be issued, and the types of share.

(*f*) An undertaking by the signatories that they do desire to be formed into a company registered under the Acts, and to undertake to purchase the number of shares against their names.

Having drawn up and signed the Memorandum of Association, it is necessary to draw up detailed Articles of Association, which control the internal affairs of the company. Such matters as the procedure to be followed at meetings, the powers of the managing director, the borrowing powers that may be exercised, etc., are considered and agreed. A set of model articles, called Table A, is printed in the Acts and becomes the Articles for any public company which fails to register any Articles. A simpler set *may* be adopted by private companies.

Registration of the Company

The promoters of the company may now proceed to register the company under the Acts. They present to the **Registrar of Companies** the Memorandum of Association; the Articles of Association; a statement of the nominal capital, on which a tax of £0·50 per cent is payable; a list of directors and their written consents and promises to take up shares, and a statutory declaration that the Company Acts have been complied with.

If all is in order, the Registrar will issue a **Certificate of Incorporation** which bestows upon the company a separate legal personality. The company can now do all the legal things that an ordinary person can do; it can own land and property, employ people, sue and be sued in the Courts, etc. Before it can begin trading however it must secure the capital it needs. With a private company this will largely be contributed by the founders anyway. With a public company it must be obtained from the public, either directly or indirectly through the institutional investors.

Classes of Shares

People with savings to spare have to be tempted to invest in an enterprise; hence the wide variety of shares and bonds offered to them. Some people want a high return on their capital, and to obtain it are prepared to run some risk. Others want security for their savings, even though the rate of interest is lower. Security is particularly difficult to ensure in inflationary times. For instance, savings in Government Securities are absolutely secure; if you leave them in for 50 years you will receive £1 back for every £1 you invested, but if that £1 will only buy 20 pence worth of goods because of **inflation** over the years you have really lost money on the investment. We say that the **Nominal Value** (nominal means 'in name only') has remained the same, but the **Real Value** (in terms of what it will purchase) has declined.

A full explanation of the types of share is given in the chapter on the Stock Exchange, but for comparison purposes a list is shown in Table 2.

How a Company is Formed and Financed

Fig. 4. shows how most public companies are formed. Starting in a small way, often as a family business and operating as a private company, they expand to the point where they can fulfil the strict requirements of the Stock Exchange Council.

When permission to deal in their shares is accorded to the Stock Exchange dealers by the Council, the company can invite the public to subscribe for shares. The new capital thus made available enables the firm to expand its activities and achieve the advantages of large-scale production.

Invitations to the public to subscribe for shares are made in a **prospectus** which is a full and frank account of the history of the company to date, its profit record, and every detail likely to be of interest to an investor trying to assess his risks in making an application for shares.

This prospectus must be registered with the Registrar before the public are invited to subscribe.

Certificate of Trading

Before a public company can begin to trade it must secure a **Certificate of Trading**. This is issued by the Registrar when registration is finally completed by lodging with him the following documents:

(*a*) A statement that the minimum capital has been subscribed.
(*b*) A statement that the directors have paid for their shares.
(*c*) A statutory declaration that the Companies Acts have been complied with.

The **minimum capital** is that amount of capital stated in the prospectus as being the minimum which, in the director's opinion, is necessary for the success of the enterprise. If this minimum is not reached, all the capital collected must be returned to the shareholders. Directors can ensure a successful commencement of trading if they have the issue

Table 2. Comparison of Different Types of Share

Type of investment	Reward earned	Degree of risk	Who buys them	Who issues them
Ordinary Shares	Equal share of profits; hence nickname 'Equity Shares'	Carry the main risk	(*a*) Well-to-do investors who want big returns. (*b*) Institutional investors, for a balanced portfolio. (*c*) People interested in capital gains, rather than revenue profits	Private and Public Companies
Deferred Ordinary Shares. (Founder's Shares)	Share of profits after Ordinary shares have had some (say 10%) profit	Same as Ordinary Shares	They are taken by the vendor of a business when he sells it to a company, as an earnest of goodwill	Public Companies chiefly, but also Private Companies
Preference Shares	Definite rate of Dividend (say 7%), but only if profits are made	Less than Ordinary Shares as they *usually* have a prior right to repayment	Investors seeking security rather than large dividends	Public and Private Companies
Cumulative Preference Shares	As above, but if profits are not earned in one year the dividend accumulates and is not lost	As above	As above	As above
Participating Preference Shares	After taking the fixed rate (say 7%) these shares earn extra dividend if the Ordinary shares get more than 7%	As above	As above	As above
Debentures (Loans to companies; Debentures are not really shares)	Fixed Rate of interest (say 6%), payable whether profits are made or not	Very small	Timid people wanting a secure investment	Public and Private Companies, if permitted by their Articles

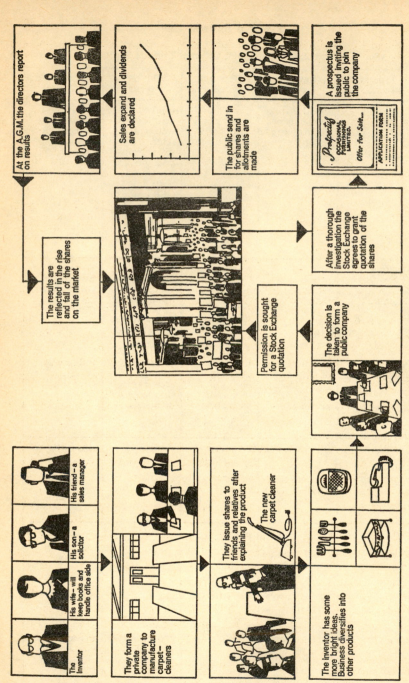

Fig. 4. The formation of a company

The Inventor

His wife — will keep books and handle office side

His son — a solicitor

His friend — a sales manager

They form a private company to manufacture carpet-cleaners

They issue shares to friends and relatives after explaining the product

The new carpet cleaner

The inventor has some more bright ideas. Business diversifies into other products

The decision is taken to form a public company

Permission is sought for a Stock Exchange quotation

After a thorough investigation the Stock Exchange agrees to grant quotation of the shares

A prospectus is issued inviting the public to join the company

Prospectus
OCCASIONAL FURNISHING LIMITED.
Offer for Sale...
APPLICATION FORM

The public send in for shares and allotments are made

The results are reflected in the rise and fall of the shares on the market

At the A.G.M. the directors report on results

Sales expand and dividends are declared

underwritten by financiers prepared to buy the shares should the public not do so.

(7) Holding Companies

Where a company has acquired control of another company by the purchase of 51 per cent of its voting shares it is said to be a **Holding Company.** This is one way of building up a large-scale business, and it has certain advantages. It takes advantage of specialization within an industry. For example, where in years gone by a motor-vehicle manufacturer may have found it convenient to allow a specialist firm to supply him with particular components, a growth in the size of his own business may make it desirable to bring the subsidiary firm within his own direct control. By purchasing 51 per cent of the voting shares, control can be secured and the subsidiary company brought within the direct influence of the parent company.

The integration may permit the smaller company to preserve its goodwill while sharing in the large-scale benefits, research, technical, marketing and welfare economies achieved by the parent firm. The parent firm can gather under its wing subsidiaries in the raw-material, transport, component-supply, marketing, advertising, and research fields which will ensure that it is never starved of raw materials, components, or markets. This is known as **vertical integration:** integration from top to bottom of an industry. The same process enables a holding company to diversify into other fields besides its major field, and thus avoid bad times when its major industry is experiencing declining activity.

Whether such large groups of companies are socially desirable is a debatable point. They are generally able to achieve economies of scale, and as such are probably desirable as a contribution to the general problem of production, which is to secure maximum satisfaction of 'wants' from a minimum input of the world's scarce resources. Whether this compensates for the monopoly-like nature of the enterprise is a matter the reader should consider without prejudice. What the Companies Acts attempt to do is to protect the **minority shareholders** of such companies. For example, it is easy for the Holding Company to pursue a policy which deliberately limits its dividends, to the detriment of the minority shareholders. Their right to protest at the Annual General Meeting is of little use to them in view of the 51 per cent of the voting shares in the hands of the Holding Company. Such shareholders are given rights under the Acts which entitle them to appeal to the Board of Trade against unfair treatment. The accounting requirements of the Act also provide that a Holding Company, in its published accounts, must clearly reveal the extent to which it controls other companies. New investors, buying what are clearly minority shares, will at least know the situation, and invest elsewhere if they prefer to buy shares which will have some chance of influencing managerial policies.

(8) The Combination of Business Units—the Trend Towards the Absorption of Small Businesses into Large Units

In the past, all businesses began in a small way because of the necessity to accumulate capital. Nowadays, in a wealthy nation, firms can actually start off as large-scale enterprises, provided that enough interested people, called shareholders, can be found to furnish the capital. Many of these shareholders are insurance companies, banks, and investment companies. Such firms are called **institutional investors.** They collect savings from people, investing them wisely for the good of the saving public.

In every project there is what is called an **optimum** size, or perfect size. For instance a watch-repairing business is usually very small, its size depending on the population of the town in which it is set up. A hydro-electric power station, on the other hand, usually has to be of very great size indeed because of the high cost of generators and distribution grids. The optimum size of businesses changes over the years, particularly with changes in transport. For instance, brickworks used to be found in almost every area of Britain where clay was available, because it was so difficult to move bricks over large distances. Now that we are able to move loads cheaply and easily by rail and road, a few large-scale centralized brickworks have replaced the numerous small local brickfields, and the hand-made brick has virtually disappeared in the face of competition from the wire-cut precision-made version.

Today there is a great tendency to increase the size of businesses in nearly all trades, manufacturing, building, wholesale, and retail. The advantages of large-scale projects are very great, especially in the retail trade. In particular the techniques of mass production require very large-scale operation. If one man is going to perform only one process, we must have a great many workers to achieve the advantages of specialization.

There is therefore a tendency for small businesses to grow into bigger businesses, and for them to be **absorbed** by the bigger firms. There is also a tendency for firms to **amalgamate** to form a bigger firm, and there is a tendency for similar firms to co-operate with one another for good reasons (greater economies) or bad reasons (price fixing). Such associations are called **cartels** (a German word), or **trusts** (an American word). On the whole, the domination of an entire industry by one firm is probably undesirable, because it leads to monopoly profits. In many countries such huge firms are banned by law, but in Britain they are controlled fairly effectively by other methods. The difficulty is to prevent the huge firm abusing its powers while at the same time encouraging efficiency by allowing firms to reach the optimum size.

If we try to increase size we may do so either horizontally or vertically.

Vertical integration tries to control all the stages of a particular product. Examples are found in many industries. In the shoe industry some firms make the shoes, distribute them and sell them in their own retail shops. Some tea firms own tea estates, process tea in their own factories, import it, blend it, package it and deliver it to the shopkeeper. Some oil companies own oil fields, tankers, refineries, delivery vehicles, and garages where the refined products are sold.

Horizontal integration is where firms try to control all aspects at one level. For example, wholesalers try to gain control of wider and wider areas; multiple shops take over small businesses all over the country; and chain stores set up branches in every town.

(9) Non-Profit-making Units

A certain number of business units are non-profit-making clubs and societies. They are formed to confer upon their members certain benefits in the way of club facilities, discount trading, or value for money. Such clubs and societies often make profits on the year's trading, but these are not profits in the normal commercial meaning of the word. They really represent overpayments by the members for the services they have received, and are usually called 'surpluses'. Examples of such business units are the Working Men's Clubs of the north of England, and the Co-operative Societies. Co-operative Societies are fully described on page 42.

(10) The Public-Enterprise Sector of the Economy

In Britain, about two-thirds of the economy and about five-sixths of commerce is conducted by the private-enterprise firms already described. The remainder of the activities of the economy are conducted by socially owned enterprises. Some, like the Army, Navy, and Air Force, are clearly the sort of institutions that the State itself should control. Others have tended to be performed by the State because they are non-profit-making, and as such are unlikely to be attractive to businessmen. Such activities as education, medical care, and sanitation are best operated as socially provided amenities for the benefit of all citizens.

In the commercial field certain goods and services are by their nature monopolies. Among these **natural monopolies** are gas, electricity, and water supply. The capital costs of such enterprises are too great for competition to be possible. We do not install three sets of gas pipes into our houses in order to be able to enjoy Jones's, Smith's, or Robinson's gas according to which is the 'best buy' this morning.

Transport is another natural monopoly. It would be uneconomic to run two railway lines from London to Reading, or two different sets of half-empty buses along a country road. These natural monopolies have, for economic, political, or social reasons come to be run in the United Kingdom by nationalized institutions, or the municipal authorities, who provide the services required at reasonable prices.

Table 3: Comparison of Private-Enterprise Units

	Aspect	Sole Trader	Partnership	Limited Partnership
1	Name of firm	Any name provided it is either the proprietor's true name or their names, or has been registered under the Registration of Business Names Act, 1916		
2	How formed	By commencing business without formality except (1) above	By agreement, which may be oral or written; limited partnerships must be registered	
3	Control of the firm	Proprietor has full control	Every partner is entitled to manage	Only the general partner(s) can manage the business
4	Liability for debts	Liable to the limits of personal wealth	Jointly and severally liable for debts to limits of personal wealth	General partners fully liable; limited partners not liable beyond the capital contributed
5	Relationship between owner and business	The business is the owner, or owners, and has no separate legal existence		The business is the same as the general partners; the limited partner is not the business
6	Membership of firm	One	Two or more	Two or more
7	General powers	At will	At will, subject to agreement; if no agreement, Partnership Act 1890 applies	
8	Transfer of ownership	By sale of 'goodwill'	Only with unanimous consent	
9	Controlling Acts	None	Partnership Act, 1890	Limited Partnership Act, 1907
10	Disbanding of firm	At will or by bankruptcy	Firm may go bankrupt or be dissolved by notice or mutual consent	
11	Advantages	Independence. Personal control of staff and granting of credit. Decisions acted upon at once	Increased capital. Days off and holidays possible. Wider experience of partners. Privacy of affairs	Limited liability for some partners. Larger capital
12	Disadvantages	Long hours no holidays. Illness affects conduct of business. Unlimited liability. Small capital.	Unlimited liability. Death or retirement ends firm. Profits must be shared	Unlimited liability for the general partners. Also as for partnerships

Comparison of Private-Enterprise Units (continued)

	Limited Companies	
	Private	Public
1	The registered name, registered under the Companies Acts, 1948 and 1967, ending in the word 'Limited', as a warning to future creditors	
2	By registration under the Companies Acts, with due legal formality	
3	Directors control the company. Members have no control at all, but may elect a new board at the Annual General Meeting if they wish to do so	
4	Limited liability for all members – only liable to the limit of capital contributed	
5	The business is a separate legal personality from the members	
6	Minimum two, maximum fifty (excluding employees)	Minimum seven, no maximum limit
7	As laid down in Memorandum of Association and Articles of Association	
8	Shares may only be transferred with consent of fellow shareholders	Shares are freely transferable
9	Companies Acts, 1948 and 1967	
10	Company may go into voluntary or compulsory liquidation	
11	Limited liability Death of shareholders does not affect the firm. Capital can be found from fifty members. Privacy to some extent on affairs	Limited liability Death of shareholders does not affect the firm. Very large capital can be collected.
12	Publication now required, but since February 1972 turnover need not be revealed unless it exceeds £250,000. Only fifty members.	Full public knowledge of affairs

Advantages of Public Enterprises

(*a*) They provide socially necessary facilities like education, sanitation, etc., which private enterprises will not provide because these facilities tend to be non-profit-making.

(*b*) They are the best way to provide services which are a natural monopoly.

(*c*) Capital can be provided by taxation and rate assessment, as well as by borrowing, with Government guarantees about interest and repayments.

(*d*) The provision of services without a principal emphasis on profit-making renders the goods or service cheaper than otherwise they would be. This amounts to a social subsidy enjoyed by domestic and business consumers.

(*e*) The large-scale operations performed enable great use to be made of the economies of scale.

Disadvantages of Public Enterprises

(*a*) There is a conflict between economy of operation and adequacy of service, which it is difficult to reconcile. For example, the public will demand as perfect a service as possible, but will complain loudly if they have to pay too much for it. Some people claim that the recent modernization of British Railways to provide an efficient service, especially on particular routes, was money misspent because it occurred at a time when traffic of all sorts was deserting the railways for the roads. Comparable expenditure on roads would have promoted the efficiency of the economy far more, they argue.

(*b*) Dis-economies of scale occur, particularly if the enterprise is very large or closely controlled by local or central government. This involves an excessive degree of caution on the part of managers fearful of being blamed for innovations they otherwise would introduce.

(*c*) Politicians and councillors may know little of business, and may influence the enterprises along unbusinesslike paths.

(*d*) Waste is encouraged since losses are borne by the ratepayers or tax-payers.

(*e*) If political repercussions are likely, or if the enterprise is subject to political or parochial pressures, it may not develop in the best way for the industry.

(*f*) State-operated services often have the opportunity to discriminate against privately-owned firms in the same line of business. For instance BOAC and BEA (now British Airways) were for many years able to prevent competitive civil airlines from operating services that were later proved to be desirable and beneficial to the nation as a whole.

However one feels about the desirability or otherwise of State-run enterprises, some degree of State ownership seems to be inevitable. Over a wide range of activities, nationalized industry appears to operate cer-tainly as well as, and possibly better than, the private-enterprise indus-try it has replaced.

Municipal Undertakings

Commercial enterprises run by Borough and County Councils in-clude such units as municipal swimming baths, bus services, piers and seaside entertainments, theatres and community centres. The capital costs are usually borne by borrowing against the general security of the rates; the idea is to price the facilities to the public at such a figure as to recover both the operating costs and the interest and capital repayments, during the lifetime of the asset.

Nationalized Industries

The major nationalized industries in the United Kingdom are coal, gas, electricity, atomic energy, steel, and some transport. Many other undertakings, while not actually nationalized, are run as public corpora-tions which carry out most of the activities in their particular fields. For instance, while there are many civil airlines, British Airways handles the vast majority of the business. A nationalized industry in Great Britain is formed by the expropriation of the assets of all existing firms in the industry in return for adequate compensation, and the setting up of a Board to run the industry under an Act of Parliament bestowing the necessary authority. The industry is expected to run as a business venture, making enough profit, taking one year with another, to pay the interest on the Government stock issued to finance the compen-sation.

Organization and Control of Public Enterprises

No hard and fast rules about the organization and control of these enterprises have been laid down, since every enterprise is controlled by its Act of Parliament which aims at devising the organization most suited to the particular industry. Probably the most general features are as follows:

(a) The industry has been set up to operate as a commercial business, without day-to-day parliamentary control of its activities. Any type of Civil Service Organization is deemed to be too slow-moving for the conduct of what must generally be an essentially industrial undertaking.

(b) Taking one year with another, the business is expected to be economically self-sufficient. The phrase 'taking one year with another' means that rates and charges to the public shall be such as to achieve an overall cover of expenses, but a loss in a particular year is not important if subsequent years will recoup the loss. This has not always been the case, especially where very heavy initial debts were taken on to pay compensation to former owners. In these cases Parliament has simply been forced to free the industry from debt by writing off the losses to the Exchequer.

(*c*) Parliamentary control of the industry is achieved by

(i) The annual publication of accounts which are scrutinized by the Public Accounts Committee.

(ii) An annual debate; one day of parliamentary business is given up to a debate on the industry's affairs. In fact these days are not always used for their true purpose, for by tradition the opposition has the right to choose some other topic of business if it is felt that there is little cause for criticism of the industry.

(iii) The designation of a Minister to exercise general control of policy; he has no right to query day-to-day administrative matters.

(*d*) Parliament usually sets up a Consumer's Council of interested parties to represent the consumer and raise questions about the service and its charges. There are no shareholders able to vote the Board out of control, though the Minister may remove the senior officials. Security of office promotes a proper career structure within the industry and ensures a regular supply of qualified and experienced personnel for senior posts.

EXERCISES SET 2

(11) Types of Business Unit

1. Do you consider that there is any place today for the sole trader? Are any legal requirements necessary before starting such a business?

(*R.S.A. II*)

2. Explain the differences between the sole-trader type of business and the Public Limited Company, with reference to the ownership and management of capital.

(*R.S.A. I*)

3. A garage is owned by two partners, both of whom are skilled motor mechanics. It offers the following services: garage service, petrol and oil, tyres and accessories, repairs; it employs four other mechanics, a porter, and two petrol-pump attendants. Each partner tends to feel responsible for all that is done, and as a result there are frequent disagreements when they give conflicting instructions to employees and advice to customers. Discuss this problem in the light of what you know about a partnership, suggesting ways of solving the problems.

(*R.S.A. I*)

4. What is meant by the phrase 'nationalized industry'? Why are industries nationalized, and are there any disadvantages?

5. Why is it necessary or advisable for partners to have a Partnership Deed or Articles of Partnership? What information would such a document contain?

6. A Private Limited Company may decide to 'go public'. What does this mean? Why do such firms change their business organization in this way?

7. What are the important differences between partnerships and Private Limited Companies? Why do these types of organization exist?

8. Write briefly about the following:

(*a*) the principle of limited liability; (*b*) a company prospectus; (*c*) quoted shares; (*d*) general partners.

9. A, B, and C are partners, with capitals amounting to £8,000, £4,000, and £2,000 respectively. There is no special Partnership Agreement. What rights and duties does each of the partners have? If the profits earned in a year totalled £3,700, how much would each partner receive?

(R.S.A.)

10. Explain the main differences between the rights enjoyed by Mr. Dixon, a shareholder in a retail co-operative society, and those of Mr. Richardson, an ordinary shareholder in a public limited liability company.

(R.S.A.)

11. What are the important differences between partnerships and private limited companies? What justification is there for the existence of these two kinds of business organization?

(Associated Examining Board)

12. Mr. George, Mr. Andrew, Mr. Patrick, and Mr. David are partners in an estate agency. There has never been a formal partnership deed to determine their respective rights. Advise the partners as to the rights and responsibilities of each in respect of (*a*) the management of the business (*b*) sharing profits and losses, and (*c*) the payment of partnership debts.

(R.S.A.)

13. Why do sole traders sometimes convert their businesses into private limited liability companies and the latter sometimes convert themselves into public limited liability companies?

(University of London)

14. Describe briefly the different forms of business unit in this country. Why has no one form driven out all the others?

(University of London)

15. (*a*) In what way does a national publicly owned industry differ from a public limited liability company? Mention appropriate examples in your answer.

(*b*) If the former is unprofitable, on whom does the loss fall?

(University of London)

CHAPTER THREE

RETAIL TRADE—MAKING GOODS AVAILABLE TO THE FINAL CONSUMER

(1) Introduction

If commerce is concerned with the movement of goods from producer to consumer, it would appear to be logical to start at the point of production and follow the movement through until the goods reach the final consumer. By starting with retail trade, we are beginning at the end. The justification for doing so is that everyone is familiar with the retail shop and by starting here we can move from what is best known towards the branches of commerce that are less known.

The shop is the place where goods can be obtained to meet everyday household needs. Some goods come directly to our homes, e.g. milk and newspapers. Probably the most characteristic feature of a civilized town is its shops. Without shops there would be little point in going to the town. To some extent it is true that the wealth and prosperity of a people can be judged by the number of retail outlets that offer goods to the people, and the variety of the articles they display.

In 1971 there were 472,991 establishments in Britain engaged in retailing. About 390,000 of these were run by self-employed persons. Altogether 2,541,430 persons were employed in retail trade. On average each small shop had four employees and an annual turnover of £21,000; each multiple had an average of 12 employees and a turnover of £87,000.

(2) Meaning of the word 'Retail'

The word 'retail' is from the old French word *retailler*—to cut again. This is the most important function of a retailer, to buy in large quantities and cut up into small quantities. The grocer may buy a whole cheese and cut it up into small pieces of $\frac{1}{2}$ lb or less. The butcher buys whole carcases of pigs and sheep, and cuts them into various joints.

Even if there is no actual cutting up to do the retailer will still break bulk in other ways. Remember that in a mass-production world the factory is turning out very large quantities of goods. It wishes to clear the production lines quickly by disposing of these goods to large-scale merchants called wholesalers. The bulk has to be broken down, and the last link in the chain is the retailer. He may buy in grosses and sell single

Table 4. Establishments, Turnover, and Persons Engaged in Retail Trade (Census of Distribution—1971 adapted)

Kind of Business and Form of Organization	1971		
	Establish-ments	Turnover	Persons engaged
	Number	£'000	Number
TOTAL RETAIL TRADE . .	472,991	15,610.730	2,541,430
Co-operative Societies . . .	15,413	1,107,999	132,204
Multiples	66,785	6,083,560	814,666
Independents	390,793	8,419,171	1,594,560
Types of Outlet			
Food	202,582	8,357,729	1,274,494
Confectionery, etc. . . .	52,064	1,305,875	275,458
Clothing and Footwear . . .	81,279	2,371,766	403,744
Other Shops	139,490	3,870,542	600,100
Market Stalls	31,790	146,965	37,829
Mail Order	771	632,585	59,816
Services (hairdressing, etc.) . .	61,090	400,919	281,434

packets. Sugar for instance arrives at the retailer's shop in packets of 56 lb each. It is the retailer's task to open the pack and put the 56 × 1 lb bags or the 28 × 2 lb bags on the counter for sale to the housewife.

Although we are so familiar with the idea of retail trade, there is still a great deal we need to know before we can fully understand the vital part retail traders play in commerce.

(3) Definition of Retail Trade

Retail trade is that part of commerce where goods are sold to the final consumer.

(4) Persons Engaged in Retail Trade

Not all the people engaged in retail trade are traditional retailers performing the full functions of a retailer. There are many wholesalers these days who act as retailers by selling goods direct to the consumer. This is a recent development since the Resale Prices Act of 1964 has finally ended Resale Price Maintenance. This is dealt with more fully on page 59. We also have many manufacturers today who sell to the general public by **mail order**, or even direct from sales departments in factories. The traditional pattern of the retail trade has changed very greatly in the last 20 years. Among the different types of retail trader we must include:

(*a*) Small-scale retailers operating as sole traders or partnerships.

(*b*) Large-scale retailers operating as limited companies, and often performing wholesaling as well as retailing functions.

(*c*) Co-operative societies, which are often manufacturers, wholesalers, and retailers.

(*d*) Wholesalers selling direct to the consumer by mail order or through discount-trading schemes.

(*e*) Manufacturers selling direct to the consumer either by mail order or to personal callers who live in the locality.

(5) The Functions of the Retailer

The chief functions of a retailer are:

(*a*) To provide a local supply of goods.
(*b*) To break bulk.
(*c*) To serve the public personally.
(*d*) To prepare goods for resale.
(*e*) To arrange hire-purchase finance.
(*f*) To provide after-sales service.
(*g*) To act as a liaison between the consumer and the manufacturer.

The chief points about each of these functions will show the retailer's services to the consumer.

(*a*) *Providing a local supply*. We need the goods we purchase to be available near our homes, or near enough for us to go to get them. A *local* supply becomes more important the heavier things are, and we often require them to be delivered to the house. Few people would buy a wardrobe if the furniture dealer said 'Very well, madam, I'll wrap it up.' We should not order half a ton of coal if we had to carry it away. Even 7 lb of potatoes is too heavy to carry far.

Local supply also becomes very important when we buy an item frequently. We do not want to travel far if we forget a box of matches. Meat, vegetables, groceries, petrol and oil, ironmongery, and many similar items are best supplied in the shops local to housing areas. We are prepared to go a little farther for furniture, television sets, or motor cars. We rarely find a full choice of television sets and radiograms in local shops: instead we go to the Town Centre where the greater number of customers makes it worthwhile for a tradesman to offer a wide selection. This is also a convenient centre to base a servicing depot, since most consumer durables need servicing during their working life. For fashionable items such as ladies' clothes we are usually prepared to go to a really big town, but we cannot normally afford to do this more than once or twice a year.

(*b*) *Breaking bulk*. This means buying in large quantities and selling in smaller quantities. The grocer may buy a gross of tablets of soap and sell in single tablets. The greengrocer buys potatoes by the sack, but he retails in pounds, or kilos.

(*c*) *Serving the public personally*. Personal service varies between different retailers according to the individual characteristics of the trader. One retailer will be of great help to his customers, advising them of particular lines that are satisfactory, or cheaper, or more suitable. He may give credit to customers who are having a hard time; he may open up after hours in an emergency, or he may work longer hours to accommodate housewives wishing to shop after work. Delivery to the customer is a service that is often performed by the retailer. Sometimes it is absolutely essential, for instance with furniture, and sometimes merely for the customer's convenience. All these activities will promote goodwill, and perhaps bring the retailer extra profit in the week, or a higher price for his business if he should sell. Another retailer might put his own convenience before his customers and do as little as possible. Obviously this will affect his takings adversely.

(*d*) *Preparing goods for resale*. This is often part of breaking bulk. When the butcher cuts up a pig or the grocer slices a side of bacon, he is preparing it for sale and breaking bulk at the same time. More and more of this preparation for sale tends to be done in the factories today; for instance sugar is usually pre-packed, so is tea. Other forms of preparation are the assembly of goods into finished form; for instance bicycles arrive in parts, or at least with the pedals turned inwards to save packing space.

(*e*) *Hire-purchase finance*. Hire-purchase is dealt with separately in Chapter 5. It is part of many people's daily lives to buy goods on 'HP'. By making the necessary arrangements the retailer ensures that his customers are able to obtain the goods and pay for them over the period of hire.

(*f*) *After-sales service*. This service is an essential part of selling consumer durables, e.g. TV sets, refrigerators, washing machines, spin driers, cars, radio sets, cooking appliances. Even the best of these suffer unexpected failures of one sort or another. Service keeps them in working order. Often they are guaranteed for one year, and the manufacturer is obliged to repair them free if they break down.

(*g*) *Liaison between the consumer and the manufacturer*. By letting the manufacturer know what his customers think about the goods they buy the retailer keeps the manufacturer informed of criticisms of his product. He may also convey to the public the views of the manufacturer by warning them of misuse of the product for which the manufacturer will not be held liable. For instance, many garments are sold with washing instructions which must be followed if the manufacturer is to be held liable for any defects; similarly, many technical products will not be repaired under guarantee if it is obvious that the purchaser has tried to repair them himself. Such an exchange of views very often results in improvements in the design of a product, greater durability, greater safety and greater reliability.

Exercises Set 3

(6) The Functions of the Retailer

1. Discuss what 'local' means with regard to each of the following items, with particular reference to the distance you would normally expect to go to

fetch a supply for your household: paraffin oil; potatoes; hot water; aspirins; a new two-piece suit; electricity; bread; ice cream; fuel oil for a hot-water system; washing-up liquid; wallpaper; a bedroom suite; tomatoes; baked beans; a rhododendron plant; a washing machine; frozen peas.

2. Suggest suitably sized orders to be placed (*a*) by a retailer to a wholesaler, and (*b*) by a housewife (4 in family) to a retailer for the commodities named below. An example is given.

Commodity	Bulk order by retailer	Order by housewife
Paraffin oil	200 gallons	½ gallon
Bread		
Cheese		
Biscuits		
Packets of detergent		
Matches		
Newspapers		
Tobacco		
Cigarettes		
Cough drops		
Oranges		
Potatoes		
Butter		
Lettuces		
Radishes		
Television sets		

3. In what ways might a retailer serve you personally? Is personal service increasing or decreasing?

4. How do various traders prepare goods for sale? Consider especially (*a*) the butcher; (*b*) the grocer; (*c*) the timber merchant; (*d*) the garage; (*e*) the furniture dealer; (*f*) the confectioner.

5. What is hire-purchase? Discuss the types of goods for which hire-purchase is desirable.

6. What sorts of goods require after-sales service?

7. Your local council is planning a new estate of 400 houses. There is to be a shopping centre of ten shops. Which retailers do you think should be allowed to have a shop? Give reasons.

8. Write a short account of how the following people prepare goods for resale: a butcher; a greengrocer; a grocer; a chemist.

9. What is the origin of the word 'retail'? Name five functions of the retailer. Which of these functions do you consider the most fundamental in retail trade?

10. Compare the services given by a general store in a small village and a large furniture store in a busy town centre.

(7) Types of Retail Outlet

We can divide the main retail outlets into three distinct classes as follows:

Retailers without shops—pedlars, hawkers, and street-market traders.
Retailers with shops—sole traders, partnership traders, multiple shops and chain stores, department stores, supermarkets and hypermarkets. *Retailers who are not really retailers*—'wholesale retailers' and mail-order businesses, wholesalers selling to privileged groups at a discount, and 'manufacturer–retailers' selling directly from factory to consumer.

Let us take a closer look at these divisions and subdivisions.

(8) Retailers without Shops

Pedlars. Pedlars are traders who carry their wares about and sell to the customer at his or her own front door. The pedlar's trade has largely died out in Britain where most housewives can now reach a shop regularly.

Hawkers. Hawkers are traders who use a cart or van to bring goods to their customer's door. In greengrocery this is very common still. A recent development is the hawking of paraffin from door to door from a small bowser. Hawkers must have a licence from the local Authority.

Street-market traders. Many retail street markets have been in existence since the Middle Ages. The law governing these markets is very ancient. It is called *Market Overt*, from the French word *ouvert*, 'open'. It is generally known how unwise it is to buy goods from people who offer them at bargain prices, because such goods may be stolen or smuggled. Anyone buying in these circumstances is deemed to realize that he may be receiving stolen goods. Certainly if the true owner claims the goods the buyer must give them up. At best he has been a fool, and has lost his money; at worst he may be charged with receiving. His title (right of ownership) to the goods is defective, since if the vendor had no right to them, neither has the buyer. The law of *Market Overt* protects a person who buys in open market. If you buy where all can see, you are deemed to buy honestly, and hence you do get a good title to your purchases.

Market traders hire a stall in the market from the local Borough Council for a few pence a day, and therefore have very small overheads. As a result prices tend to be lower, but it is also true that some goods may be of sub-standard quality.

(9) Retailers with Shops

Independent Small Traders

These are people in business on their own account, or in partnership; they used to be the backbone of retail trade in Britain. They now account for about half the total trade done; the rest is carried on by large-scale organizations.

The traditional shopkeeper still has much to offer the customer, especially with personal service, temporary credit, longer shop hours and locality. He is at a disadvantage with price competition, display, and hygiene. He has less capital available to improve premises and layout, and he cannot buy on such favourable terms as the large-scale firms, because he orders in smaller quantities.

The small retailers have attempted to overcome some of these disadvantages by forming special large-scale organizations. These are discussed later under the heading 'Large Scale in the Retail Trade'.

Co-operative Retail Societies

The first successful 'Co-op' store was founded in 1844 in Toad Lane, Rochdale, by 28 weavers nowadays remembered as the 'Rochdale Pioneers'. The idea was to buy foodstuffs at wholesale prices and sell them (to members only) at market price. Profits were divided among

Fig. 5. The Rochdale Pioneers' historic store as it was in 1844

members in proportion to the value of their purchases. The share-out (dividend) took place twice a year. By 1845 there were 74 members, the turnover was £710, the profit £22.

At this time many of the shops in the northern industrial towns were owned either by the mill owners or by shopkeepers who were under the influence of the mill owners. The general shortage of coins and reliable bank-notes meant that workers were often cheated of part of their earnings, in the following way. The first group of workers were paid in the morning and were then quickly sent to the shop to spend their money at once, so that the coins could be used later the same day to pay other workers. This reduced the workers' chances of choosing goods carefully. The Rochdale Pioneers showed how to avoid dealing at all with the 'company stores'.

Most of the following principles adopted by the Rochdale Pioneers in 1844 are today recognized by Co-operatives throughout the world.

(*a*) Open membership

(*b*) Democratic control (one member, one vote)

(*c*) Distribution of the surplus in proportion to purchases

(*d*) Payment of limited interest on capital

(*e*) Political and religious neutrality

(*f*) Cash trading

(*g*) Promotion of education

The Co-operative movement spread rapidly. Societies were set up in towns all over the United Kingdom. In 1862 the members voted to set up a wholesale society, the Co-operative Wholesale Society. This society not only supplied the retail societies like any ordinary wholesaler, but ran factories, farms, transport services, and even tea gardens to provide everything the retail societies needed. The retail societies joined the wholesale society in exactly the same way as the ordinary members joined the retail society. All the profits of the C.W.S. are shared among the member retail societies, and all the profits of the retail societies are shared among the members. Thus in the end all the profits return to the members of the retail societies whose purchasing power actually keeps the Co-operative movement going. In 1972 there were about 11 million members in 270 retail societies. Sales were £1,290 million. Half of these were sales of groceries.

The Co-operatives have always been motivated by social objectives. Although members have a share in the capital of the society, and one member may have up to £1,000 capital in most societies, each member has only a single vote. This is quite different from a capitalist firm, where those shares that do carry voting powers are usually accorded one vote each.

The advantages of co-operation in retail trade can be listed as follows:

(*a*) The customers who shop at the Co-op get good quality products at fair prices, and a share of all the profits made.

(*b*) They share in the democratic control of the society, though this is less easy today as societies grow bigger. The lay-director, concerning himself with policy matters as the elected representative of the members, is less influential in the modern conditions than in former times.

(*c*) A range of benefits for members and employees includes such items as help with education, convalescence after illness, youth camps for children and assistance with funeral expenses.

(*d*) At one time the societies had a 'private market' of their members, who supported the societies for idealistic as well as practical reasons. Today this is less true, with the dividend replaced by trading stamps which attract customers who are not members. The Co-operative stores have just passed through a rather difficult period owing to the changing pattern of retail trade. A discussion of this period is given on pp. 52–65.

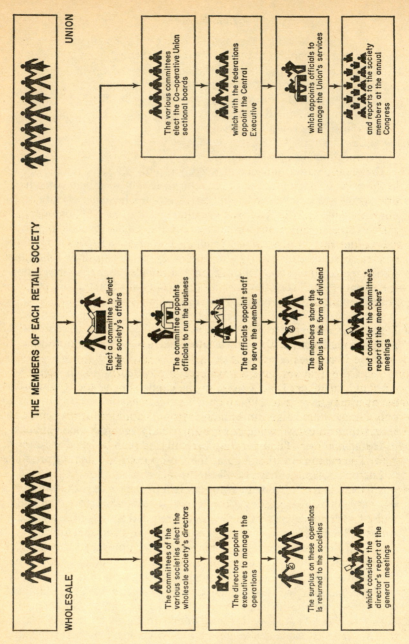

Fig. 6. How democracy works in the Co-operative movement

How Democracy works in the Co-operative movement

This diagram gives only an approximate idea of the movement's structure, but it shows clearly how the ultimate control of the co-operative system lies in the hands of the members.

In the left-hand column the detailed method of management in the C.W.S. differs from that in the Scottish C.W.S., but the control by a democratically elected board of directors is the same.

In the centre column, the system of staff appointments varies slightly from society to society, but the general principle is common to all.

In the right-hand column the Central Executive of the Co-operative Union comprises nine elected retail society representatives, plus eight nominees of the C.W.S. and two nominees of the S.C.W.S. The Co-operative Union has a separately elected Parliamentary Committee which comprises representatives from Sectional Boards, the Central Executive, the Co-operative Party, the Co-operative Press and the two Wholesale Societies. The Co-operative Union also has the following departments: Legal, Finance, Taxation, Publications and Information, Labour and Industrial Relations, Research and Statistics, and Education.

Multiple Shops and Chain Stores

Under these headings we study a type of shop which will be familiar to most readers. There are several similar types of organization but their chief feature is that they are all large-scale organizations run from a Head Office. They are practically all Limited Companies, not sole-trader or partnership organizations.

In the **multiple-shop** type of establishment a Head Office acts as administration section and warehouse, buying goods in large quantities at very favourable rates, and sending them round to a large number of branches. These branches may all have the same name, the Head Office name, or they may have kept the names of the original businesses which have been taken over. The reader may find, if he inquires, that shops in his own area which he thought were private traders are actually owned by a Limited Company. One way to find out is to ask for a bill with some purchase. The bill is bound by law to reveal the true owners' names.

This type of multiple shop has many branches, but they often deal in only one class of goods, say groceries, or furniture.

The **chain-store** types of shop have a similar organization and many branches, but they also have many shops under one roof. The chain store or variety store was originally developed in America, and perhaps F. W. Woolworth & Co. Ltd. is the best-known example. When we enter a branch we expect to find ourselves in a stationer's, grocer's, toy-shop, ironmonger's, electrical-supplies store, draper's, chemist's, horticultural supplier's, and lots more.

It is very convenient to buy so many goods in one store, especially when quality goes with low prices. Because of the large orders they place, variety stores are able to command high-class goods at attractive prices.

Chain stores do not hide behind the names of firms they take over in order to preserve the goodwill. Instead they spread goodwill from branch to branch by keeping uniform shop-fronts which always look the same in every town. The customer who is out of his own home area, seeing the familiar shop-front, recalls the wide variety of goods available at reasonable prices, and presses in to make his purchases.

Department Stores

Sixty years ago the department store was the latest thing in retail trading. It was many shops under one roof, and each department vied with every other department to increase its share of the business. Catering for the well-to-do customer, and with ladies' fashions as one of its chief attractions, the department store relied on attracting its customers into the centre of the big cities. The West End of London is the best known of these areas, with heavily carpeted luxurious department stores, offering personal attention to the customer and guaranteeing to supply anything within reason at a moment's notice. One such store has the telegraphic address 'EVERYTHING LONDON'.

For some years after the Second World War the department stores declined in importance because the distribution of wealth in the United Kingdom changed. They were slow to adjust to these changes and lost trade as a result. More recently they have improved the attractiveness of their stores, particularly to young people, who tend to be better paid these days. The establishment of 'in-store' boutiques, record counters, etc., has increased their sales to this fashion-conscious sector. It is still true to say that a day's shopping in the department stores of our major cities is a pleasant and enjoyable event.

Supermarkets

Supermarkets are self-service cut-price chain stores. They cut out personal service by shop assistants, offer many different types of goods and cut the price of items wherever possible. They present the fiercest competition to all types of shops because of this price-cutting policy. At present there are still some types of goods on which Resale Price Maintenance applies, but the vast majority of goods are now freed from restrictive sales practices by the Resale Prices Act, 1964. For a full discussion of Resale Price Maintenance see page 57.

Supermarkets are large-scale organizations run from Head Offices by Limited Companies.

The policy of 'loss leaders' pursued by supermarkets means cutting the price of some popular article very much below the market price, in order to attract customers to the shop. The shopkeeper is relying on his customer buying other items at the same time. Sugar was a good choice for a 'loss-leader', since it is required every day in most families. If a housewife got into a habit of shopping at a store which sold sugar for much less than most other shops, the losses on sugar would be more than compensated by the extra custom received. Its high price has now reduced its use as a loss-leader.

Hypermarkets

A new type of large retail outlet is now being introduced. It has already proved extremely successful on the Continent. It consists of very large retail premises, usually at a main cross roads in an outlying area, with large car parking facilities. It avoids the high cost of town centre premises and rates, catering for the car owning customer. It offers (*a*) easy parking (*b*) every type of goods (groceries, consumer durables, clothing, hardware etc.) (*c*) extremely competitive prices (*d*) self service (*e*) credit card facilities and (*f*) off-peak shopping hours. The name 'hypermarket', or very large market, seems appropriate. Despite some opposition from established retailers sites are slowly becoming available for these new firms.

(10) Retailers who are not really Retailers

Wholesale Retailers

Mail-order firms. Selling by mail order originated in the United States of America as a solution to the problems of customers who lived far away from the nearest shop. The shop-window for the mail-order firm is its catalogue, which is expensive to produce and to distribute, but which presents the customer with a very wide range of goods attractively displayed. Unlike stock in some shops, it does not need dusting, or rearranging more often than once a year, and there is no chance of the clothes and fabrics displayed becoming shop-soiled or faded. Thus it is in many ways a very satisfactory shop window.

Not all mail-order firms issue catalogues. Very successful businesses worth millions of pounds have been set up using newspaper advertisements. This type of advertisement can be seen in any popular newspaper, particularly on Saturdays.

In Great Britain, where shops are plentiful, it might seem unnecessary to have mail-order firms at all, but they offer one attraction which most shops do not offer, and that is hire-purchase of non-durable goods. Many families are glad to spread their payments for clothing, footwear, soft furnishings, linoleum, etc., over a period.

The usual period of credit in Great Britain is 20 weeks, in which case the weekly repayments amount to 0·05 in the pound. If the customer sends her payments regularly, she soon becomes a credit-worthy customer and entitled to re-order at any time. Whatever is unpaid from the previous order is added to the price of the new article, and the total is paid for over the next 19 weeks. In this way the housewife is always in debt but always able to order more goods if required.

Two things are required if this system is to work satisfactorily for all parties: the goods must be of high quality and value for money, and bad debts must be kept to a minimum. The mail-order firms establish nationwide links by having housewives who act as agents in every street. These housewives collect the weekly payments from their friends who are customers and remit them to Head Office weekly in return for a commission of about 10 per cent. This reduces the bad debts, but of course managers of such types of business expect a higher rate of bad debts than ordinary shops.

The mail-order business is an example of the elimination of the retailer by the wholesaler. The mail-order firm is simply a huge warehouse, often with its own private post office built in for convenience of both the firm and the Post Office authorities. It takes the profits of the normal wholesaler and retailer and also gets extra profit because it is usually doing such large-scale business that it can buy in extra large quantities at very favourable prices.

At the same time it has certain additional expenses to take into account. Postage is a large item, especially as goods are usually sent on 'sale or return'; commission has to be paid to the agents, and as already mentioned bad debts are fairly high.

Discount Selling to Privileged Groups

A second way of eliminating the retailer has been developed since the Resale Prices Act, 1964. It is the wholesale warehouse which opens its doors to privileged groups of people, but has been careful to tie the bonds of privilege very loosely so that in fact almost everyone can buy in this way. For instance, most Trade Unions have this privilege extended to their members and this lets in almost the entire nation. Discounts of about 10 per cent to 25 per cent or even higher are allowed, and payment is by cash, or in some cases by hire-purchase.

The privileged nature of the customer to some extent reduces bad debts, but as most of the business is for cash the bad-debt losses are very small anyway.

Direct Selling by Manufacturers—the Elimination of both Wholesalers and Retailers.

In recent years a very determined attack upon both wholesalers and retailers has been made by some manufacturers in the durable consumer goods industries who have adopted a policy of direct selling straight from the factory to the consumer. Contact with the consumer is made by advertisements in the newspapers.

The manufacturer reaps all the profits that would normally be made by the wholesaler and the retailer, as well as the manufacturing profit which he would normally make. This enables him to cut the price to the consumer very considerably—in effect to share his extra profit with the householder who purchases the goods for less than the normal retail price.

This sounds a highly profitable way of running a business, but although many fortunes have been made by this method of direct selling, it is not all profit. The services usually performed by the wholesaler and retailer have still to be performed; bulk must be broken, storage provided, transport arranged and payment collected, so that some of the extra profits are used up in these ways.

Is the Elimination of the Retailer Desirable?

We saw in Chapter One that, when people specialize, productivity rises and general efficiency increases so that total available surpluses rise. The wholesale and retail trades are specialized branches of commerce, and if we eliminate them we reduce specialization. The knowledge, experience, and skill of the specialist wholesaler or retailer is lost, and the manufacturer has to develop his own ability to perform the functions previously performed by specialists. These functions cannot be avoided, as explained above.

If a manufacturer ceases to specialize, it seems certain that there must be some loss of efficiency. He will have to warehouse his goods instead of the wholesaler doing it. He will have to transport them instead of the wholesaler doing it. He will have to display pictures of his machines in advertisements instead of in shops, and he must demonstrate them through his local representatives. He must service them after sale, arrange hire-purchase finance and so on. Clearly, the extra money earned will not be all profit. Setting up local servicing centres entails great expense.

It therefore seems certain that, while personal fortunes may be made in this way, there could well be an overall loss to society by the reduction in specialization. The whole country may lose even though individuals benefit.

The same is true of mail-order firms. The cost of sending goods in separate parcels may be excessive and wasteful in a society which already has an efficient distribution system.

Against these arguments it may be said that society benefits indirectly in other ways. The housewives who can afford a washing machine only directly from the factory, or new clothes only on extended credit from the mail-order firms, gain morale-boosting pleasures from their new possessions which react upon the economy in favourable ways.

Exercises Set 4

(11) The Pattern of Retail Trade

1. Choose a word or phrase from the list on the right to fill the blank in each of the following sentences:

(a) The usual place where consumers obtain supplies of goods is a . . .

(b) The French word *retailler* means . . .

(c) A person who sells goods from a cart or van is a . . .

(d) To allow people time to pay for goods is called giving them . . .

(e) Department stores try to attract customers into the big . . .

(f) . . . shops set up a branch in every busy shopping centre.

(g) Price-cutting by . . . is a feature of modern retail trade.

(h) A commodity which is sold at a loss in order to attract customers is called a . . . . . .

(i) Mail-order firms are wholesalers who . . . the retailer.

(j) Chain stores have many branches and each branch is . . . under one roof.

hawker
eliminate
cities
supermarkets
shop
credit
many shops
to cut again
loss leader
multiple

2. Old Tom has run a bicycle shop for many years, supplying new and secondhand bicycles and spare parts to the people of the neighbourhood. He has been well known for his obliging attitude for many years, and has given many a youngster a hand to fit a new outer cover, mend a puncture, or fix a three-speed gear. Often he has made no charge for his services.

A new supermarket has opened next door to Tom's shop and proposes to sell new bicycles, on which there is a good rate of profit, at cut prices. They will not sell spare parts, or carry out any service of the bicycles they sell, because the profit is very small on such items.

Discuss whether such competition is fair to Old Tom, or of real benefit to the community.

3. What are the functions of a retailer? Does a supermarket provide all these functions? What does it offer the public that a traditional shopkeeper is unable or unwilling to offer?

4. Distinguish between a department store and a chain store. What are the differences between them as to: (a) the range of items sold; (b) the prices of the goods they sell; (c) their situation geographically; (d) the personal service they offer?

5. Write a short paragraph each about three of the following:

(a) pedlars; (b) hawkers; (c) Co-operative Societies; (d) multiple shops; (e) traditional retail outlets; (f) mail-order houses; (g) hypermarkets.

6. What do you understand by elimination of the retailer? Which kinds of firm in the retail trade eliminate the retailer and how do they attract the customer?

7. 'Last year the Co-operative Societies made profits of £50 million.' 'No one makes a profit in the co-operative system of retailing, but the shopper simply puts money by when he makes a purchase which he regains on dividend

day.' Explain these two statements, and show that they do not really contradict one another.

8. How does a small retailer serve the people in the community where he has his shop? What reward does he get for his services? Which functions does the small retailer perform that a multiple shop or chain store would not usually offer?

9. Describe the organization of a retail Co-operative Society.

10. What factors would you take into account when selecting a site for: (*a*) a supermarket; (*b*) a launderette; (*c*) a hypermarket?

11. How would you account for the large number of retail concerns in Britain? Say with reasons, if you think their number could be reduced without inconvenience to consumers.

(R.S.A.)

12. Describe briefly the chief forms of retail organization and explain why they may all exist in any one shopping area.

(University of London)

13. What changes in shopping habits are being brought about by self-service? To what extent do you think self-service shopping will develop further? Give reasons.

(University of London)

14. (*a*) In what ways does a retail co-operative society differ from a chain store or multiple shop organization?

(*b*) What is the relationship of a retail co-operative society to the Co-operative Wholesale Society?

(University of London)

15. The small retailer suffers from certain disadvantages compared with the modern large-scale retailer. What are they? What attempts are being made by small retailers in conjunction with their suppliers to overcome these disadvantages?

(University of London)

CHAPTER FOUR

THE CHANGING PATTERN OF RETAIL TRADE

(1) Introduction

During the last 50 years the pattern of retail trade has changed out of all recognition. At the end of the First World War retail trade was still dominated by the small shop, run by the independent sole trader or by two partners. Such proprietors were skilled in their trade, they knew how to break bulk, wrap a wide variety of goods, make secure paper packets out of a sheet of paper without string or glue, could weigh and measure and change money, add up quickly and so on. The local Co-operative shop and the department stores of the big cities were their only competitors.

Today many of these old skills have disappeared. The grocer who sells a wider variety of goods than ever before knows very little about many of them, since they arrive pre-packed and readily available to the customer. The whole tempo of retail trade has been speeded up as a result. An assistant who cannot herself add up very well produces excellent printed copies of bills correctly totalled by means of an automatic till. This may even subtract for returned 'empties' and often indicates which department each item came from.

(2) The Causes of the Changes in Retail Trade

The chief causes of this revolution in retail trade are as follows:

(*a*) The branding of goods under specialized brand names such as Bisto, Atora, Saxa, Cerebos, Paxo, etc.

(*b*) The technological revolution in both products and marketing.

(*c*) The employment of women on a national scale has reduced the time available for household shopping to a few hours per week for many families.

(*d*) The more even distribution of wealth in our society.

(*e*) The virtual abolition of Resale Price Maintenance under the Restrictive Trade Practices Act, 1956, and the Resale Prices Act, 1964.

(*f*) The growth of large-scale enterprises in the retail trade, particularly the self-service store.

(*g*) The changing nature of Co-operative retail trade.

(3) The Effect of the Branding of Goods on Retail Trade

The branding of goods is the selling of these goods under a 'trade

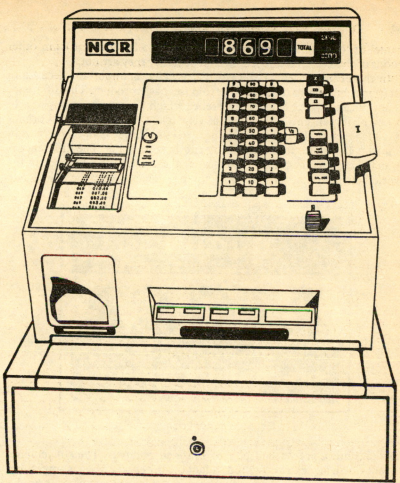

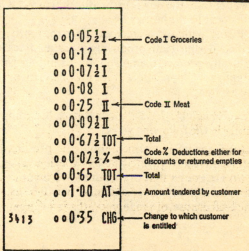

Fig. 7. A mechanized till and the bill it produces. (*The machine itself works out the change to which the customer is entitled*)

	o o 0·05½ I	← Code I Groceries
	o o 0·12 I	
	o o 0·07½ I	
	o o 0·08 I	
	o o 0·25 II	← Code II Meat
	o o 0·09½ II	
	o o 0·67½ TOT	← Total
	o o 0·02½ %	← Code % Deductions either for discounts or returned empties
	o o 0·65 TOT	← Total
	o o 1·00 AT	← Amount tendered by customer
3413	o o 0·35 CHG	← Change to which customer is entitled

name' or 'brand name' so that they appear to be different from other goods of the same name, even though basically they are not.

In the definition above the word 'basically' is important because in fact most brands do differ subtly from the basic product. The difference is not purely a psychological difference which we have been duped into believing is real. This is the point of view taken by most critics of branding, that in fact the difference is not real at all, but is purely a 'conditioned belief' put into our heads by subtle advertising. The difference is in many cases real enough, for instance there is all the difference in the world between potatoes heavy with mud, purchased from the retail street

Fig. 8. A branded commodity

market, and a pre-washed bag of branded potatoes. The convenience is well worth any extra cost, and in fact the pre-washed bag is sometimes cheaper than the unwashed natural product. Countless similar examples will occur to the housewife.

Firms with secret recipes, or secret processes of manufacture, or skilled design staff producing unique styles of furniture or clothing, naturally protect themselves by branding their image. 'G-Plan' is as unique as 'Chippendale', and no one criticized Chippendale for branding his image.

How branding affects the consumer. Branding is beneficial to the consumer in the following ways:

(*a*) He is well informed about the product both by the right kind of informative advertising, and by experience.

(*b*) He knows that the product will be uniform in quality. One packet of a particular branded commodity will be exactly the same as any other packet because the manufacturer is at great pains to keep the quality exactly the same. There is no need to inspect the goods before purchasing them; the manufacturer can be relied on to deal at once with any complaint.

(*c*) Branding increases the rate of turnover. This is of great importance not only to the manufacturer but also to the consumer who gets a

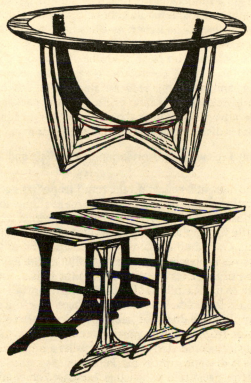

Fig. 9. 'G-Plan'—a famous brand of furniture

fresher product because stock is sold and replaced more frequently. Large-scale manufacture reduces the cost per unit.

(*d*) Asking for branded items by name saves time in the selection of goods and in the making up of orders.

On the other hand there are some cases where the branding process is clearly against the public interest, in that the extra cost to the housewife is excessive compared with the extra benefit. An inquiry into the detergent industry in Britain established that the branding of detergents under different names was wasteful, and suggested that the detergent industry should reduce its advertising budget by 40 per cent and its prices by 20 per cent. In the United States drug prices have been forced down by government activity aimed at reducing the 'me-too' branding of drugs. This happy American phrase refers to the practice of taking a new antibiotic invented by some other manufacturer, altering its chemical structure very slightly without altering its basic therapeutic effect, and claiming that 'we've got a new antibiotic too'. The 'new' drug is patented as if it really were new, and marketed at high prices with expensive advertising campaigns. Society is no richer, and has had to afford unnecessary expense which it would rather have spent in other ways.

The effect of branding on retail trade has been very great. By packaging goods in the factory, the retailer is saved the necessity of weighing, measuring, and wrapping separate items. The advice the retailer formerly gave his customer is now printed on the packet, or conveyed by mass-media advertising. Often the customer serves himself, and all the retailer does is display the goods and take the money.

(4) Effect of the Technological Revolution in Products and Marketing on Retail Trade

Equally important in its effect on the retail trade has been the change to mass-production techniques. We can now make things so cheaply that repairing them is not really worth while. No one wants the ironmonger to repair a kettle for him these days, we throw the old kettle away and buy a new one. One famous scientist coined the phrase 'The Effluent Society', a pun on Professor Galbraith's 'Affluent Society', to describe our present way of life. Every year we sink in the seas around our coasts enough rubbish to make a pile as high as Mount Everest.

The effect on retail trade has once again been to reduce the services the retailer supplies. He does not need special skills to sell us another kettle. The quick-frozen chicken portions retailed from an ice box can be sold as easily by a confectioner or grocer as by a butcher. The division between trades is disappearing as marketing packs remove from the retailer any need for specialized knowledge. Increased convenience, greater hygiene, and lower prices often result because, while the organization behind the retailer is more complex than ever, it is highly specialized and very efficient. At the same time, a decline in the skills required by the individual retailer has resulted in a different, less intelligent and less skilled class of worker being adequate for the retailer's purpose.

(5) Effect of the Employment of Women on Retail Trade

Out of a total of 25,639,000 people at work in Great Britain (excluding Northern Ireland) in June, 1970 more than 9 million were women, of whom more than half were married. In 25 years the proportion of married women at work has increased threefold.

There are many explanations of this change in employment, and it has had many effects upon the life of the families whose mother goes out to work. In retail trade this has taken the form of a preference for self-service stores. The housewife who does her shopping during a short work-time lunch period or during a busy week-end when she has to catch up with the household chores, has no time to wait while an assistant fetches and carries things for her which she could just as easily collect herself. The technological revolution has enabled the housewife to serve herself more easily than a retailer can serve her. The self-service store (see page 58) is the solution to the problems of the working housewife.

(6) Effect on Retail Trade of a More Even Distribution of Wealth

Since 1945 a feature of British life has been a more even distribution of wealth, achieved partly by changes in the wages structure, and partly by changes in the tax structure. Whatever we may feel personally about the desirability of a more even wealth distribution, its effects on retail trade have been far-reaching.

The first of these effects has been a decline in the luxury services provided by the great department stores for the very rich section of the population. There are fewer very rich people about and the luxury services offered do not appeal to lower income groups, who are not so easily attracted to the fashionable shopping areas, and who are very price conscious.

The second effect has been the rapid expansion of all retail outlets catering for the mass of the population, especially where cost consciousness goes with quality goods. The multiple shops and the chain stores have expanded very rapidly in response to the greater incomes of the masses. Profits are to be made, if not more easily at least more regularly, in serving these very large groups of customers.

The third effect has been the relative decline of Co-operative trading. The reasons for this are dealt with on page 62.

The final effect of this redistribution of wealth has been a growth in the sales of goods on hire purchase. The hire-purchase system (see p. 71) has taken firm root in the economy as the only certain way for lower income groups to purchase the durable consumer goods on which our present prosperity and standard of living are based. The moral, and even religious, antipathy to hire purchase has yielded in the face of incontrovertible common-sense arguments in favour of this method of purchasing capital assets out of income.

(7) Abolition of Resale Price Maintenance
The Early History of R.P.M.

By about 1895 competition in the retail trades had become so fierce that many firms could not keep in business without cutting quality. Adulteration of food was common: for example, chalk was mixed with flour, and bran was mixed with wholemeal flour. Clearly, cut prices are no advantage if they involve cutting the quality of the goods. Low food prices also hold wages down, and give employers unfair arguments for refusing wage increases.

A chemist, Glyn Jones, who had a shop in the East End of London devised **Resale Price Maintenance** (R.P.M.) as a way to prevent price cutting. He persuaded suppliers of chemists' sundries to put R.P.M. clauses in their contracts of sale. It was made a major condition of the contracts that the goods should not be sold below the price laid down by the manufacturer, and retailers who were in breach of this contractual clause could be sued. The price had to be maintained at the 'fair' retail price.

In practice the manufacturers also developed the custom of refusing to supply anyone who cut their prices, so that he could not obtain replacements for the stock sold. It might be thought that there was little point in the manufacturers' doing this, since it would make little difference to them whether their goods were sold at cut prices or not. In fact it does affect them because retailers who are being forced to sell goods at cut prices owing to fierce competition soon turn on the manufacturer and insist that he cuts his profit margins too. If he then has to cut quality in order to make a living the public are not really benefiting from the cut price at all. Also there is a tendency for cut prices to force some retailers out of business, with a consequent reduction in the number of selling points for a manufacturers' goods, and a decline in convenience to the shopper.

For many years the manufacturers successfully defeated the attempts of some retailers to increase their share of any given market by cutting prices. From 1895 to 1945, in a period of stable money values, the general lack of prosperity kept profit margins and business down. Only since 1945, when it has become the chief function of governments to arrange prosperity for the people, has a change occurred.

The decisive breakthrough in the Resale Price Maintenance situation occurred in 1956 with the passing of the Restrictive Trade Practices Act. This act was introduced as a result of the high profits being made by the self-service shops. To see how this came about let us look at the history of self-service.

The Development of Self-Service Shops in Britain

In 1948 the Royal Arsenal Co-operative Society opened the first specially designed self-service store in this country. Customers selected the goods they required, took them to the cashier and paid for them, surrendering their ration coupons at the same time. This proved to be highly popular with busy workers, and highly profitable to the Co-operative Society, which made the full R.P.M. profit on all goods sold. However, there is nothing objectionable about high profits in a Co-operative Society, because the high profits are returned to the customers as dividend.

Within a few years other retailers copied the self-service idea, and began to make 'excessive' profits because the R.P.M. clauses in their contracts were still forcing them to maintain the resale prices. The result was a growing public outcry against the practice of maintaining resale prices, which resulted in the Restrictive Trade Practices Act of 1956. This Act made a small breach in the R.P.M. system. Against protests sponsored by small traders everywhere, it prohibited dealers in groceries from enforcing contractual agreements whereby goods were withheld from any firm which was known to cut prices. In other words, a manufacturer could still put in a clause requiring the person supplied not to resell to the general public at lower than the maintained price, but if he resold to another retailer the price-maintenance clause could not be enforced. It could not 'run with the goods'. This permitted a breakthrough in the grocery field to end the high profits achieved under maintained prices. In other fields, for instance confectionery and tobacco, the retail lobby was sufficiently strong to prevent the 1956 Act being applied.

The Growth of Supermarkets

The direct result of the 1956 Act was the widespread growth of price-cutting supermarkets in the retail grocery trade. These shops are large-scale, self-service stores operating in busy town centres where they combine a fierce price-cutting policy with a large turnover. They attracted the price-conscious poorer class of customers, now for the first time in history enjoying reasonable incomes and the use of adequate personal transport giving access to the town shopping centres. The small retailers in the 'neighbourhood' shops were faced with very severe competition.

The effect on the Co-operative shops was even more pronounced, and rather sad, for self-service had been a Co-operative discovery, which in a dozen years had turned round to deal its discoverer a serious blow. Over 50 per cent of all the Co-operative trade has always been in groceries. Despite widespread appeals to the public to 'shop at the Co-op' and not to desert a movement that had served them well for over a century, the Co-operative share of trade declined. Customers preferred an 'instant' dividend in the form of cut prices.

Membership has declined by about 1 per cent per annum since 1965, and fell by 4% in 1970 (mainly due to the elimination of dual memberships as local societies amalgamated, and the balances for disposal have fallen from as much as 10 per cent in the immediate post war years to only 1·8 per cent in 1970. The major re-organisation this has necessitated in the Co-operative Societies is further discussed on page 62.

The Resale Prices Act, 1964

Resale Price Maintenance in Britain has now been virtually ended by the rules laid down in the Resale Prices Act of 1964. This permits the manufacturer to lay down restrictive clauses in his contracts of sale, and even permits these restrictive clauses to 'run with the goods', thus reversing the rules laid down in the 1956 Act. In return for this right, the manufacturer must register the restrictive practice with the Restrictive Practices Registrar, who will then decide whether the practice is one that should be brought before the Restrictive Practices Court, as being *prima facie* against the public interest. The manufacturer will then have to justify his practice to the Court. In fact the Court has proved to be extremely hard to convince that a restrictive practice is in the public interest.

Firms who wished to register restrictive practices were given until December 31st, 1966, to do so. After that date prices, on new products for instance, cannot be enforced and goods may be sold by the retailer at whatever price yields him a profit. Firms have therefore taken to putting 'Recommended Retail Price' on their products, to give some guide to the retailer. The 1964 Act does however give some protection to a manufacturer whose products are persistently used as 'loss leaders' to attract customers into the supermarket. The firm in these circumstances has a limited right to withhold supplies from the offending retailer.

Several thousand restrictive practices were registered under the Act. Very few have been recognised as being in the public interest. The arguments used in favour of R.P.M.—loss of convenience as small shops close, and reductions in quality as profit margins fall—have not followed the Court's decisions to free retailers to charge what prices they like.

Effects of the Abolition of R.P.M. on the Retail Trade

The retail trade has become fiercely competitive as a result of these developments, and many small-scale retailers have been forced out of business. The disadvantages to the public are borne chiefly by the least well organized and least vocal consumers such as old people, married women with young children and disabled persons, who make the greatest use of the local shops. (Younger people and more active people can drive or take the bus to town to do their shopping and enjoy cut-price benefits.) These more vulnerable people are the hardest hit when a retailer closes down due to competition from the supermarket or other large-scale retailers. Before we can examine the full effects of the abolition of R.P.M. we must consider the change to large-scale operations in the retail trade.

(8) Large Scale in the Retail Trade

In discussing the types of retail trade carried on today we find that the pattern of retail trade is changing and that more and more large-scale trading is being carried on. 'Large scale' is an economic term which means big firms with big organizations.

Retail businesses can be classified according to size as follows:

Small Scale	Large Scale
(a) Pedlars	(a) Co-operative stores
(b) Hawkers	(b) Department stores
(c) Retail-market stallholders	(c) Multiple Shops
(d) Sole-trader shops	(d) Chain stores
(e) Partnership shops	(e) Supermarkets
	(f) hypermarkets
	(g) Mail-order firms
	(h) Discount sellers to privileged groups.
	(i) Direct selling by manufacturers

An examination of this classification shows that in the 'small-scale' list we find most of the declining types of retail trade, whose influence yearly becomes less important—the pedlar, the hawker, and the small trader.

Advantages of Large-Scale Trading

(a) The bigger businesses, with many branches, have a greater total turnover than a single shop; hence they are able to get the benefit of bulk purchasing. The trader who is buying goods by the hundredweight will pay more than the trader buying by the ton. The larger the order, the cheaper the unit price.

(b) Bigger businesses can afford specialist buyers for each department, well trained with wide knowledge of the class of goods to be purchased. This means that the goods purchased will be of better quality. Often the small retailer has to buy his goods from a commercial traveller who is a high pressure salesman while he is himself busy with customers and cannot give the matter his full attention. The specialist buyer from a large-scale firm is less likely to buy unwisely.

(c) Big firms can get the advantages of specialization at all levels. For instance, in the grocery trade one man will cut ham all day, another will wrap it up; another will cut cheese all day and so on. The waste from poor cutting will be reduced and the eventual profit will rise.

(d) Organization and planning will often devise ways of doing work more quickly or more economically. Shops can be planned to accommodate the maximum number of customers. Loudspeaker aids can be introduced for 'pushing' certain types of produce at times when it is particularly desirable to sell it. On a Saturday afternoon supermarket loud-speakers can often be heard urging customers not to forget bananas, tomatoes, and other perishable items. These may go bad if left over the week-end unsold.

(e) Staff can be trained on special courses.

(f) Mechanized tills, accounting and statistical controls, comparative shopping with rivals up and down the High Street, stock controls, and other devices can be introduced at all levels to promote efficiency.

(*g*) Large-scale firms can usually borrow money on more favourable terms than small traders.

(*h*) Economies in transportation facilities, under the personal super-vision of the company's own staff, can be achieved.

(*i*) The cash basis of activities cuts bad debts; and where hire-purchase is involved, the formation of legal departments becomes an economic proposition.

(*j*) Special departments can secure good sites, appraise their value at regular intervals and achieve capital gains on revaluation of property.

(*k*) Control of subsidiary sources of supply to ensure good standards of quality is easily achieved. Marks & Spencer, for example, lay down clear standards of work for their suppliers and insist on this standard being maintained.

Disadvantages of Large-Scale Trading

(*a*) There is a decline in personal service. For instance, a small retailer will often supply half a dozen screws for a household job, for a few pence. The large-scale retailer has these same screws in pre-packed polythene bags costing much more, for say two dozen screws: the rest tend to be wasted.

(*b*) Self-service involves losses by theft, and the retailer must employ store detectives, one-way mirrors, etc., to control pilfering.

(*c*) Staff lose personal touch with the employer, and tend to feel that they are just cogs in a big machine.

(*d*) It is not very easy to find managers of the right quality for large-scale stores. One supermarket chain claims to have adopted the policy of 'first finding a good manager, then building him a store'.

Effects of Large-Scale Trading on Retail Businesses

The large-scale firms have been expanding their share of the trade at the expense of the independent traders and the Co-operative Societies. The small traders find it difficult to compete with the large-scale enter-prises if this involves cutting profit margins, because the old profit margins were fixed at levels which gave small traders no more than a reasonable income. If they cut their profit margins the likelihood is that the return on their businesses will be reduced to the point where it simply is not worth their while to continue. What the small retailer has been able to do to meet this competition is discussed on page 65. The effect on the Co-operative Societies must now be given attention.

(9) Co-operative Trading Today

The Co-operative Societies have been through a period of difficult competition, and their share of retail trade is declining. This is a result of a change in the pattern of retail trade following the introduction of self-service stores—originally a Co-operative innovation. Whereas in

1951 the Co-operatives accounted for one-sixth of the total U.K. retail trade, by 1961 the figure had dropped to one-ninth, and by 1966 to less than one-tenth. In 1972 Co-operative trade was 8% of U.K. trade.

The reaction of the Co-ops to cut-price competition was slow when supermarkets first began in 1956. For idealistic reasons going back to its early history the Co-operative movement has always favoured 'honest' trading, i.e. good quality products at fair prices. Price cutting was presumed to involve a lowering in the quality of the goods, but in fact in the new retailing situation this did not prove to be the case.

For some time after price cutting began in the town-centre supermarkets, the Co-operatives either ignored it or relied on loyalty to the Co-operative ideal to maintain their trade. In any case it did not affect the small Co-op shops in the localities. It did drastically hit sales in the town-centre Co-operative stores, whose grocery departments saw trade that had been theirs for generations turning to the cut-price stores.

As a result the Co-operative Societies have had to review their traditional organization and enter the 1970s with a new approach on many aspects of their movement. The most interesting points are as follows:

Aspects of the Co-operative Position Today

Declining idealism. It is a regrettable fact that the introduction of the Welfare State has robbed the Co-operatives of much of their support. The days when ardent co-operators trudged weary miles to attend the quarterly meetings are gone. Today less than 1 per cent of Co-operators take any interest in their organization, and it is sometimes necessary to introduce employees to find a quorum under the rules. The Co-operative movement views with serious concern this general apathy among members.

It is also true to say that the Co-operatives have always done best when times were bad. Again and again in the nineteenth century when depressions occurred the poorest workers turned to the Co-ops for the bare necessities of life. At a time when the management of prosperity is a major concern of governments it seems inevitable that the Co-operative share of trade must decline.

Dividends by Trading Stamps. Traditionally the Co-operatives had to record the purchases made by customers and give a receipt at every payment. The carbon copies of these receipts involved enormous labour costs in totalling the purchases of each customer, and issuing a dividend warrant every six months. This expensive system has now been largely abandoned, and replaced by a **Dividend Trading Stamp Scheme**. This is operated on a national basis by the Co-operative Wholesale Society, saving the local societies large sums in administration costs.

Improved Distribution Methods. The local societies which formerly formed the backbone of the Co-operative movement were unable to achieve the economies of large-scale activities. The recent change-over to larger regional societies (see below) has enabled improvements in distribution to be achieved. The C.W.S. is at present organizing a chain of regional grocery warehouses which will provide a very efficient method of distribution.

The Regional Plan. In 1967 the Regional Plan called for the amalgamation of smaller societies, and the establishment of 49 regional societies instead of the 625 then existing. This process has been proceeding apace, and the number has now been reduced, in 1973, to only 200 societies in England and Wales. Three of the regional societies are actually in existence.

The regional plan is a grouping of societies in such a way as to form a catchment area within which the inhabitants do almost their entire shopping. This may reflect the geographical nature of the terrain, the transport facilities available, the urban concentrations, etc. At the centre of each region will be one or more towns with a population of at least 100,000 inhabitants. By the amalgamation of independent societies it is hoped to consolidate these regions gradually into viable economic units. Capital will be judiciously employed to develop the facilities in the key towns, while the societies are reducing and disposing of surplus facilities elsewhere. It is not easy to effect these re-arrangements because Co-operative Societies are associations of individuals, and members must agree to the proposed changes, but it is hoped that a clear understanding of the situation will persuade members of the necessity of the reforms. In the North-East of England one very large society, much bigger than the region envisaged in the Regional Plan, has come into existence. This has led to a re-thinking of the Plan itself. In England and Wales only 45 societies will eventually remain. A new plan for Scotland will reduce the 80 societies to only 5 regional societies.

Rapidly changing fashions. With greater wealth came increasingly aggressive marketing of new materials, styles, and fashions in a whole range of goods, but particularly in ladies and teenage fashions. These styles are often the product of highly personal flair by individual masters of their craft, whose ideas are then quickly mass-produced by specialist firms.

This sort of competition hit the Co-op hard, because durable quality was no longer really required, style was the thing. A movement that was founded to provide clothing, footwear, and furniture that would last found it difficult to adapt to a situation where durability was scorned. To be stylish was everything: fad today and fade tomorrow. To meet this challenge the C.W.S. has improved both the productions, presentation and packaging in use, and has done much to give the movement a new image. Coupled with this, a face-lifting operation on older stores and careful design of new premises has done much to improve the general atmosphere in which co-operators shop.

Antiquated personnel policy. It was traditional in the Co-operative stores that the employee shall learn his business the hard way by working his way up. This policy is out of step with modern trends where so many of the brightest young persons pursue their education past the normal school-leaving age in sixth form colleges, technical colleges, polytechnics and universities. There are fewer and fewer good young people prepared to start with their foot on the very bottom rung of the ladder. This meant that the Co-op was finding it more and more difficult to compete.

One of the best arguments in favour of the Regional Plan is that it enables the Co-ops to become large enough to provide specialist posts at all levels of management, so that an attractive career structure can be offered to well-educated young people. A movement that has always been able to command the services of the very best types of workers has now to attract them by offering comparable rewards with other enterprises. In doing so it may replace the rather inbred traditional Co-op management by one with wider experience of competitive retail trade. There are signs that this is already beginning to happen.

(10) The Pattern of Retail Trade Today

In Fig. 10 we see that between 1961 and 1970 the total value of retail trade done increased by 53 per cent (two thirds of it due to increases in prices and not to increased turnover). While multiple shops and mail-order trading expanded by 89 per cent and 143 per cent, respectively, the more traditional large-scale firms such as the department stores and the Co-operative societies increased by only 44 per cent, and 13 per cent respectively, while the independent small retailers increased by 29 per cent. Two-fifths of the total trade was shared between 400,000 small firms. Another two-fifths of total trade was shared between only 700 large firms. In the face of this sort of competition the small retailers have had to defend themselves as best they could.

(11) The Retailers' Reply to Competition from Large-Scale Outlets

Retailer Co-operation. Bulk purchase is the key to cheaper retail prices. The manufacturer, wholesaler, or grower supplying a retailer will reduce the unit price for very large orders, because transport, finance, warehousing, and other costs are reduced. One reply of the small retailer to the multiple shops is to buy in very large quantities, but this can be done only in co-operation with fellow retailers. This is the solution of the 'Spar' (Society for the Protection of the Average Retailer) and 'Wavy Line' grocers. By setting up their own purchasing and distribution network these associations can buy in bulk and share the advantages of large-scale organization.

Not only the produce itself but the aids to efficient operation employed by the multiples can be made available to the small retailer. For

SHARES OF TOTAL 1961
Total £9,140m.

SHARES OF TOTAL 1970
Total £13,579m.

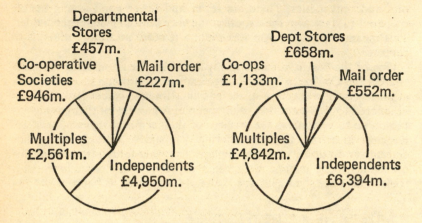

SALES AT CURRENT PRICES
PERCENTAGE INCREASES IN SALES 1961 — 70
Index 1961 = 100

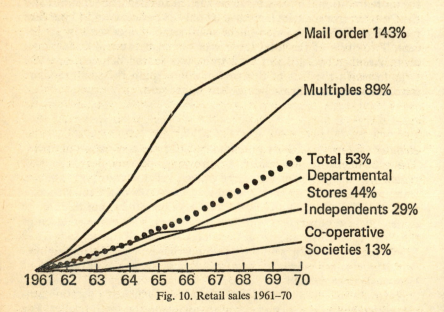

Fig. 10. Retail sales 1961–70

instance, paper bags can be bought in bulk, printing of cut-price labels and 'special-offer' notices can be undertaken in a large way. Similarly, a group of retailers like this can obtain more favourable terms from manufacturers of shop fittings, weighing machines, etc., and from sign-writing firms and Finance Houses. In general the retailers can achieve most of the economies of large-scale operation without quite abandoning their independence.

Compound trading. In former times small-scale retailers were careful not to offend fellow traders by encroaching on their types of business. A stationer would not sell ice-cream and a grocer would not sell tobacco. The retailer today feels less compunction about moving into another field of trade if his competitors are multiple shops, for they pay little regard to *his* feelings. There is a tendency therefore today for the range of goods handled by small retailers to widen, and be less specialized. This is called **compound trading**.

The traditional channels used, with goods moving from manufacturer to wholesaler to retailer, are also being abandoned more and more. Retailers often deal directly with growers and manufacturers, and find the **'cash and carry' warehouse** more suitable to their needs in the new situation created since the Resale Prices Act, 1964.

The 'cash and carry' warehouse. This is a formidable development, whose owners compete with the traditional wholesaler. The basis of their activities is a wholesale super-supermarket, operated exactly like a supermarket but dealing in bulk. After closing his shop for the day, the retailer goes in person to the 'cash and carry' wholesaler, who supplies him with a 'float' to go around the warehouse and pick out what he wants. After selecting the stock he needs, he pays at the cash desk like any other supermarket customer. By opening the warehouse after ordinary working hours, at week-ends or early in the day, the wholesaler gives the retailer the chance to buy at cut prices and therefore to sell as low as his rivals in the multiple shops. Today the cash and carry warehouse is beginning to open its doors to ordinary consumers, especially those who have purchased a deep-freeze. The retailers may yet find this new form of competition very unpleasant—the customer who buys half a bullock, ready jointed, will not be visiting his local butcher very frequently.

(12) Trading Stamps

Trading stamps were first used in Britain in 1880 when the Blue Stamp Company was founded. In 1896 Thomas A. Sperry & Shelley B. Hutchinson began the same system in America. Stamps are now used in 90,000 American stores, while in England alone there are about 30 trading-stamp companies.

The basic idea of trading stamps is that they are a way of returning a small percentage of the profit to the customer, in a form he will remember with pleasure. Actually it is a discount of about 2–2½ per cent. This is much less than is given by many cut-price shops, but of course stamps are often given in addition to cut prices.

The trading-stamp system is a good example of *specialization*. The stamp firm sells the stamps to the retailer for the 2½p in the £1 discount. If a customer spends £1, he gets 40 stamps and these entitle him to a 2½p gift. If he fills a book (32 × 40 stamps in a book) he thus gets an 80p gift.

How can the trading-stamp company afford to offer a gift worth 80p when it received only 80p from the retailer? The answer is that, by buying the gifts in bulk orders and thus getting cheap rates, the stamp company's income comes from the price difference (profit) on the gift.

Advantages to the customer. The customer gets a gift of his choice as a bonus for trading with shops that give the stamps. By special arrangement, gifts of an unusual nature can be obtained; for instance, some charitable bodies collect stamps and use them to buy invalid carriages or similar expensive items.

Disadvantages to the customer. The customer has to redeem the stamps, either by post or by going to the redemption centre. He may finish up with goods he did not want, because the company usually reserves the right to send something else if a particular line is out of stock. He therefore might do better if the cash was refunded direct to him by the shopkeeper. The Trading Stamps Act now requires that customers shall have the right to exchange their stamps for cash, but the cash value is about half the value obtained when taking a gift; the way the system operates would otherwise make it difficult for the trading-stamp system to continue if cash was generally demanded in full, since the stamp-firm must cover its overheads.

Advantages to the retailer. The retailer is offering his customers an incentive to encourage them to enter his shop and return there regularly. A customer who starts a book of stamps wants to go on and fill it. This may bring the retailer £32 worth of business. It makes a 'steady shopper' of a passer-by.

Because it is a regular steady attraction to customers, the retailer can cut out other 'stunt' adverts, special-promotion features, etc.

Secondly, giving stamps helps to reduce bad debts, since bills which yield a bonus of trading stamps tend to be settled in preference to other bills. This saves book-keeping, lawyers' fees, and interest on bank overdrafts.

Disadvantages to the retailer. The retailer loses 2½p in the £1 (of course, he may do more trade to make up for this loss). Also, he has to bother with the stamps: this may waste employee time, slow down the cash tills, and brings risks of theft by employees, etc.

(13) The 'Hire-Rather-than-Buy' Retailer

A very recent development in retail trade is the hire shop. The laundrette, which enables customers to hire washing machines, spin driers and dry-cleaning machines has been one of the fastest growing branches of retail trade in the 1960s. Here the equipment hired is used on the premises. An equally rapid growth may develop in the 1970s in the field of hire of equipment for use in the hirer's own home. Obvious examples of suitable apparatus are power sprayers for home decorations; power drills and saws for do-it-yourself activities; post-hole borers and other gardeners' aids etc. Camping equipment is an obviously expensive item which is only used a few times a year. In off-seasons the householder has it lying idle in his garage. The hire retailer, who has already used it much more intensively during the season, uses the off-season break to repair, reproof and renew where necessary.

(14) Will the Small Trader ever Disappear?

This seems highly unlikely. Business size is limited to some extent by the market. Supermarkets which handle jewellery, for instance, are very few in number because the demand for jewellery is small. In the same way, village shops are big enough to cater for local demand and are unlikely to be replaced by a supermarket, although they are beginning to be taken over by multiple-shop organizations.

Retail trade has always been a way for the independent, hard-working man to start in business. It is what we call a nodal point (a growing point) of business. An enterprising individual who sees an opportunity to provide a useful commodity or a useful service can step into this field relatively easily, and by hard work and self-denial build up a thriving business.

Exercises Set 5

(15) The Changing Pattern of Retail Trade

1. List the types of retail establishment which are large-scale outlets. Which of these would you consider traditional, and which have only developed in the last few years?

2. What changes in shopping habits are being brought about by self-service? To what extent do you think self-service shopping will develop further? Give reasons.   (*University of London*)

3. What do you understand by mail-order business? What explanation could you give for the recent rapid expansion of mail-order business?

4. What part is played in the retail field today by: (*a*) the small independent retailer; (*b*) the department store; (*c*) the supermarket: (*d*) the Co-operative retail society?

5. What problems face the Co-operative Societies at the present time? You

should deal in your answer with (*a*) cut-price competition and (*b*) stylish teenage fashion, as well as with other problems that occur to you.

6. 'Resale Price Maintenance ensures that all the public receive their goods at a fair price'. . . . 'The abolition of Resale Price Maintenance will lead to the public receiving their goods more cheaply'.

Explain both these points of view and say what you know about the present position with regard to Resale Price Maintenance.

7. What are the advantages and the disadvantages of large-scale organization in the retail trade?

8. What arguments can be advanced for and against trading-stamp schemes?

9. You are considering setting up in a grocery business on your own account after returning from abroad. What considerations enter into your choice of a site?

10. A manufacturer of children's clothing receives a proposal that in future he should work solely for a particular chain of stores, which would take his entire output. What considerations are likely to enter into his decision on this suggestion?

11. Five grocers in the town of Middleham each run a separate business as a sole trader. Three of them, Atkins, Barnes, and Cook, are trying to persuade the other two, Drake and East, to join them in attempts to compete more successfully with the grocery chains. Briefly outline the arguments they may use.

12. What are the advantages of 'branding' goods? Consider the retailer's, the customer's, and the manufacturer's points of view. Are there any disadvantages?

13. Cut-throat competition in the retail trade will eventually result in inconvenience to the consumer and unfair profits to the large-scale firms. Discuss.

14. If large-scale trading has such advantages, why are many small retailers able to continue in business? Discuss.

15. Describe the changes taking place in the forms of retail distribution in Britain.

16. What are the advantages of hiring rather than buying in the 'do-it-yourself' home decorating field? Refer in your answer to (a) ladders, (b) paint brushes and (c) blowlamps, as well as any other items you feel are important.

(R.S.A.)

CHAPTER FIVE

HIRE-PURCHASE TRADING AND CONSUMER CREDIT

(1) Introduction

In many fields of trade today the customer requires the loan of money to finance goods purchased and must obtain this money from a bank or finance house of some sort. All such loans of money are controlled by the Consumer Credit Act 1974, which set up an Office of Fair Trading under a Director General of Fair Trading whose duty it is to keep such arrangements under constant review. Before looking at his duties some discussion of the place of consumer credit in the economy is desirable.

We live in a mass-production society where the production of goods is arranged in such a way that very large outputs can be achieved. These can only be disposed of to consumers if payment is arranged out of income, on some sort of instalment method. At first this was held to verge on immorality, because the idea of the poorer classes enjoying the use of expensive durable consumer goods which had not been paid for was repugnant to those who advocated thrift as the great virtue. Gradually this idea has been eroded away; partly by a general redistribution of income which has increased taxation heavily, making thrift less attractive; but more by the discovery that poverty breeds social unrest, and that in the management of general prosperity thrift is positively harmful. To keep factories busy and men employed we need to spend, not save. Hire purchase has therefore become a great boon to the economy, but it is worth listing some of the difficulties of consumer credit, so that we can see why controls have become necessary.

(*a*) Aggressive businessmen can easily persuade unsophisticated people, particularly housewives, to purchase goods which they do not really require and cannot afford. So-called 'doorstep sales' are particularly suspect, and in Britain there are now special controls.

(*b*) In signing a legal agreement to purchase, the ordinary householder commits himself to a contract which he probably does not fully understand, and which may be prejudicial to his true interests.

(*c*) If goods are to be delivered without any payment being necessary, poor people will easily be tempted to order more than they can afford. Government policy, except in times of severe unemployment, when the economy needs every possible encouragement, is therefore directed to ensure reasonable deposits.

(*d*) Rates of interest in hire purchase tend to be a little higher than in other fields, because of the speculative nature of the business, i.e. there are many bad debts. However, because of the doubling-up effect, the true rate of hire-purchase interest is much greater than at first appears. Special control of this aspect is also necessary. The doubling-up effect is explained later in this chapter.

(*e*) Since property is placed in the possession of people who do not own it but have only hired it—until the last instalment is paid—the possibility exists that unsuspecting third parties may be misled into buying from the hirer goods that the hirer has no right to sell. Some protection of the innocent private buyer is desirable.

Consumer credit arrangements are a mixed blessing. They confer great advantages on the purchaser, the retailer, the financier and the manufacturer, but are open to abuse by the sophisticated and legally advised, so that the consumer requires protection because of his relatively vulnerable condition when surrounded by astute and aggressive salesmen.

For this reason statutory control of hire purchase has existed in Britain since 1938. A major Hire Purchase Act was passed in 1965, and is still the effective law on Hire Purchase. As the various sections of the Consumer Credit Act 1974 are implemented by Orders, new regulations will be introduced. It is unlikely that this will happen before 1977.

(2) Duties of the Director General of Fair Trading

The Director General of Fair Trading has the following duties:

(*a*) To license all businesses where consumer credit is given or goods are hired, after ensuring that the persons to whom licences are given are fit and proper persons to carry on this type of business. He must keep the licence under review and may renew, withdraw or suspend it for improper conduct. The word 'credit' means cash loan or any other type of financial help. The first applications for licences are currently being considered.

(*b*) To superintend the working of the Act and any regulations made under it, and to enforce it if necessary.

(*c*) To advise the Secretary of State for Prices and Consumer Protection of any matters in the social and commercial development of the country which may require action regarding the provision of consumer credit.

(*d*) To disseminate information and advice for the benefit of the general public.

(*e*) To present an annual report.

(3) Types of Credit Controlled by the Consumer Credit Act 1974

The Act lists the following types of credit agreements which are controlled:

(*a*) A *personal credit agreement*, which is an agreement between one individual (a debtor) and another (the creditor) by which the latter provides the former with credit of any amount.

(*b*) A *consumer credit agreement*. This is a personal credit agreement, where one person (the creditor) provides credit to the other person (the debtor) up to a limit of £5,000. It does not apply to certain exempt agreements, such as those made with Building Societies, Trade Unions, Local Authorities, etc., about the purchase of land and dwelling houses.

(*c*) *Running-account credit*, where a sum of money is specified to which the debtor can turn from time to time as required so long as he does not exceed the credit limit.

(*d*) *Credit token agreements* are agreements whereby a card voucher, coupon or similar object is given to an individual who is then able to obtain goods, cash or services on credit by producing it either to the creditor or to some third party such as a shopkeeper or hotelier, or even a mechanical device such as a cash dispenser.

(*e*) *The Hire-Purchase Agreement* is an agreement which bails goods to the intending purchaser, the property in the goods passing to the bailee when the terms of the agreement are fulfilled. A bailee is any person who comes into possession of other people's goods. When I agree to sign a hire-purchase agreement I agree to hire goods from their owner, paying for them by instalments and finally purchasing them for a purely nominal sum at the end of the hire. The situation is complicated by the fact that retailers can rarely afford to finance the transactions themselves, so that the agreement is often concluded with a **consumer credit business**, the retailer merely acting as the agent of the credit business. In the past, finance companies have proved to be quick to assert their rights and aggressive in the collection of sums due. The Office of Fair Trading is designed to overcome this type of abuse and encourage a more professional attitude.

(*f*) A *Credit-Sale Agreement* is an agreement to sell goods by instalments not being a conditional-sale agreement (see below). With this type of agreement the sale is an ordinary sale of goods, the property passing to the new owner at once. It is usually used for sale of clothing and similar articles where repossession is undesirable because the goods have ceased to be worth re-selling.

(*g*) A *Conditional Sale Agreement* is one for the sale of goods or land by instalments where the passing of the property to the buyer is conditional upon the payments being completed. It is therefore like a hire-purchase agreement except that the buyer is a bailee under a contract of conditional sale instead of a contract of bailment.

(*h*) *A consumer hire agreement.* This is an agreement made with an individual to hire goods to him, which is not a hire purchase arrangement—in other words the hirer will never become the owner of the goods.

(4) The Advantages of Hire Purchase

(*a*) *To the consumer.* It enables him to enjoy the possession of the goods before he has paid for them. By arranging repayments over a period of time he is able to budget for the purchase of expensive capital items out of weekly or monthly earnings. This may promote his family's health (comfortable furniture, vacuum cleaners, bathroom and toilet fittings). It may provide entertainment and education (television sets, radios, recording equipment, and encyclopedias). It may save waste and promote economy (refrigerators, cooking equipment, gas and electrical appliances). It may facilitate the mobility of his labour (motor vehicles and personalized transport).

(*b*) *To the retailer.* It increases turnover and enhances the profitability of his enterprise. This is reflected in a general reduction in profit margins in the competitive atmosphere of retail trade, so that the general public benefits by lower prices, whether or not they buy by hire purchase.

(*c*) *To the financier.* Hire purchase is a rewarding field of financial investment today, because, despite the chance of bad debts, the rewards earned are higher than the normal rates of interest. Although the Act of 1974 provides for the courts to step in and supervise 'extortionate agreements' this does not mean that the court will not allow a rate of interest which reflects the risks involved.

(*d*) *To the manufacturer.* By increasing the sales of products it enables a more fully specialized system of production to be employed with a consequent reduction in unit costs.

(*e*) *To the general community.* Modern consumer societies are based on the mass production of things most people want, and hire purchase keeps demand high and the general community prosperous. If the hire-purchase system did not exist, the general level of prosperity would fall and a decline in national income would follow from the inevitable decrease in specialization.

(5) The Protection of the Consumer in Britain

In 1962 the Moloney Committee Report on Consumer Protection made over 200 recommendations to protect the consumer. The Hire Purchase Acts of 1964 and 1965 provided for this as far as hire purchase was concerned. The 1974 Consumer Credit Act will repeal these Acts when it is implemented in the next eighteen months. The regulations then made may alter some of the details about documents, etc., given in this chapter. The Act certainly raises the limit of credit transactions covered from the £2,000 mentioned in (*a*) below to £5,000.

Neither the 1965 Act nor the 1974 Act protect companies, since it is assumed that they are able to protect themselves.

The chief points are:

(*a*) *The upper limit of value of goods covered by the Act is £2,000.* Under the original H.P. Act of 1938 the limit was £50, subsequently raised to £300. By raising the limit to £2,000 most cars are now inside the protection of the Act.

(*b*) *The lower limit is £30 on credit-sales agreements*—but on certain matters it is dispensed with. This is to cover mail-order sales of clothing, etc., freeing it from the need for a written legal agreement and the right to return the goods, but keeping it within other (more important) protective clauses.

(*c*) *Declaration of cash price.* Before making a hire-purchase agreement the seller has to tell the buyer in writing the cash price of the goods, so that he knows how much he could save by postponing purchase until he has the ready money. These requirements are satisfied if (i) the price is in the agreement, or (ii) it was stated in writing separately, or (iii) it was written on the goods and these were inspected by the buyer, or (iv) it was in the advertisement, catalogue or price list.

(*d*) *The memorandum.* Under the Act the memorandum is very important, for a hire-purchase agreement is enforceable only if a note or memorandum is available in writing. This must contain the following:

This document contains the terms of a hire purchase agreement. Sign it only if you want to be legally bound by them.

Signature of Hirer ....

The goods will not become your property until you have made all the payments. You must not sell them before then.

(iv) A statutory notice of the hirer's rights under the Act.

The memorandum must be signed by the hirer or buyer *in person*, and by the owner or his agent. A wife cannot sign for her husband, even if she has her husband's authority.

The following rules must be adhered to regarding the delivery to the hirer of the statutory copy of the agreement:

(I) if the agreement is signed at the trade premises of the seller, one statutory copy;

(II) if the agreement is signed anywhere else, for instance in the customer's home, or on his doorstep, or in a car on the public highway, two statutory copies, one at once and the second copy by post. Also any hirer can have a further copy, showing the amount owing at the time, whenever he wishes on payment of £0·12½.

(*e*) *Rights of cancellation*. No right of cancellation exists on a contract made in usual trade premises.

A right of cancellation exists on all contracts signed elsewhere, i.e. doorstep sales, etc. Such a sale will be cancelled if the buyer gives notice within four days of receiving the second statutory copy. He then has a lien on the goods for recovery of his deposit and the return of any goods part-exchanged. (A lien is a right to retain goods until all sums due in connection with the abortive sale have been restored.) If the goods part-exchanged have been sold or destroyed, the buyer has a lien for their trade-in value. The buyer who has changed his mind need not return the goods to the shop, but may wait for them to be collected. He is responsible for their safe-keeping for 21 days; after that time he ceases to be liable to take care of them.

(*f*) *Right of the hirer to terminate the agreement*. At any time the hirer or buyer may terminate the agreement, but if he does so he must pay half the price (unless the Court decides that the loss suffered by the owner is worth less), or what is due if the contract has already passed the half-way mark. The hirer must also pay for any damage done to the goods. Any clause in the agreement increasing the hirer's duties and making them more onerous than the Act requires is void. This right to terminate the agreement is a great protection to the consumer who gets into difficulties, for he can always escape from the agreement by giving notice to the trader. Giving notice to the trader is deemed under the Act to be the same as giving notice to the finance company. The trader must pass the message on to the finance company.

(*g*) *Restriction of the right to retake goods*. The Act creates a special class of *protected goods*. Goods are 'protected' under the Act if (*a*) they were sold under a hire-purchase or conditional-sale agreement, (*b*) one-third of the price has been paid or tendered, and (*c*) the hirer has made no attempt to terminate the agreement.

Such goods are protected by a restriction on the owner's right to recover the goods without a **court order** being obtained from the County Court. At such proceedings the Court may:

(i) Order the specific delivery of all or some proportion of the goods, bearing in mind how much has been paid.
(ii) Order the hirer to pay the outstanding balance in such a way as it deems fit, or it may order a new agreement according to the detailed rules laid down in the Act.

Once such action is begun no further payments are due until the Court makes its order. The right of the owner has been restricted in this way by law, and cannot be contracted out. *If the owner retakes possession without authority:* (*a*) the contract is automatically ended; and (*b*) the hirer is entitled to recover, under an action for money had and received, all sums paid on the agreement and possibly also for trespass.

Sale of goods under H.P. by the hirer. This is a breach of contract, and probably a crime too. The owner has a right to recover the goods unless they are a motor vehicle, when the special protection given to private purchasers may prevent him re-asserting ownership.

The 1964 Hire Purchase Act contains a section not repealed by the 1965 Act which says that if a *private buyer* buys a car which is later found to be subject to a hire-purchase agreement he does get a good title to the car so long as he bought without knowledge that it was on H.P. This rule does not apply to a motor trader, since he can always check whether a vehicle is on H.P. through his trade organization.

In conclusion, at the time of writing (March 1976) only three items of the 1974 Consumer Credit Act have actually been enforced.

(*a*) Prohibition of credit brokers and similar people canvassing for business in homes, workplaces, etc. It is illegal to organise any meeting or appointment to discuss loans other than on business premises.

(*b*) Restriction of the charges made by mortgage brokers for putting consumers in touch with mortgage sources.

(*c*) All consumer credit businesses to be registered.

(6) Organizing Property—Hire Purchase Controls as an Instrument of Government Policy

Because hire purchase is so attractive to the masses it is a useful tool with which the Government can control the economy. If a depression exists, and the Government wishes to promote employment, it can ease the hire-purchase controls. This usually means that the hire-purchase deposits required by law are reduced, and the periods of repayment lengthened. This will permit thousands of people to obtain goods for which they had been saving, and will promote sales of consumer durable goods. This will mean more employment in the factories where such goods are made, and the incomes enjoyed by the new employees will promote trade in other fields of production. Conversely, if over-full employment is producing inflation, with rising prices and rising wage demands, a tightening of hire-purchase controls will reduce the demand for goods and services, cut employment and give a deflationary effect in the levels of business activity.

The effectiveness of hire-purchase controls has been reduced somewhat in recent years. The use by an increasing number of people, of the ordinary banking system of personal loans and overdrafts, has enabled them to pay cash for goods. The repayments are made to their bankers rather than to a Hire-Purchase Finance Company. This is usually less expensive. The use of systems like 'Barclaycard', with its instantaneous overdraft to reliable customers, also circumvents the H.P. system.

The sale of goods at discount rates to privileged customers by whole-salers, bypasses the retail trade altogether, and represents a further incentive to the purchaser to borrow money and pay in cash. For poorer people the system of Trading Checks, which are paid for in the follow-ing 20-week period to a 'tally man' who calls at the customer's house, also permit 'cash' dealing instead of hire purchase.

EXERCISES SET 6

(7) Hire Purchase

1. What do you consider to be the chief advantages of hire purchase to the consumer and the retailer?

2. Define a hire-purchase agreement. What safeguards does the 1965 Hire Purchase Act give to a man who buys a car, valued at £650, on hire purchase?

3. Write short notes (about 5–8 lines each) on (a) a credit-sale agreement, (b) the right of the finance company to repossess goods sold on hire purchase, and (c) the protection given to a private buyer of a motor vehicle subsequently found to be on H.P. and unpaid for.

4. What do you understand by 'doorstep hire-purchase sales'? Why are these undesirable, and what controls over them are contained in the 1965 Hire Purchase Act?

5. What is the effect of hire purchase on the division of labour in factories?

6. 'People who disapprove of hire purchase may benefit from the system even though they never use it themselves.' Explain.

7. (a) Assess the importance of hire-purchase facilities (i) to businesses, and (ii) to retail shoppers.

(b) What measures to safeguard the hirers were introduced in legislation in 1964 and 1965?   (*University of London—adapted*)

8. Consumers who purchase on instalments are protected by regulations (a) as to the total price paid, (b) as to the place where the purchase is made, (c) as to the right of the seller to re-possess the goods. Explain these rules.

9. Write short notes (4–5 lines each) on: (a) hire purchase agreements; (b) doorstep sales; (c) sale of a motor vehicle which is on H.P. to a private buyer; (d) the 1974 Consumer Credit Act.

10. 'It is wrong to buy goods on "Hire Purchase" which you cannot afford to buy for cash.'

Discuss this view of credit trading, bringing out clearly the advantages and disadvantages of the hire-purchase system.

CHAPTER SIX

THE WHOLESALE TRADE

(1) Introduction

Wholesale trade in the United Kingdom has been through a period of change as the retail trade has been modified by the Resale Prices Act of 1964. Traditional ways of marketing through wholesalers are often by-passed by manufacturers and growers, who sell direct to retailers, or to the public. Wholesalers themselves have branched out into new fields of activity, like selling direct to the consumer by mail order. It is therefore difficult to lay down a definition that applies to all wholesalers today, and unwise to specify which activities a wholesaler will perform.

Traditionally a wholesaler is a person who buys in very large quantities and sells in bulk to retailers, performing in the intermediate period the functions of warehousing and transportation. Today these functions may also be performed by the manufacturer, or the purchasing organization of a large-scale retailer.

Whoever handles the distribution of primary and secondary goods, it is obviously as important to have an efficient distribution system as it is to have efficient production. Distribution expenses amount to about 40 per cent of retail prices. Whether manufacturers handle these matters themselves or hand them over to the specialist attentions of wholesalers, the public have to pay the distribution costs as an increase in the retail price. A new management technique—physical distribution management—seeks to keep these costs as low as possible.

(2) Position of the Wholesaler in the Chain of Commerce

Wholesalers are businessmen who handle goods in the intermediate position between the producer and the consumer, but traditionally they have always dealt in large quantities, e.g. whole cheeses or whole carcasses. They have left the cutting up of 'whole' units into smaller quantities to the 'retailers'. The traditional distribution chain has therefore been:

Producer ⟶ *Wholesaler* ⟶ *Retailer* ⟶ *Consumer*
(growing or (transport, (breaking (consumption)
manufacturing) warehousing) bulk, display)

Since the transport and warehousing of goods is a very involved and lengthy process, it is not unusual for several wholesalers to be involved

79

in the movement of the goods, handing them on from one to another. The term **middlemen** has been applied to these traders, since they stand between the producer and the retailer.

(3) Evolution of the Middleman

Where production and consumption are carried on in the same locality there is usually little need for a 'middleman' to arrange the transport and exchange of goods. Middlemen before the industrial revolution were therefore mainly involved in the luxury trades, especially imported luxuries like furs, wine, and silk. They were also a feature of the 'staple' trades, of which wool and spices were the most important.

As the agricultural and industrial revolutions developed, and as transport problems were solved by the use of canals and eventually railways, the change to a more specialized production led to greater distribution problems. Wholesalers became involved in vast movements of goods. Market-garden and agricultural production increased; meat, poultry, milk and milk products were available in greater quantities. Fishing and whaling increased, while the volume of manufactured goods rose year by year. New classes of wholesaler arose in the produce markets, in the coal trade, in groceries, drapery, furnishings, ironmongery, and above all in the import–export trade.

Merchants, Agents, Brokers, and Factors

Some of these middlemen were mercers, or *merchants* as we should call them today. A merchant buys the goods he handles and is therefore a true owner of them, selling at a price which takes into account the original cost and the service rendered. Others act only as intermediaries between the producer and the retailer, selling the goods on a commission basis. Such men are called *agents*. Strictly speaking, an agent is anyone who does something on behalf of another. In commerce we call them 'mercantile agents'. These are defined in the Factors Act of 1889 as persons 'having in the customary course of his business as an agent the authority either to sell goods, or to consign goods for the purpose of sale, or to buy goods or to raise money on the security of goods'.

The two commonest types of mercantile agent are brokers and factors. The difference between them is a difference in the extent to which they handle goods. *Brokers* merely sell the goods for their principals, and delivery of the goods sold is left to be arranged later, for the broker does not have them in his possession. The *factor* on the other hand is in possession of the goods, selling them for his principal, delivering them up to the buyer for payment, and rendering an account, less his commission for the sums due.

(4) Functions of the Wholesaler

The functions of traditional wholesalers are as follows:

(*a*) To remove from the manufacturer the burden of marketing his goods by taking bulk supplies from him, and settling promptly with cash. The risks of production are therefore greatly reduced, since it is now the wholesaler who is bearing the risks.

(*b*) To assume the risks of the enterprise begun by the manufacturer but which he has now relinquished. These risks are: (i) that the goods will not be needed because there is no demand: (ii) that they can be disposed of only at a lower price than the cost price to the wholesaler; (iii) deterioration; (iv) theft and misappropriation, which are specially high when goods are in transit; (v) bad debts.

(*c*) To transport the goods from the point of production to suitable depots in market areas, and possibly from the depots to the retailer's shop.

(*d*) To warehouse the goods, in such a way that they will not deteriorate or be stolen, in the time gap before they are bought by the retailers.

(*e*) To market the goods by advertising, demonstrating, or displaying them in ways appropriate to the class of goods concerned. This may also involve other processes such as packaging, blending, and branding.

(*f*) To grant credit where required to retailers whose resources are limited, so that goods can be sold before payment is required.

(*g*) To act as liaison between retailers and producers conveying the views of each to the other.

(*h*) To even out the flow of goods in times of glut or shortage by taking supplies into stock or releasing them from stock. This is the speculative function which keeps prices steady irrespective of natural or man-made interferences with supplies.

All these services are useful to the other parties involved, and to the general consuming public. They may be classified as follows:

(5) Services to the Manufacturer

(*a*) The wholesaler removes goods in large quantities as they are produced, thus clearing the production lines.

(*b*) He eliminates the need for a marketing system with all that involves in terms of warehousing space, distribution network, sales staff, accounting records, and debt collection.

(*c*) By paying promptly the wholesaler reduces the working capital required by the manufacturer.

(*d*) By warehousing the goods the wholesaler bridges the time gap between production and consumption, leaving the manufacturer free to concentrate on his specialized activities.

(*e*) By selling under his own brand name the wholesaler often relieves the manufacturer of the need to advertise his product.

(6) Services to the Retailer

(*a*) The wholesaler breaks bulk to a reasonable size, selling in quantity but not large quantities.

(*b*) He gives credit to certain classes of retailer, thus reducing the amount of capital needed by the retailer.

(*c*) He often grades, pre-packs, and prices goods. This reduces the retailer's work and enables him to serve customers more quickly.

(*d*) By carrying stock which is readily available he reduces the capital and space required by the retailer. The retailer stocks only the goods that 'turn over' quickly. Slow moving items are ordered as required from the wholesaler.

(*e*) The wholesaler displays a variety of goods from hundreds of manufacturers and demonstrates or displays them as necessary. At the warehouse the retailer can therefore see not only the lines he normally handles but the latest inventions and designs.

(*f*) In many cases the wholesaler operates a fleet of vehicles and delivers goods to the retailer as and when required.

(*g*) He chooses a convenient situation and opens at convenient hours.

(*h*) He often helps the retailer to meet cut-price competition from the multiple shops and chain stores by selling to him at cut prices, providing the retailer is prepared to accept a reduction of services. This usually means 'cash and carry'; no credit is given, and the retailer transports the goods to his premises in his own van.

(7) Services to the Public

(*a*) By assuming the speculative function of buying goods when they are plentiful and releasing them when they are in short supply, the wholesaler enables the consumer to obtain a steady flow of goods throughout the year, at steady prices.

(*b*) By specializing in distribution the wholesalers ensures that goods reach the consumer in the right quantities at the right times in the most economic way, so that the price to the consumer includes the smallest possible element of distribution costs.

(*c*) As an intermediary between retailer and manufacturer or grower he conveys the views of each to the other so that complaints from consumers reach the manufacturer and grower and result in a general improvement in products.

(*d*) The convenience of the public is served by the increased number of retail outlets kept in existence to serve them against the competition of large-scale retail outlets which are viable propositions only if established in town centres.

(8) Types of Wholesaler

The pattern of wholesale trade is changing but the main types are as follows:

(*a*) *Traditional wholesalers*
(i) Large general wholesalers operating very large warehouses. Showrooms in suitable centres enable retailers to see the goods in comfort, but

orders are filled from the warehouse. Commercial travellers are also employed in sales areas remote from the showrooms.

(ii) Specialist wholesalers operating in a more limited field but carrying a detailed inventory in their particular sphere of trade.

Both the above may operate on a national scale.

(iii) Regional wholesalers serving a particular area. These wholesalers operate in the perishable field as well as in manufactured goods, delivering prepared foods, frozen foods, fruit and vegetables, meat, etc. Each of these is a specialized field.

(iv) Local wholesalers, operating on a small scale, and dealing in goods from the produce exchanges or as service and spares agents in the consumer-durable fields.

(b) *'Cash and carry' warehouses* operating in the cut-price groceries and general retailing fields. The emphasis is on self-service, absence of credit facilities, breaking bulk to the requirement of the individual retailer, convenience of opening hours to suit the retail trade and absence of delivery facilities.

(c) *Retailer-protection wholesalers* operating in the cut-price grocery field as co-operative enterprises. Such organizations as Spar (Society for the Protection of the Average Retailer) and Wavy Line offer advantages to the small trader, in the form of favourable discounts, national advertising and services to promote goodwill.

(d) *The Co-operative Wholesale Society* is the largest unit in wholesale trade, catering for the needs of the retail societies who are its members. Its influence extends further than the normal wholesaling function, into manufacturing, farming, dairying, tea planting, and transport.

(e) *Mail-order wholesalers* sell direct to the consumer in his own home, eliminating the retailer. One of the fastest growing fields of wholesale trade, the mail-order houses are really general wholesalers on a national scale. Their chief attraction to the consumer is short-term credit; the basis of their activities being the credit-sale agreement. This is a form of short-term hire purchase, and the 20-week payment period for non-durable goods such as clothing and footwear is attractive to the lower income groups. Mail-order firms operate through 'home agents' working on commission. In fact the system is now so widespread that almost every housewife is her own agent.

(9) Warehousing

The mass-production system depends upon producing in anticipation of demand. It is no longer necessary to order a pair of socks to be knitted for you, or to place an order for a motor vehicle with a manufacturer. Millions of pairs of socks and thousands of motor cars are produced each month in anticipation of demand. The heavy investment required has to be planned in advance to produce a certain output. It follows that whether the orders come in or not the goods will roll off the production line. Warehousing is the method used to store the goods until they are required. The demand may be seasonal, as with raincoats and umbrellas. It may be related to a particular festival, like the demand for greetings cards, decorations, crackers, gifts, and toys at Christmas.

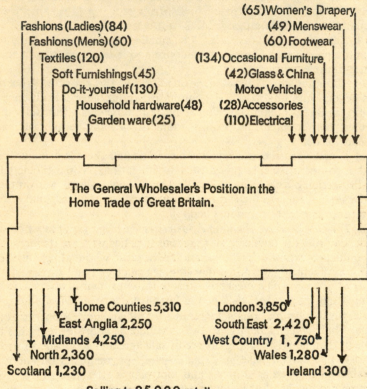

Buying From 1,000 Manufacturers.

Fashions (Ladies) (84)
Fashions (Men's) (60)
Textiles (120)
Soft Furnishings (45)
Do-it-yourself (130)
Household hardware (48)
Garden ware (25)

(65) Women's Drapery
(49) Menswear
(60) Footwear
(134) Occasional Furniture
(42) Glass & China
Motor Vehicle
(28) Accessories
(110) Electrical

The General Wholesaler's Position in the Home Trade of Great Britain.

Home Counties 5,310
East Anglia 2,250
Midlands 4,250
North 2,360
Scotland 1,230

London 3,850
South East 2,420
West Country 1,750
Wales 1,280
Ireland 300

Selling to 25,000 retailers
Reaching 5,000,000 Consumers.

Fig. 11. How the wholesaler fulfils his functions

Fireworks are wanted for Guy Fawkes' Day, or the 4th of July, or Bastille Day, or Independence Day, according to custom.

The storage of manufactured articles between the time they are produced and the time they are used is in most cases an essential part of the production process. Goods have not been 'produced' in the economic use of that word until they reach the consumer. Just as efficiency is essential in the manufacturing process, it is vital in the distribution process.

The specialist wholesaler removes the responsibility of the warehousing process from the manufacturer, sets him free to concentrate on the technological processes and takes over the risks and the work of transporting the goods geographically and through time.

(10) Organization of a Wholesale Warehouse

Fig. 12 shows a typical large-scale organization in the wholesale trade. It is a Limited Company, run by a board of directors, most of whom are only part-time directors. The board exercises general control of policy, reviews trends in business and determines major modifications in the conduct of its affairs.

Day-to-day affairs are controlled by the Managing Director. Probably the Chief Accountant is also a director with full-time services to be performed. These two full-time directors represent the board in everyday affairs and report to the board where necessary. In emergencies they contact the Chairman, but ordinarily they report on the routine developments at the monthly board meeting.

The three aspects of the organization are:

(*a*) The specialist departments, buying the various classes of goods, transporting them and storing them as they become available, receiving orders for them and dispatching them to their destinations.

(*b*) The financial department, controlling the availability and employment of the capital of the enterprise and ensuring that profit margins are adequate.

(*c*) The general administration department, controlling the organization itself, handling such routine matters as staffing, wages and salaries, training, etc.

The Specialist Departments

(*a*) *Buying departments*. There will be a degree of specialization here depending upon the classes of goods dealt with. The buyers have considerable responsibility: in certain trades they must be alert to changes in fashion and taste; they must know the best sources of supply, the trends in demand, the cost build-up of the product and the likely profit margin to be earned. Liaison with the sales departments is essential if expectations are to be realized.

(*b*) *Transport departments*. Manufacturers today have provided a tremendous range of vehicles for particular purposes. Specialist vehicles promote distribution efficiency. A wholesaler picking up goods in bulk will be taking advantage of large-scale transport, motorway networks, and railway freightliner services. His deliveries to retailers will be made in smaller vehicles. On either side of the warehousing function is the transport function. (*Transport and Distribution Made Simple* deals in detail with this area.)

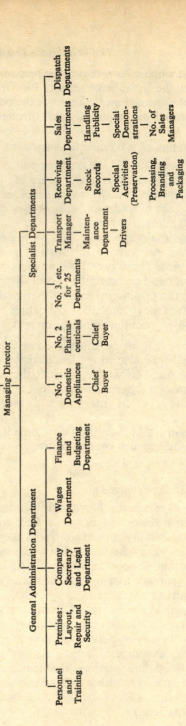

Fig. 12. The Organization of a wholesale warehouse

(*c*) *Receiving department.* On arrival goods are checked and discrepancies reported. The goods are then handed over to the warehouse department which will deal with them. This may mean merely that they will be stacked on shelves, or they may be treated to preserve them, refrigerated perhaps, or some re-packaging and branding may take place. Forklift trucks may be used to handle the goods, and computerized systems of selection for sales orders may also be employed. This is particularly helpful in fields such as pharmaceuticals, where one firm has established the 1,400 most frequently used lines on a computerized system. Uncommon items are picked out by hand and added to the order before it leaves for the packing department.

(*d*) *Sales departments.* The wholesale trade is highly competitive, and a firm must keep contact with its customers and be on the look-out for new business. Selling departments handle publicity, trade advertising, specialized demonstrations and features and also staff the warehouse showrooms to meet customers, show them lines that are available, follow up telephone inquiries, etc. A wide variety of systems is used for the processing of orders, invoicing, assembly of the goods, packing and dispatch.

(11) The Bad Reputation of 'Middlemen'

The term 'middlemen' has come to have overtones of unscrupulousness attached to it. Certain political groups hold that 'middleman' is synonymous with 'profiteer'. How true is this, and how did the situation arise?

In earlier times communications were so poor and transport facilities so limited that merchants were carrying considerable risks when they undertook a 'trading venture'. This old name for a commercial undertaking speaks for itself. Also in early days when credit facilities were less well developed, and usury frowned upon, one of the middlemen's main functions was to finance the undertaking. This he did by paying promptly for the goods supplied, and often in advance of supply, while he also waited until the retailer had sold the goods before receiving payment himself. For this reason it often arose that both producer and retailer were in debt to the merchant, or *brogger*, as he was called. The word brogger has changed into 'broker' and to have the 'broker's man in' is to have one's home sold up to pay debts.

Many of the early capitalists were middlemen who accumulated their wealth in the favourable position in which they found themselves. The man who is in the middle of a productive process is favourably placed to exploit others. He can refuse to buy the product from the producer unless the price is low, and he can refuse to sell it when he has acquired it unless the price is favourable to him.

Today the middleman is not able to exploit either the producers or the consumers in quite the same way, but he may nevertheless make quite enormous profits at certain times. If he performs the speculative function, buying in times of glut and selling in times of shortage, he may make tremendous profits out of a situation which has developed of its own accord and was not engineered by him. To the taunt of the politician that his enormous profits are causing the shortage, he will reply that the shortage is causing his profits. His activities as a matter of fact are not causing the shortage, but relieving it. He may also point out that if prices had fallen, so that he lost on the transaction, no one would have sympathized with him.

If the middleman is a little maligned here, it is perhaps regrettable. The student of commerce at least should see the point that the activities of middlemen, whether it is transport, warehousing or risk-bearing are all useful functions. Even if the middleman is eliminated someone will have to perform these functions, and to the extent that he is not a specialist, society will be the poorer, not the richer.

(12) Should We Eliminate the Wholesaler?

An almost unanimous 'yes' from the mass of ordinary people would probably greet this question. It seems elementary that if the middleman is cut out the 'honest' producer and the consumer must benefit. The producer's reward will be greater, and the consumer would get the goods

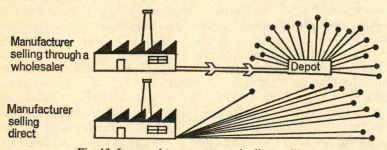

Fig. 13. Increased transport costs in direct selling

more cheaply. In fact this does not necessarily follow. As already mentioned, the wholesaler's functions have still to be performed and they are now to be performed by a non-specialist. Consider direct selling by manufacturers as distinct from selling through the wholesaler.

Fig. 13 illustrates the non-specialist nature of the delivery involved in this type of selling. The point is that increased *social costs*, not borne by the producer or the consumer but spread over the whole community, will creep in. Bigger traffic jams, bigger road programmes, more accidents and hospital treatment, busier funeral parlours may result from a decrease in specialization. Remember that specialization is the key to increased wealth. If the specialist uses his favourable position to reap super profits the tax system usually returns these to the mass of the people anyway.

(13) Achieving Economies in Distribution

(a) Fewer depots and larger 'drops'

One effect of trying to eliminate the wholesaler is an all-round effort to improve efficiency in the distribution network. It now seems that about 80 per cent of grocery turnover can be reached through only about 1,600 central buying points. This means that actual deliveries made to depots are fewer in number, and that each delivery is larger in size. This change coincides with transport developments which are particularly suitable for large-scale 'drops'. Container services both by liner train and by specialized road vehicles, faster and larger than in earlier days, are appropriate to this type of freight.

Full utilization of vehicles also requires improved loading and unloading facilities at each end. Another big development in the transport field is that more and more vehicles are being equipped with hoist apparatus that enables the driver to unload his vehicle by himself without the need for under-utilized lifting equipment at the depot. We have had lifting tackle on ships for a very long while now, so that ships can load and unload in ports where the facilities are poor. This idea has now been carried over to the vehicle, with consequent improvements in turnround time.

Transport has also been effective in eliminating some depots, since the improvement of roads and the motorway development increases the catchment area of each depot. A few main depots therefore can deal with a region where formerly many small depots were required.

(b) Stock control

Another aspect of economies in distribution concerns the stock. Inevitably much of the warehouseman's capital is tied up in stock. To some extent it is his function to hold slow-moving stock and thus save the retailer valuable space on his shelves. Idle stock is not profitable however, and anything the warehouseman can do to keep stock down to the minimum will increase the efficiency of the undertaking.

Computers can now be used in stock control, but for firms unable to afford to buy computer time to study the problem, the rule is to discover the stock replacement time, i.e. how long it takes for an order to be filled. Suppose it takes two weeks. The warehouseman must then keep a fortnight's average sales in stock. Whether he orders at exactly that time interval may depend on the discount he gets. It may for instance pay him to order monthly supplies if by doing so very favourable rates of discount can be obtained.

A reduction in the number of depots will almost certainly affect the total stock levels of slow-moving stock. Imagine a firm with 60 depots each serving a very small locality, which reduces the number of depots to 20. The stock held, of a slow-moving line, will need to be only a little larger than was held at one of the original depots to cater for the needs of the much bigger area now being supplied. This will release capital tied up in stock and reduce losses by pilferage. Insurance premiums may also be reduced.

(c) Eliminating the small order

If a retailer finds he can obtain 24-hour delivery service from his wholesaler he will tend to order frequently in small quantities. In this way he is economizing on the capital tied up in his business, and placing a heavy burden on the wholesaler. The wholesaler's expenses on delivery, invoicing, accounting and debt collection rise correspondingly, and may exceed the profit on the small order placed. The proud boast of a sales manager that his firm always delivers within 24 hours may lead eventually to a multiplicity of small orders. Ruthless pruning of these orders is the best way to promote the efficiency of a wholesale business, which is ideally a large-scale business.

(14) A Page to Test You on the Wholesale Trade

Answer	Question
—	1. What is a wholesaler?
1. A wholesaler is a person who buys in bulk, transports and warehouses goods in bulk as necessary, and sells in fair bulk to retailers.	2. What is a middleman?
2. A middleman is a person who performs some useful function in between the grower or manufacturer and the retailer.	3. What sort of functions might a middleman perform?
3. Transport, warehousing, finance, risk-bearing, prevention of deterioration, marketing, branding.	4. What are the wholesaler's services to the manufacturer?
4. (a) Clears the production lines. (b) Pays promptly for goods taken. (c) Warehouses the goods until required. (d) Assumes the risks. (e) If he brands under his own brand name he extends the manufacturers' market.	5. What are his services to the retailer?
5. (a) Breaks bulk. (b) Delivers to retailer. (c) May give credit. (d) May grade, pre-pack and brand. (e) Displays a wide variety of goods from many manufacturers. (f) Carries slow-moving stock. (g) Acts as a liaison between the retailer and the manufacturer.	6. What are the chief types of wholesaler?
6. (a) National general wholesalers. (b) Regional general wholesalers. (c) Specialist wholesalers. (d) Local wholesalers. (e) The Co-operative Wholesale Society. (f) 'Cash and carry' wholesalers. (g) 'Retailer-protection' wholesalers.	7. Is it desirable to eliminate the middleman?
7. Not really. He offers useful services to both producers and retailers.	8. Who would perform these services if the middleman did not exist?
8. They would have to be performed by the manufacturer, or grower, on one side, or the retailer on the other.	9. How many did you answer Correctly? Go over the list again.

EXERCISES SET 7

(15) The Wholesale Trade

1. What are the functions of a wholesaler in the chemist's sundries field?

2. What are the most usual types of wholesaler to be met in the home trade? What part do wholesalers play in the distribution of goods?

3. 'Middlemen are performing a useful function which helps everybody.' . . . 'Middlemen are more likely to help themselves than to help the public.'
Discuss these contrasting views of the activities of middlemen.

4. Distinguish between a merchant and a mercantile agent, bringing out clearly the part played by each in the wholesale trade.

5. Efficient operation in the distributive trades is as important as efficient operation in factories. How may a wholesaler seek to improve the efficiency of his distribution network?

6. What is a 'cash and carry' warehouse? Describe its advantages to the retail trader. Are there any disadvantages?

7. The sales manager and the accountant of a large wholesale undertaking may have very different views on the service that should be offered to the retailer. Discuss the points of view of these two people over the ideal service to be offered.

8. Distribution geographically is relatively straightforward, distribution over the time period from the present to the future is not so easy. Explain these two forms of distribution.

9. Explain the functions of the wholesaler. Discuss the probable effect on the future of wholesalers of the changing forms of modern retailing.

(University of London)

10. Messrs. Brown & Wilson, Ltd. describe themselves as *wholesale warehousemen* of patent medicines and toilet preparations. Describe their services (*a*) to the manufacturers (*b*) to the retailers of their goods. *(R.S.A.)*

11. Enumerate the several types of wholesale middlemen in English business today, adding brief notes on the services they render to the home manufacturer. *(R.S.A.)*

12. State the principle reasons why retailers and wholesalers should turn over their stock-in-trade as quickly as possible. Outline the methods which could be adopted by each to increase the rate of turnover and say if these methods could be applied to all trades. *(R.S.A.)*

13. (*a*) Why are wholesale warehouses needed?

(*b*) Describe the organization of a wholesale warehouse and show how it helps to fulfil the purposes mentioned by you in your answer to part (*a*) of this question. *(University of London)*

14. (*a*) Describe three services which the wholesaler provides for the retailer.

(*b*) Give two reasons why the wholesaler is becoming less important in the distribution of goods.

(*c*) Why are many small retailers forming voluntary groups? *(East Anglian Examination Board)*

15. How do wholesalers and retailers facilitate the flow of goods to the final consumer? *(University of London)*

CHAPTER SEVEN

IMPORT TRADE

(1) Introduction

Trade between nations takes place because:

(*a*) for climatic and other reasons no country is able to produce all the natural products it needs;

(*b*) there are economic advantages (connected with the international specialization of labour) in refraining from the production of some commodities.

Clearly Britain cannot grow cotton or jungle hardwoods, and although some products like tobacco can be grown here the finishing processes cannot be completed before winter sets in. Similarly we cannot mine ores that are not buried in our soil. Nature has been haphazard in the way she has distributed her resources.

At one time Britain produced enough wheat to feed her own people and even exported it to the Continent at certain times. Britain still grows excellent crops of wheat, probably the best in the world, yet she could grow still more. She does not do so because she can import wheat more cheaply from other countries. Britain can therefore enjoy a higher standard of living if she takes advantage of the international specialization of labour. She has herself concentrated on secondary and tertiary production, i.e. manufacturing and services, and may be said to grow her wheat in automobile factories and in the offices of banks and insurance companies.

Trade is a two-way affair in the modern world, and no nation can hope to sell its own goods abroad unless it is prepared to buy goods in return. A nation which wishes to import must also be prepared to export and must keep her exports of such a quality and at such reasonable prices as will enable her to achieve a **balance of trade.** If a balance of trade cannot be achieved, some other way of paying for the excess imports must be devised. These matters are dealt with later (see page 317).

(2) The Pattern of Import Trade

Fig. 14 shows the 1973 figures for the import trade of the United Kingdom.

Almost one half of Britain's imports are primary products, foods, fuel, and raw materials. The other half consists of various types of manufactured goods. We should certainly expect the bulk of Britain's imports to be primary products, for her own natural resources have been largely used up in the 200 years since the Industrial Revolution began, but in recent years we have imported more manufactured goods.

Most of the primary goods come from the less-developed regions of the world, from Commonwealth countries which were formerly part of

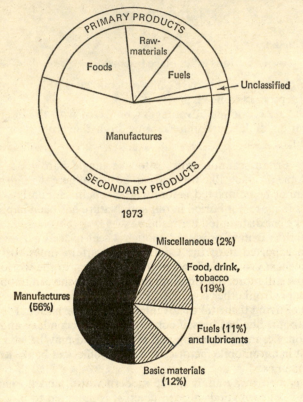

1973

Total value £15,855 m. (c.i.f.)

Fig. 14. The Import Trade of the U.K. 1973

the British Empire, from the Middle East, the Far East, Africa, and South and Central America. The semi-manufactured and manufacturd goods come mainly from the advanced nations in Europe and the United States of America. In many cases they are goods we could produce for ourselves, but because some nations have special skills in design or manufacture we enrich the variety of goods available to home consumers by importing them in exchange for British products which incorporate *our* special skills.

The import trade handles these very different types of product in different ways. Primary commodities are brought in as **bulk cargoes** as far as possible, and are usually handled by middlemen whose function is to finance, transport, and warehouse these goods until they are required. This is the type of goods handled on the **Commodity Markets**, which are dealt with fully on page 102. Where there is a need to ensure regular supplies of the raw material, or where a particular firm has built up a 'most favoured customer' link with overseas, **direct importation** by a manufacturing firm may be the usual thing,

Imports of secondary (manufactured) goods are not usually dealt with by middlemen, since technical knowledge is often important. Such products are usually imported either directly by the importing organization of the firm that will sell the product, or by agents appointed to handle the goods in this country by the overseas manufacturer. The latter may also set up his own office in this country to handle his export trade, and to stage exhibitions and displays of his goods.

(3) Specialists in the Import Trade—Merchants, Agents, and Brokers

Merchants buy goods on their own account. *Agents* make deals on behalf of other businessmen who are therefore the principals to the contracts which the agent has arranged. *Brokers* are middlemen who specialize in bringing together people in a particular market who are anxious to trade but, because of lack of knowledge of the market, do not know whom to trade with.

These specialists operate in most markets, but are particularly useful in import and export trade where distance, language difficulties, and expense would often prevent a small trader from making his needs known.

An import merchant with connexions in a particular country or group of countries will buy goods or produce from growers or manufacturers. By paying promptly he can often buy at competitive prices, for he is relieving the foreign exporter of the risks of the enterprise. He transports, warehouses, and displays the produce, and by dealing on the commodity markets, or direct with large-scale retailers or wholesalers, disposes of the goods at a profit.

An import commission agent deals with goods for foreign exporters on a consignment basis. This involves the import of the goods by the agent at the overseas dealer's risk. The agent will sell the goods at the best price he can obtain, using his expert knowledge of the British market. He will then render a document called an 'Account Sales' to the foreign exporter showing the gross proceeds, the commission deducted, and possibly a further deduction for *del credere* commission. *Del credere* means 'of the belief'. The agent believes he has found a buyer who will honour his bargain in due course. By accepting a *del credere* commission the agent agrees to assume the risk of any debts. The overseas manufacturer or grower is clearly unable to follow up a debt as easily as a person in the importing country. Having deducted these commissions, the agent remits the net proceeds to his overseas client.

Import brokers are experts in the technical details of the produce in which they deal, and are able to find buyers for foreign growers seeking a market, and supplies at the right price for home buyers who lack the

---

ACCOUNT SALES
By R. Gilbert & Co.,
70, St. Mary Axe,
London

1st February 19...

In the matter of 200 tons Chrome Ore ex S.S. *Silver Star*, sold by order and account of Rio Mining Co. Ltd.

Discharged from vessel 198 tons 10 cwts
Tare of bags   10 cwts

198 tons   @   12·00 per ton   =   £
                                            2,376

Charges
Ocean Freight @ £3·125 ton × 200   =   625·00
Dock Dues, etc.   =   85·50
Marine Insurance   =   22·50
Brokerage @ $1\frac{1}{4}$% on £2,376   =   29·70
Commission @ $2\frac{1}{2}$% on £2,376   =   59·40

                                           822·10

Net proceeds as per draft enclosed   1,553·90

E. & O. E.
London, 1st February 19...
(Signed) R. Gilbert & Co.

Fig. 15. An Account Sales in the import trade

knowledge of world markets which the broker possesses. A broker who knows his product will be able to advise that, in the present world shortage of a particular commodity, a similar, but not identical, product will do almost as well, and where supplies are to be obtained. His reward is a commission known as **brokerage.**

(4) Restrictions on Free Trade in Imports

If every nation specialized in the things it does best the wealth of the world would be at its greatest, and an optimum position in production would be reached. Goods would be produced in the country with the greatest economic advantages in that class of goods, and the resulting output would be traded freely around the world.

In fact it is difficult to get nations to agree to allow **free trade** in this way, because it condemns many countries to being primary producers only. For example, the United States during the nineteenth century was very much opposed to free trade, and pursued a **protectionist policy** which protected her home industries even though this meant a lower standard of living for her people. The present prosperity of the United States is the result of the strong industrial tradition created in that century. Today the United States is a strong advocate of free trade, but other nations are not so keen.

Britain plays what part it can in promoting free trade, but is adversely affected if other nations 'dump' their goods on the British market. To 'dump' goods is to sell them abroad at a lower price than they are being sold at home, in order to earn foreign exchange. If this is done it represents unfair competition to the home industries of the nation on which they are dumped. It is particularly serious for Great Britain, which in any case usually faces a very high import bill for necessary foodstuffs and raw materials. Systems of **import licensing, exchange control,** and **customs procedures** help to control imports.

Import licences. The Board of Trade issues import licences which cover the import of all goods into the United Kingdom, but in many cases the only use made of them is for statistical purposes, an *open general licence* being given on schedules of goods which may enter the country unrestrictedly. For goods not listed on the schedules, a *specific licence* has to be obtained. Specific licences limit the import of the commodity to a certain quantity, or value. This is not always satisfactory, for if quota licences of this sort artificially restrict the supply of goods available, the price rises and the foreign exporter receives more money for the goods. If the limit is set on the value of the goods, the limit is reached before the foreign exporter has supplied the usual quantity, since every unit is more expensive. If we restrict the prices by law a rationing system has to be brought in, and a 'black market' may develop. Licensing is one device for keeping control of the volume of imports. Another device is exchange control.

Exchange control. When we try to buy goods from overseas we have to pay the foreign exporter in his own currency, or in a currency that is acceptable to him. Some countries will accept Sterling pounds as a satisfactory medium of payment, but other countries will not. They prefer to be paid in dollars or in gold. Whatever we import must therefore be paid for in foreign exchange of some sort. For many years it has been getting more difficult for Britain to earn all the foreign exchange she needs. The system of exchange control rations out the available foreign currency. It is operated by the Bank of England, whose role is explained on page 185.

Customs procedures were at one time a method of raising revenues for the exchequer, but the duties collected today are relatively insignificant, and customs duties have become more important as a method of controlling imports. There are two types of duty; *specific duties* are imposed

on a commodity per unit of quantity imported, irrespective of the price
at which the goods were bought; *ad valorem duties* are imposed on the
value of the merchandise. By variations in the duty rates a country can
give 'most favoured nation' treatment to a particular country or group
of countries, as Britain did for many years to Commonwealth countries and as she does to the E.E.C. countries today.

(5) Documentation of Import Cargoes

A full explanation of the documentation of overseas cargoes is given
in the chapter on Export Trade (page 136) but a word here on customs
procedures is necessary. Goods arriving in the United Kingdom must
be entered for customs clearance on a form known as an 'Entry'. These
entries are made on forms for

(*a*) *non-dutiable goods:* here the interest is largely a statistical one, to
discover trends in the import trade.

(*b*) *dutiable goods:* here the interest is also statistical, but the inspection of goods and collection of duty is the chief purpose.

Possession of the consignment cannot be obtained from the shipping
company until the necessary documents are presented to them. One of
these documents is the *Bill of Lading* which represents the title to the
goods. The other is a copy of the 'Entry' form confirming that the duty
has been paid. Different entry forms are used for different classes of
imports. Details of the correct form to be used may be found in the
Customs and Excise Tariff, a volume published by Her Majesty's
Stationery Office. 'Entry' forms are usually prepared in quadruplicate,
one copy for the importer, one for the Exchange Control, two for the
Customs, who return one copy to the importer on payment of duty. It
is this copy, with the Bill of Lading, which secures delivery of the goods
from the shipping company.

Some goods carry a **value added tax** as well as a customs duty. When
these classes of goods are imported value added tax must also be paid on
entry, and the appropriate adjustments made (for a full description of
VAT see Appendix).

(6) Re-exports, Transhipment and Process Inwards Relief

Customs duties represent an increase in the price of goods to home
consumers. An anomaly therefore arises where goods are not consumed
at home but are re-exported. Their price would be increased by the
amount of the duty, and this would render British goods less competitive
in overseas markets.

In practice goods for re-export and for transhipment (transfer to
another vessel for onward delivery to an overseas port) are entered on
special 'Entry' forms and are entitled to 'Same State Relief'. This
name comes from their being exported in the same state. In addition

to this, where an import pays duty and is manufactured into a finished product which is subsequently exported, the exporter can claim a **'process inwards relief'**, formerly called 'drawback', from the customs authorities. Primary imports embodied into secondary exports are therefore free from customs duty, thus keeping their export prices as competitive as possible.

(7) Bonded Warehouses

The payment of duties is a very considerable cost to some firms. For instance the tobacco industry in Britain pays about £1 million every day in duty. The duty is payable in advance, before entry is allowed, and firms therefore have considerable quantities of capital tied up in this duty. To reduce the burden somewhat a system of **bonded warehouses** permits the landing of cargo on which duty has not been paid. The owners of such warehouses give a bond to the authorities promising not to release goods from the warehouse until the duty has been paid and a customs officer is present. The bond names a penalty to be paid should any infringement occur.

Importers may own their own bonded warehouse, or may simply hire space in one when required. The advantage is that goods can be graded, sorted, and, in some countries, even manufactured while in bond, the duty being payable only on removal of the goods for sale on the home market.

(8) Entry to the European Economic Community

Upon entry to the European Economic Community the United Kingdom began a transitional period which will eventually lead to 'free circulation' of British goods in the Community, and 'free circulation' in Britain of goods produced in the other member countries. During the transitional period tariffs will be progressively reduced. Since 1973, in order to signal to customs authorities that goods are entitled to special rates of duty additional documents have been required for both imports and exports to comply with the Community transit (C.T.) system. This system gives evidence of entitlement to preferential tariff rates. The simple **'movement certificate'** provides evidence that the goods are in free circulation in the country of export. Since EEC countries have no customs duties between one another, goods in free circulation in one country may circulate freely in another. With new member states during the transitional period the regulations require goods moving between new member states and original members to pay the special 'intra-Community rates' prevailing at the time.

A fuller system, designed to be used as a transit document across several frontiers, is the T form procedure. These transit forms, T1, T2 and T3 signal to the Customs authorities whether goods are to be admitted free, at the intra-Community rate or at the rates for dutiable goods.

(9) A Page to Test You on Import Trade

Answers	Questions
—	1. Why do most countries import goods?
1. (*a*) Because Nature has not spread her bounties evenly around the world. (*b*) Because climatic differences favour particular crops or industrial processes. (*c*) Because of the international specialization of labour.	2. How are primary products imported most economically?
2. In bulk, carried in bulk carriers such as oil tankers, ore carriers, refrigerated meat carriers, etc.	3. Who handles such cargoes?
3. The merchants and brokers operating through the Commodity Markets.	4. How are secondary manufactures usually imported, and why?
4. Through agents, because they can (*a*) deal with the technical details; (*b*) find the customer on the home market; (*c*) take over the *del credere* risks.	5. What are *del credere* risks?
5. The risks a creditor runs that he will not be paid, i.e. the bad-debt risks.	6. How is the import trade controlled?
6. By (*a*) licensing; (*b*) exchange control; (*c*) customs entry procedures.	7. What are the types of licence?
7. (*a*) Open general licences; (*b*) specific licences; (*c*) quota licences.	8. What forms do the Customs require?
8. (*a*) Entry forms in duplicate; (*b*) value added tax forms if necessary.	9. What is 'drawback'?
9. A reclaim of customs duty paid on imported goods which are embodied in manufactured goods exported to consumers abroad.	10. What is a bonded warehouse?
10. It is a warehouse where imported dutiable goods can be stored, sampled, and treated even though duty has not been paid.	11. What is a movement certificate?
11. It is a certificate used in the community transit system to certify that goods are in free circulation in the exporting country.	12. How many did you answer correctly? Go over the list again.

EXERCISES SET 8

(10) Import Trade

1. What special difficulties face a manufacturer whose raw materials have to be obtained from overseas? How may he overcome these difficulties?

2. Explain the part played by (*a*) merchants, and (*b*) agents, in the import trade of Great Britain.

3. 'Middlemen in the import trade assume both the risks and the transportation problems.' What do you understand by this, and how do these activities benefit (*a*) the British importer and (*b*) the foreign exporter?

4. What is a bonded warehouse? Explain why it might be of greater use in the import of wine than in the import of transistor radios.

5. Why is it necessary for Great Britain to control the volume of imports? In what ways is this control achieved?

6. What do you understand by (*a*) an open general licence; (*b*) a specific licence; (*c*) a quota licence?

7. Besides a commission on the goods sold an import agent often receives *del credere* commission. What functions does he perform for the overseas seller which entitle him to receive these commissions?

8. Describe the pattern of United Kingdom imports revealed in Fig. 14.

9. Why does a country import certain goods, and not import others? Illustrate your answer by reference to (*a*) your own country; (*b*) one other country.

10. 'Brokers use their expert knowledge of markets to bring buyers seeking supplies into contact with suppliers seeking customers.' Explain.

11. Goods which are in free circulation in a country which is a member of the European Economic Community may circulate freely in the other member countries. Explain, referring in your answer to 'movement certificates'.

CHAPTER EIGHT

MARKETS

(1) Definition

A market is defined as a place where buyers and sellers are in contact with one another to fix prices.

This contact may be established directly, e.g. where retailers buy supplies at the wholesale produce markets such as Smithfield or Billingsgate; or indirectly through specialists, such as the brokers and jobbers on the London Stock Exchange. Physical presence in the market is not necessary; indeed, the Foreign Exchange Market is largely conducted by telephone.

Generally speaking, the major markets are such specialized affairs, and dealings are conducted in such large quantities, that the general public are ill-equipped to deal upon them. For instance, the minimum contract for wheat on the Liverpool Wheat Exchange is 125 tons, and the minimum contract for sugar is 50 tons on the London Sugar Futures Market. Such markets are called **highly organized markets**, and only experts may deal on them.

These highly organized markets stand at the very centre of civilized life today, and Britain's continued prosperity is closely linked to the expertise developed in the markets of the City of London, Liverpool, Manchester, and other centres.

(2) Types of market

In this chapter and the ones that follow no reference will be made to traditional type of retail market already dealt with on page 41. The types of market which lie at the root of the prosperity of the British nation are markets dealing in a specialist way with the major commodities required by an advanced industrial nation. The major markets are listed below:

Commodity Markets

(*a*) The London Metal Exchange in Whittington Avenue, where copper, tin, lead, and zinc are bought and sold.

(*b*) The London Tea Auctions in Plantation House, Mincing Lane.

(*c*) The London Commodity Exchange Group in Plantation House. This is a group of commodity markets, some of which have been established for a very long time. Others are very recent, like the London Fishmeal Terminal Market and the London Vegetable Oil Terminal Market, both of which were set up in 1967. An interesting case which illustrates the dynamic nature of market institutions is the London Shellac Trade Association, which ceased to trade in 1966. This market, which formerly handled enormous transactions, has been affected partly by technological change (gramophone records are no longer made from shellac), but more seriously by price control in India. This has resulted in merchants obtaining the commodity at a fixed price whatever orders they place, so that there is little point in laying in stocks when the commodity is cheap. For this reason speculation ceased to be possible and the market in 'futures' has ceased.

The other products dealt in on the London Commodity Exchange group markets are:

(i) Cocoa

(ii) Coffee

(iii) Copra the dried 'meat' of the coconut, rich in vegetable oils, (used in the manufacture of margarine and soap).

(iv) Fishmeal (made chiefly from anchovies caught in millions off the coast of Peru. Fishmeal is very rich in protein and has become vital to the broiler industry, one of the fastest growing sections of Britain's intensive agriculture).

(v) General Produce. This very old market was the original market for many commodities which now have a separate market to themselves, such as rubber, coffee, tea, and cocoa. Its members still handle over 100 commodities, of which pepper and spices, aromatic oils, bristles, hair, gum, waxes, mica, and ivory are examples.

(vi) Jute (a coarse fibre from Bengal used in making sacking and carpets).

(vii) Rubber

(viii) Sugar

(ix) Vegetable Oils. This market deals in soya-bean oil, and it is hoped to extend the market to deal in other vegetable oils in due course.

(*d*) The London Wool Top Futures Market, where semi-manufactured wool for future delivery is bought and sold.

(*e*) The Fur Market, in Beaver House, Garlick Hill.

(*f*) The London Wool Exchange in Coleman Street.

(*g*) The Uncut Diamond Market run by the Diamond Corporation in Holborn Circus, and the Hatton Garden Market associated with it.

(*h*) The English Grains Market in the Corn Exchange, Mark Lane.

(*i*) The Gold Bullion Market in St. Swithin's Lane.

(*j*) The Silver Bullion Market, Great Winchester Street.

(*k*) The Manchester Royal Exchange, where cotton and rayon yarn, and cloth are dealt with.

(*l*) The Bradford Wool Exchange, where 'tops' and 'noils' are bought and sold.

(*m*) The Liverpool Cotton Exchange, traditionally the market for raw cotton.

(*n*) The Liverpool Wheat Exchange.

Financial Markets

(*a*) The Stock Exchange in Throgmorton Street.

(*b*) The Discount Market, centred around Lombard Street and Cornhill.

(*c*) The Foreign Exchange Market, in which a few authorized dealers exchange pounds for foreign currencies.

N.B. The term 'Money Market' is often used, but there is no such market. It refers to the whole range of banks and merchant banks.

The Insurance Market centred around Lloyd's.

The Baltic Exchange in St. Mary Axe, where shipping and air freight space can be chartered or hired.

Wholesale Produce Markets. These are very widespread, but the London ones are famous and attract produce from a wide area. They are:

(*a*) Covent Garden, the fruit and vegetable market. This market has now been moved to a location outside central London.

(*b*) Spitalfields, the East End fruit and vegetable market.

(*c*) Smithfield, the meat market.

(*d*) Billingsgate, the fish market.

The situation of the London Markets can be seen on the map of the City of London, Fig. 16.

(3) Methods of Dealing

The methods of dealing in the British commodity markets vary greatly because they are the result of a century or more of dealings in the particular commodities concerned. To some extent the method of dealing is affected by the commodity itself.

Where a product has, or can be given, a uniform standard quality, dealings are made much easier, because the dealers know with certainty what they are buying and selling. For example, on the London Metal Exchange the commodities dealt in are called Standard Copper, Standard Tin, etc. The quality of these products can be scientifically tested and established.

Tea on the other hand is insusceptible to standardization. The quality varies not only from growing area to growing area, but also seasonal differences in rainfall, etc. make the product different from year to year in the same area. Even on a given bush the leaves vary from poor to top quality. Similarly no two sheep give wool that is alike. Some sheep are contented and docile, with a good fleece, while others are temperamental and grow a poor quality fleece. Products such as tea and wool must therefore be sampled by the buyers before they can decide on a fair price.

In particular, if a commodity can be standardized so that dealers

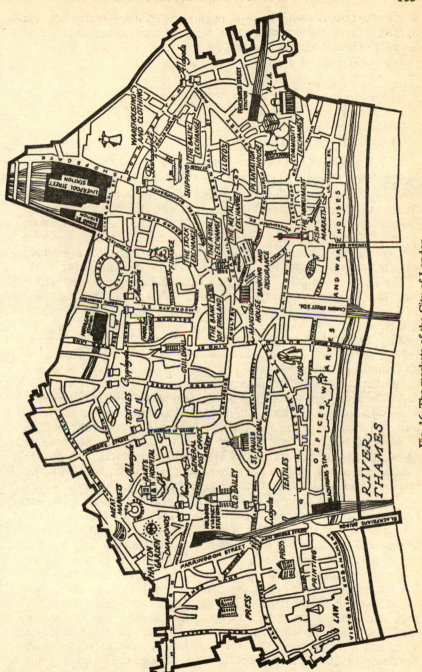

Fig. 16. The markets of the City of London

know with certainty what they are buying and selling, it makes possible a 'futures' market. Futures markets are particularly useful in reducing the risks of business life (see page 109).

The chief types of dealing are:

(a) Auction sales
(b) Ring trading
(c) Challenging
(d) Private treaty
(e) A special case—diamonds.

Auction sales occur where the product is not susceptible to standardization. It must be sampled beforehand if the buyers are to decide a fair price for the goods. At the London Tea Auctions in Plantation House the buying brokers sit round in tiered seats while the brokers representing the tea growers in India and Ceylon mount the rostrum to auction their lots. The buying brokers know which particular lots they require and have decided the limits of prices to which they will go. The highest bid wins, but sellers may specify a reserve price below which they will not sell.

The London Wool Exchange is situated in Coleman Street not far from the Guildhall. Wool arriving from New Zealand and Australia, the Falkland Islands and South Africa is laid out for inspection for two days. The buyers from Yorkshire and from Europe inspect it to determine its quality. The auctions are conducted by a representative of the Committee of London Wool Brokers, and sales are made to the highest bidder. At times of international tension the bidding can be noisy, because of the importance of wool for military uniforms.

A different type of auction has been experimented with in some of the wholesale produce markets, which, it is claimed, gives the grower a fairer price for his goods. For instance, where lettuces or cabbages are in plentiful supply buyers have no need to bid keenly against one another, and the produce is sold at rock-bottom prices. The grower suffers and, unless the low prices are passed on to the housewife, the retailer makes good profits at the expense of the grower.

The new system features an illuminated board on which prices are marked in a ring—say from 25 pence downwards in new pennies. As the operating key traverses a series of studs, the prices light up—25 pence, 24 pence, 23 pence, etc. The buyers are each given a push-button which will stop the mechanism. As the prices fall a buyer who has the price of 18 pence per bag as his top price may watch to see if he will be able to buy at that price. Just as he is about to press the button, another buyer stops the mechanism at 19 pence per bag. This buyer is asked how many bags he requires. He may say 60 bags. 'There are 156 bags left, gentlemen' says the auctioneer, starting the mechanism again. The would-be buyer may revise his bid to 19 pence. Just as he is about to bid, someone else does so at 20 pence. He takes 100 bags: 'There are 56 bags only left

Fig. 17. Tea auctions at Plantation House

gentlemen'. It is an auction in reverse. Whether or not it is really successful in giving the grower fairer prices, it is distinctly unpopular with some traders, and it probably has raised the prices of produce to the retailer.

Ring Trading is a method of trading used at the Metal Exchange and the Sugar Exchange in Plantation House. The name originates from the use of a chalk ring on the floor in years gone by to separate the buyers from the sellers.

In the Metal Exchange the ring now consists of a circle of curved benches, and there are 40 members who take their seats at 12 noon for the first of the three daily sessions. Dealings are allowed for five minutes only in each metal, and are started by the Secretary of the Exchange with the hanging up of a notice bearing the name of the metal to be dealt in and the appropriate words; for example 'Tin, gentlemen, tin'. Members with tin to sell shout their offers, and those wishing to buy approach the seated sellers. Clerks standing behind make a note of the deals concluded. After five minutes the notice is changed, and the cry 'Copper, gentlemen, copper' is heard.

Besides these open-market periods when trading takes place in a very public way, private contracts are concluded outside market hours between dealers who wish to get their books straight or to complete unfilled orders. This may be done in the centre of the Metal Exchange floor, or in private offices, or by telephone.

At the Sugar Exchange a white circle is marked on the floor and buyers and sellers meet inside the circle to make binding deals. Sugar prices fluctuate very widely because sugar is a vital food and changes in the international situation may cause demand to rise suddenly. Also a large proportion of cane sugar is grown in the West Indies where hurricanes can destroy a whole island's crop in a few hours. This raises prices throughout the world. The Sugar Market at Plantation House is one of the most modern in the world with soundproof telephone boxes and closed-circuit television to help the dealers.

In the Coffee Market at Plantation House a similar method is used. It is called 'open outcry' on the floor of the market, and calls are made four times a day at 10.45 a.m., 12.30 p.m., 2.45 p.m., and 4.50 p.m. The wide range of qualities and varieties on offer in world coffee markets makes 'trading in actuals' a complex operation, and dependent entirely on the sellers and buyers honouring their contracts. For instance, if the grade, size, roast or 'cup' of a consignment of coffee proves to be different from the original sample, disputes can and do arise. There is no arbitration body to decide such disputes, probably because no one has more knowledge of the product than the dealers themselves.

Challenging. The London gold and silver bullion markets are less boisterous because the number of dealers authorized to deal in these metals is limited. The half-dozen brokers sit around a small table and challenge one another until a firm price is agreed. This is said to be the price at which gold has been 'fixed' for the day, and the room where the brokers sit is therefore called the 'Gold Fixing Room'.

Private Treaty. This is the method used by the dealers on the Stock Exchange, the Baltic Exchange, the Foreign Exchange Market, the Corn Exchange and the Insurance markets. In the Copra Market the business is done mainly in the offices of the firms themselves. In the General Produce market private treaty now fixes the price of most of the bargains. In the Rubber Market the floor of the house is used to conduct business, but it is by private treaty and not open outcry.

Despite the fact that the bargains they strike are private contracts between the parties, fierce competition exists in these markets and the public are therefore assured of a 'fair' price for the arrangements the dealers are making on their behalf.

Diamond Market. Some 85 per cent of all newly mined rough gem and industrial diamonds are sold through the London-based Central Selling Organisation (CSO), whose companies sort, value and sell rough diamonds to the world's major diamond-cutting centres and industries. Companies within the CSO enter into agreements with the various diamond producers to purchase their entire output. In times when certain categories (there are over 2,000 of them) are in excess of demand, the CSO will hold them in reserve and offer them for sale only at a rate at which world markets can absorb them. This has created price stability for diamonds, confidence in the diamond industry and also ensured that the producers do not have to worry about fluctuation in demand.

When the diamonds reach the CSO in London they are sorted and valued according to size, colour, shape and quality before they can be sold. Industrial diamonds are sold through Industrial Distributors (Sales) on a day-to-day basis to meet the demands of modern industry. Gem diamonds are sold at the ten annual sights held by The Diamond Trading Company. The Company's customers are advised of the sights and send in their requirements which are equated against present stocks. They will then come to London to inspect their diamonds, although they cannot argue about the price except in the case of a large stone. The customer can refuse to take the entire parcel but cannot merely take any particular part of it; however, should an error in valuation occur this would be rectified.

In Hatton Garden, close to the CSO offices, there are many traders in diamonds both rough and polished. There, diamonds are available in much smaller quantities than those supplied by the CSO.

Most of the diamonds are re-exported and are an important foreign exchange earner for the United Kingdom.

(4) 'Spot' Markets and Futures Markets

Markets which deal in goods for prompt delivery are called **'spot' markets** because the goods are there on the spot and can be delivered upon payment. This is true of tea, raw wool, gold, and diamonds.

Futures markets, or terminal markets, are markets where the goods being bought and sold are not available yet, but will become available in the future. It is of the greatest importance that 'future' prices should be firm, both to the buyer and the seller. Since an understanding of 'futures' is essential to our study of commerce, let us see why the buyer of copper, or tin, or rubber needs to have firm prices for his goods, even though he does not want them for three months, or six months.

The Importance of 'Future' Prices

(*a*) *To the buyer.* Imagine a manufacturer who is submitting a tender for the supply of copper piping, radiators, and boilers for a heating installation. The job is to be carried out in July, but tenders must be submitted by 1 March. In deciding his price for the job the manufacturer will need to know his raw-material prices. However, these fluctuate day by day: today's price will not do for the basis of the contract, unless he can actually buy the copper today and keep it. This would tie up his capital, and present him with storage problems. If he can find someone who will sell him 'future' copper, for delivery in July at a firm price, he will be able to submit his tender. That tender will include a profit on the contract. Should the price of copper rise above his 'future' price it will not affect him. The supplier will still have to supply at the agreed price. Should the price of copper fall our buyer will have to honour his agreement to buy, even though he could buy more cheaply on the open market. This will not worry the buyer, because he will still earn a reasonable profit from the contract.

The real risk that is worrying the buyer therefore is the possibility of a rise in price, since this would destroy the profitability of the contract unless he can shield himself against it. We shall see in the next paragraph that the seller is worried in the opposite way.

(b) *To the seller*. Suppose the supplier of the copper mentioned above is the selling organization of a nationalized industry in Zambia. The industry has wages to pay, development to finance, transport and processing charges to be met. It will feel happier if some at least of its eventual output is sold already. To sell 'futures' at firm prices gives the industry a guaranteed market for some of its output. The chief worry facing producers is the prospect of a fall in the world price of their goods. If the 'bottom falls out of the market' the producers may face serious losses. It is for this reason that they are willing to accommodate buyers anxious to insure against the opposite type of risks.

A futures contract is essentially a transaction between two parties who require to cover themselves against opposite risks, one fearing a rise in price, the other a fall.

(c) *To the speculator*. Besides the actual producers and consumers in the 'forward market' speculators are also active. They provide much of the stability in the markets, since, like all speculators (see page 213) they buy when others are selling and sell when others are buying. The one thing a speculator does not want is to receive 25 tons of standard copper, but he is perfectly happy to buy it 'at 3 months forward' in the hopes of selling the ticket for it to someone in urgent need of copper, at a profit to himself.

Hedging Operations

All the activities mentioned above are known as 'hedging' operations on the markets. A hedge is a protection against the bitter winds that blow, and a 'hedge' on the markets is a protection against the bitter economic blows that fate sends against us.

Suppose that a manufacturer agrees on 1 May to deliver cotton yarn on 1 July, the price to be decided by the ruling price of cotton on that date. The raw cotton on 1 May costs £500, and in the normal course of events the yarn will fetch £1,000, which is enough to cover wages and expenses and leave a profit.

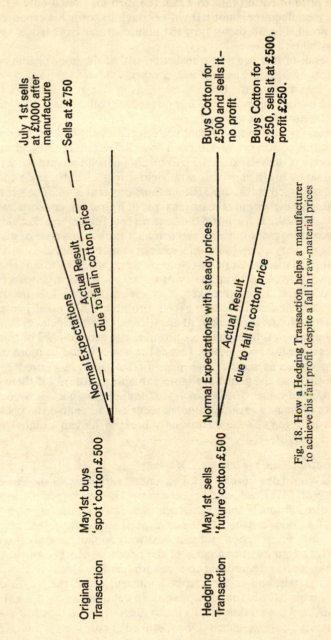

Fig. 18. How a Hedging Transaction helps a manufacturer to achieve his fair profit despite a fall in raw-material prices

Original Transaction

May 1st buys 'spot' cotton £500

July 1st sells at £1,000 after manufacture

Sells at £750

Normal Expectations

Actual Result
due to fall in cotton price

Hedging Transaction

May 1st sells 'future' cotton £500

Normal Expectations with steady prices

Actual Result
due to fall in cotton price

Buys Cotton for £500 and sells it – no profit

Buys Cotton for £250, sells it at £500, profit £250.

If the price of cotton falls to £250, the yarn may fetch only £750, so that the manufacturer is not left with enough to cover his expenses and yield a profit. Fig. 18 shows how the manufacturer can 'hedge' against this possibility.

The result of this hedging transaction is that the poor results on the manufacturer's main business are compensated by the profits on his 'hedge'. By taking on the hedging transaction alongside the main transaction he assumes an equal and opposite risk to offset the risk he cannot avoid on the main transaction.

Imagine that the price of raw cotton had changed in the opposite direction, i.e. cotton prices had risen to £750. His main transaction will now be very profitable, since he will be able to sell the yarn for £1,250. Unfortunately his 'hedge' will now yield a loss of £250, since to keep his promise to sell cotton for £500 he must buy it at £750. The net result will be that he makes only the original profit he had hoped to make. This is fair enough. What the normal dealer on the 'futures' market wants is to safeguard his main business; security is the chief purpose of his activity. The primary aim is to limit losses, not to make profits.

Terminal markets are not therefore gambling markets, although some people do gamble on them. They are markets where risks can be reduced. Where risks are reduced enterprise is encouraged. Like insurance, the activities of the 'futures' markets promote the general prosperity of the nation to the enrichment of all citizens. One particular example of the way in which futures markets promote the general level of business activities is the financial aspect. Just as the banks would be more willing to accept goods as security (see page 142) if they are insured against fire and theft, so the goods are more valuable as security if there is no fear of a fall in value. Goods which are the subject of a hedging contract therefore command greater value as security and enable the trader to conduct a larger volume of business because he can obtain greater financial support.

Standardization and the 'Futures' Markets

In the Wool Tops Futures Market, a new market established since the Second World War, we have a good example of the connection between standardized products and futures dealings. If we are dealing on a 'spot' market, the goods are there for us to inspect, sample, taste, etc. If we are dealing with 'future' goods we can deal with confidence only if we can predict with certainty the quality of the goods we shall be buying. The product must be standardized to a certain quality. This is not too difficult with metals, and cotton can be standardized on the length of the fibre. With wool it was found impossible to define a standard for futures contracts, and the market has to be conducted on the basis of a semi-manufactured article, called Dry Combed Top. This product has a fibre fineness of 22·5 microns, and a fibre length of 6·2 cm hauteur and a barbe of 7·7 cms. It makes a satisfactory commodity to deal in without actual inspection and sampling.

Details of the British Terminal Markets are summarized in Table 5.

Table 5. British Terminal Markets

Market	Basic commodity for 'future' contracts	Price quoted in	Minimum contract
Plantation House (Rubber)	No. 1 Ribbed Smoked Sheet Rubber	New pence per kg	5 metric tons
Plantation House (Cocoa)	Good fermented Ghana	£ per metric ton	5 metric tons
Plantation House (Coffee)	Sound native Uganda Robusta	£ per metric ton	5 metric tons
Plantation House (Raw Sugar)	Raw Sugar	£ per metric ton	5 metric tons
London Wool Top Futures	Dry Combed Top	New pence per Kg	2,250 Kgs.
London Metal Exchange	Standard Copper	£ per metric ton	25 metric tons
	Standard Tin	£ per metric ton	5 metric tons
	Standard Zinc	£ per metric ton	25 metric tons
	Standard Lead	£ per metric ton	25 metric tons
	Silver 0·999% fine	Pence per troy ounce	10,000 ozs (10 bars)
Baltic Exchange	Coarse Grains Maize (varieties)	£ per ton (2240 lbs)	100 tons
Baltic Exchange	Coarse Grains Barley (varieties)	£ per ton (,,)	100 tons
Silver Bullion	0·999% fine	Pence per troy oz.	2,000 ozs. = 2 bars
Liverpool Wheat Exchange	Varieties	£ per ton	125 tons
Liverpool Cotton Exchange	Varieties	Pence per kilo	at will

Settling Futures Contracts

The vast majority of futures contracts are not pressed to maturity. The manufacturer who has hedged disposes of the hedge when the risk run on his normal contract comes to an end, without serious fluctuations in price having occurred. By selling the futures contract he liquidates it without physical delivery of the commodity having to take place. Despite the high probability that the contracts will never come to maturity the risk is always there, and the market traders are alert to the need to preserve their good names by ensuring that deals are honoured.

Terminal contracts are therefore registered with the London Produce Clearing House, on standard forms provided by the Clearing House and in accordance with the rules of the Terminal Market concerned. Both buyers and sellers are required to lodge with the Clearing House a deposit which is held until the contract is liquidated. If the price moves against either party, so that the deposit would not be great enough to buy him out of his difficulty, he must increase the deposit by paying in a 'margin' which is reclaimed if prices recover in his favour.

Like all clearing houses the London Produce Clearing House eliminates intermediate buyers and sellers to establish who is finally dealing with whom. These actual contracting parties will be involved in the final settlement.

EXERCISES SET 9

(5) Markets

1. What is a market? Why does the market play such an important part in advanced economies? Illustrate your answer with reference to either the London Metal Exchange or the London Tea Auctions, Mincing Lane.

2. Why is it undesirable from the point of view of (*a*) the diamond producers, and (*b*) a retired actress with money invested in diamonds, that there should be a free market in diamonds?

3. How does a 'futures' market help a manufacturer in his pursuit of ordinary business?

4. 'Speculators help everybody' . . . 'Speculators help themselves at everybody else's expense.' Is either of these statements true? Discuss whether they could both be true at the same time.

5. What do you understand by a 'highly organized market'? Why is it undesirable for the general public to do business on these markets, except through an authorized agent?

6. How does a lettuce grown in a market garden 100 miles from your home reach your tea table within 24 hours of being cut?

7. Tea is not susceptible to standardization. What do you understand by this, and how does it affect the way that tea is marketed?

8. 'Hedging is like gambling, but at the same time different from it.' Explain.

9. Explain how a broker on a commodity market would fulfil an order for a client.

10. Why are auctions used to sell some commodities but not others? Which commodities are sold by auction, and why is it the most appropriate method?

11. Describe the work of two wholesale produce markets or exchanges. Explain how they perform a useful function in commerce.

(*University of London*)

12. Write short accounts of: (*a*) The London Metal Exchange; (*b*) The London Commodity Exchange Group.

13. Explain why a futures market is of great importance to a manufacturer estimating for a contract which will probably not be started for three months.

14. Write short paragraphs on each of the following: (*a*) open outcry; (*b*) hedging operations; (*c*) the London Tea Auctions; (*d*) Dry combed top.

15. What is meant by a 'minimum contract'? Explain why the system of minimum contracts makes it impossible for the ordinary public to operate on the 'Commodity Markets'.

CHAPTER NINE

THE BALTIC EXCHANGE

(1) Introduction

One of the most important markets in the City of London today is the Baltic Mercantile and Shipping Exchange, known simply as the Baltic Exchange. Like Lloyd's it originated in a coffee house, or rather two coffee houses, much frequented by ships' masters and merchants in the import–export trade. The countries around the shores of the Baltic Sea have traded with Britain since medieval times, in particular supplying grain and tallow to the British market. At one time this trade was in the hands of the Hansa towns of North Germany, but when the Hansa were driven out in 1602 British merchants began to deal direct. The trade with the American colonies grew up about the same time, and from 1744 onwards the coffee house where the merchants met was called the Virginia and Baltic.

From 1823 onwards the Baltic Club has had rules and regulations for its members. The basis of its operations is the verbal contract, which is binding upon members. As we shall see later 'My word is my bond' is a motto found to lie at the root of activities of many highly organized markets. Today, in splendid premises in St. Mary Axe, the Baltic Exchange is the centre of the following important markets.

(*a*) The Freight Market, where cargoes are arranged for ships and ships are found for cargoes.

(*b*) The Air Freight Market.

(*c*) The Grain Futures Market.

(*d*) The Oil and Oilseeds Market.

(2) The Freight Market

All over the world are cargoes waiting to be shipped and ships delivering cargoes. Some of these ships are liners, operating on regular routes from one port to another, with intermediate calls at one or two other ports. Others are 'tramps', prepared to go anywhere in the world with a cargo, so long as it is a profitable journey. Competition is fierce in this international business.

The Freight Market on the Baltic Exchange is a highly organized market where those in search of a vessel to carry cargo can find those with cargo space available. The specialists who deal in this market are as follows:

(*a*) *The chartering agents*, who represent the merchants and other organizations anxious to charter ships. The word 'charter' means a 'document of rights'. Charters may be **'voyage charters'**, which are usually arranged to carry a particular cargo for a particular voyage, or **'time charters'**, which give the charterer rights over the vessel for a period of time. On voyage charters the cost of the charter is calculated per ton of cargo carried. On time charters the charge is based on the deadweight tonnage of the ship. The charterer has to pay all the running expenses of the vessel itself, including the fuel bill and the port dues, but excluding services and wages on the vessel.

(*b*) *The shipbrokers*, who represent the shipowners. They are naturally looking for cargoes that will give the best return on capital invested by the owners they represent.

(*c*) *Independent brokers*, who handle the business from both points of view, arranging ships for cargoes and cargoes for ships.

These specialists are engaged in continuous negotiations of a complex nature. They know where vessels are at any moment, what cargoes are becoming available and for which destinations. By calculating the probable yield from each potential charter they can decide which to try for, and as a result of negotiations conclude as satisfactory a deal as possible. Both (*a*) and (*b*) above, on occasions, handle business from both points of view, like the independent brokers.

(3) The Air Freight Market

In the section of this book about air transport (see page 273) attention is given to the changes that are beginning to take place in the concept of air freighting. No longer is air freighting confined to small packets of industrial diamonds, or perishable cargoes such as fruit and flowers.

The Baltic Air Freight Market operates very similarly to the sea-freight market just described. It has the same classes of specialists, known as charterers' agents and owners' brokers. They find aircraft for cargoes and cargoes for aircraft, and generally try to promote the 'tramp' activities of the 100 or more aircraft operators throughout the world. One of the defects of using aircraft is the need to return to a home base, particularly for the regular servicing, which is so essential if safety standards are to be maintained. 'Round-trip' costs can make air freighting prohibitive. The Baltic Air Market can often fill an empty return journey with at least a partial cargo by diverting an aircraft on its return flight to some airport where goods or passengers are waiting.

In particular the Baltic Air Market has done much to establish the same high standards of business usage in the air-freight market as it has established in the ordinary freight market, and the Baltair 1962 Air Charter Party, prepared by the Documentary Committee of the Air-brokers' Association, embodies their experience in this field.

(4) The London Grain Futures Market

Grain is one of those primary commodities which are peculiarly susceptible to price fluctuations, and in particular to slumps caused by over-production. As a result many governments now control the growing of wheat to restrict output and the marketing of wheat to preserve world prices. This has done much to reduce the activity of the Baltic Exchange in wheat, since uncertainty of price has been eliminated and there is little point in speculators operating. Nevertheless, the Baltic Exchange is still important in the wheat trade, because of Britain's primary position as a world importer of wheat. The ships to move these imports are chartered on the Freight Market.

In barley, on the other hand, there is still a good deal of free trading since prices are not fixed by government regulation. This means that the speculator can fulfil one of his chief functions; carrying risks. In the grain market the risks carried are those of (*a*) carrying the goods through time, (*b*) changes in market value, and (*c*) directing goods uneconomically either geographically or in time, i.e. the misjudgement of markets, taking expensive cargoes to places where they are not required.

Perhaps the chief value of a futures market lies in the expertise of its buyers and sellers. These men, who assume the responsibility of carrying enormous financial risks, are more likely to get the world's market requirements right than other people who are not prepared to back their judgment with their own savings.

Dealing on the Grain Futures Market is of the 'Ring' type (see page 107), with business hours 11.30–1 p.m. and 2.45–4.15 p.m. Bargains must be struck in the Ring during the official sessions so that there is complete knowledge of reigning market prices. The chief use is for hedging transactions so that actual losses, due to changes in grain prices after contracts have been entered into, can be avoided by the distillers, poultry-food manufacturers and other buyers.

(5) The Oil and Oilseeds Market

This market deals in the primary commodities that give us (*a*) vegetable oils, widely used these days in the preparation of margarine, synthetic cooking fats, paint, and linoleum, and (*b*) the 'cake' left after the extraction of oil; this is used in cattle and poultry feeds. Although some of the main producing countries have built crushing plants and export their own oil and cake, large quantities of linseed, castor seed, soya beans, groundnuts, and cotton seed are still dealt in through members of the Baltic Exchange.

(6) Ancillary Activities

Allied to the other activities of the Baltic Exchange are several ancillary activities which give the Baltic its unique position as a shipping exchange. We should notice in particular the parts played by sale and purchasing brokers who buy and sell ships, the dry-dock and ship-repair specialists, the average adjusters and ships' valuers who assist in preparing and settling insurance matters, and the bunkering agents. Finally, the Exchange itself can find, from among its senior members, **arbitrators** with specialist knowledge of international reputation who will assist in the settlement of disputes which otherwise might lead to expensive and protracted litigation.

Recent Trends

The present trend towards bulk carriage of iron ore and coal to the expanding steel industry, located in M.I.D.A.'s (see p. 262), has resulted in the building of large bulk carriers from 50,000 tons to 500,000 tons carrying capacity. Many of these vessels are capable of fulfilling contracts to carry millions of tons of the raw material over a period of years. Although many of these contracts are negotiated through members of the Baltic Exchange, many are done directly between the bulk carrier owner and the steel manufacturer. They use a system of charges based on 'Worldscale'. This is an agreed standard charge for a return journey. Thus Worldscale 260 means that a charter has been agreed at 260 per cent of the standard Worldscale charge per ton. At Worldscale 260 a vessel loading at Mena-al-Ahmadi and discharging at London would be chartered at a freight rate of £9.56 per ton since the Worldscale rate for this voyage is £3.68 per ton.

EXERCISES SET 10

(7) The Baltic Exchange

1. What is the Baltic Exchange? Outline some of the main commercial activities of its members.

2. 'All over the world ships are looking for cargoes and cargoes are waiting for ships.' Explain the part played by chartering agents and owners' brokers in bringing vessels and cargoes together.

3. What is the Air Freight Market? Explain how its activities may reduce the cost of flying out relief crews to ships abroad.

4. Although the London Grains Futures Market is still important, it deals mainly in barley, rather than in wheat. Why is this so? Explain why the Baltic Exchange is still of immense importance to wheat importers.

5. What is a charter party? Distinguish between a voyage charter and a time charter.

6. The highly organized markets lie at the very centre of the prosperity of the British nation. Explain how this is so, referring in particular to the activities of the Baltic Exchange.

7. Explain the activities of the following members of the highly organized markets: (*a*) chartering agents (*b*) stockjobbers (*c*) underwriters (*d*) average adjusters.

CHAPTER TEN

THE EXPORT TRADE

(1) Introduction

For the last quarter of a century Britain has been preoccupied with the problem of selling its goods overseas. British politicians have exhorted businessmen to export, using slogans like 'We must export or die'. The monthly trade figures are watched with anxious care to detect the slightest improvement, and government agencies encourage exports in every way. The reasons are well known. Britain is a densely populated country of 55 million people, living on an island whose natural resources have been largely used up in two centuries of industrial activity. Although our skills and techniques are as good as, or even better than, ever before, they can only be used if we import raw materials in great quantities. Much of our food supplies are imported too, to take advantage of the cheap food grown by other nations. These imports must be paid for by exports.

A comparison of Fig. 19 shown below with the diagram of imports on page 94 will show that our **balance of trade**, Imports *versus* Exports, was unfavourable. In 1973 we had a deficit on our balance of trade of £3395 million, on the figures shown in these two diagrams.

Make-up of UK exports, 1973

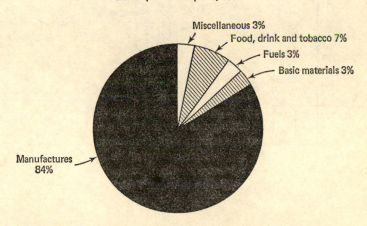

Total value £12,460 million

Fig. 19.   British Exports in 1973.

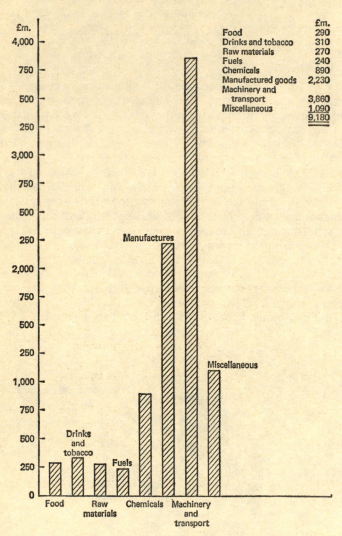

Fig. 20. British Exports 1971 (valued f.o.b.)

1973 was not a very good year for British exports, despite strenuous efforts to reduce the *trade gap*. The figure of more than £3,000 million is very large, but for some years the trade gap has been £1,000 million or more. 1973 was the year the United Kingdom entered the Common Market and imports from the Community rose steeply.

Seven-eighths of British exports are manufactured articles, and over 40 per cent are machinery and transport equipment.

The traditional exports of Great Britain were cotton and woollen goods, but today textiles represent only one-twentieth of our exports, and much of these are made from synthetic fibres such as nylon. Coal, once the very backbone of British export trade, contributed a mere £14

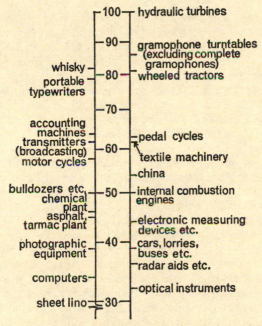

Fig. 21. British Export Achievements in certain products
(Figures show percentage of output exported)

million, whereas petrol and oil exports totalled £340 million. By contrast with these declining industries our export of non-electrical machinery was £2,400 million. Transport equipment earned us £1,560 million; electrical equipment £800 million; chemical products £1,300 million; and scientific instruments £360 million.

Like commerce itself, the export trade is dynamic, restless, and changing. We have to keep up with the trends in world trade if we are to narrow the trade gap as far as possible. Some of these trends are illustrated in Fig. 20, while the achievements of British exporters in particular fields are shown in Fig. 21.

Despite these very creditable performances in particular industries, Great Britain must still do more, not only to sell overseas, but also to compete in the home market with other sophisticated nations whose exports to us form part of the import bill which is the cause of the adverse trade gap. If home-produced goods are as well designed, as well serviced and as cheap as those of our overseas competitors we shall be able to reduce the trade gap from both sides, by an increase in exports and a decrease in imports. To do this we must overcome the problems of foreign trade.

(2) Problems Facing the Exporter

(*a*) *Language*. When we enter an export market we must expect to translate the packaging, informative literature, and technical handouts into the language of the country concerned. We must have salesmen who are able to speak the language fluently and qualified to sell the product in that language.

(*b*) *Standardized units*. There are a great many technological problems arising from the use in different countries of different units of length, weight, capacity, voltage, screw threads, etc. People have been killed because of electrical miswiring caused by the ambiguous colour coding of leads. In Great Britain we have recently changed over to adopt a colour coding for wiring which is acceptable internationally. We are also adopting metric units of length, weight and capacity. This will enable our manufacturers to supply both home and overseas markets. Previously export orders had to be made to different specifications from goods for the home trade.

In North America and many Middle Eastern countries the domestic electricity supply is 110–120 volts only, and the frequency is 60 Hz; in Britain it is 240 volts and 50 Hz. This means that special motors, transformers and other equipment are needed if a British firm is to succeed in this export field. One of the reasons that Britain is changing over to metric units is to enable us to adopt the same threads, and the same units of length, weight, and capacity as our competitors abroad.

(*c*) *Currency*. Clearly, prices of goods sold abroad have to be converted into the currency units of the country where they are to be sold. Since rates of exchange fluctuate, particularly in some politically unstable countries, the prices decided upon may prove to be insufficient to yield a profit if the rate of exchange alters. An exporter who contracts to supply goods at a fixed price may find that this contract price is no longer satisfactory. Britain herself has devalued the pound twice in 20 years, and has recently allowed the pound to 'float', so that we cannot claim to be free from this sort of exchange fluctuation ourselves.

(*d*) *Licences and other documentation.* There are a host of regulations to fulfil in most branches of the export trade. Not only may a licence be required before goods can enter a foreign country, one may even be needed from this country before they proceed overseas. This may partly be for statistical purposes only, but certain strategic materials may not be exported, while political embargoes are often imposed by the Government or by the United Nations. The importing country may be pursuing a protectionist policy, or it may be restricting imports to a quota to help its balance of payments. Import duties may make the price of a British export prohibitive and the exporter may find he is unable to sell the goods.

(*e*) *Risks of the export trade.* These are numerous. We have the sheer physical hazards of crossing oceans by sea or air, the corrosion that comes to iron and steel products from the salt air spray, the chance that goods will be damaged in rough weather or even jettisoned to save the vessel. There are the risks of theft at the docks, or in transit; the risks of non-payment by the buyer or refusal by his government to release foreign exchange. Even where these risks can be assumed by insurers or *del credere* agents, the premiums paid, or the commission given, eat into profit margins and make export trade less attractive than home trade.

Against this formidable list of problems can be set the very great rewards to be won by successful overseas trade where sound arrangements can be made with foreign buyers.

(3) The Channels of Export Trade

The four main channels for exporting are: (*a*) selling from the United Kingdom; (*b*) selling via overseas agents; (*c*) selling from an overseas sales base, established as an extension of the United Kingdom firm; (*d*) licensing an overseas producer to manufacture and sell one's product.

A few words about each of these is desirable.

(a) Selling from the United Kingdom

There are several ways by which the home producer can export without himself having to go abroad. Many overseas firms have buyers permanently based in this country as a buying mission. This is particularly true of countries like the U.S.S.R. which have large central planning bodies anxious to purchase technological or other equipment. Such buyers are highly sophisticated and well trained, quick to detect weak points in a product or excessively priced goods. On the other hand, they are placing orders for millions of people, and the rewards from a contract may be well worth while even if they are competitively priced; while the risks of non-payment are reduced. Other overseas buyers fly in from time to time, especially where a trade is seasonal, like the fashion trades. Still others inquire through government agents direct to the Board of Trade Export Intelligence Department, which channels inquiries to firms likely to be able to supply the overseas buyer.

The Board of Trade publishes a daily bulletin which lists the inquiries received, and also lists export opportunities arising from the activities of organizations like the International Bank for Reconstruction and Development, the North Atlantic Treaty Organization, overseas governments and municipalities, etc.

Export houses are specialist firms which act like the export department of a large firm, securing orders from abroad. They take care of the many technical details involved in the export trade, such as shipping, packing, insurance and finance. In many cases they take full responsibility for the order, confirming that they will honour the price payable when the goods are supplied to their warehouses. In this way the order becomes an order from the export house, and the exporter has no worries at all about payment. This type of firm is called a *confirming house*. Often these firms receive their orders in the form of 'indents' from abroad. These require them to find a supplier who can supply the goods needed.

Freight forwarding agents provide services rather similar to those of the export house, expediting the movement of, and payment for, exports. Home-based exporters can also sell by sending chief executives on sales visits to suitable overseas markets.

(b) Selling by Overseas Agents

A firm wishing to export may employ a sales agent in a foreign country, authorizing him to make contracts for the sale of goods on their behalf with customers in his own country. Another method is to appoint a representative who, while not actually selling himself, undertakes to find, appoint, and supervise selling agents in his own country, authorizing them to make contracts on behalf of the exporter. The great advantage of these sales agents is that they are home nationals of the country concerned so that problems of language, currency, etc. are reduced, but they must be trained in a number of ways. They should be able

(i) to understand the product, its uses, potential markets, etc.

(ii) to state the range, variety of performance, etc. of the product.

(iii) to judge each customer in the market and help him develop his sales of the product to the maximum.

(iv) to know the documentation necessary and any changes that may be developing.

(v) to keep track of credit-worthiness by a personal knowledge of their customers.

(vi) to report regularly to their principals.

(vii) to resist pressures to cut profit margins.

(c) Selling from an Overseas Sales Base

Where the volume of trade that can be done with a country is very great, the use of home-based selling techniques, or the use of overseas agents is rarely satisfactory. Home-based techniques cannot penetrate a market deeply, and agents often act for more than one firm. The presence of at least one full-time actively interested person is necessary to develop an overseas market to its full extent. The difficulty of finding British staff who speak the language, and are prepared to live abroad most of their lives, is such that the appointment of foreign nationals as full-time employees is often preferable. Many countries view the activities of foreign firms with more sympathy if their enterprises offer employment to home nationals.

Familiarization with the product and training in sales methods can be achieved very easily by bringing the employee over to Britain for briefing and instruction. He may well change the attitudes of home staff to the market with which he is familiar, and lead to the general integration of the foreign market as just one more sales area in the firm's marketing scheme. This is the first step towards a global marketing outlook, which is typical of the forward-looking international company.

(d) Licensing an overseas Manufacturer to Produce and Market Products

These days so many countries are trying to set up their own secondary industries, and move out of the primary producing field only, that companies can often make larger profits from selling their product designs than from selling their products. If we sell a patent right we often finish up by selling a factory, because the design is always to some extent protected by the technique and expertise of manufacture.

Some firms are not even aware that expertise is a marketable commodity. They think that it is essential to protect their future by secrecy about their techniques. In fact the reverse often proves to be true. The highly secretive firm finds that its competitors have developed research departments of their own and have discovered the secrets for themselves. The firm that sells or licenses its patent rights to other firms abroad is able to afford more expenditure on layout and research and is able to keep ahead of its competitors more easily. A carefully worded licensing agreement which includes 'minimum-payment' royalty rights, reciprocal licensing rights on patents developed by the overseas company and similar matters can prove to be a very lucrative export. It moves the firm into the 'invisible-export' field *and earns income without adding to the country's import bill for raw materials to be manufactured.*

(4) The Finance of Foreign Trade

Like all trade, foreign trade is dependent upon someone financing the venture, and who provides the finance will depend very much upon the sort of commodity being exported and the competitive state of the market. Where the export is a consumer commodity, long-term finance is undesirable and the ordinary commercial arrangements for finance will prove adequate. Where the export is a capital project, e.g. a power station or an oil refinery, the country purchasing will usually expect long-term credit so that the project itself contributes, once it is working, to the repayments. If overseas competition from countries like the United States, Germany, Japan, the Soviet Union, or China is fierce, it may be necessary to seek Government financial support in some way. In this respect the Government does not provide financial aid itself, but by the Export Credit Guarantees Department (E.C.G.D.) gives guarantees which will be accepted as collateral security by the ordinary banks and Accepting Houses. These matters are best considered from the point of view of the duration of credit given.

Self-financing. Many firms take on the finance of their own sales, regarding capital tied up in this way as part of the normal employment of their funds. The reward for this use of the firm's capital is included in the profit margin on the sales, or added as an extra charge made if payment is delayed by the buyer. Where a firm moves into exporting and finds that it needs financial help, it should first consider whether some increase in its permanent capital is required. This may be secured by a new issue on the Stock Exchange, or by the issue of debentures.

Finance of Short-Term Business (*Less Than Two Years' Credit*)

(*a*) *Overdrafts and loans.* The exporter who cannot afford to finance his own sales will usually find his ordinary commercial bank willing to advance, either by overdraft or loan, limited sums of money at six months' credit on consumer goods, or longer on light-engineering durable goods. The banks have agreed to lend to exporters at rates which are rather more favourable than those which they offer to the home market. These advances require security, and an E.C.G.D. policy will often be regarded as satisfactory security for this purpose. (The security lies alongside the debt. If the debt is not paid the security can be 'realized' to pay the creditor. See page 142 for a fuller explanation.)

These policies, which are dealt with on page 131 give a guarantee of payment, usually up to 90 per cent of the value of the order. With such a policy the exporter can assign the policy to the bank who are thus secure for up to 90 per cent of the value of the risks. They do have recourse to the borrower if the loss suffered proves to have been due to events not covered by the policy. The banks set limits to the loans and overdrafts they are prepared to sanction, so that an exporter who has reached this limit already, or who wants complete non-recourse financing, must look elsewhere.

(*b*) *Non-recourse finance.* This term refers to the complete assumption by a finance company of all risks of non-payment. Under no circumstances can the finance company have recourse to the exporter, who receives payment—obviously at a reduced rate—while the finance company collects the full amount from the buyer overseas. Naturally such services are more expensive than ordinary overdrafts and loans. They are best carried out by finance companies associated with the international banks. Because of their overseas branches very often employing native staff as well as U.K. expatriates, they are in a position to assess the credit-worthiness of the buyer and to pursue him for any bad debt through the intricacies of his own legal system. This is similar to the function performed by Export Houses, already discussed on page 124.

A further example of non-recourse finance is the 'comprehensive guarantee of payment' system, operated by the Export Credit Guarantees Department. Exporters who have been dealing with E.C.G.D. for at least a year and who are selling on less than two years' credit can buy these policies for a little more than the ordinary E.C.G.D. policy. The Department gives a guarantee directly to the bank financing the export sale. In the event of non-payment the bank has recourse to the Department, and not to the exporter, who is thus relieved of all worries about non-payment for the order.

(*c*) '*Open-Account*' *methods of payment by overseas buyers.* Where a British exporter has good relations with an overseas buyer, built up over many years, he may operate just like a home trader. The overseas buyer will make payment direct to the overseas branch of the exporter's ordinary commercial bank. Pending such payments the bank will often either credit the exporter's account at once with the funds due to be paid, or at least loan money against the expected sums. An E.C.G.D. policy will again prove extremely good security for such a loan.

(*d*) *Bills of Exchange: How a Bill of Exchange is used to settle indebtedness.* Consider a British exporter, Engineering Ltd., who receives an order from Australia for 60 bus engines, valued at £10,000. Having undertaken the purchase of raw materials, etc. and made the engines, Engineering Ltd. ships them on the S.S. *Southern Star* to the Australian Bus Co. Having kept their part of the bargain they would now like to be paid for the engines. On the other hand, the Australian firm has not yet received them, and is unwilling to pay until they arrive. A **Bill of Exchange** is a commercial form of payment which will satisfactorily solve this problem. A bill of exchange is defined as follows, in the Bills of Exchange Act, 1882.

'A Bill of Exchange is an unconditional order in writing, addressed by one person to another, signed by the person giving it, requiring the person to whom it is addressed to pay, on demand, or at some fixed or determinable future time, a sum certain in money, to, or to the order of, a specified person, or to bearer.'

As can be seen from Fig. 22, this is an unconditional order, signed by a director of Engineering Ltd., requiring the Australian Bus Co. Pty. to pay him 90 days after January 21st the sum of £10,000. For historical

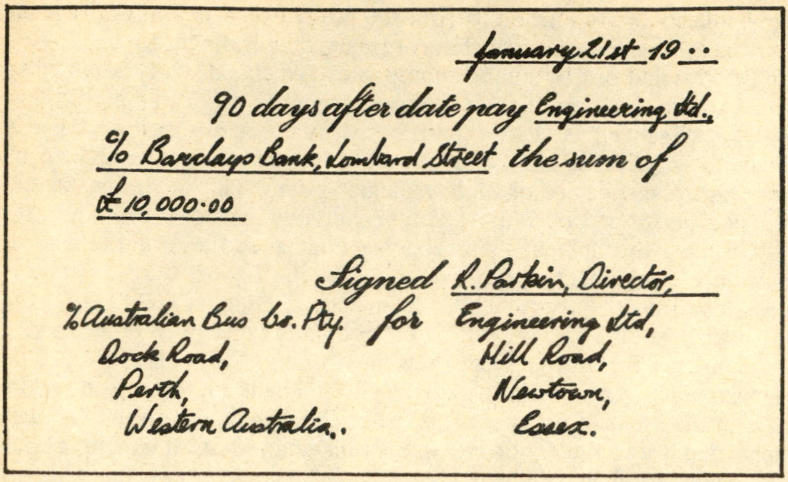

January 21st 19..

90 days after date pay Engineering Ltd.
c/o Barclays Bank, Lombard Street the sum of
£10,000.00

Signed R. Parkin, Director,
c/o Australian Bus Co. Pty.   for   Engineering Ltd.
Dock Road,   Hill Road,
Perth,   Newtown,
Western Australia..   Essex.

Fig. 22. The Bill of Exchange

reasons associated with bad transport facilities in the early days, a debtor on a Bill of Exchange used to be allowed 'three days of grace' to pay the debt. This has now been discontinued and it would therefore now be due on the 90th day after January 21st, which is April 21st (except of course in Leap Year when it would be April 20th).

When such a bill is made out it can be used to collect payment from the overseas debtor. He will not have the Bill of Lading (which he needs to obtain to collect the goods from the ship owner) released to him until he 'accepts' the bill. This means he writes on it his agreement to pay it. He then collects the goods, and pays for them on the due date by honouring the bill. Meanwhile Engineering Ltd. have been allowed to get their money by drawing a bill for the same amount on the London bank. Fig. 23 explains exactly what happens.

NOTE TO FIG. 23

(*a*) Engineering Ltd. manufacture the goods and deliver them to the shipowner with a copy invoice and a Bill of Lading. The master returns the Bill of Lading signed to acknowledge that the goods have been shipped in good order and condition.

(*b*) Engineering Ltd. have also arranged an insurance policy at Lloyds to cover the shipment. They now draw up a Bill of Exchange requiring the Australian buyer to pay for the goods on the due date, and present it (with the other documents) to the London correspondent bank named by their overseas customer.

(*c*) The London bank agrees to help Engineering Ltd. by accepting a bill of exchange for the same amount as the foreign bill lodged with them for collection. Engineering Ltd. can discount this bill at once and use the money.

(*d*) The London bank sends the documents of title to Australia and releases them to the Bus Co. when they accept the original Bill of Exchange. They hold the bill until the due date and collect the money.

(*e*) If the goods arrive safely the Bus Co. collects them at the docks.

(*f*) If they are lost at sea the Bus Co. claims the insurance money.

(*g*) On the due date the Bus Co. honours the Bill; the money is sent to London and used to clear up the acceptance credit opened for Engineering Ltd.

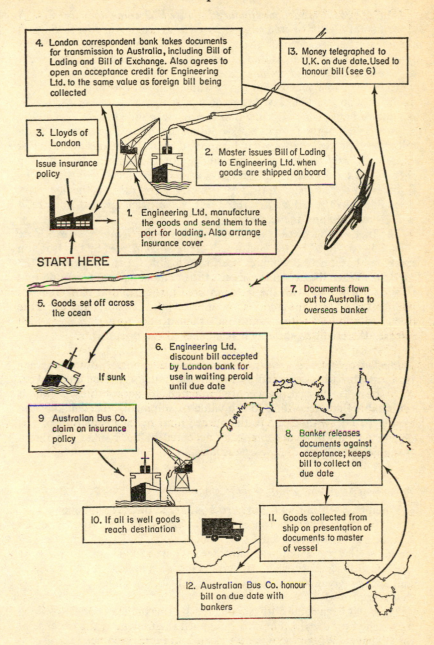

4. London correspondent bank takes documents for transmission to Australia, including Bill of Lading and Bill of Exchange. Also agrees to open an acceptance credit for Engineering Ltd. to the same value as foreign bill being collected

13. Money telegraphed to U.K. on due date. Used to honour bill (see 6)

3. Lloyds of London

Issue insurance policy

2. Master issues Bill of Lading to Engineering Ltd. when goods are shipped on board

1. Engineering Ltd. manufacture the goods and send them to the port for loading. Also arrange insurance cover

START HERE

5. Goods set off across the ocean

7. Documents flown out to Australia to overseas banker

If sunk

6. Engineering Ltd. discount bill accepted by London bank for use in waiting peroid until due date

9 Australian Bus Co. claim on insurance policy

8. Banker releases documents against acceptance; keeps bill to collect on due date

10. If all is well goods reach destination

11. Goods collected from ship on presentation of documents to master of vessel

12. Australian Bus Co. honour bill on due date with bankers

Fig. 23. Financing overseas trade with a Bill of Exchange

(*e*) *Overseas transactions financed through documentary credits.* A documentary letter of credit is a device for arranging export trade with the maximum security for the exporter. When approached to supply goods, the exporter agrees to do so provided the foreign customer opens an *irrevocable letter of credit* in his favour with a reputable bank. The word 'irrevocable' means that the customer cannot cancel it without the exporter's permission. The letter of credit is sent to the exporter by a London bank, which is known as the 'correspondent bank' because it acts on behalf of the foreign bank holding the funds. The letter of credit tells the exporter exactly what he must do to obtain the money. For example, it will tell him exactly what goods to supply; where to ship them; what documents to produce and other details. Provided he fulfils every requirement of the letter of credit and submits the necessary documents to the bank after the goods have been shipped, the credit will be released and the exporter paid.

The best arrangement is a *confirmed irrevocable letter of credit*. Here the credit arranged by the customer's bank is *confirmed* by the London bank, so that it actually makes itself responsible for the payment to the exporter. When the exporter presents the documents, and it is found that they conform fully with the letter of credit, the London bank releases payment at once. If the credit is unconfirmed the London bank takes the documents lodged with it and sends them to the foreign bank, which releases the credit as soon as it has checked the documents.

London acceptance credits. Sometimes an exporter doing regular business abroad is regarded as so reliable that the Merchant Bankers who specialize in acceptance are prepared to accept bills within a reasonable limit according to the value of shipments. This enables the exporter to draw funds up to the agreed limit by means of Bills of Exchange which will be automatically accepted by the banker and therefore enjoy a high standing when discounted.

Finance of Medium-Term Export Business

When payment for an export order is spread out over a longer period than two years, the risks inherent in the finance of the project rise. To finance such projects, even for very sound firms of the highest credit standing, the banks require guarantees. These are usually provided by the E.C.G.D. on specific contracts. Each case is looked at on its merits, and **specific guarantees** are issued to the banks to cover each contract that is approved.

There has been some criticism of British firms in the export field which have relied on the E.C.G.D. to safeguard themselves at the expense of the taxpayer. Where there is no risk of loss there is no need to be cautious, and some overseas countries with autocratic governments have been encouraged by exporters to buy capital assets for prestige reasons irrespective of whether their countries could afford the project concerned. The exporter knows that he is unlikely to suffer, for the E.C.G.D. is acting as guarantor. It is the Department that will have to come to terms with the bankrupt government overseas eventually. Certainly the Department scrutinizes each project closely, but has not gone as far as appraising the whole national economy of the country concerned.

Where specific guarantees are made on longer-term contracts, it is usual to finance on **fixed rates of interest.** Fixed rates of interest have the advantage of being known throughout the lifetime of the contract, and enable firm contract prices to be agreed.

Finance of Long-Term Contracts

Long-term contracts are usually for large-scale capital projects such as power dams, transport systems, oil refineries, and petrochemical installations. Such projects are often financed by international organizations like the International Bank for Reconstruction and Development. The exporter winning part of the contract will be paid in cash, the financing body assuming the responsibility for collecting repayments from the country concerned.

(5) The Export Credit Guarantees Department

The E.C.G.D. is a separate Government department under the same minister as the Department of Trade, charged to operate on commercial lines following the advice of its advisory council of bankers and businessmen. Set up in 1919, its activities are now very widespread and deal with approximately £5,000 million of exports each year.

The Department insures exporters against some major risks of export trade. These are: (i) the risk that the buyer fails to pay; (ii) the risk that he will be prevented from doing so because of exchange controls imposed by his government; (iii) the political risk that import licences may be revoked; (iv) the risk of war; and (v) other risks.

Like all insurance policies, the premiums collected from the vast majority of trouble-free exporters are used to reimburse the unfortunate few whose reasonable business expectations are disappointed. Because of its worldwide network of commercial and diplomatic informants, the credit ratings of about 150,000 buyers in nearly 200 countries are available in the Department's records. Such wide knowledge enables risks to be accurately predicted and premiums to be arranged at minimum rates.

The policies available fall into three groups, as follows:

(*a*) Comprehensive policies for continuous export business. Here the contracts are often for 'production' goods, usually with many contracts of small value. Insurance of each contract would be time-consuming, and a blanket cover is provided for the coming year or two-year period.

(*b*) Specific policies for larger export contracts.

(*c*) Special policies for unusual export contracts. This group includes a special policy to cover escalating costs during inflation, a policy to insure earnings of an 'invisible' nature, i.e. export of services, and a policy to cover exporters dealing with State trading organizations.

Comprehensive Policies

These policies are general policies giving cover against a number of risks to exporters who sell abroad in a continuous and repetitive way. The exporter insures either all his exports, or all his exports in certain markets only, against the full range of risks for one or three years ahead. He furnishes the Department with estimates of his exports for the period concerned, the markets and buyers and the credit terms he hopes to arrange. Using their records, the E.C.G.D. will then prepare a quotation of so much per £100 of goods for each country or destination. Any limits set by the Department beyond which they will not be prepared to give cover with a particular buyer are included in the quotation. After accepting the quotation the seller submits monthly records of goods sold and is invoiced for the premium.

Table 6 opposite shows the risk covered, the percentage of loss paid and the time of payment.

Comprehensive policies can also be extended by endorsement to cover a wide variety of other risks, for instance risks that an overseas subsidiary of a holding company may not pay for goods supplied, or that a British export house may not pay for goods supplied to it for foreign customers

Specific policies for large capital projects

These E.C.G.D. policies are negotiated as the contract itself proceeds, because without a guarantee of this sort the tender itself is difficult to prepare. By making it clear that policies are available for that particular market, and the likely rate of premium, the Department assists the manufacturer in pricing the contract. This tentative suggestion for a guarantee policy crystallizes into a firm offer as the negotiations approach the final stage. Note that the Department here is unable to spread the risk over a large field of other business, and premium rates therefore tend to be higher than for comprehensive policies.

Modified special policies are also available to cover special types of risks, notably for the sale of aircraft and aero-engines, for the sale of ships and constructional works for overseas governments. Here the exporter contracts not only for the export of goods but also for the export of services, and may be left as employer with contractual obligations to employees should the contract be cancelled or frustrated.

Special Forms of Cover

(a) *Escalating Cost Cover*. Inflation has made it difficult to predict the cost of contracts, and some spectacular bankruptcies have occurred as a result. It is now possible to cover rising costs on large contracts (over £2 million), provided they are long-term contracts with non-E.E.C. countries. The cover is at present only about 70 per cent.

Table 6. Insurance against export risks

Risk covered	Percentage paid in the event of loss		When payable
	Before Shipment	After Shipment	
(1) Insolvency of buyer	90%	90%	On proof of insolvency
(2) Failure to pay within 6 months	90%	90%	Six months after
(3) Failure to take delivery	90% of loss on re-sale less 18% of full invoice price		One month after re-sale
(4) Government exchange control	90%	95%	Four months after the event
(5) Cancellation of import licence	90%	95%	Four months after the event
(6) War between United Kingdom and the buyer's country	90%	95%	Four months after the event
(7) War or revolution in the buyer's country	90%	95%	Four months after the event
(8) Export licensing controls in the United Kingdom	90%	95%	Four months after the event
(9) Extra transport or insurance charges	90%	95%	Four months after the event
(10) Any other cause of loss occurring outside the United Kingdom and out of the control of the buyer, or seller, and not insurable elsewhere	90%	95%	Four months after the event

(b) Cover for the *export of services* is provided both by comprehensive and specific policies similar to those outlined already. 'Invisible' items include insurance, shipping, consultant services, and supervision of maintenance on capital projects.

(c) Cover for *State-Trading Companies' contracts* is given where the exporter has a contract with this type of purchasing organization, usually in Communist countries, and the organization defaults. Called 'arbitration cover', the usual policy covers any award made to an exporter who is given a favourable decision by an independent arbitrator, but is unable to persuade the customer to honour the arbitrator's award. The E.C.G.D. does not cover default caused by the failure of the exporter to honour his contract in some particular.

(6) Government Aid for Exporters

The Government department concerned with promoting the export trade is the Department of Trade, which has an Export Intelligence Headquarters in London. It also has nine regional and three district offices throughout the British Isles. It maintains links with the commercial officers of the Diplomatic Service in over 200 embassies and consulates overseas, and publicizes British exports and tourism.

Market Intelligence for British Exporters. The Department of Trade *Export Intelligence Service* supplies registered firms with a daily computer print-out of any contract anywhere in the world of interest to them. It also supplies on request:

(*a*) Assessments of particular markets for particular products.
(*b*) Current tariff and import regulations.
(*c*) Current labelling and marketing requirements.
(*d*) Details of overseas contracts put out to tender.
(*e*) The commercial standing of overseas traders.
(*f*) Regulations regarding manufacturing under licence.
(*g*) Advice on exporting safeguards.
(*h*) Advice on exporting to Communist countries.
(*i*) Statistical data on prices, production figures, etc. in various countries abroad.

Promotion of Overseas Trade

Introducing a product to an overseas market is not easy, and the Government offers a certain amount of assistance to exporters. Among the assistance offered are the following:

(*a*) Advice on finding a suitable translator. The Central Office of Information has a Foreign Language Section which advises on the choice of a translator, preferably one resident in the country concerned. This can be arranged through the Diplomatic Service, at no charge to the exporter except that he must pay the actual translator's fee.

(*b*) Two special groups, the *Overseas Projects Group* and the *Commercial Relations and Exports Division*, assist British exporters in a wide variety of ways to obtain overseas contracts and sell their products abroad. Some financial help is available with preparing tenders.

(*c*) 'British Weeks' are held at intervals in overseas countries to show British products to overseas buyers. Organized on a joint Government Industry basis, they offer financial assistance to firms wishing to take part. In a recent year the Board of Trade helped 4,500 firms to display goods in 41 countries at over 200 trade fairs, 250 British store promotions, and nine British Weeks.

(*d*) The Central Office of Information spends considerable sums promoting overseas sales. The methods used exclude paid advertising, but do involve the use of B.B.C. services, circularizing overseas official bodies and foreign journalists in Britain. These facilities are free to firms wishing to make use of them.

Government Activity to Free Trade

If we are to earn the maximum possible from our export trade our goods must be free to enter other countries, and not be obstructed by tariff barriers. Usually countries will lower tariffs only if some reciprocal concession is made in return. This inevitably leads to a degree of international specialization. The country that produces a particular class of goods most cheaply will specialize in that class of goods. Any activity to free trade which permits us to sell abroad the kind of goods that we make best must therefore introduce a blast of competition to home industries that are not as efficient as overseas producers. Free trade is a two-edged sword; it enables us to cut our way into an overseas market only to the extent that overseas producers can compete here.

There are several groups of nations, each of which offers its members reciprocal trading advantages. These may be **free trade areas, or customs unions.** The major groups are the European Economic Community, E.F.T.A., the Commonwealth, Comecom (the Communist Economic Community) and even the United States which is really a free-trade area established many years ago. Britain has been part of the European Free Trade Association, and part of the Commonwealth. She has recntly joined the European Economic Community, or Common Market countries. Two other E.F.T.A. countries, Denmark and the Irish Republic, also joined, but Norway decided against joining after proposing entry in 1972. Britain now enjoys tariff advantages in the enlarged market, though only at the expense of her privileged position in E.F.T.A. and the Commonwealth. It remains to be seen what impact on British trade will be made by the changed role of Britain in the world. World-wide negotiations through G.A.T.T., the General Agreement on Tariffs and Trade, led in 1967 to agreements on what is called the 'Kennedy Round'. This is an agreement, the negotiations for which were started by the late President Kennedy, to gain all-round reductions in tariffs between the major trading nations. A further series of discussions about further reductions is now (1975) taking place. (See *Economics Made Simple* for a fuller discussion of Free Trade Areas.)

Export Finance and Insurance

Although the Government cannot help directly in the finance of overseas trade, since this would be against the spirit of international agreements on free trade, it can do much indirectly to assist. The Bank of England has advised the ordinary banks, at a time of credit squeeze, to look more favourably on credit to exporting firms than to firms in the home trade. The **British Overseas Trade Board** of the **Department of Trade** will advise exporters on the sources of export finance, while insurance of export credits are covered by the Export Credit Guarantees Department policies (see page 131).

Resolving Commercial Disputes

Exporters sometimes become involved in disputes overseas which threaten to become legal disputes unless resolved amicably. The Export Services Branch and the Commercial Officers overseas are available to appraise contracts where differences arise and resolve problems before they become legal in character. Legal disputes cannot be considered by these officers.

(7) Documentation of Overseas Trade

Overseas trade has to be particularly well-documented since government controls on both goods and finance are usually strict. Traditionally, merchants have devised their own documents to suit their own needs, and have hesitated to adjust their own practices to fit in with those of other merchants. In the last few years it has become increasingly obvious that much routine clerical time was being wasted in completing forms that carried the same information, but differently placed on each form. In 1962 the Board of Trade set up a Joint Liaison Committee to investigate the whole problem of export documentation, with a view to preparing an 'aligned series', i.e. a complete set of documents of standard size with the same information in the same position. Modern duplicator techniques permit all the documents to be run-off from a 'master document', and where certain details are not required on a particular form a mask is fitted over the 'master' which obliterates the details not required. The Board of Trade's booklet *Simpler Export Documents* illustrates how the system works.

The main documents used in the export trade are: (*a*) The Bill of Lading; (*b*) The Customs Declaration C273; (*c*) The Port Rates Schedule; (*d*) The Shipping Note; (*e*) The Certificate of Origin; (*f*) The Insurance Certificate; and (*g*) The Air Waybill.

In addition the European Community requires special Community Transit documents. (See page 99.)

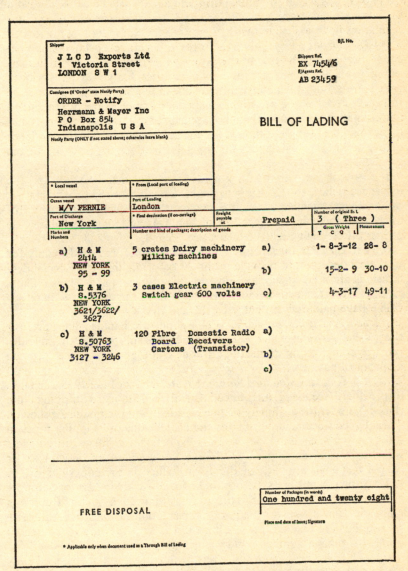

Fig. 24. A Bill of Lading from the Recommended Aligned Series

In 1970 a Simplification of International Trade Procedures Board (SITPRO) was set up to guide, stimulate and assist the rationalisation of international trade procedures, and the documentation and information flows associated with them (see the Shipping Note below).

(*a*) *The Bill of Lading.* This is the most important export document because it represents the title to the goods while they are on the high seas, purchase of which transfers the ownership of the goods. It has been called a quasi-negotiable instrument, but in fact it does not possess the full characteristics of a negotiable instrument, since it does not transfer a better title of ownership than was possessed by the transferor. It has three functions: (*a*) it is a receipt for the goods shipped; (*b*) it is evidence of the contract of carriage; and (*c*) it is the document of title to the goods.

It is usually accompanied by other documents, the invoice and the insurance policy, so that the set gives the owner for the time being not only a clear statement of what he owns (the invoice) but the proof of ownership and shipment (the Bill of Lading) and indemnity in the case of loss on the high seas (the insurance policy).

(*b*) *The Customs Declaration Form C273.* This is required mainly for statistical purposes, to provide monthly export figures, etc. Special declarations are used when claiming 'process inwards relief'. This relief is given to exporters whose goods are made from imported raw materials which have paid duty on entry to the country.

(*c*) *The Port Rates Schedule.* When goods are handled the Port Authority charges rates which are payable by the shipper. These schedules must be completed in duplicate, and one will then be returned stamped as proof of payment.

(*d*) *The National Standard Shipping Note.* On April 1st, 1975, the U.K. Sitpro Board (see above) introduced its National Standard Shipping Note (NSSN), under the authority of the National Shipping Note Authority. This aligned document eliminates the use of different shipping notes in different ports, and can be used by exporters and forwarding agents when delivering cargo to any British port, container base or other freight terminal. Supplies of the form, which is the copyright of the U.K. Sitpro Board, may be obtained from a wide variety of shipping and commercial stationers. This note is submitted to the Receiving Authority which receives the goods for shipping. It tells the Authority what goods are handed into their care, the ship they are to be loaded on to, the marks, numbers, and measurements, etc.

(*e*) *The Certificate of Origin.* Certificates of origin are needed only where a **Free-Trade Area** is afraid that its tariffs to non-members will be avoided by circuitous routings. For instance if Germany allows British goods in duty free, but charges Swedish goods a tariff, a Swedish firm might seek to evade the tariff by sending the goods to Britain first and having them re-exported to Germany. A certificate of origin is usually issued by the Chamber of Commerce to certify that goods have been either entirely, or largely, manufactured in the country stated.

(*f*) *The Insurance Certificate.* This is a certificate proving that a policy has been taken out either with Lloyd's or with an insurance company to cover the goods while in transit.

(*g*) *The Air Waybill.* Under the Carriage by Air Act, 1961, which revises the rules made at the Warsaw Convention in 1929, every consignment of goods by air must be covered by an Air Waybill in three parts. Part One is marked 'For the Carrier' and signed by the consignor. Part Two is marked 'For the Consignees' and travels with the goods. It is signed by both the carrier and the consignor. Part Three is signed by the carrier and returned to the consignor. We thus have each of the parties receiving a copy of the Waybill signed by other parties to the transaction. Article 8 of the Act specifies exactly what details must be completed on the form, so as to bring the carriage within the protection of the Convention rules. It must also carry a statement that the carriage is subject to the rules relating to liability laid down in the Convention. A properly completed Air Waybill limits a carrier's liability to 250 francs per kilogram, which is by international agreement the same as £7·64 per kilogram.

Up-to-date advice on export documentation in particular countries is obtainable from the Department of Trade Export Services and Promotions Branch.

EXERCISES SET 11

(8) The Export Trade

1. Why is the export trade of such importance to Great Britain? Describe the measures the Government has taken to encourage exports.

2. What factors tend to discourage the British manufacturer from exporting? How does the Government help in overcoming these difficulties?

3. What are the chief risks of the export trade? What can a businessman do to overcome these risks, or make them less hazardous?

4. What methods of dealing with a foreign market can be used by a British businessman?

5. Discuss the part played by the Export Credit Guarantees Department in the encouragement of overseas trade.

6. Why is overseas trade still desirable even when we are importing goods we could make, or grow ourselves?

7. What is a Bill of Exchange? How does it help in the overseas trade of this country?

8. What part do the banks play in the finance of foreign trade?

9. Write short paragraphs about: (*a*) accepting houses; (*b*) confirming houses; (*c*) export houses; (*d*) freight forwarding agents.

140 Commerce Made Simple

10. What are the factors which make the work of a business engaged in foreign trade more onerous than that of one trading only in the home market? How are importers and exporters helped by the commercial banks?

(University of London)

11. What are the problems, not found in the home trade, which confront importers and exporters? How are they overcome?

(University of London)

12. What are the functions of (*a*) manufacturers' agents, (*b*) brokers? Give examples. What are the special obligations of each of these types of business?

(University of London)

13. A firm sells its products both at home and in many countries abroad. What problems will the foreign sales department have, which the home sales department does not have? *(University of London)*

14. How does the export trade of the United Kingdom benefit from the services of (i) export merchants, (ii) the Board of Trade, (iii) the Export Credits Guarantee Department? *(University of London)*

15. What methods are commonly used by small manufacturers in this country to sell their goods abroad, without the expense of setting up an overseas base? *(University of London)*

CHAPTER ELEVEN

THE GENERAL FRAMEWORK OF THE BANKING SYSTEM

(1) Definition of a Bank

A bank is an institution which collects surplus funds from the general public, safeguards them and makes them available to the true owner when required, but also loans out sums not required by their true owners to those who are in need of funds and can provide security.

(2) The Basic Functions of Banking

These are:

(*a*) The collection of surplus funds from the general public.

(*b*) The safeguarding of such funds.

(*c*) The transfer of these funds from one person to another, without their leaving the bank, by means of the **cheque** and **credit-transfer** systems.

(*d*) The lending of surplus funds not required by the present owner to other customers who are in need of funds, in return for interest and collateral security. The interest is shared between the bank (a reward for its services) and the true owner (a reward for *not* using his money).

(3) How the Basic Functions of Banking were Developed

(*a*) *Lombard Street*

The first bankers in Britain were Lombards, from the Plains of Lombardy in northern Italy. Here had grown up a group of independent cities called the Lombard League. Merchants and traders from this cradle of European liberty came to do business in the City of London, and their home, Lombard Street, is still the centre of British banking. The Lombards, after a century or so of business in London, were eventually made bankrupt because they loaned money to kings who did not repay the loans.

After the departure of the Lombards, banking came to be conducted by the goldsmiths as a sideline to their normal activities in the bullion and jewellery fields. The early goldsmiths had to have large vaults which were soundly built and heavily guarded. The idea grew up of letting one of these goldsmiths take care of your wealth if you had more than you could safely defend yourself.

The person who deposited his surplus funds with the goldsmith became known as a 'depositor' and naturally paid for the privilege of having his money defended in this way. These payments were called 'bank charges'. The depositor who needed funds, to pay wages or debts, could call at the bank and collect such sums as he required.

(b) Origin of the Cheque System

Before long it became clear that unnecessary risks were being run by depositors who needed to pay money to creditors. The depositor had to collect the money and deliver it to the creditor who promptly had to return it to the bank. Why not simply order your banker to transfer funds from your deposit to the creditor's deposit? This was the origin of the cheque system. A cheque is an order to a banker to pay money from your account to, or into the account of, another person without the need for the money to leave the safety of the bank. (Fig. 26 illustrates this.)

(c) Origin of Bank Credit

The goldsmiths soon noticed that only a very small proportion of the funds of each depositor was in use regularly, being drawn out and paid in as funds were used or received. The proportion left on permanent deposit was about 92 per cent of the average depositor's funds. It seemed sensible to lend some of this money to people anxious to borrow for industrial and commercial reasons.

The two requirements for a sound credit policy are:

(i) that the depositor whose funds are being used shall be content to leave them on deposit without making sudden demands upon the bank. To encourage this it is usual to pay him interest on the deposit.

(ii) that the borrower shall be credit-worthy, and shall offer—if requested—some security. This may take the form of a guarantee from some credit-worthy person, or the deeds of a house or a piece of land. The latter is sometimes called collateral security, security lying alongside the debt. Life assurance policies are often used as security for small debts, and provided the surrender value is great enough they offer good security to the banker.

During the course of the Industrial Revolution the banks had much to do with finding the necessary funds to finance the mines, mills, and shipyards on which the prosperity of Britain was built (see Fig. 27). The banks' role today in fostering the prosperity of the nation is considered on page 145.

(4) The English Banking System

The English banking system is a tripartite system like a three-layer cake. The three parts are:

(a) The Bank of England, a 'State Bank' or 'National Bank'.

(b) Specialized banking institutions, such as the Discount Houses and Merchant Banks, which deal only with special customers providing funds for special purposes.

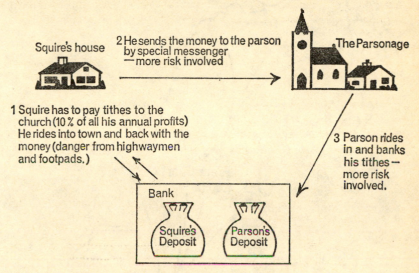

Squire's house

2 He sends the money to the parson by special messenger — more risk involved

The Parsonage

1 Squire has to pay tithes to the church (10 % of all his annual profits) He rides into town and back with the money (danger from highwaymen and footpads.)

3 Parson rides in and banks his tithes — more risk involved.

Bank

Squire's Deposit   Parson's Deposit

Fig. 25. Payment without the cheque system

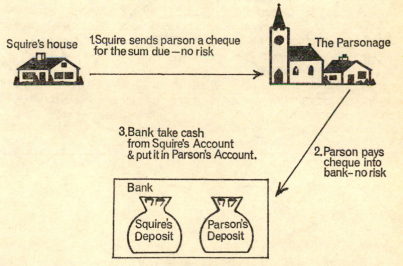

Squire's house

1.Squire sends parson a cheque for the sum due — no risk

The Parsonage

3.Bank take cash from Squire's Account & put it in Parson's Account.

2. Parson pays cheque into bank— no risk

Bank

Squire's Deposit   Parson's Deposit

Fig. 26. Payment with the cheque system

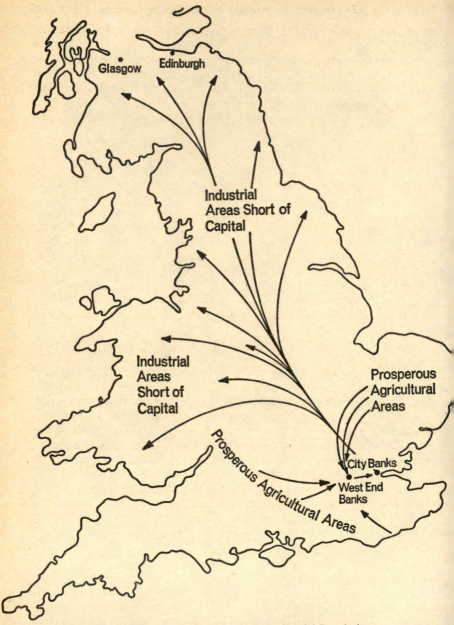

Fig. 27. How the Banks fostered the Industrial Revolution

The prosperous agricultural aristocracy banked with the fashionable West End banks. The West End banks loaned the money to the City of London, and the City banks loaned it to the Industrial Areas of the North of England.

(*c*) The Commercial, or Joint-Stock Banks, which deal with the general public.

The Bank of England is dealt with in Chapter 15. The specialized banking institutions are dealt with in Chapters 13 and 14. This chapter deals with the commercial or joint-stock banks which are used by the general public every day.

(5) Commercial or Joint-Stock Banks

In the eighteenth century the banking system developed as a means of providing the capital for the agricultural and industrial revolutions. Not only goldsmiths, but merchants, landowners, and other well-to-do people practised banking as a sideline and gradually developed the necessary expert knowledge.

Since a single banker was limited by his personal capital, the idea of partnerships in banking was adopted from an early date, and hence the name **Joint-Stock Banks.** It soon became clear that a bank that was too small and localized in its connections was likely to go bankrupt if hard times hit that particular area. For instance, banks in farming areas that were severely hit by floods might be bankrupted if all the depositors withdrew their funds at the same time to replace cattle, machinery, and fencing lost in the flood. This led to the amalgamation of banks in different localities to give a broader base to the bank.

The advantages of amalgamations, both with regard to the stability of the banking system and economical operation in other ways has reduced the number of banks over the years, so that by the 1920's England had only the 'Big Five' and six smaller banks. In recent years further amalgamations have occurred. Two of the 'Big Five', Westminster and National Provincial, have merged with Coutts and Co., and District to form the National Westminster Group. Another, Barclays, has merged with Martins; and the remaining three smaller banks, Glyn Mills, National and Williams Deacon's, have formed the National and Commercial Banking Group. Midland and Lloyds are the other big banks. These eleven banks were once called the **Clearing Banks,** because together, and in co-operation with the Bank of England, they operated the Bankers' Clearing House. There are now six chief Clearing Banks. (See p. 191.)

(6) Importance of the Commercial Banks

The place of the commercial banks in the British economy is a very important one. They stand at the very centre of business activity and can promote prosperity or deflate the economy into unemployment almost at will. For this reason the banks are closely controlled in their credit policies by the Bank of England, which is itself influenced and controlled by the Treasury. This is dealt with later, on page 185, but a preliminary understanding of how bank credit operates to inflate or deflate the economy is desirable.

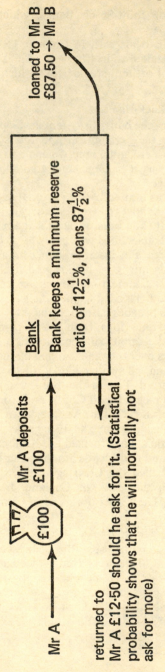

Fig. 28. A simple view of bank loans (banks loan to customers the money that other depositors do not want to use)

In June 1971 the commercial banks had made advances total-ling over £5,700 million in ordinary loans and overdrafts. Another £1,200 million was invested in more permanent ways, in industrial and commercial firms. Some idea of the importance of the banks in the day-to-day business of the country can be seen from these figures.

(7) Simple and Sophisticated Views of Bank Lending Policy

The lending policy of the banks depends upon that simple idea men-tioned earlier (page 142) that some, if not most, of the funds people de-posit in the bank are left idle. The early bankers observed that only about 8 per cent of their customers' funds were likely to be demanded in cash at any time. This was called the **cash ratio.** In September 1971 the Bank of England instituted new rules raising the ratio of its assets which a bank must keep in cash or near cash (in case the depositors want the money back) to $12\frac{1}{2}$ per cent of the **eligible liabilities.** This is called the **minimum reserve ratio.** Consider the situation shown in Figs. 28 and 29.

We might think that if £87·50 is lying around idle, the bank might prudently lend it to someone short of money, charging him interest on the loan. In fact, the bankers take a much more sophisticated view of what that £100 means to them. Mr. A has given them £100. They have it in the bank. They therefore have enough cash to form the *minimum reserve ratio* ($12\frac{1}{2}$ per cent) of a total deposit of £800. Of course no one has actually deposited £800. Mr. A has deposited only £100. The bank can therefore now lend up to £700 to Mr. B. Mr. B receives this as a deposit in his account, but he also has to open up an equal, and oppo-site, loan account of £700, so really his 'deposit' is not a deposit at all. But it very quickly becomes one, because Mr. B borrowed the money to use. He spends the money on a new car. The garage proprietors who sold him the car deposit the £700 as a real deposit: they are unaware that it is borrowed money. This is where the banker's statistics give him confidence. He knows that the garage proprietors will demand only 8 per cent of their deposit. It is most unlikely that they will demand as much as $12\frac{1}{2}$ per cent, the amount kept in reserve. Meanwhile the bank is making a nice profit from the interest on £700 it never really had. Figs. 28 and 29 should clarify the financial aspects of these transactions.

We can now see what effect the creation of purchasing power by the banks has on the economy. Mr. A saved £100, of which he spent only £12·50. It enabled Mr. B to buy a £700 car and Mr. C to spend £87·50. In other words, an expenditure of £800 has been based on £100 of sav-ings. If the banks pursue such policies unchecked the people of this country will be permitted to live at a higher level than they are really entitled to, and problems will arise with our Balance of Payments.

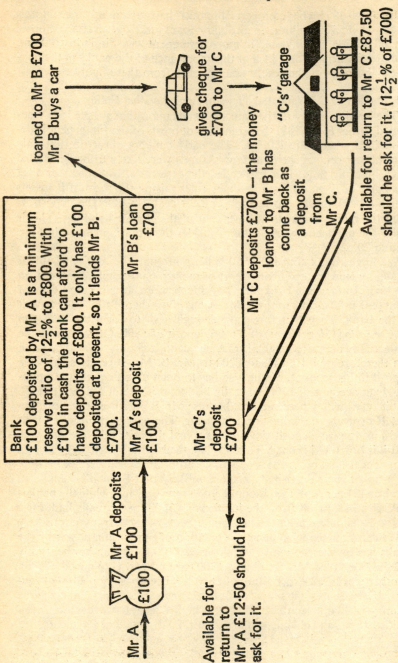

Mr A → £100

Mr A deposits £100

Available for return to Mr A £12·50 should he ask for it.

Bank
£100 deposited by Mr A is a minimum reserve ratio of $12\frac{1}{2}$% to £800. With £100 in cash the bank can afford to have deposits of £800. It only has £100 deposited at present, so it lends Mr B. £700.

Mr A's deposit £100

Mr C's deposit £700

Mr B's loan £700

Mr C deposits £700 — the money loaned to Mr B has come back as a deposit from Mr C.

loaned to Mr B £700
Mr B buys a car

gives cheque for £700 to Mr C

"C's" garage

Available for return to Mr C £87.50 should he ask for it. ($12\frac{1}{2}$% of £700)

Fig. 29. A more sophisticated view of bank loans (banks create credit, lending out far more than the sums deposited with them)

(8) Liquidity and the Banks

Before the 16th September 1971 banks maintained a cash ratio of 8 per cent and a liquidity ratio of a further 20 per cent. This liquidity ratio was usually in the form of money 'at call' or 'short notice' with various firms in the discount market who guaranteed to repay it quickly. Since September 1971, the banks have been required to keep only a minimum reserve ratio of 12½ per cent and further reserves can be called for by the Bank of England. These 'special deposits' will be called if banks pursue such generous credit policies that their deposits are likely to exceed the cover given by the minimum reserve ratio.

The banks are always concerned about liquidity, and many of their investments are 'near-cash' investments. **'Near-cash' investments** are investments which can be turned back into cash immediately if necessary. In this type of investment the bank can ask for only a low rate of interest, below current bank rate. The banks are unlikely therefore to expand credit to the theoretical limits shown in Fig. 29, since this type of loan to customers is very illiquid. By lending at least some of their funds in more liquid 'near-cash' loans they are likely to keep their lending down to about 3 times what is really deposited.

(9) How Banks Earn a Living

Bankers earn a living by lending money at interest, and also by charging for certain services that they perform for their customers. In lending money they have to balance their natural desire to make a good living with the necessity to play safe and maintain a good liquidity position. Liquidity and profitability are direct opposites; one cannot have both at once. If we lend money for long periods we earn a lot of interest, but if we lend so much that we have to stop our customers getting their money out when they want it we will be very unpopular.

The two triangles Fig. 30 (a) and (b) show the assets of one of the 'Big Four' banks from two different points of view. Fig. 30 (*a*) shows the assets as they are normally listed on the bank's balance sheet in the *order of liquidity*, i.e. with the most liquid items first and the permanent and long-term assets as the base of the pyramid. A solid and reliable structure, a pyramid. The second part, Fig. 30 (b), shows the same pyramid inverted. The assets are now in the *order* of *permanence*. The whole banking structure is poised upon the tiny cash holdings. If the general public eat into this cash base by withdrawing funds unexpectedly from the bank, even for the most worthy reasons, the whole unstable edifice of banking could come crashing down, and with it the economy of the nation.

At the beginning of each World War the British Government's first act was to close the banks. They feared that while people were worried and agitated about their own and the country's situtation, they might withdraw funds which would ruin the banking system. In a few days, when the public had grown accustomed to the idea of being at war, the

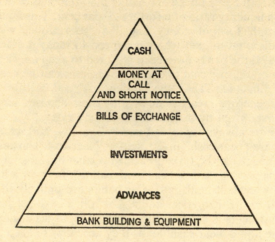

Fig. 30(a). The 'stable View' of banking
The assets are arranged in order of liquidity.

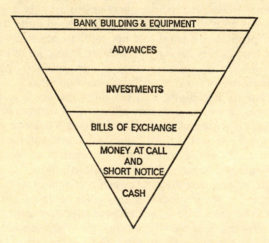

Fig. 30(b). The 'unstable View' of banking
The assets are arranged in order of permanence.

banks re-opened without any serious effects upon their liquidity. Successful banking depends upon confidence—confidence in the political and economic stability of the whole country.

EXERCISES SET 12

(10) The General Framework of Banking

1. Define a bank. What are its basic functions and how does it perform them?

2. Write about five lines on each of the following topics: (*a*) depositors; (*b*) the origin of the word 'bank'; (*c*) security on a loan; (*d*) minimum reserve ratio; (*e*) Lombard Street; (*f*) the 'Big Four'.

3. 'The British banking system is a tripartite system, with the specialized banking institutions sandwiched in the middle.' Explain.

4. 'When Mrs. Brown deposits £1,000 with her bank it represents at least £3,000 worth of possible deposits to them.' Explain this statement, mentioning the phrases 'minimum reserve ratio' and 'liquidity'.

5. 'Banking depends upon confidence: if the depositors cannot be persuaded to leave their money where it is the whole system collapses.' Explain.

6. Explain how the working of the cheque system and traders' credit facilities of the commercial banks can be regarded as a system of book-keeping between the banks and their customers.

(University of London)

7. Name the items which appear on the assets side of the balance sheet of a joint-stock bank and indicate why they appear in a certain order.

8. 'Savings make deposits, but loans make deposits too.' Explain.

9. Distinguish between balance sheets written in the 'order of liquidity' and the 'order of permanence'. Show how the first gives an appearance of stability to the banking system while the second gives an appearance of instability.

10. 'Cheques have become the simple method of paying money, so that bank notes are now the small change of the monetary system.' Why has this come about?

CHAPTER TWELVE

THE SERVICES OF THE BANKS TO COMMERCIAL FIRMS AND PRIVATE INDIVIDUALS

(1) The Services of the Banks Today

Bankers' services cover an enormous range of activities today. A full list would include:

(*a*) Current-account services, such as:
    (i) transfer of moneys by the cheque system
    (ii) transfer of moneys by standing orders
    (iii) transfer of moneys by the credit-transfer system
    (iv) permission to run an overdraft
    (v) bank loans
    (vi) night-safe facilities
    (vii) banker's draft facilities.

(*b*) Deposit-account services

(*c*) Savings-account services

(*d*) Other services, such as:
    (i) foreign exchange activities for importers and exporters
    (ii) acting as intermediaries in dealings with stockbrokers
    (iii) executorship and trustee services
    (iv) safe-custody
    (v) insurance
    (vi) income tax advice to customers
    (vii) services in the export field
    (viii) credit ratings and credit worthiness
    (ix) economic information on overseas markets etc.
    (x) cash dispensers and cash points
    (xi) banker's Credit Cards
    (xii) discounting Bills of Exchange
    (xiii) investment management services

(2) Current-Account Services

(*a*) *Introduction*

Banks extend current-account services to anyone whom they regard as reliable. A new depositor, unless recommended by his employer, will be asked for a reference, and if this proves satisfactory the bank will accept a deposit from him which will be entered in his current account. A cheque book will then be issued free of charge. Stamp duty on cheques was abolished in February 1971.

Once he has received his cheque book the customer may use the cheques to order the banker to pay out sums of money from his current account. The name 'current account' comes from the French word *courrant*, 'running', and implies that money is being paid into, and paid out of, the account as often as the customer finds convenient. The balance of the account changes from day to day as the various transactions proceed. The usual method of paying money into an account is by means of a **paying-in slip**, while the **cheque** is the usual way of withdrawing money from the account.

(b) Paying in money to a Current Account

When a current-account customer wishes to pay money into his current account he makes out in duplicate a paying-in slip. These slips are provided to customers in handy booklets of about 20 slips, or they are available on the counter in single form; the customer takes two so that he has a duplicate. Some banks now include these slips in the back of their cheque books. The slips have the coded number as on the cheques, so that they can be mechanically sorted. Fig. 31 shows a paying-in slip.

When the slips are completed, the customer presents them to the cashier who checks them and accepts the sum paid in. The cashier stamps and initials both the stub and the credit slip, tearing off the latter which will be recorded on the customer's account, and returning the paying-in book with the stub of the entry as a receipt for the amount paid in.

The paying-in book is a useful record of sums paid in, but it is not complete because it is possible to deposit money in other ways. For instance, many people have their salaries paid direct to the bank these days by credit transfer. Many dividends and sums of money paid as interest on bonds and debentures are paid direct to the holders' current accounts in the same way.

The depositor can pay money into his account at any branch in the country, so that the system is very convenient. If the customer cannot get to the bank himself an employee or friend can make the deposit. The stub represents a receipt for the safe delivery of the money and cheques deposited, because of course it bears the bank stamp, and the cashier's initials as proof.

(c) Withdrawing money from a Current Account

Money can be withdrawn from a current account by means of a cheque. The cheque may instruct the paying banker to pay in cash, or to transfer the sum concerned to the account of some other customer.

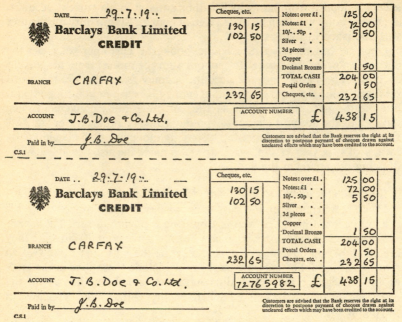

	Cheques, etc.				
Barclays Bank Limited **CREDIT**			Notes: over £1 .	125	00
	130	15	Notes: £1 . .	72	00
	102	50	10/-. 50p . .	5	50
			Silver . . .		
			3d pieces . .		
			Copper . .		
			Decimal Bronze	1	50
BRANCH CARFAX			TOTAL CASH	204	00
			Postal Orders .	1	50
	232	65	Cheques, etc. .	232	65

DATE 29.7.19..

ACCOUNT J.B.Doe & Co. Ltd.   ACCOUNT NUMBER   £ 438 15

Paid in by J.B.Doe

C.S.1

Customers are advised that the Bank reserves the right at its discretion to postpone payment of cheques drawn against uncleared effects which may have been credited to the account.

	Cheques, etc.				
Barclays Bank Limited **CREDIT**			Notes: over £1 .	125	00
	130	15	Notes: £1 . .	72	00
	102	50	10/-. 50p . .	5	50
			Silver . . .		
			3d pieces . .		
			Copper . .		
			Decimal Bronze	1	50
BRANCH CARFAX			TOTAL CASH	204	00
			Postal Orders .	1	50
	232	65	Cheques, etc. .	232	65

DATE .. 29.7.19..

ACCOUNT J. B. Doe & Co. Ltd.   ACCOUNT NUMBER 7276 5982   £ 438 15

Paid in by J.B.Doe

C.S.1

Customers are advised that the Bank reserves the right at its discretion to postpone payment of cheques drawn against uncleared effects which may have been credited to the account.

Fig. 31. A paying-in slip with stub

(d) Cheques

A cheque is defined as 'a bill of exchange drawn on a banker payable on demand'. Bills of Exchange are rather complex documents, so at present it is better to regard a cheque merely as an order to a banker to pay money to a named person, or order, on demand. ('Or order' means that the named person can order the bank to pay someone else. If I have a cheque from T. Brown in which he orders the bank to pay me £10, I can sign away my rights to the £10 by writing 'Pay R. Peacock' on the back of the cheque, and signing my own name after it. The bank will then pay R. Peacock instead of me.)

Cheques may be written on any piece of paper, or indeed on anything —one well-known character in legal fiction is alleged to have written a cheque on a cow. These days bankers prefer cheques to be of a certain size because they have to be dealt with by machines. Very often the cheques have magnetic codes printed on to them which assist the machines to sort them. Odd bits of paper do not fit the machines, and there are peculiar difficulties about processing cows.

It must be clearly stated who is going to sign cheques, and specimen signatures must be lodged with the bank. This helps to ensure that forgeries do not go undetected. Quite often two signatures are required, thus making it more difficult for employees to embezzle money.

Advantages of Paying by Cheque

(i) It is just as easy to pay £1,000 as it is to pay £1. Payment by cheque eliminates the need for counting and checking banknotes—a time-consuming business if a sum of £1,000 is paid in £1 notes.

(ii) A cheque can be safeguarded by crossing it. Even if it is stolen it is impossible for the thief to obtain cash.

(iii) Often the money never leaves the bank, so it is extremely safe.

(iv) In some countries, including the United Kingdom (by the Cheques Act of 1957), the paid cheque acts as a receipt. It is proof, once it has been paid, that the money has been received.

Explanation of the Four Cheques Shown in Fig. 32

(i) An **open cheque**: An open cheque (one that has no crossing) can be cashed at the bank by anyone who presents it and says he is the payee, in this case T. Jones. He will have to endorse it. This means he must sign on the back when he cashes the cheque. Although this is not much of a safeguard it does have a deterrent effect on thieves, because endorsement by a person other than the payee is forgery, which is a serious crime.

There is an even more unsafe cheque, called a **bearer cheque**, which is made out 'Pay Bearer'. This is very unsafe indeed and does not require endorsement, because the name of the bearer is not important. Anyone who presents it is entitled to payment on it. Generally speaking it is safer to cross a cheque, and banks issue books of cheques that are already crossed for those who prefer to play safe.

(ii) A **general crossing**: A cheque with two lines across it, with or without '& Co.', is said to be 'generally' crossed. It will only be cashed across the counter of the bank if the presenter is known to the cashier as the drawer-customer or his accredited representative; otherwise it must be cleared into a bank account. It is therefore much safer than (i), but it can be cleared by anyone so long as T. Jones has endorsed it (written his name on the back). Notice that it is possible to pay this cheque into any account. It does not have to go into the account of the man named on the cheque, T. Jones. This is because it is an **order cheque**. At the end of the line it says 'Pay T. Jones .... or Order' This means that if Jones endorses it 'Pay R. Brown' and signs his name, the bank concerned will obey the order, and pay R. Brown not T. Jones.

The Rules about Endorsement are as follows:

No endorsement is necessary if the payee pays an order cheque into his own account. If the payee orders the bank to pay someone else, he must endorse the cheque. The new payee will also endorse it when he pays it into his account. An endorsement in blank, i.e. T. Jones, makes the cheque payable to bearer.

BARCLAYS International

12th July 19__   20-50-80

Barclays Bank International Limited
4 Water Street Liverpool

Pay T. Jones ———————————— or Order

Fifty Pounds ——————— £50 ————

W. SMITH

W. Smith .

⑈000000⑈ 20⑆5080⑈ 12345678⑈

BARCLAYS International

12th July 19__   20-47-35

Barclays Bank International Limited
Knightsbridge Branch
16/18 Brompton Road London SW1

Pay T. Jones ———————————— or Order

Fifty Pounds ——————— £50 ————

W. SMITH

W. Smith

⑈000000⑈ 20⑆4735⑈ 12345678⑈

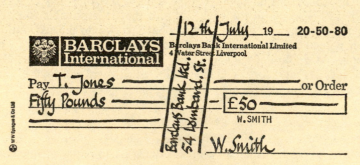

BARCLAYS International

12th July 19__   20-50-80

Barclays Bank International Limited
4 Water Street Liverpool

Pay T. Jones ———————————— or Order

Fifty Pounds ——————— £50 ————

W. SMITH

Barclays Bank Ltd., 54 Lombard St.

W. Smith

⑈000000⑈ 20⑆5080⑈ 12345678⑈

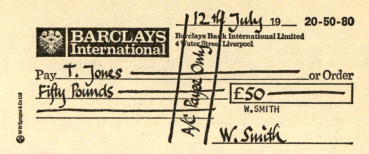

Fig. 32. Safeguarding a cheque

(iii) A **special crossing**. Where a cheque has the name of a banker filled in on the face of the cheque between the crossed lines it is said to be 'specially' crossed. Such a cheque will normally be cleared into the account of the payee in the bank named on the cheque. However, this is not absolutely necessary, unless the drawer of the cheque also writes 'not negotiable' on the cheque.

(iv) An **'A/c payee' cheque**. Where a cheque has the words 'A/c payee' written on the face of it, the indication is that the drawer wishes to restrict the cheque. If the cheque is paid into any other account the bank is 'put upon inquiry' over the circumstances, i.e. it will be liable to the payer if an unauthorized person should collect the money. The bank must inquire whether the payee has given authority for the cheque to be cleared through the account of the person who has paid it in.

'Not Negotiable' Cheques

Where a cheque is marked 'not negotiable' it loses the properties of a negotiable instrument, the chief of which is the ability to transfer a better title of ownership than that of the original giver. Any person receiving a cheque of this sort from a transferor knows that he takes it subject to any defects in title of the transferor. He is therefore put upon his guard to ensure that the transferor really does own the cheque.

Dishonoured Cheques

Where a cheque is presented for payment and the drawer does not have the funds to cover it, the cheque is said to be dishonoured. It is an offence fraudulently to pass cheques that will not be honoured, and this explains why the bank is careful to ask for a reference before it accepts a deposit and issues a cheque book.

Dishonoured cheques are returned by the bank marked R.D., which means 'Refer to Drawer'. The correct action to take with such a cheque is to approach the drawer and ask for an explanation. If it is a mere oversight on his part he will either arrange for the bank to honour it or pay in funds to cover it. We then re-present the cheque for payment and all should be well. If we cannot get a satisfactory explanation of his behaviour we may of course take legal action, or ask the police to deal with the criminal side of the matter.

Post-dated Cheques

These are cheques made payable on a later date than the present date. People who are paid their salary monthly by cheque sometimes send post-dated cheques, which will fall due at the end of the month, when their salary will have reached the bank. Banks do not like this practice, but it is not illegal. We are only ordering the banker to pay out our money at a later date than the present.

(e) Bank Charges

The bank usually charges for the use of the account, which gives them considerable work to do, but the size of the 'bank charge' depends upon the amount of money left in the account. Where a firm has sizable balances on a current account which is not a particular busy account, it is quite common for the bank to waive charges. They also are considerate in helping charitable or socially valuable organizations, by keeping accounts free of charge.

(f) Standing Orders

If a cheque is an order to a banker to pay money, a 'standing order' must be very similar to a cheque. In fact it is an order to pay a sum of money regularly on a given day of the month. This is the easy way of settling regularly recurring payments such as mortgage repayments, hire-purchase transactions, rent and rates.

Most large service organizations such as the electricity and gas boards will accept standing orders for a reasonable sum towards electricity bills and gas bills. They usually have an arrangement whereby they will settle any under- or overpayment once a year. Insurance brokers are now accepting standing orders for insurance cover on motor vehicles, and many organizations like the Automobile Association prefer the annual subscription to be paid in this way.

Bankers offer this extremely useful service for the same charge as they would make for clearing an ordinary cheque, and it is a great convenience to the millions of current-account customers who use it.

(g) The Credit-Transfer System

The principle of the credit-transfer system is payment directly into the bank account of the payee. The transfer may be executed by a standing order, a traders' credit or a counter credit. The payee is not informed

FROM BARCLAYS BANK LIMITED **bank giro credit** ⌘

_____LIVERPOOL_____BRANCH   DATE___27th July, 19··.___

CODE NO.	BANK AND BRANCH TITLE (as given in List of Sorting Code Numbers)	ACCOUNT	AMOUNT
20-93-59	Barclays, West End	G. M. Brown A/C NO. 72485018	£ 55·65

By order of___Lewis Electrics Ltd.___   Ref.___187/5___

CT 23

Fig. 33. A bank giro credit slip

about it immediately but discovers it when he asks for a bank statement.

A growing use of this system is in the payment of wages. The procedure is to present the bank with a list of employees and the sums due to them. For each employee a credit-transfer slip like the one in Fig. 33 is prepared and sent to the bank. The sums due are transferred to the credit of the employees' accounts. The total of these payments is debited to the employer's account, one cheque being written for the whole sum due. This is a very useful way of paying many sums at once, since cheques usually have to be signed by two directors of the firm, and instead of hundreds of cheques to be signed only one need be used. Clearly the credit-transfer system is a very safe and simple way of paying wages. Wage packets do not have to be made up with notes and coins, security guards are not needed to fetch the money from the bank; there is no counting of money and less chance of a mistake.

Credit transfers can also be used to settle accounts at the end of the month, and many firms encourage the practice by supplying a credit-transfer form on the statement sent to the debtor, who can thus transfer the amount due direct into the bank account of his creditor.

The general public who do not have bank accounts are able to use this system too if they present the credit-transfer slip at the counter, pay the money that they wish to transfer to the cashier, plus a charge of $2\frac{1}{2}$p for each payment.

(*h*) *Clearing payments*

Whether we use a cheque, a standing order or a credit transfer the bank has to perform a service which involves taking money from one person's account and putting it into the account of another person. In Fig. 26 we saw this being done in the very early days of banking when banks were small, local affairs and both accounts were available in the bank. Today we have a rather more complicated situation which covers three possible alternatives, which are:

(i) Both payer and payee live in the same town and bank at the same branch (say Barclays branch at Grays, Essex).

(ii) Both payer and payee live in different towns but use different branches of the same bank (Mr. A banks at Barclays, Grays, Essex, but Mr. B banks at Barclays in Bristol).

(iii) The payer and payee use different bankers (Mr. A banks at Barclays, Grays branch, while Mr. B banks at Midland, Bristol branch).

Figs. 34 and 35 show the clearing procedure in each of these cases.

(*i*) *Overdrafts and Loans*

Overdrafts are a convenient way of lending money to a customer without going through the formal procedure of completing documents for the actual loan of the money. Loans are a more formal way of advancing funds to a customer, by means of a special loan account.

Considerations taken into account before granting overdraft or loan facilities. Bank lending policies are dictated by a number of considerations, of which the most important are (*a*) Government policies aimed at controlling the economy, and (*b*) banking policies aimed at maintaining the balance between liquidity and profitability (see page 147). A third set of considerations centres on the personal position of the borrower and the security he can provide.

The bank manager will already be pursuing his ordinary business life in a climate dictated by Government policies which have been conveyed to him by directives from Head Office. These may include:

(i) A complete ban on loans or overdrafts (credit freeze).

(ii) A directive to reduce bank lending within certain total figures. These usually involve him in reducing the amount of new loans made compared with a previous period. For example for every £100 repaid by earlier borrowers he may be allowed to lend only £50 in the new period. This is often called a 'credit squeeze', it reduces loans for inessential projects but does not entirely forbid them.

(iii) A directive to lend freely or even generously wherever customers ask for money. This will expand the economy out of a slump if serious unemployment exists. This might even be permitted in an area of severe unemployment at a time when a credit squeeze was being applied in other parts of the country.

(iv) A Government directive to lend in particular fields of activity, for instance the export field, may influence the banks in favour of a particular borrower.

Government restrictions apart, the bank has its own affairs to keep in order. It can only lend to the point where its liquidity has been reduced to the minimum, at about the 30 per cent figure. If it pursues too gen-

Case B. Head Office Clearing
Drawer & Payee live in different towns
but do use the same bank.

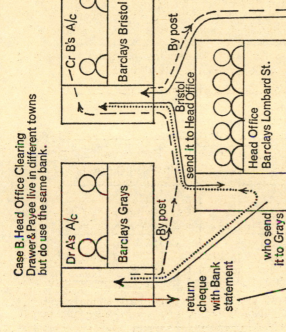

By post

Cr B's A/c

Barclays Bristol

Bristol
send it to Head Office

Dr A's A/c

Barclays Grays

By post

Head Office
Barclays Lombard St.

who send
it to Grays

return
cheque
with Bank
statement

Mr A ⟶ pays Mr B ⟶ Mr B pays it into
£10·00 — —→ his Bristol Branch

Case A. Branch Clearing
Drawer and payee live in the
same town & use the
same bank.

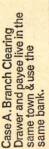

Dr A's A/c Cr B's A/c

Barclays Bank,
Grays

By hand or
by post

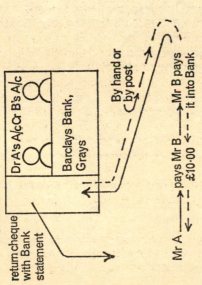

return cheque
with Bank
statement

Mr A ⟶ pays Mr B ⟶ Mr B pays
£10·00 — —→ it into Bank

Dr. = Debit entry in the account named.

Cr.= Credit entry in the account named.

Fig. 34. Clearing a payment where both payer and payee use the same bank.
In each case the line of dashes indicates the path that would be taken by a dishonoured cheque.
The dotted line represents the return of a clearing document (claim for unpaid).

NOTE: Since both payer and payee bank with Barclays there is no need for any money to move at all. The total deposits with
Barclays are unchanged, but Mr. A now has less on his account, while Mr. B's balance has increased.

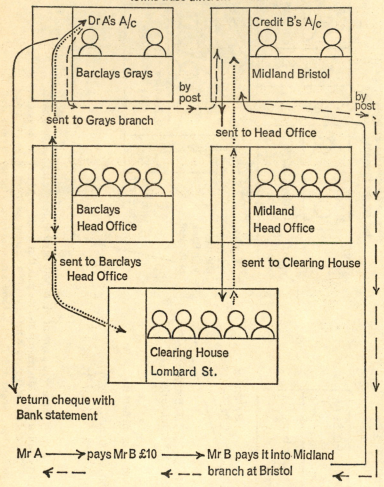

Case C. A Bankers' Clearing House Clearing
Drawer and Payee live in different
towns & use different banks.

Dr A's A/c

Barclays Grays

by
post

Credit B's A/c

Midland Bristol

by
post

sent to Grays branch

sent to Head Office

Barclays
Head Office

Midland
Head Office

sent to Barclays
Head Office

sent to Clearing House

Clearing House
Lombard St.

return cheque with
Bank statement

Mr A ⟶ pays Mr B £10 ⟶ Mr B pays it into Midland
                              branch at Bristol

Fig. 35. Clearing cheques where the payer and payee have different bankers

NOTE: The important point here is that in both these cases funds will have to move
from one bank to another for Barclays total deposits will fall by £10, while Midland's
total deposits will rise. To follow the clearing mechanism see p. 191. Again the line
of dashes shows the return path of any dishonoured cheque. The dotted line shows
the path taken by a 'claim for unpaid'.

erous a loan policy it will endanger its liquid reserves, losing liquid assets to other banks. This will soon result in Head Office issuing a directive reducing loan levels until the liquidity position is restored. It will have to forgo desirable profits on the money it could lend because it must keep liquid funds available.

Personal considerations include:

(i) The credit-worthiness of the borrower and his record of personal integrity in financial matters.

(ii) The purposes for which he requires the loan. For instance, the purchase of business premises is often considered a valid reason for granting a bridging loan to tide the customer over the interval between paying the deposit and receiving a mortgage. A holiday cruise might be viewed less favourably as a reason for granting a loan.

(iii) The general expectations of profitability in the business concerned; the likelihood of competition and the overall volume of business expected.

(iv) The type of security offered may encourage the bank to grant

P.R. STEINER ESQ.

Barclays Bank Limited

STATEMENT OF ACCOUNT

170, FENCHURCH STREET, E.C.3.

60554553

P.R. STEINER ESQ.,
ELMHURST,
FOREST ROAD,
PINNER,
MIDDLESEX.

DIARY

POST   1969/ 8

CUSTOMER'S NOTES	DETAIL	PAYMENTS	RECEIPTS	DATE	BALANCE
	BALANCE FORWARD			3JUN	256.13
	777064	0.80		5JUN	255.33
	067	19.00		6JUN	236.33
	003850	7.87		9JUN	228.46
	777066	90.70			
	068	1.00			
	069	5.00		13JUN	131.76
	777070	35.56		16JUN	96.20
	STANDING ORDER	10.00		17JUN	86.20
	777071	4.00			
	777072	4.25		18JUN	77.95
	BANK CHARGES	0.53		20JUN	77.42
	BANK GIRO CREDIT		196.17	26JUN	273.59
	074	32.00			
	COUNTER CREDIT		18.40	30JUN	259.99
	ABBEY.NTL.BLDG.SOC				
	LC.4289 STO	33.53		1JUL	226.46
	075	250.00		2JUL	23.54DR
	COUNTER CREDIT		50.00	3JUL	26.46

DIV DIVIDEND   STO STANDING ORDER   BGC BANK GIRO CREDIT   DDR DIRECT DEBIT   OVERDRAWN BALANCES ARE INDICATED BY THE LETTERS DR

Fig. 36. A Current Account that shows an overdraft at one point

the loan. If it is valuable, with a ready market, the bank runs little risk of loss.

(v) The proposed duration, and rate of repayment.

Overdrafts. These simply permit the customer to overdraw on his account, in other words take out more than the amount of his original deposit. No special method of repayment is necessarily laid down but a time limit is set on the overdraft. In any case all overdrafts can theoretically be terminated at any time by the bank. During a credit squeeze, for instance, the bank may require the overdraft to be repaid or drastically reduced. Banks charge interest on the overdraft usually at a rate 2 per cent above the **minimum lending rate** charged by the Bank of England to official borrowers. Except for very small overdrafts the banks do ask for some sort of security.

Fig. 36 shows such an account, where the customer has overdrawn. The mechanical type of book-keeping used provides a continuous balance on the account automatically adjusted as receipts and payments are entered. Where the account changes to an overdraft, the machine prints the letters DR to show that the customer is now a debtor of the bank. At one time it also printed the balance figured in red from that point on, until a receipt of money from the customer cleared the overdraft and the machine returned to the use of black ink. Modern computer systems do not always indicate overdrafts in red.

Loans. When a customer receives a loan, slightly more formal arrangements are made. The customer is interviewed by the bank manager and signs a simple loan agreement, together with a repayment standing order. The amount of the loan, say £300, is actually credited to the customer's current account, which therefore should not need to be overdrawn. An equal, and opposite, debit entry is made in a special **loan account**. This debt is then repaid by taking money from the customer's account each month under the standing order, until the loan is repaid. Interest is charged every six months on the outstanding balance, and has to be met at once by the customer. Banks do not like spreading interest over the period of the loan, as Building Societies do, for example.

(j) Night-safe Facilities

Current-account customers who wish to bank moneys after closing hours are able to do so through the night-safe system. The basic idea here is that moneys collected after the banks close are put into a leather bag with the paying-in slip in duplicate. The bag is locked and is put into the night safe. The night safe consists of a small opening in the bank wall giving access to a chute which leads down into a strong room or vault. Protective devices inside the locked door prevent anyone possessing a key from getting out what has been put into the safe.

The customer takes his locked bag to the bank, opens the night safe with the key provided, pushes it past the safety devices inside, which are like a one-way valve, and re-locks the door. Next morning the bags are opened and their contents are credited to the appropriate account.

This service is very useful to multiple-shop organizations who require managers to bank their daily takings except for a small float of change for the tills next day. By ensuring that all sums are banked the Head Office achieves day-to-day control of the business, and managers who are too lazy to cash up, or are taking unauthorized time off from work can be detected.

(k) Banker's Draft Facilities

A banker's draft is like a cheque drawn by the bank on itself. It enables a customer to offer persons or firms to whom he is in debt a document in payment with the absolute authority of a big bank behind it. These drafts can be used when a trader deals with a wholesaler for the first time, or when he offers payment in a foreign country. Whereas a personal cheque would probably not be acceptable to a foreigner, a draft backed with the authority of one of the 'Big Four' probably would be. A 'traveller's cheque' is therefore a special type of banker's draft.

(3) Deposit-Account Services

Deposit accounts are accounts in which individuals and firms deposit cash resources that are not needed at present. They bear interest at 2 per cent less than the bank rate. The bank loans these funds out to borrowers usually at $2\frac{1}{2}$ per cent more than the bank rate, the interest being shared therefore with the depositor. Since the bank is using these moneys it cannot always regain them at short notice, and in theory the bank is supposed to be given 7 days' notice before money is withdrawn. In fact the bank usually waives this notice, but charges 7 days' interest instead on sums drawn out.

Unlike a current account, a deposit account does not carry the right to use a cheque book. Credit slips are used by the depositor who may pay in cash, postal orders, or cheques.

(4) Savings-Account Services

These are intended for the small saver. They earn interest at a low rate. They enable the small saver to put money away for particular purposes, such as holidays.

Of these three types of account, the most commonly used is the current account. Many customers with current accounts probably have either a deposit account or a savings account where reserves can be accumulated.

(5) Other Services offered by the Banks

(*a*) *Foreign-exchange services.* The bank will secure foreign currency for customers about to travel abroad, within the limits set by the exchange control regulations in force at the time. They will also arrange foreign exchange for exporters and importers (see pages 93 and 119). By international agreement a 'Eurocheque' scheme which started in 1970, enables cheques up to £30 in value to be cashed in many European countries.

(*b*) *Stockbroker services.* The banks, through their connections with stockbroker firms in London, will act as brokers for customers who wish to buy and sell shares. This is very important for some business firms who wish to invest spare capital which is being accumulated for plant-replacement reserves, dividend-equalization reserves and pension funds. The banks operate through a broker in the usual way, sharing the commission with the broker so that the cost to the customer is no greater than it would be normally.

(*c*) *Executorship services and trustee services.* When people die their relations may be put to considerable difficulty if a proper will has not been left and an executor appointed to carry out the wishes of the deceased. Problems often arise because aged and infirm people overlook matters which are vital.

A bank is generally more reliable and better equipped than any individual to act as an executor or trustee, particularly if money is to be invested for beneficiaries who are not yet old enough to receive it. This is called a **trust**, and such trusts are safest in the hands of organizations like banks which are impartial, offer safeguards against embezzlement and negligence, and treat the trust as strictly confidential.

(*d*) *Safe-custody and safe-deposit services.* Banks will take care of the personal property and documents of customers who provide a locked box to be kept in safe custody in the vaults. A few banks offer safe-deposit facilities, with special compartments for the long-term retention of customers' valuables. The banks do not accept responsibility for theft, but theft is very unlikely, and insurance is easily and cheaply arranged because of the secure circumstances.

(*e*) *Insurance services.* Most banks have Insurance Departments which will arrange all types of insurance, including life, marine, fire, traders' comprehensive, and house owners' and householders' comprehensive Policies. These Insurance Departments have close links with Lloyd's brokers and are therefore able to secure competitive quotations for most classes of business.

(*f*) *Income tax services.* Banks will assist individuals with tax problems and employ specialists who will advise on income tax and surtax. In addition to the usual matters, such as personal and child allowances, banks also cater for the special tax requirements of business and professional persons.

(*g*) *Services in the export field.* These are discussed in detail on page 125.

(*h*) *Credit ratings and credit worthiness.* Some firms who are about to sign contracts with people they have not previously dealt with, like to know whether the other contracting party is financially sound. They may also like to be able to prove to other firms that they themselves are financially sound. Most banks have special departments which preserve records of business over the years. This information is not necessarily secret, having usually been accumulated by regular examination of the published accounts of the firms concerned. Anyone can see such records at the offices of the Company Registrar on payment of 5p. For a small charge banks will supply a report on any firm on their files, and will issue a credit rating for any firm that asks for it. A credit rating is a certificate that a firm is itself financially sound. It is not a check-up on another firm, but a proof of one's own stability.

(*i*) *Economic information.* Even this list of services to business firms does not cover all the matters banks deal with, for the whole range of economic life is covered by bank activities.

Banks are interested in everything people do everywhere. They employ expert observers who analyse business trends, study political developments, forecast government reactions to situations and try to make the complex business of life less risky and more certain. This information, informed discussion, and comment is published regularly in the bank reviews. These are free to interested persons, and may be obtained from the Head Offices of the bigger banks.

(*j*) *Cash dispensers and cash points.* Cash dispensers pay out cash to accredited customers from a cash dispensing machine outside the bank. They are available 24 hours a day. 'Cash points' in the main banking-hall are more sophisticated cash dispensers linked to computers. Here the machine is able to check the state of the customer's account. If the computer confirms that he is in funds the money will be released. In both cases a coded card and number are given to customers wishing to operate the machine.

(*k*) *Banker's credit cards.* Credit cards are now issued by most banks to customers with sound credit ratings. A sound credit rating depends not so much on the balance kept on deposit as on the degree of responsibility shown in handling money matters. Credit cards can be used to withdraw cash at other branches than the customer's usual one; to pay bills in restaurants and motels; and are sometimes used to prove identity when paying by cheque in shops. Perhaps the most widespread and convenient of all is the Barclaycard system.

The Barclaycard system enables a customer to pay in shops, hotels, garages, theatres, and cinemas and to draw cash at any branch of Barclays when the customer is away from home. An embossed card is used to record the customer's code on to the invoice provided at the Barclaycard shop or garage. The customer pays no extra but the shopkeeper pays a charge which may be up to 5 per cent. At the end of the month the customer is sent an account which he may pay without charge within 25 days. After that time 2 per cent interest is added per month. Continuous credit up to an agreed limit is available. At least 15 per cent, or a maximum of £6 must be met at the end of any month. Barclaycard is an extremely convenient service for shopkeepers and customers alike. Access cards provide a similar service.

(*l*) *Discounting Bills of Exchange.* As explained fully on page 174 the use of inland bills of exchange is increasing as a source of funds. The ordinary commercial banks act for their customers in arranging the discounting of such bills with the discount market firms.

(*m*) *Investment Management.* Many customers with funds to invest rely on the expert knowledge of the bankers in the management of their portfolios. For a consideration the banks will provide details of investment prospects, will purchase and sell shares on the Stock Exchange through their brokers and advise clients about unfavourable developments.

EXERCISES SET 13

(6) The Banks' Services

1. By means of the cheque system traders may make payments to their creditors safely, cheaply, and conveniently. Justify this statement, giving examples which illustrate it clearly.

2. 'Cheques are the safe way to make payments.' 'Owing to disappointments in the past we regret we are unable to accept cheques in payment.' Explain these contradictory statements.

3. What services are offered by the bank to a small trader?

4. A small trader protests to his bank manager: 'My bank charges for this half-year are £5·50, which I find works out to about five new pence a cheque. It is clearly far too much.' Justify the charges as if you were the bank manager.

5. Draw and make out an open cheque to R. T. Smith, for £273·54. The Bank is Newtown Bank Ltd., Basildon, Essex, and the date is today's date. Use your own name as drawer.

6. Make out suitable bank paying-in slips, in duplicate, for the payment into your account of £57·50 in various sorts of cash, and £172·40 in cheques. Invent names for the people who have sent you the cheques, and choose figures for each cheque to come to the total given.

7. (*a*) I draw a cheque, payable to AB Company Ltd., which is crossed. I write in the crossing: 'Northern Bank, Ltd., Westminster Road, W.C.1 branch, AB Company, Ltd. a/c'. Explain the effect of this crossing.

(*b*) I draw a cheque, payable to 'Self' which is crossed. What must I do further before presenting this cheque at the bank counter for encashment?

(*c*) I receive a cheque from a customer, which is crossed 'not negotiable'. Can I pass this cheque on to one of my creditors in payment of a debt I owe him? Explain fully. (*R.S.A.*)

8. What is the fundamental work of a joint-stock bank? State briefly the additional services it renders for the convenience of its customers.

(*R.S.A.*)

9. What are the essential features of a cheque? Distinguish between: (*a*) a crossed cheque and an open cheque; (*b*) the crossing 'not negotiable' and the crossing 'Midland Bank, Leicester Square branch, AB a/c'; (*c*) an Order cheque and a Bearer cheque. (*R.S.A.*)

10. (*a*) What different kinds of customers do these banks serve:

      (i) savings banks (Trustee and Post Office)
      (ii) commercial banks
      (iii) merchant banks

(*b*) What services does each type offer to its customers?

(*c*) How do the banks obtain the funds to pay interest and/or dividends to their customers and investors? (*University of London*)

CHAPTER THIRTEEN

THE DISCOUNT MARKET

(1) Introduction

The 'Discount Market' consists of 11 firms who are members of the London Discount Market Association and 3 or 4 other smaller firms, not members of the Association, who are simple bill-brokers and do not have a large portfolio. They specialize in 'bill broking', i.e. the provision of short-term money by way of discounting bills to borrowers who require funds which they expect to be able to repay within three months. This is a specialized form of banking. The discount market provides a market-place where those who have surplus money, the use of which they are prepared to sell, can meet those prepared to buy the use of this money. The smallest unit for money on the market is £10,000, but occasionally lower amounts are used.

Today the savings of the nation are increasingly concentrated in the hands of institutional investors, such as banks, insurance companies, and building societies, who assume the responsibility of caring for, and earning interest on, the savings of the ordinary public. As this is a competitive world they are becoming more and more sophisticated in their outlook. Money is not allowed to lie idle, even for 24 hours, if profits can be earned with it on the world's markets. Someone can usually be found willing to borrow money at a worthwhile rate of interest even for terms as short as 1–3 days. The discount houses are borrowers of this kind, taking *call money* from investors. Every institutional investor has a 'balanced portfolio' of investments of different types. Some of the short-term investments in their portfolios will have been purchased from the bill brokers of the London Discount Market Association. The commonest short-term investments are **Treasury Bills, Bank Bills, Trade Bills of Exchange, Short Gilt Edged Securities,** and **Corporation Stocks,** and more recently **Sterling Certificates of Deposit.** Some houses also deal in **Dollar Certificates of Deposit** and **Foreign Currency Bills.**

(2) Bill-Broking

Bill-broking may be defined as dealing in money; taking it from those who have a surplus and distributing it to those who have need of it, by using the Bill of Exchange as described above. When we take money from people we must pay interest on it in due course, so that if we lend it out to people who have need of it we must clearly lend at a higher rate of interest than we are to pay to the person from whom it was obtained.

The difference between the borrowing rate and the lending rate is the source of the profits of the discount house.

If this profit margin is to be kept to a minimum there is no room for expensive paper records of transactions. Almost all the deals are by word of mouth only, but, once given, the discount banker's word is his bond. In a single day as much as £1,500 million may be handled by the market, with very little fuss or formality.

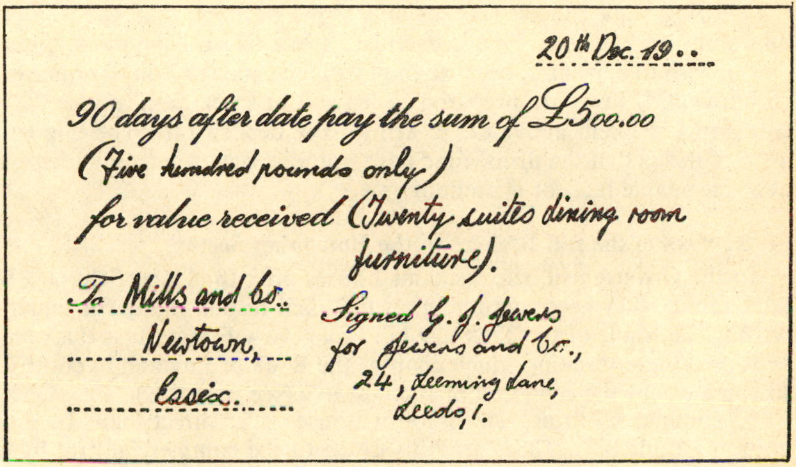
20th Dec. 19..

90 days after date pay the sum of £500.00 (Five hundred pounds only) for value received (Twenty suites dining room furniture).

To Mills and Co.
Newtown,
Essex.

Signed G. J. Jewers
for Jewers and Co.,
24, Leeming Lane,
Leeds, 1.

Fig. 37. An Inland Bill of Exchange

Flexible behaviour is absolutely essential to the bill broker. Changes in prices on the commodity markets or rates of interest anywhere in the world may lead to a strong demand for money, or cause a glut of money to be available. These trends must be reflected in changed interest rates or a lot of money will be lost. The important rate is the **minimum lending rate,** which is fixed at ½ per cent above the Treasury Bill rate for the previous Friday, rounded up to the next ¼ per cent. This is the minimum rate at which the Bank of England will discount bills to the discount houses.

(3) Services of the Bill Brokers to the Lending Sector

Bill brokers are prepared to borrow money from anyone who has a surplus and they agree to repay it as required. Money that is to be repayable on demand is known as **'call money'** because it is on call at any time. **'Short-notice'** money is usually repayable in a few days.

To the banks, bill brokers offer a secure outlet for liquid funds which can still be regarded by the banks as part of their minimum reserve ratio. The basic rate of interest is about 1⅝ per cent below the minimum lending rate but the actual rate depends upon supply and demand. It is therefore quite profitable to the banks to lend this money at negligible risk. The brokers also buy from the commercial banks those bills of exchange which the banks have discounted for customers and do not wish to keep to maturity. Such bills are promises to pay made by commercial firms, and re-discounted by the banks to the discount market.

To commercial firms wishing to lend money the discount houses offer the clearing-bank deposit rate, usually 2 per cent less than the Bank's minimum lending rate. This is useful to firms which have money, but do not wish to deposit it, because they will have to give 7 days' notice of withdrawal. If firms are prepared to leave it at seven days' notice they can earn $\frac{1}{4}$ per cent above the clearing-bank deposit rate. The importance of this is that the firms' funds are not idle, but are earning interest at a reasonable rate for shareholders.

(4) Services of the Bill Brokers to the Borrowing Sector

To the Government, the discount houses offer the loan of the short-term money they need; assuming an informal responsibility for underwriting the whole of the Treasury bill issue every Friday. It is this conventional understanding which enables the Bank of England to control to some extent the economy of the country (see page 185).

To commercial firms, the discount houses offer direct loans by discounting trade bills. These are bills given to the commercial firm by a customer who promises to pay later. By discounting these bills the commercial firm is able to obtain the money at once, less a certain rate of interest. If a discount broker is not sure that the firm's bill is reliable, he may ask that a merchant banker or accepting house adds its name to the bill. The discount houses also sell short-term stock investments through the Stock Exchange to both commercial firms and institutional investors who are building a balanced portfolio of investments. The commercial firms may do this in order to build up a pension fund, or a sinking fund with which to purchase new plant and machinery when present equipment becomes obsolete or unfit for use. By selling such firms Treasury bills and short-term gilt-edged securities, the discount houses earn useful profits, but also save their customers a good deal of risk and trouble. They also supply banks with bank bills and trade bills for portfolio purposes. A word about this type of business is desirable.

Bank Bills are bills that have been accepted or endorsed by a reputable bank. As such they are very reliable, and are discounted at a competitive rate called the **Fine Rate**. This is an agreed minimum rate below which the 11 houses will not buy bills. There is no maximum rate, so a bill broker who could get more than the fine rate would take it. Since the market is very competitive it is unlikely he would be able to do so often; his customer would go elsewhere.

Trade Bills are bills not signed by a bank. They are usually drawn to cover a particular transaction and are more risky than a bank bill. On the other hand they are also more profitable. If these bills are passed on by the discount house to banks building a balanced portfolio, the discount house accepts full liability on the bill. If the bill is dishonoured, the discount house immediately puts the customer in funds and looks to the parties to the bill to give satisfaction. It may therefore be said that the discount houses lend respectability to many commercial transactions and thus oil the wheels of commerce. One point about these trade bills is that they are sometimes for small amounts, mere hundreds or thousands of pounds.

(5) How the Discount Market Operates

The portfolio of investments that a firm in the discount market owns is earning interest at varying rates of interest. Gilts earn more than the minimum lending rate, bank bills just above it and trade bills somewhere between $\frac{1}{8}$ and 2 per cent above this rate. At the same time the discount market itself has borrowed the money from the banks, at rates varying from $1\frac{5}{8}$ per cent below to minimum lending rate, or from commercial firms at 2 per cent below, i.e. the Commercial Bank Deposit Rate. Naturally, like any other borrower from the bank, the discount market firm has to provide **security**, hence large parts of its portfolio of investments are actually lodged as security with the banks to whom they are in debt.

If this situation continued for a few months or longer the profits earned by the discount-market firm would be the difference between the interest they earn and the interest they have to pay out. In fact the situation never stays static for even one day. First, the discount-market firms have promised to lend the Government money every day, by buying Treasury bills for which they tendered the previous Friday. Next, the banks always 'call' money in the mornings to pay out the sums they have agreed to lend to the public, the commercial firms and the Government, and also to pay tax moneys paid to them which they now have to hand on to the Treasury. If the banks do this it makes the discount-market firms very short of cash in the morning. Later in the day the banks will probably have cash to spare because depositors have paid in money during the day. The discount-market firms have to telephone round desperately to get the cash they need before 2.30 p.m., which is the closing time for borrowing from the Bank of England. Great excitement develops as they try to obtain the funds they need, ringing round on their private switchboards to raise the money: there is no time to ask a telephonist to get them a number, seconds might mean that someone else will get half a million pounds first.

At 2.30 those bankers whose attempts to raise the cash they need have been unsuccessful must present themselves at the Bank of England to borrow what they need. They have been 'forced into the Bank', and if the Bank is anxious to raise interest rates all round it will charge them minimum lending rate, or even more. This is sad for the market for they have already loaned the money to someone at less than this rate, and are therefore going to lose money. If, on the other hand, the Bank of England does not wish to force interest rates up it will not allow the discount houses to be 'forced into the bank'. It will ease the shortage of cash in the market either by buying directly from the discount houses any treasury bills or bank bills they wish to dispose of, or by buying such bills from the clearing banks, who promptly lend the cash to the discount houses. This relieves the shortage indirectly.

(6) Recent Developments in the Discount Market

The history of bill-broking is a history of adaptability to changing conditions in the money market. In the early days of the Industrial Revolution inland bills were a major source of currency, and bill brokers earned a steady living by helping to sort out uneven situations in the money market. As branch banking developed these uneven situations were adjusted by the Head Offices of the big banks, and the bill brokers turned to foreign bills, i.e. bills drawn in London to settle international indebtedness. During this period the saying grew up that 'a good bill should smell of the sea'.

In recent years there has been a considerable increase in the use of inland bills to finance internal trade and provide working capital, particularly in the more profitable, but more speculative, hire-purchase field. This has increased the part played by the bill broker in developing the economy of the nation. A succession of credit squeezes has made loans and overdrafts from the ordinary banks more difficult to obtain. Businessmen have had to turn elsewhere to secure funds, and the inland Bill of Exchange has been one way to obtain them.

A recent development too is the issue by local authorities of short-term bills and bonds with a life of one to four years. These enable the local authorities to fund some of their short-term debts, against the security of the rates. The time chosen, one to four years, lies conveniently between the three-month Treasury and Trade bills and the five-year period usually chosen for short-term government bonds.

In September 1971 new arrangements made by the Bank of England with the Discount Houses included the following points:

(*a*) The Discount Houses agreed to keep 50 per cent of their funds in government or local government bills and bonds.

(*b*) They also agreed to tender each week for the entire Treasury Bill tender.

(*c*) The Bank agreed to continue to confine 'last resort' lending facilities to the Discount Houses only (see page 188). (*Contd. on p. 176*)

(7) A Page to Test You on the Discount Market

Answers	Questions
—	1. What is the Discount Market?
1. It consists of eleven firms who are members of the London Discount Market Association.	2. In what way is it a market?
2. It is a means whereby those with surplus money, the use of which they are prepared to sell, can meet those in need of money prepared to buy its use.	3. Do the discount-market firms operate as agents or as principals?
3. As principals. They borrow the money themselves and then relend it to others, by way of investments.	4. At what rate do they borrow?
4. (a) From banks between 1⅜ per cent below and minimum lending rate (b) From commercial firms at the Clearing Bank Deposit rate.	5. At what rate do they lend?
5. Slightly above these rates—perhaps ¼ per cent or a little more.	6. From whom do they borrow?
6. (a) From the commercial banks. (b) From commercial firms. (c) From other institutional investors.	7. To whom do they lend?
7. (a) To the Government. (b) To the banks. (c) To commercial firms, and Financial Houses.	8. Why are all bargains made by word of mouth?
8. To save expense and keep the price of borrowing money (interest) down.	9. What part does the discount market play in the gilt-edged market?
9. It buys and sells the short-term gilt-edged security with about five years to run. This keeps the short market active and helps the public deal in these securities with confidence.	10. List the types of paper securities the discount market deals in. List them in order of length of life.
10. Treasury Bills—up to 3 months. Bank Bills —up to 6 months. Trade Bills —up to 6 months. Foreign currency bills—Ditto. Sterling certs. of deposit—up to 2 yrs. Dollar certs. of deposit—up to 5 yrs. Local Government Bills and Bonds —one to four years. Short-term gilt edged—five years.	11. How many did you answer correctly? Go over the list again.

In 1973 the Bank of England recognized that the 1971 arrangements were causing serious difficulties in the money market. In particular the requirement to hold 50 per cent of their funds in government or local government bills and bonds was forcing up the price of these securities. This arrangement was therefore discontinued. Traditional operations on the Discount Market have been greatly affected by the changes made in 1971, and the Market is still going through a rather difficult period. This is nothing new in the history of this market. It is only by adapting to changing conditions that bill-brokers maintain their positions as vital operators at the centre of the short-term money market.

EXERCISES SET 14

(8) The Discount Market

1. 'I am a bill broker by trade; one who evens out the surpluses and shortages of money.' Explain.

2. Write a short account of the probable life of a bill of exchange drawn at three months on J. Mills, a timber dealer, by A. Rosner, an importer of softwoods.

3. The Bank of England keeps the money market short of cash by setting the Treasury Bill offers at a high figure. This enables the Bank to control the money market and the economy to some extent. Explain.

4. What services do the members of the London Discount Market Association render to (a) the Banks (b) the Finance Houses?

5. As 2.30 approaches, the discount market 'phones desperately to all possible sources of finance to avoid being forced into the Bank of England. Explain

6. 'Even a millionaire must deposit security when he borrows money.' What is security? What sort of security might the following people deposit in order to borrow money? (a) a householder; (b) a dealer on the discount market; (c) a Trade Union involved in a big strike.

7. What is the 'Discount Market'? Describe its functions, and explain how the firms on the market earn a living.

8. What are (a) Treasury Bills, (b) Bank Bills, (c) Trade Bills? Explain who issues each of these, and why.

9. A financial market is just like any other market-place. Explain, referring in your answer to the Bills Discount Market of London.

10. 'If the bank will not lend me money I shall turn to the discount market, even if it is more expensive.'

'I shall not borrow from the bank, for the discount market is cheaper.' Are these two remarks both valid? Explain.

CHAPTER FOURTEEN

THE MERCHANT BANKERS

(1) Introduction

The term 'merchant banker' is very widely used today, but is properly applied to the 17 members of the Accepting Houses Committee. These 17 City houses include such famous names as N. M. Rothschild & Sons, Samuel Montagu & Co. Ltd. and Baring Brothers. The name 'merchant banker' refers to their origin as mercantile houses specializing in the export of British products, particularly cotton cloth, and the import of any products of the countries where they were established. This involved remitting money from one country to another, and the bill of exchange on London became the means of financing the import and export trades. The merchants concerned became well known as absolutely reliable firms whose signature on a bill would make it readily discountable on the money market.

Some of the 17 merchant bankers are still active as merchants: one owns subsidiary companies in the timber trade; one is active in the coffee trade; one has business houses in Australia, America, and Africa. The change to banking developed as the number of firms trading with overseas territories increased. Many of these new firms found that they lacked the respect and trust enjoyed by the well-established houses, so that their bills of exchange were less readily discounted. The solution was found to be the accepting of these traders' bills by one of the older well-established firms, for a consideration in the form of commission. Gradually the merchant became a banker specializing in the accepting of bills for other merchants.

A second interest of these firms became the issue of foreign bonds for overseas governments who lacked capital. The issue of these bonds was only possible if the names of famous houses appeared in association with the issue. The merchant bankers arranged for a quotation on the London Stock Exchange, and handled the issues which were subscribed for by British and overseas investors. The London Foreign Bond Market was an international market and a source of 'invisible earnings' of foreign exchange. For balance-of-payments reasons the issue of foreign bonds is not carried on today.

(2) The Functions of Accepting Houses Today

(a) *Finance of Home and Foreign Trade*

The Accepting Houses are still the specialist financiers of foreign trade, and the accepting of bills of exchange drawn on London is still one of their primary functions. Alongside the Foreign Bills has grown up a widespread use of inland bills, already explained on page 174. This growth in inland business has occurred because of the more competitive rates of interest charged on bills of exchange, which are essentially short-term money and therefore provide a ready, and reasonably priced, source of funds to businessmen.

It must not be overlooked, however, that the essential feature of a bill is its self-liquidating nature. That is, by the time the bill falls due, the trading venture it was designed to finance should have been completed and should have provided the funds for settlement of the bill. Bills are not intended to form a long-term financial alternative to bank loans or overdraft facilities. They are simply a method whereby the exporter receives his payment and the importer enjoys a period of credit, while the goods are in transit, being unloaded, going through customs formalities, etc.

(b) Issuing of New Shares

As foreign-bond issues decreased in the unsettled international situation of the 1930s, the merchant bankers turned to home issues. Very considerable increases in the scale of British business took place before the start of the Second World War, and the demand for large sums of capital presented problems to industry. These problems were solved by handing over to the merchant bankers the new issues of shares. The Issuing Houses Association has over 50 members, so there are many issuing houses which are not accepting houses. The accepting houses had a long experience of issuing foreign bonds, which made them particularly suitable for undertaking new issues.

New issues are made by offering shares and debentures in these ways:

  (i) direct to the general public, through a prospectus,
 (ii) through an issuing house, by an 'Offer for Sale',
(iii) through an issuing house, which 'places' the shares with one or two institutional investors who it knows have funds available.

(c) Helping the Exporter to Hedge against Currency Fluctuations

By adopting the device of 'pre-shipment credits' the merchant bankers give the exporter an opportunity to hedge against currency fluctuations. When an overseas exporter has made a contract for the sale of goods to a British importer he is entitled to a certain sum in sterling. By opening a credit for him against which he may draw, even in advance of shipment, the overseas exporter can sell the sterling he is due to receive at once and thus avoid the risk of exchange fluctuations. He has converted the sum due to be received into his own currency. He could of course have executed a forward exchange transaction to sell his sterling at an agreed price when it finally arrives, but he may lose on the price he is offered. Under pre-shipment credits he is actually put in funds at once, and the discount lost on the bill he draws will usually be less than the combined losses on his forward transaction and any borrowing he might otherwise do to tide him over until he received his sterling payment.

(*d*) *Confirming*

A confirming house operates as an intermediary between an overseas buyer and his British supplier. It confirms the order, sending it to the British manufacturer as if it was an order from the merchant banker. The British manufacturer supplies the goods to the confirming house, which pays for them, ships them to the overseas customer, and secures payment for the goods in its own name.

(*e*) *The Gold and Silver Bullion Markets*

These markets are operated by one or two of the merchant-banking firms, in association with certain independent brokers. All the accepting houses handle bullion; the price of gold is fixed daily at a meeting whose chairman is the representative of one of them which owns a refinery.

(*f*) *Take-overs and Mergers*

An increasing number of mergers and take-overs occur in business today, to achieve the advantages of large-scale activities. Merchant bankers are frequently called in to assist in the involved financial arrangements necessary, and to advise how these arrangements may be kept within the code of conduct drawn up by the City Working Party on Take-overs and Mergers. (See p. 221.)

(*g*) *Other Functions*

As bankers, the accepting houses naturally perform banking functions for clients. Being engaged in international trade, they have close links with the shipping world, the insurance markets, the foreign-exchange market, and the money market. Export Credit Guarantees (see page 131) are of interest to them, particularly in the field of long-term capital projects, where the sums involved are so large that a consortium of banks is necessary to finance the venture. A recent activity of great importance is the issue of international euro-bonds, sometimes in dollar units (eurodollars) but also in Swiss francs, deutschmarks, and other units. The merchant bankers are very active indeed in the issue and marketing of these euro-currency bonds, and place about 15 per cent of all such issues. In 1969 about 4,000 million dollars were borrowed on such issues by the businessmen and governments of the world.

EXERCISES SET 15

(3) The Merchant Bankers

1. What do you understand by the term 'Accepting Houses'? Explain the part they play in commerce today.

2. 'A merchant banker may be more banker than merchant, but he will generally know much about particular businesses and something about most businesses.' Explain the position of merchant bankers in commerce today.

3. What is an issuing house? Explain the services it offers to businessmen.

4. How is gold fixed? Explain the importance of gold in the modern world.

5. A confirming house is an intermediary between a British exporter and his overseas buyer. Explain what part it plays.

CHAPTER FIFTEEN

THE BANK OF ENGLAND AND THE CONTROL OF THE BANKING SYSTEM

(1) Introduction

Fig. 38. The 'Medallion' of the Bank of England

The Bank of England was founded in 1694, to lend money to the Government. It was given a monopoly of joint-stock banking and became the Government's bank. It was at this time not a nationalized institution but a private bank which wielded great influence partly because of its close relationship with the Treasury. Just over a century later Sheridan, the dramatist, described the Bank as 'an elderly lady in the City, of great credit and long standing'. Possibly this description of the Bank led James Gillray, a cartoonist of the day, to depict the Bank in a famous cartoon called 'The Old Lady of Threadneedle Street in danger'. It showed the Prime Minister, Pitt, attacking the Bank to obtain money for the Napoleonic Wars. The old lady was putting up a spirited resistance. The nickname stuck, and has been in popular use ever since.

In 1844 the Bank Charter Act reorganized the Bank of England, splitting it into two parts: the Banking Department and the Issue Department. The Banking Department dealt with banking operations as they affected the Government, the commercial banks, the money market and the few private firms who banked with the Bank of England. The Issue Department was charged with seeing that bank notes were issued as required by the public within the limits set by the gold reserves and a small *fiduciary issue* of £14 million. A 'fiduciary issue' is one that has no gold to back it but is backed only by other coin and securities. So long as Britain kept on the gold standard the promise on a note 'I promise to

180

pay the bearer on demand the sum of x pounds' meant that the customer who preferred to have gold could have it. Today the promise refers only to credit in the form of other notes and coin, or an entry in a bank account.

The separation of the Bank into two departments is of little significance today except for accounting purposes. The weekly **Bank Return** reproduced in Fig. 40 shows the accounts in two sections. Note that in the issue department, the 'Notes Issued' total £5,418,913,670, none of which is now backed by gold. The entire note issue is therefore fiduciary issue, backed by paper securities. This means that the Bank of England has a large portfolio of stocks which helps it play its part in

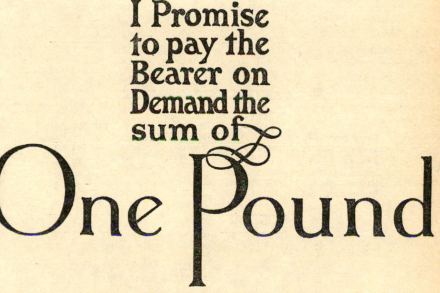

Fig. 39. The traditional promise on a Bank of England note

the management of the gilt edged market. This is fully discussed on page 185.

In 1946 Parliament brought the Bank of England into public ownership. The Governor, Deputy Governor, and 16 Directors who form the Court of Directors are appointed by the sovereign on the recommendation of the Prime Minister. No longer can it be claimed, justifiably or otherwise, that the Bank prevents the implementation of desirable social policies. The Treasury is helped to implement government policies through the Bank which controls in various ways the credit policies of the commercial banks in their relations with the public.

BANK OF ENGLAND

Wednesday the 19th day of March 1975

ISSUE DEPARTMENT

	£		£
Notes Issued:		Government Debt	11 015 100
In Circulation	5418 913 670	Other Govt.Securities	4528 905 081
In Banking Department	31 086 330	Other Securities	910 079 819
	5450 000 000		5450 000 000

BANKING DEPARTMENT

	£		£
Capital	14 553 000	Govt.Securities	1417 557 899
Public Deposits— including Exchequer, National Loans Fund, National Debt Commissioners and Dividend Accounts	25 095 522	Advances and Other Accounts	288 105 285
Special Deposits	942 970 000	Premises, Equipment and Other Securities	76 304 403
Bankers Deposits	359 253 306	Notes	31 086 330
Reserves and Other Accounts	471 377 835	Coin	195 746
	1813 249 663		1813 249 663

Dated the 20th day of March 1975

J.B.PAGE, Chief Cashier

Fig. 40.   The weekly 'Return' of the Bank of England

(2) The Functions of the Bank of England

The Bank of England is a central bank, or national bank, charged with the control of the banking system in the interests of the nation. In the last 25 years one of the key functions of government has been the management of prosperity. Most nations are preoccupied with this, and an indispensable requirement is a central bank which can control the general activities of the ordinary banks.

The chief functions of the Bank of England are to act as the Government's bank in the widest possible sense, anticipating where possible the banking problems that may arise and examining those that do arise. It then undertakes the appropriate operations in the money, capital, and foreign-exchange markets. A full list of activities includes the following:

(*a*) *The Bank's role as Banker*

    (i) Bankers to the Government.

    (ii) Bankers to the banks and the money market.

    (iii) Bankers to foreign central banks and international organizations.

    (iv) Bankers to a residue of private customers.

    (v) Managers of the note issue for the British Isles (Scottish and Northern Ireland banks still issue their own notes, but the numbers are comparatively small).

    (vi) The registration of Government stocks, and the servicing of the National Debt.

    (vii) Operating the exchange control system to protect the gold and foreign exchange reserves.

(*b*) *The Bank's operations in the markets*

    (i) The implementation of Government policy to control the economy by controlling the money market for short-term loans.

    (ii) The implementation of Government policy in both the long- and short-term loan markets by varying minimum lending rate.

    (iii) To meet the Government's long-term borrowing requirements by open-market operations in Government Stocks; this may also influence the lending policies of the commercial banks.

    (iv) Managing the Exchange Rate to protect the pound.

(*c*) *The Bank's influence on policy*

    (i) Because of its influential position in the financial affairs of the country, the Bank is able to give useful financial advice to the Treasury, to assist in forecasts of the economic situation and the balance-of-payments position.

    (ii) It often advises on capital structure and the finance of companies.

    (iii) It participates in the international activities of such bodies as the International Monetary Fund and the International Bank for Reconstruction and Development.

It is now necessary to consider each of these activities in detail.

(3) The Bank in its Role as Banker

(*a*) *Bankers to the Government.* The main Government account is the central Exchequer Account at the Bank, to which all Government revenues are eventually credited, and from which all Government payments originate. Other major ministerial accounts are also kept at the Bank and the major expenses of Government departments are disbursed through these accounts.

The Bank does not lend money to the Government, except on a small scale, overnight. If the Government needs funds because tax moneys have not yet been received in sufficient volume, it borrows the sums required by issuing Treasury bills or by selling stocks. Treasury bills are short-term securities, offered for sale by tender every Friday, repayable three months after issue. The Bank's function is to balance every day the sums received against the sums needed, never allowing idle balances to accumulate. If moneys are received in excess of requirements, the Bank buys back Treasury bills, adding them to its portfolio, to save interest payments on them. This reduces the burden of servicing the National Debt. Longer-term borrowing is effected by selling gilt-edged securities on the Stock Exchange.

(*b*) *Bankers to the banks.* The Bank of England are bankers to the commercial banks, and also to the discount and accepting houses. There are also a number of overseas banks with accounts at the Bank of England. The ordinary commercial banks maintain about 4 per cent of their assets in cash with the Bank of England. In Fig. 40 (see p. 182) these cash deposits were over £359 million. As the 'Bankers' Bank' the Bank of England assists in the day-to-day settlement of indebtedness between the banks (see page 191). The need to preserve their cash reserves gives the Bank of England a method of influencing the credit policies of the commercial banks. This is called 'open-market operations' and is discussed on page 185.

(*c*) *Bankers to foreign central banks and international organizations.* About 90 overseas central banks and international bodies such as the International Monetary Fund have accounts with the Bank of England to facilitate a wide variety of international transactions. Such central banks are primarily concerned with influencing affairs in their own countries to promote trade and prosperity so far as possible. Former Sterling-Area countries keep much of their reserves in London; others keep substantial working balances to assist home nationals desiring sterling. The Bank of England will advise on the investment and use of these funds, making arrangements of use to both Britain and the country concerned.

(*d*) *Bankers to a residue of private customers.* In earlier days the Bank did accept accounts from private persons and some famous families have dealt with the Bank for over 200 years. The Bank also provides banking facilities for its own staff. This residue of private banking is at least helpful in reminding the Bank of the sort of problems faced by the ordinary bankers. The Bank does not open new private accounts today, except for employees.

(*e*) *The Bank and the note issue.* Bank of England notes are legal tender to any amount. This means that we can buy anything we like and pay for it with bank-notes if we have them. In fact most of us today pay by cheque because of the great convenience of paying only one peice of paper instead of counting out hundreds of notes. Bank-notes have therefore become the small change of the money system. For large amounts we pay by cheque. Even so the number of notes in circulation is very great. As the central note-issuing authority, the Bank has a great deal of work to do just changing dirty notes for new ones. New notes are issued and worn notes withdrawn in very large numbers every day. The ordinary banks pay in bundles of dirty notes and draw bundles of clean notes daily, so that fluctuations in their deposits with the Bank occur as a result.

(*f*) *The Bank as registrar of Government stocks.* In the same way as companies must register the transfer of stocks from one stockholder to another, someone must register the transfer of gilt-edged securities. The Bank performs these activities as registrar of Government stocks, stocks of nationalized industries and public boards. It also pays dividends when they fall due on about 200 stocks, worth about £20,000 million, on about $2\frac{1}{2}$ million accounts. This means about five million dividend warrants per year, and about three-quarters of a million stock transfers.

(*g*) *The Bank as it operates the exchange-control system.* The Exchange Control Act of 1947 authorized the control of the use made of foreign exchange by persons wishing to transfer funds out of the Sterling Area referred to in the Act as the 'Scheduled Territories'. The Bank acts as the Government's agent in the administration of exchange control, and employs over 500 of its staff on this type of work. Many types of exchange-control applications are in fact dealt with by the ordinary banks under powers delegated to them by the Bank of England. Such banks are known as authorized banks. Some similar powers have been delegated to Stock Exchange firms in connection with transactions in securities, and to travel agents in the routine work of administering travel allowances.

(4) The Bank's Operations in the Markets

(*a*) *Controlling the Economy by Controlling the Money Market.*

The discount market consists of 11 firms of **discount houses** who operate in the field of short-term loans. They are members of the London Discount Market Association. They discount bills of exchange to private and institutional borrowers, and also tender for Treasury bills in the weekly tenders.

Readers who are not familiar with the idea of a 'tender' should note that it is an offer to buy at a certain price. A Treasury bill, which is a three-month bill offered by the Treasury as security for a loan, might be worth, at the end of three months, its full face value of say £10,000. If a discount house tenders for this bill it might offer to buy it for £9,850. This offer, if accepted by the Bank means that the money market will lend the Government £9,850 and will receive in return, in three months' time, £10,000. The extra money is clearly the interest on the loan, earned by the discount house. If another discount house tendered at £9,875 the Bank of England would accept this offer instead, because it is a better offer as far as the Treasury is concerned; the interest to be paid will be £25 less than in the previous example.

Discount houses who lend money in this way are not lending their own funds, but money they have borrowed elsewhere. The market is highly competitive and the margin of profit that they earn is small. For instance a firm might borrow a million pounds from one of the commercial banks at 6 per cent and lend to the Treasury at $6\frac{1}{4}$ per cent.

What the discount houses do is very important in the economy of the country. If businessmen can borrow cheaply from the discount houses they will proceed with many activities and the economy will be prosperous. Too buoyant an economy may lead to inflation. When inflation seems likely, the Bank of England indicates that it is displeased with the 'cheap' interest rates prevailing by refusing to relieve any money shortages that may develop in the discount-market, except by loans at minimum lending rate or above. The discount houses are very sensitive to the Bank's displeasure, and raise their interest rates to choke off some of the demand for funds.

If the Bank is to operate successfully, it suits it if there is an initial shortage of funds in the market. This shortage can be imposed on the discount-market for one reason only: there is an informal understanding that the members of the London Discount Market Association will bid for the whole of the Treasury bills on offer, so that if no other bidders are in the market the entire Treasury bill offer will be taken up. This means that the Bank is able to set the weekly offer figure at such a level as to keep the money market rather short of cash.

If the money market is short of cash, the firms in the money market will have to borrow from someone, and if they cannot borrow from anyone else they will be 'forced into the Bank'. In fact what really happens is that the Bank is in a position to lend to the money market as the **lender of last resort.** If it does not wish particularly to interfere with the economy as it is developing at present it will lend the discount market funds at very reasonable rates, or buy back Treasury bills until the discount-market's books balance. It may buy these bills back direct from the discount-market firms (this is called 'direct' assistance), or buy them back from the commercial banks—who promptly lend the cash they have just received from the Bank of England to the firms in the money market (this is called 'indirect' assistance). Sometimes many millions of pounds is provided in a single day in this way.

If the Bank does not approve of the way the economy is developing it refuses to help the discount houses in this way. The discount houses are forced to balance their books by borrowing direct from the Bank, or obtaining an overdraft against a deposit of securities. The rate of interest charged may be minimum lending rate, or even more. It may make many of the transactions into which they have entered unprofitable to the discount houses. It is therefore called a 'penal rate', since the losses can be very heavy. Fear of being 'forced into the Bank' causes the discount houses to raise their rates of discount to their customers and discourages the 'boom' that is developing in the economy. This is explained further in the section on minimum lending rate.

(*b*) *Influencing the Economy through both the Long-term and the Short-term Loan Markets by the Lending-Rate Mechanism.*

Minimum lending rate is defined as **the rate at which the Bank will re-discount first-class Bills of Exchange.** It replaces Bank Rate, which was formerly announced every Thursday. It is found by adding $\frac{1}{2}$ per cent to the Treasury Bill rate. announced the previous Friday, after rounding up to the nearest $\frac{1}{4}$ per cent.

The significance of a change in minimum lending rate is that all other rates of interest are affected: a rise leads to a rise in general interest rates

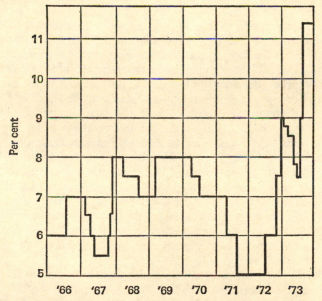

Fig. 41. How the Bank Rate has changed over recent years
(In October 1972 Bank Rate was changed to minimum lending rate—see above)

over the whole field of credit. More expensive loans from banks, finance houses, and building societies will lead to changes in the demand for consumer goods and producer goods. Economists would say 'the marginal project will not be proceeded with'. The marginal project is the project that is only just going to make a profit under present conditions. If this project suddenly has to face increased interest charges it will cease to be profitable and the businessman will abandon it for the present. Thus a rise in interest rates will discourage investment and reduce demand for consumer goods, while a fall in interest rates will encourage investment, increase demand for consumer goods and provide employment for people who are out of work. It will also have an effect on overseas capital. This is discussed on page 191.

How minimum lending rate takes effect. The Bank of England is the **'lender of last resort'**, to whom bill brokers in difficulties must turn to borrow. The bill brokers, pursuing their normal Discount Market activities, inevitably come up against times when they are short of funds, because the commercial banks have themselves run into difficulties. The discount houses, taking money from those who have it to spare, and lending it to those who need funds are borrowing 'short' to lend 'long'. They borrow money at very short notice from the commercial banks. Since it is at short notice, they borrow more cheaply than the ordinary borrower. The banks know that they are running no risk and can even count this short-term money as liquid assets, part of their $12\frac{1}{2}$ per cent minimum reserve ratio.

At the first sign of a change in their liquidity the commercial bankers look round to see where they can obtain cash. Naturally the first group they turn to are the firms in the discount market who are under contract to repay at once. If the commercial banks recall their loans made to the discount market, the discount houses will be 'forced into the Bank', i.e. forced to borrow at minimum lending rate from the Bank of England. This may destroy the profitability of the bargains struck by these firms. Commercial necessity therefore makes these firms keep their discount rates to customers in the region of minimum lending rate. A rise in minimum lending rate is therefore reflected in a rise of interest rates from the discount houses to their customers. In order to prevent these customers from switching to the commercial banks, the commercial bankers also raise their rates of interest to borrowers.

The changes in such rates also affects the long-term capital market, for if the yield on short-term loans is altered, investors will move funds in or out of the short-term market with consequent effects on the prices of gilt-edged securities and industrial shares.

In Fig. 41 the rapid fluctuations which have taken place since Bank Rate changed to Minimum Lending Rate have caused confusion in the Discount Market. Critics of the new system argue that the Bank of England has lost some of its control.

A further effect of minimum lending rate is dealt with on page 191.

Special-deposit requirements. If the Chancellor feels that bank credit policies are too easy, and that as a result more businessmen and private individuals are receiving loans than is desirable, he can ask the Bank of England to require **special deposits** from the commercial banks.

This scheme was first used in April, 1960. The usual order is for 1 per cent of the banks' total deposits to be deposited with the Bank of England and frozen there until such time as the Chancellor sees fit to release them. This represents about £220 million of cash removed from the banks' pockets. It is a very serious blow at their liquidity and causes a severe tightening of credit. After some time without special deposits the Bank called for 1 per cent (£220 million) in November 1972, and this was raised to 6 per cent by 13th November, 1973.

Conversely, if unemployment becomes serious, and the Chancellor wishes to ease credit policies, he may release special deposits. This is usually done in ½ per cent steps; even this will enable much more generous loan and overdraft facilities to be made available.

(c) Influencing the Economy by Open-market Operations in the Gilt-Edged Market.

The Gilt-Edged Market is an active market in Government stocks. The sale of these stocks is used to finance the long-term borrowing of Government departments and nationalized industries. The 'trustee status' of such stocks assists the market in maintaining active interest in gilt-edged securities. The main object of the Bank's activities here is to promote the sale of long-term stock and keep the market healthy so that this type of long-term loan will always be available to the Government.

All purchases and sales are made through the Government Broker and are largely authorized by the Issue Department. From time to time the Bank's portfolio is restored by new issues of stock. Most of these new issues cannot be sold at once to the general public but are taken up by the Issue Department. **Funding** is a chief aim of the Issue Department. It may be defined as persuading citizens and institutions to lend money on a long-term basis (creating a fund) instead of only for a short term. If people lend for a short term they may spend the money when it returns to them in a few months. In inflationary times this tendency to spend will make the situation worse.

A secondary effect is that, if the Bank engages in open-market operations successfully, its activities will have repercussions on the liquidity of the commercial banks, and will force them to pursue credit policies in line with Government policy. Open-market operations involve the sale or purchase of Government securities on the open market. Suppose the Government Broker sells gilt-edged securities from the Issue Department portfolio to the general public through the Stock Exchange. The buyers of these securities will pay by cheques drawn on their current accounts. This will reduce the balances deposited with the Bank of England by the commercial banks, which are part of each bank's minimum ratio. There is a loss of liquidity by the banks and a consequent reduction in the loans they can make. Because the cash lost has been acting as the reserve ratio for a much larger volume of deposits, they will have to reduce loans by about three times the amount of the loss in cash. Such a credit policy would reduce inflationary pressure by reducing the amount of money consumers could obtain.

Reflating the economy by open-market operations. If on the other hand business is bad and unemployment is spreading the bank can encourage prosperity to return by buying Government securities on the open market. If the Government Broker buys gilt-edged securities and pays cash for them, the sellers of the securities will receive cheques from the Treasury to bank in their ordinary accounts. These increased cash deposits will encourage the bankers to go ahead with loans to businessmen wishing to expand, or private people wishing to buy cars, houses, washing machines and television sets, etc. The increased business activity resulting from this more liberal credit policy will lead to a reduction in unemployment and a return to more prosperous times.

(d) Managing the Exchange Rate to Protect the Pound

For many years the rate of exchange between the £1 and other currencies was arranged under a system of fixed par values. This means that the exchange rate was not allowed to fluctuate outside certain rather narrow limits without the Bank of England stepping into the market in order to prevent it exceeding or falling below these limits.

Suppose the rate of exchange of the pound against the dollar was 2·40 dollars = £1, with a 1 cent fluctuation allowed on either side. Imagine that the value of the £1 was dropping against the dollar. World bankers were not prepared to give 2·40 dollars for a £1 but only 2·39 dollars or 2·38½ dollars. As the lowest point that fluctuations were allowed to reach was 2·38 dollars, it follows that someone had to 'support the pound' i.e. buy pounds on the market.

If the Bank of England stepped in and bought pounds at 2·38½ dollars it would help the price of the £1 recover. If it did not recover, if people all over the world who had pounds decided to sell them even at 2·38 dollars, we had what was called a 'run on the pound'. If the Bank went on buying, buying, buying, we had a 'drain on the reserves'. In these circumstances serious action was needed. Borrowing from the International Monetary Fund helped recovery by enlarging our reserves. The speculators who had sold and sold and sold (in the hopes of buying pounds back more cheaply later) would 'burn their fingers'. The price recovered and they had to buy back at higher prices than they sold at. Sooner or later if they wanted to buy British goods or insure on the British market they needed pounds. The Bank hoped when it supported the pound that recovery would set in, and when it did the Bank would be able to sell pounds and rebuild the gold and dollar reserves.

Fixed exchange rates have been abandoned at present but the Bank is still actively supporting the pound at times when it displays weakness against other major currencies due to speculative pressure.

One final aspect of Minimum Lending Rate, often the most important today, is its effect on so-called **'hot money'**. Hot money is money invested by international speculators who are looking for a high rate of interest combined with security. It is difficult to get both at the same time. If a run on the pound begins to develop, these speculators make the situation worse by rushing out of the danger zone to invest somewhere safer than Britain. Others will rush out of pounds in the hope of returning later at a cheaper rate. Raising the minimum lending rate will encourage them to keep their money in pounds, since the interest to be earned is better than elsewhere.

(5) The London Bankers' Clearing House

The London Bankers' Clearing House consists at the time of writing of 6 clearing banks but other banks do receive assistance.

The 6 clearing banks are:

Barclays	Midland
Lloyds	Williams and Glyn's
National Westminster	Coutts & Co.

Coutts & Co., while preserving its position as a clearing bank, has become part of the National Westminster group.

History of the Clearing House. About 1730 Child & Co., a firm of goldsmiths, issued the first printed goldsmith's note, the forerunner of the modern cheque. The use of these notes gradually became more commonplace, until clerks had to be employed to go on a daily round of other banks presenting the notes that had been paid in and asking for cash in exchange. To save many separate calls at business houses all over the City and West End, the idea soon arose of hiring a room, the expenses of which would be shared. In 1773 an entry in the books of Martin's Bank reads 'Quarterly charge for use of clearing room 19*s*. 6*d*.'; less than £1 for 13 weeks. Eventually a clearing house was built in 1833.

The present Clearing House is on the same site, at 10 Lombard Street, London, E.C.3. It is still run in the same way, being wholly owned by the clearing banks who contribute to the cost in proportion to the volume of business handled on their behalf. About 1,250 million cheques and credit transfers are cleared every year.

How the Clearing System Works—Settling the Net Indebtedness

There are really three quite simple ideas behind the clearing system. *Idea No. 1.* All that a bank needs to settle is its 'net indebtedness'.

Wednesday 26th November 1828

Debtor **CLEARING HOUSE.** Creditor

Debtor £	s.	d.		Creditor £	s.	d.
			ATTWOOD...	393	15	5
			BARCLAY....	7106	2	1
			BARNARD...	4022	10	1
21582	1	8	BARNETT....			
1456	18	5	BOND........			
			BOSANQUET.	3498	9	11
3867	11	3	BROWN......			
7222	16		CURRIES....			
			CURTIS......	6804	12	9
1124	5	7	DORRIEN			
			ESDAILE	57186	14	10
			FRY..........			
5405	3	3	FULLER			
43428	15	3	GLYN			
1738	10	9	GROTE.......			
6273	2	10	HANBURY....			
			HANKEY......	8788	1	1
			JONES........	61068	17	7
36	2	2	KAY..........			
64659	10	6	LADBROOKE.			
11349	19	4	LEES.			
21220	2	9	LUBBOCK....			
9462	18	—	MARTIN......			
			MASTERMAN.	37976	6	11
2730	7	10	REMINGTON..			
			ROGERS.....	7680	6	8
813	12	8	SANSOM.....			
			SMITH.......			
			VERES.......	3209	17	1
5994	4	3	WESTON.....			
			WHITMORE.	5270	9	11
			WILLIAMS ...	50541	14	3
			WILLIS	17676	14	1
208366	2	6	7/8	271224	12	8
Smith 62858	10	2	8/7			6/7/8/6/7
271224	12	8	1/8/5			

Fig. 42. An early clearing

Consider the following situation between two banks at the end of a given day:

Barclays	Lloyds
Has to pay £12 million on behalf of various customers to people who bank with Lloyds.	Has to pay £11 million on behalf of various customers to people who bank with Barclays.

There is no point in taking £12 million from Barclays' vaults to Lloyds' vaults, and then £11 million from Lloyds' vaults to Barclays' vaults. All that need to move is the net indebtedness, which is £1 million from Barclays to Lloyds.

Idea No. 2. 'Net indebtedness' among a large number of banks can be more easily settled than by the banks settling their affairs separately.

Consider the following pattern of indebtedness at the end of a day's clearing:

Table 7. Multilateral clearing through the Bankers' Clearing House

Debtor Bank	Banks to whom money is owed					
	Barclays	Lloyds	Midland	National Westminster	Coutts &Co.	Total owed
Barclays	—	£1m	—	£3m	£1m	£5m
Lloyds	—	—	£5m	—	—	£5m
Midland	£4m	—	—	£3m	—	£7m
National Westminster	—	£6m	—	—	£2m	£8m
Coutts & Co.	—	£3m	£2m	—	—	£5m
Total Due	£4m	£10m	£7m	£6m	£3m	£30m

Summary of above position			
Bank	Amount owed	Amount due	Net indebtedness to all other banks
Barclays	£5m	£4m	£1m
Lloyds	£5m	£10m	—£5m
Midland	£7m	£7m	0
National Westminster	£8m	£6m	£2m
Coutts & Co.	£5m	£3m	£2m

Settlement at the Clearing House

*London,*________________19

To the Cashiers of the BANK OF ENGLAND,

*Be pleased to CREDIT our Account the Sum of*________________

____

____

out of the money at the credit of the account of the Clearing Bankers.

£________________ ________________

Seen by me,

____

Inspector at the Clearing House. (690) 8/66—6000

Settlement at the Clearing House

BANK OF ENGLAND,

________________19

*The account of*________________________

has this evening been CREDITED *with the Sum of*________________

____

____

out of the money at the credit of the account of the Clearing Bankers.

For the Bank of England,

£________________ ________________

Fig. 43. Adjusting a banker's account at the Bank of England

These figures show quite clearly that all that is necessary for a complete settlement of all indebtedness is for Lloyds to receive from Barclays, National Westminster, and Coutts & Co. the amounts of £1m, £2m, and £2m respectively.

Idea No. 3. Since all banks have accounts with the Bank of England the safest and most convenient way for Barclays, National Westminster, and Coutts & Co. to settle their debts to Lloyds is to make a credit transfer for the amounts due to Lloyds' account at the Bank of England.

The Daily Settlement

The brilliant efficiency of the Clearing-House system can be seen if we consider what happens about 4.15 p.m. every day at the daily settlement meeting. A Clearing-House inspector receives the figures from the representatives of each clearing bank. Each has struck a Balance Sheet revealing his bank's net indebtedness to other banks as in Table 7. Of course in reality there are 6 clearing banks, but using Table 7 as a basis simplifies the discussion.

Perhaps £3,000 million has been paid by customers of the various banks to business houses and employees during the day. This is about the average daily clearing. Yet the final position shows that only £5 million needs to change hands. Over the course of any recent year, where clearings every day have been running at about £3,000 million, the net settlement has averaged about £75 million a day, or only 2·5 per cent.

When the position is clear, those banks due to receive funds make out a credit voucher like the one shown in Fig. 43. Those due to lose funds make out a debit voucher. These vouchers are then entered in the appropriate accounts at the Bank of England.

The representatives of the clearing banks report their positions to Head Office, where the top management compare the actual liquidity positions with their estimated figures. If liquidity has worsened for a particular bank, changes in loan and overdraft policies may have to be made to tighten credit, and the customer who seeks an overdraft in the weeks ahead may be met with a serious countenance and a shake of the head.

EXERCISES SET 16

(6) The Bank of England and the Control of the Banking System

1. Give an account of the work of the Bankers' Clearing House. What is its relationship to the clearing banks, and to the Bank of England?
(*University of London*)

2. Write short notes on three of the following: (*a*) the lender of last resort; (*b*) the bankers' bank; (*c*) current accounts; (*d*) The Government broker; (*e*) Legal tender; (*f*) The Friday tender.

3. Why is the Bank of England of such importance in the British monetary system? (*R.S.A.*)

4. Explain the terms 'Fiduciary Issue' and 'Bank of England Return'. What connection is there between them?

5. Once Britain's currency was backed by solid gold; now it is backed by gilt-edged securities. Explain.

6. In what ways are the joint-stock banks (*a*) connected with the central bank, (*b*) controlled by the central bank?   (*University of London*)

7. How does the Bank of England influence the credit policies of the commercial banks?

8. What is meant by 'open market operations'? How do they affect the lending policies of the banks?

9. Why is exchange control necessary? Who is responsible for operating the exchange controls, and how are they put into effect?

10. 'Gentlemen in top hats, walking down to Threadneedle Street at 2.30 p.m. to borrow money, having been forced into the bank.' Explain this sentence.

CHAPTER SIXTEEN

THE STOCK EXCHANGE

(1) Introduction

A stock exchange is a highly organized financial market where bonds, stocks and shares can be bought or sold. The London Stock Exchange is situated in Throgmorton Street within a few yards of the Bank of England, and at the centre of the financial affairs of the City of London. It is a respected and valued national institution, but it is not alone. There are independent groups of stock exchanges in other large cities, while members of the Provincial Brokers' Stock Exchange also carry on business in numerous smaller towns.

Stock-market business is world-wide, and New York, Johannesburg, Melbourne, Tokyo, Calcutta, Paris, Amsterdam, and Brussels are all famous centres of stock-exchange activity.

The function of a stock exchange is to put those who wish to sell stocks or shares in touch with those who wish to buy, so that investments can change hands in the quickest, cheapest, and fairest manner possible.

(2) Turning Fixed Capital into Cash—and Cash into Fixed Capital

When a member of the general public invests his savings by lending them to the managers of a company, he does not intend that the company shall have the use of his money for ever, for he does not know when fate may knock on his door and present him with problems. The investment as far as the investor is concerned is a purely temporary one, depending upon his good luck to some extent. If the fates are kind the investment may last for years; if the fates are unkind he, or his heirs, may wish to withdraw the investment in cash form, just like withdrawing money from a bank.

From the point of view of directors of the firm the matter is quite different. They regard the investment as a permanent one, for they spend the invested money on land and buildings, plant and machinery, transport, and other equipment. They cannot possibly return the money, for they no longer have it. They have turned it into assets, and in the process it has been 'fixed'. Fixed capital is capital tied up in fixed assets, which have been purchased for permanent use in the business. There is no point in the shareholder ringing up the secretary of the company to say that he has decided to reclaim his investment, and will call round for his

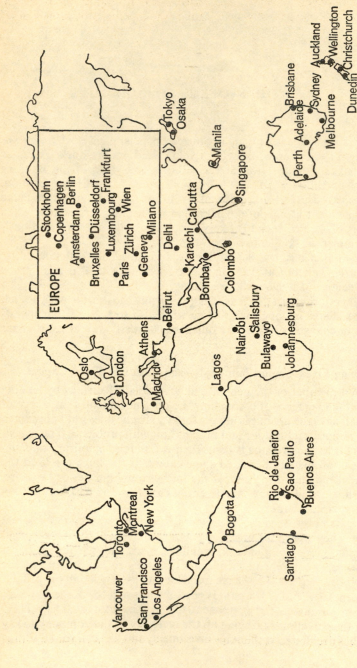

Fig. 44. A world-wide network of stock exchanges

share at 11 o'clock. The secretary has no way of 'liquefying' the fixed assets and will simply point out that the only way for the shareholder to

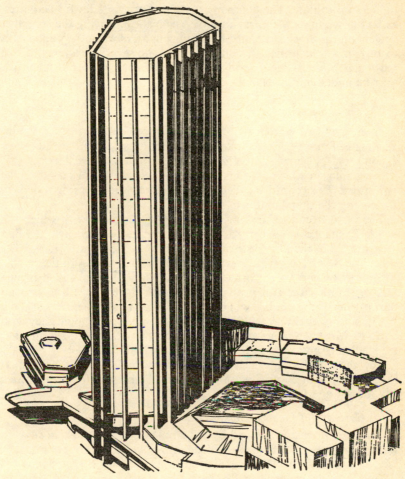

Fig. 45. *The new London Stock Exchange*

The original Stock Exchange building in London was constructed in 1801. Since then it has been rebuilt twice. The latest building, only just completed, provides the most up-to-date facilities for members. There is a tower block which provides excellent accommodation for many jobbing and broking firms, and the new market is more spacious and better equipped than any previous market.

get his money back is to sell the shares for what they will fetch in the market place.

This is what the Stock Exchange is: a market where those who wish to sell shares are able to contact those who wish to buy. The company whose shares are being bought and sold has little interest in the matter, but it will register the transfer of shares in order to keep its list of share-holders up to date. The company merely pursues its lawful activities, as laid down in its Memorandum of Association, leaving the specialist dealers on the Stock Exchange to arrange matters when the public wish to buy or sell securities. A company may, however, be interested if a particular buyer is acquiring large blocks of shares, since a take-over may be under consideration.

(3) Types of Security

A security is a written or printed document acknowledging the investment of money. The investor may merely loan the money in return for interest, or he may actually purchase a share in the enterprise that attracts him, in which case his reward is to share in the profits of the enterprise. This reward is called a **dividend,** because the profit is divided up among the shareholders.

The word 'securities' covers all kinds of investment with which the Stock Exchange is concerned. Generally speaking they are 'existing securities', i.e. they have already come into existence at some earlier date. The Stock Exchange does not itself issue new shares to the public. This function is often performed by specialist institutions called **Issuing Houses.** For a successful new issue, the Stock Exchange still has a vital part to play, for the public will be unwilling to buy the issue unless there is a guarantee that they will be able to sell them again should they wish to do so. Most new issues are therefore announced 'subject to permission to deal being given by the Stock Exchange Council'.

The main types of security are: (*a*) Government loans or bonds; (*b*) Municipal or local-Government loans or bonds; (*c*) Debentures; (*d*) Shares; and (*e*) Stocks.

(a) Government Loans or Bonds

These are documents issued by governments or public authorities in return for loans made to finance expenditures which are not at present to be met by taxation. 'War Loan' is an example, but similar loans are floated at regular intervals for peacetime purposes such as building power stations, docks and harbours, or road bridges. These securities pay a fixed rate of interest throughout their lives, and repayment is guaranteed by the Government. Such loans by British or Commonwealth Governments are called **gilt-edged securities**, because the original gilt-edged securities were recorded in a book that had gilt edges.

(b) Local Government Loans or Bonds

These are issued by local councils against the general security of the rates. Nearly all are issued to finance capital expenditure which the local authority wishes to afford now, but whose advantage will be enjoyed for several years. For instance, a municipal swimming bath will pay for itself in due course, so that this type of expenditure might justifiably be financed out of borrowing. The interest and repayments will be paid out of surplus receipts of the enterprise, after operating expenses have been paid. Such investments are very safe, and, although not quite 'gilt-edged', have **trustee status**. This means that they are so safe that they may be used by lawyers and others acting as executors of wills, who are investing trust-moneys on behalf of young persons not yet old enough to manage their own affairs. This type of investment is authorized by Section 1 of the Trustee Act, 1925.

(c) Debentures

Debentures are loans to a company. This type of security is issued to attract the more timid type of investor, because they offer almost as great security as a gilt-edged security. Timid old ladies who have been left money by their husbands traditionally buy debentures, which are secure both as to income and capital. The interest rate on a debenture is about 10 per cent these days, and after taxation earns about 6 per cent for the holder. Payment of this interest is made whether the company is making profits or not, for the money is essentially a *loan* to the company, not a *shareholding* in the company.

A simple or naked debenture carries no charge on the assets, but a mortgage debenture carries a mortgage on the assets of the company. This entitles the debenture holders to take over the assets charged and sell them should the provisions as to payment of interest and repayment of principal not be properly observed. A **Fixed Debenture** is secured on certain fixed assets, which are directly charged with the duty of repaying the debenture holders. It follows that these assets cannot be disposed of in any way by the directors without the permission of the debenture trustees. These trustees are appointed to represent the debenture holders, since it would be unrealistic to expect timid old ladies to understand what changes were taking place in a company's affairs. A **Floating Debenture** is not secured on particular fixed assets, but floats generally over the assets of a company, particularly the current assets. This type of security is best where a firm deals in huge quantities of valuable stock, but has little plant or machinery, and whose premises are not very valuable. For example, mail-order houses very often operate from premises that are not modern or well placed from the site-value point of view; yet their stocks may be enormously valuable. It would not be sensible to restrict the directors in dealing in such stocks, the sale of which is the source of the profits of the business. Instead, the floating debenture floats over the assets, and only 'crystallizes' into solid control when the directors fail to honour their bargain by not paying the interest or repaying the principal.

(d) Shares

These are documents which acknowledge investment in a company. There are many types of share, which are dealt with elsewhere in this book. The various classes are designed to attract different classes of investor (see page 25).

(e) Stock

Stock is shares that have been consolidated into one block. Every share is an individual unit which has been paid for by the shareholder. It must be transferred in one piece from one owner to the next. When

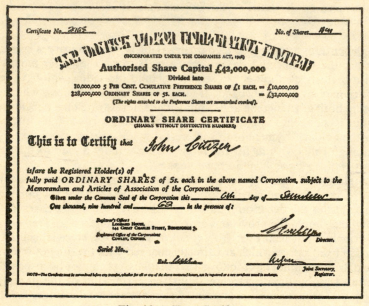

Fig. 46. A Share Certificate

shares have been paid for in full, the total number of shares can be consolidated into stock. This has certain advantages to the firm trying to keep a record of transfers. For instance if 1,000 shares are transferred from Mr. A to Mr. B the share certificate issued to Mr. B may need 1,000 serial numbers written on to it. This takes a great deal of time. If the shares have been consolidated into stock, only the monetary value needs to be recorded on the Stock Certificate.

There is really no difference at all between shares and stock today.

(4) Who owns Stocks, Shares, and Debentures?

Even in these days of high taxation and high death duties, there are still some rich people left. Many people consider that the Stock Exchange is a place where millionaries buy and sell investments in order to make quick profits at the expense of the general public. If this ever was true it is certainly not true today, for the Stock Exchange Council makes very strict regulations about manipulating the market, and disciplines dealers who engage in sharp practices. We are today a property-owning democracy; the decline in the number of rich people has been more than balanced by an increasing number of middle-class and lower-middle-class citizens, of whom about $2\frac{1}{2}$ million actually own some shares directly. About 22 million people, nearly half the population, own shares indirectly by investing money in savings banks, building societies, pensions funds, and insurance companies. The other half of the population are wives and children of the half who invest in these ways, so that practically everyone in the country is either directly or indirectly involved in the work of the Stock Exchange. At some time or other one of our representatives, a banker or insurance agent possibly, will ask his broker to sell shares on our behalf. Every time we pay insurance money someone will buy shares on our behalf.

Some of the biggest direct investors who use the Stock Exchange are listed below:

Pension and other Trust Funds	Building Societies
The National Insurance Fund	The National Savings Bank
Trade Unions	Trustee Savings Banks
Banks	Collecting Societies
Insurance Companies	Provident and Industrial Societies
Investment Trusts	Co-operative Societies
Unit Trusts	Friendly Societies

If you have money in any of these organizations, if you pay insurance on a motor vehicle, or if you save to get married, or to buy a house, the money you invest will be used to buy shares on the Stock Exchange. When eventually you need money to buy the house, to pay the wedding expenses, or to repair a damaged motor vehicle, the investor who has been saving for you will pay you back again, possibly disposing of some shares in order to make funds available.

(5) Buying and Selling Securities—a Highly Organized Market

The investor who wishes to purchase stocks or shares must approach a stockbroker who will undertake the purchase for him. The Stock Exchange is another type of highly organized market, already referred to in the chapter on Markets (see page 102). Only experts may deal on such markets, for the ordinary member of the public would not know the procedures to be followed, and would almost certainly make a bad bargain. Only the expert with experience of the market can judge what is a fair price for a share.

There are two classes of experts: brokers and jobbers who are also known as dealers. The **broker** buys and sells shares on behalf of the general public, or he may deal on his own account. When acting for the public he is an agent employed to buy and sell at the best price obtainable. Brokers are paid by the client according to a fixed scale of charges, usually 1¼ per cent or 0·0125 in the £. Brokers also give their clients advice in connection with investment affairs. They are forbidden to advertise.

Brokers execute their clients' orders by dealing with the **jobbers.** The jobber is a wholesaler of stocks and shares. A broker wishing to sell shares on behalf of a client will sell them at a fair price to the jobber who will add them to his store of securities. A broker wishing to buy shares on behalf of a client will obtain them from the jobber at a fair price. The difference between the jobber's buying price and the price at which he sells is the 'jobber's turn' (see page 222). As the market is highly competitive, it is unlikely that the profit will be excessive, especially when the risks of loss are taken into account.

Because the Stock Exchange today lists more than 9,100 different securities, jobbers cannot be expert dealers in them all. A jobber or firm of jobbers will concentrate on certain classes of shares and make a special study of them. There are always a number of jobbers dealing in each group of securities; they compete for the business brought to them by brokers, and so a competitive 'market' is created.

Often jobbers who deal in the same types of shares will stand close to one another on one part of the floor of the Stock Exchange. Thus all those who deal in Government and similar stocks will be found in the 'gilt-edged' market; and the dealers in the shares of manufacturing companies will be found grouped together in an area known as the 'Industrials' market. However, this does not always happen, and the jobbers in the bank, shipping, oil, property, and brewery shares are scattered about the floor of the Stock Exchange. It is the existence of this competitive market which ensures that the public gets a fair price for shares sold on the Exchange.

This type of highly organized market does not develop overnight. An unbroken succession of business activity since the seventeenth century has developed the customs, rules, and controlling Council of the Stock Exchange, ensuring that the public's affairs will be conducted efficiently, cheaply, and quickly.

(6) How a Bargain is Struck

As in any market a deal takes place only when the price is right. If one party thinks the price wrong he will hesitate, and if the other senses this hesitation in any way he will alter the price if he thinks he can still make a profit by doing so, or if he thinks he should cut his losses by selling at once. If he has quoted a rock-bottom price anyway he will not lower it further. As prices on the Stock Exchange vary with world

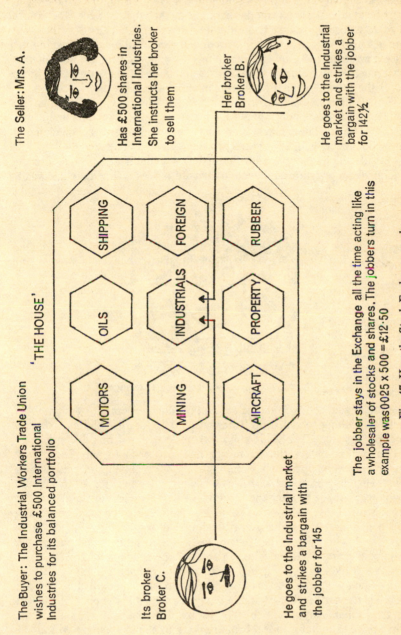

The Seller: Mrs. A.

Has £500 shares in International Industries. She instructs her broker to sell them

Her broker Broker B.

He goes to the Industrial market and strikes a bargain with the jobber for 142½

The Buyer: The Industrial Workers Trade Union wishes to purchase £500 International Industries for its balanced portfolio

'THE HOUSE'

SHIPPING FOREIGN RUBBER
OILS INDUSTRIALS PROPERTY
MOTORS MINING AIRCRAFT

Its broker Broker C.

He goes to the Industrial market and strikes a bargain with the jobber for 145

The jobber stays in the Exchange all the time acting like a wholesaler of stocks and shares. The jobbers turn in this example was 0·025 × 500 = £12·50

Fig. 47. How the Stock Exchange works

business activity, the brokers and jobbers are continually balancing in their heads the business trends throughout the world. Success or failure of firms whose shares are being dealt with, or of other firms in the same line of business; wars and rumours of wars; natural disasters; economic crises; government activities restricting or encouraging the flow of raw materials, manufactured goods or capital around the world; all these affect the present value of a share on the market.

Fig. 47 illustrates how the system works. The floor of the house, to which only brokers and jobbers have access, is shown with some of the main 'markets'. These markets consist of groups of jobbers, specializing in particular fields, and prepared to buy or sell as required.

Outside the Exchange, but of course free to enter at any time, are the stockbrokers operating from their private offices where they are avail-

"MY WORD IS MY BOND"
Fig. 48. The Motto of the Stock Exchange

able for advice and help to the general public. A member of the public, Mrs. A, wishing to sell £500 'International Industries' shares, asks her stockbroker to act for her in selling them at the best possible price.

The broker enters the Exchange and proceeds to the 'Industrial' market where he approaches one of the jobbers dealing in this type of share. He may not reveal whether he is a buyer or a seller, for this would enable the jobber to vary the price to suit the transaction and make it more profitable to himself. The jobber now quotes two prices, using new pence as the basic unit and fractions down to $\frac{1}{16}$th—say $142\frac{1}{2}$ to 145. The lower price is the 'bid' price at which he is prepared to buy. The upper price is the 'offer' price at which he is prepared to sell. Since Mrs. A's broker is trying to sell shares, he may reply 'I'll sell you 500 at $142\frac{1}{2}$'. Each will then make a note of the bargain struck in his 'bargain book'. If the broker feels that a better price than $142\frac{1}{2}$ is possible he will ask the jobber 'Anything else'. The jobber may then say $141\frac{7}{8}$. This is a worse price than before for a broker trying to sell shares. He will therefore move on to another jobber, looking for a better bargain. In this example we will pretend he is satisfied with 142½ and sells at that figure.

When a bargain has been struck a note is made of it in the 'bargain books' of the jobber and broker. Having agreed to deal at this price a jobber will always honour his bargain, for the proud motto of the Stock Exchange is '*Dictum Meum Pactum—*My Word is my Bond'. (A bond

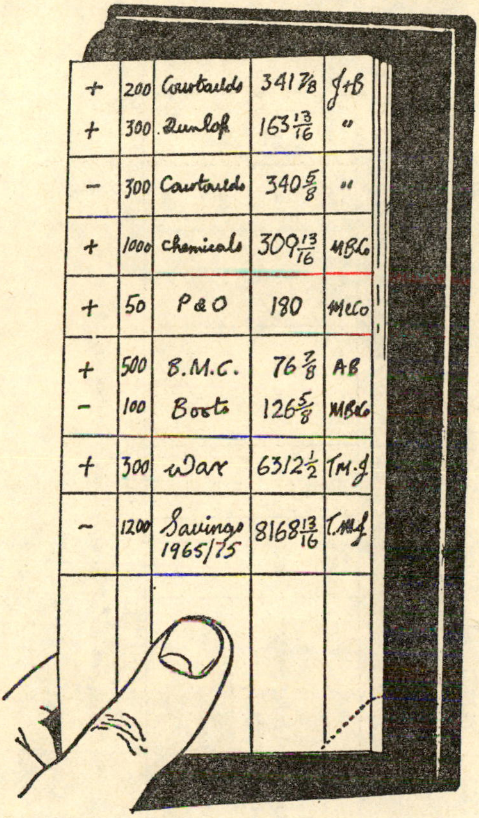

Fig. 49. A typical page from a 'Bargain Book'

is a written promise to do something. Some promises are only enforceable by law if they are in writing. An oral promise by a broker or jobber is as good as if it were in writing.)

(7) Why the Prices Fluctuate

The jobber described in the last illustration has just brought 500 shares in International Industries. Perhaps he needs some of these shares anyway to honour earlier bargains in which he was a seller. Alternatively

ANOTHER BROKER & CO.
Stock & Share Brokers

A. B. JONES　E. F. JONES
C. D. SMITH　G. H. SMITH

TELEPHONE: 01-888 88888
TELEGRAMS: BROTHER LONDONEC2.

Sold
by Order &
for Account of

Mrs A.

99 Throgmorton Street,
(AND STOCK EXCHANGE)
London E.C.2. 8th Sept. 19..

Subject to the rules and regulations of The Stock Exchange, London

Stock or Share	Stock Code	Price	Consideration	Transfer Stamps	Transfer Fees	Contract Stamp	Comm. Rate	Commission	Balance Due
500 International Industries Ltd £1 Ordinary Shares	909090	£1·42½	£712·50	-	-	0·15	1¼%	8·91	703·44

For Settlement 26th September, 19..

ANOTHER BROKER & CO.

CONTRACT
STAMP
0·15

MEMBERS OF THE STOCK EXCHANGE, LONDON

CAPITAL GAINS TAX.
THIS CONTRACT NOTE SHOULD BE RETAINED IN A SAFE PLACE TO SUPPORT POSSIBLE FUTURE TAX RETURNS.

E. & O. E.

Fig. 50. A Contract Note

this may be the fourth broker in succession that has sold him some of these shares. The jobber may wonder what is happening to International Industries. Has an adverse business or political movement developed? He will have to prevent too many of these shares being unloaded on to himself. The best way to do this is to lower his prices. The next inquiry by a broker may be greeted with the price $140\frac{5}{8}$–$143\frac{1}{8}$. If the broker buys 500 at $143\frac{1}{8}$ the jobber will have disposed of the 500 at only $\frac{5}{8}$p more than he paid for them, but he will feel happier about the shares he already holds. Evidently there are buyers about, so it is unlikely that any bad news affecting that class of share is generally known.

To operate successfully a jobber must try to balance what he buys with what he sells, so that at the end of an account period he can honour the bargains he has struck.

(8) The Contract Note

To continue with Fig. 47, Broker B now notifies Mrs. A that he has sold the shares by sending her a **Contract Note.**

This tells Mrs. A the following facts:

(*a*) That she has sold 500 shares in International Industries.

(*b*) The price at which the shares were sold, which is $142\frac{1}{2}$ making a total value of 712·50.

(*c*) The broker's commission, which varies with the value of the total transaction. This is $1\frac{1}{4}$ per cent or 1·25 pence in the £, which is the minimum commission on transactions, in shares as fixed under the rules of the Stock Exchange. For transactions under £100 a minimum charge of £2·00 is made, and for transactions between £100 and £320 the minimum charge is £4·00. Above £320 the $1\frac{1}{4}$ per cent rule applies.

(*d*) Mrs. A will also be charged for a Contract Stamp, which is a government duty on the Contract Note. No duty is payable for transactions up to £100 and 0·10 on transactions from £100 to £500. After that it rises in proportion. A buyer would also have to pay for a Transfer Stamp, which is a Government duty of 1 per cent on the value of the transaction, and possibly a Transfer Charge of $0·12\frac{1}{2}$, to the company which is put to the trouble of registering the transfer. The practice of charging for transfers is gradually dying out under pressure from the Stock Exchange Council. Mrs. A does not have to meet these charges because she is the seller.

(*e*) Finally the Contract Note notifies Mrs. A of the net amount she is due to receive from the broker for the sale of her shares, and the date of settlement. This is the date on which he will pay Mrs. A, provided that she surrenders the shares after signing the Transfer Form enclosed.

Mrs. A now checks the Contract Note and if she is satisfied returns the Transfer Form with the Share Certificates she no longer owns. Her broker will deliver them to the new owner, and pay her on settlement day.

(9) Who is the New Owner?

In the simple case chosen for Fig. 47 the new owner is an institutional investor, The Industrial Workers' Trade Union. This union has collected subscriptions from its members which will eventually be used for such purposes as the support of aged members living on inadequate pensions, the provision of convalescent homes for sick members, strike pay in the event of an industrial dispute, and so on. This union wishes to invest the subscriptions where they will be reasonably safe and at the same time profitable.

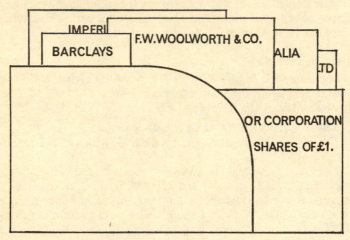

Fig. 51. A 'balanced portfolio" of investments

Since high profitability and maximum safety do not go together, the Union will invest in a 'balanced portfolio'. This is a collection of shares and stock of different types. Some gilt-edged securities, some 'blue chips' (sound, top-quality, industrial shares), some debentures, some rather risky (but often very profitable) shares in finance companies, etc. As part of its portfolio it instructs Broker C to purchase 500 shares in International Industries. Broker C approaches the jobber who has just bought Mrs. A's shares and on hearing the prices $142\frac{1}{2}$–145 says 'I will buy 500 at 145'. The jobber has made a turn of 0·025 on the shares, yielding him a profit of 12·50. The market has performed its function and all parties, Mrs. A, Broker B, the jobber, Broker C, and the Industrial Workers' Trade Union are happy with the arrangements.

(10) The Stock Exchange 'Zoo'—Bulls, Bears, and Stags

There are only two classes of member on the Stock Exchange: brokers and jobbers. Brokers act for the general public, or for the institutional buyers and sellers. Jobbers act for themselves, buying shares when there appear to be bargains about, and selling shares when it appears likely that they will fall in price. Outsiders may also act in this way, and anyone who does so is said to be a speculator. To speculate is to let one's mind wander around a situation trying to predict what will happen. A speculator is a person who backs the judgments he makes about likely developments by buying or selling shares, or other valuable commodities. Speculators operate on all markets, but on the Stock Exchange it is securities they are dealing in. The chief varieties of speculator on the Stock Exchange are known as 'bulls', 'bears', and 'stags'.

Bulls are speculators who take an optimistic view of business trends. When the market is 'bullish' the dealers are expecting prices to rise. In these circumstances it is a good thing to hold securities, because if the prices rise one will be able to get more for them. Bulls therefore step in and buy, even if they have no money. Since dealings are usually not for cash, but for the 'account', i.e. payable at the end of the accounting period in about a fortnight's time, a bull who buys now and sells before settlement day will not need to provide any money but will collect a profit on the shares he bought low and sold higher. If the expected price rise does not come, the bull may find himself having to sell at a loss, or pay up for the shares and hold them over to the next period. This is explained more fully later.

Bears are pessimistic speculators who expect a fall in share prices. They therefore sell any shares they have now, and even shares they do not have, because, if prices fall as expected, the shares will be available in a few hours or a few days at lower prices than at present. Suppose a bear has 500 industrial shares and sells them at 104. In half an hour he buys them back at 101. He now has exactly the same shares he had before but he also has $500 \times 0.030 = £15$ profit. Nothing to be gloomy about there. Suppose he did not have any shares to sell. He still sells 500 shares at £1·040 and buys them back at £1·010. He now has them to hand over to the buyer when required and he has £15 profit as well. It sounds profitable, but in fact he ran a risk. Suppose the shares had risen. He would have had to honour his obligation by buying shares at say, 107, to give to the buyer who is paying only £1·040. The loss of £15 would be rather sad for him. That is when a bear really does feel gloomy. The speculator backs his judgment, but he needs to be wealthy if he is going to weather the storms when his expectations are disappointed.

Stags are speculators who operate in the 'New Issues' market rather than on the Stock Exchange, although they must use the Stock Exchange before they can realize any profit. What a stag does is to apply for shares that are just being issued and are likely to be over-subscribed. He does not want to keep the shares, or invest in the company that is issuing them, but simply to make a profit out of the issue. The activities of 'stags' have been greatly reduced in recent years but in order to explain them we must look at a rather old-fashioned situation, when shares were issued for a small deposit called 'application money'.

Suppose the Magnificent Oil Co. is isuing four million extra shares at £1 each, payable at ten pence on application and another ten pence on allotment, 40 pence on First Call and 40 pence on Final Call. Since oil shares are very popular there is an excellent chance the issue will be over-subscribed, and many disappointed applicants will probably apply to their brokers to buy them some shares on the Stock Exchange. Mr. C, a small investor, applies for 50 shares. Mr. Stag applies for 10,000 shares. The directors decide that they will only accept the applications of people asking for 500 shares or more. This reduces the work of issuing the shares. Mr. C gets no shares, but Mr. Stag is allotted 10,000 shares which he does not really want, or intend to keep. Since demand is strong the price of these shares rises on the Stock Exchange and Mr C buys 50 of them from Mr. Stag.

There are a number of reasons why stags are less active in recent years than formerly. One is that there is something morally repugnant about a person who does not really want a share in a company being allowed to get one when his application robs poorer, but genuinely interested, small investors from securing a share in the company that attracts them. Another reason is that, in any case, the number of public issues where stags can operate is reduced with the growing influence of the institutional investor (see page 238). Many new issues of capital are not offered to the public in the traditional way which is expensive, but are 'placed'. This means that the issuing houses approach large institutional investors who are always on the look-out for sound investments at fair prices, and ask them to buy the shares. If ten of these big investors take up one-tenth of the shares each, the capital can be raised without expensive advertising and cumbersome clerical work.

The issue of shares by 'tender' is a method which eliminates the 'stag', and makes his former profits available as a premium on shares to the company that is expanding. Suppose the shares are £1 shares. The application form invites the prospective shareholder to tender for the shares by filling in, on the form, the price he is prepared to pay. The applicant who is extremely keen to become a shareholder will offer to buy at a premium, say £1·05 per share. By offering a higher price he makes sure of an allotment, and the company receives extra capital, instead of this profit being enjoyed by the 'stag'.

One final explanation of reduced stag activity is that the risk the stags run is less than it once was, and this is what makes their profits unfair. In years gone by the speculating stag was welcome because he reduced the chances that the issue would be unsuccessful. If he ordered 10,000 shares he stood the chance of not being able to sell them at once; he might have to pay up for them. This is no longer likely. Once again this is due to the presence of many large institutional investors who are always ready to buy, and keep the Stock Exchange busy. To prevent stag activity, 'tendering' and 'payments in full on application' have been introduced. By the latter system the 'stag' must find the full sum of money, not just a small part of it. This ties up his capital.

(11) How the Public Benefits from Speculation

What use is speculative activity to the ordinary member of the public who is not acting as a speculator himself? Suppose Mrs. Smith, whose husband has just died, urgently needs to sell 500 shares, but no one will buy them because the general public feel the firm she has invested in is not in too sound a position. Mrs. Smith could be in real difficulty. If a speculator steps in and buys the shares her problem will be solved. Of course he is only going to buy them at a price which he hopes will yield him a profit, so that Mrs. Smith will perhaps get rather less than she hoped for, but not very much less. This is because there are many speculators in competition with one another. If the price drops a little, one of them will snap up the shares Mrs. Smith is offering. It is really the presence of speculators that makes the whole market system work. Speculators buy when others are selling, and sell when others are buying, and make a little profit in the process. While doing so they render an invaluable service to small investors by smoothing out the 'booms' and 'slumps' in the market. This is made clear in Figs. 52 and 53.

At points *A* the public are buying and demanding the share. No one is willing to sell, so the price rises steeply.

At points *B* the public are losing confidence in the share. Prices are falling and a general lack of confidence may mean that the price will fall a long way.

If speculators were present they would begin to sell when the share prices rose, so as to make a profit while they could. This would stop the market rising so quickly, and would smooth off the boom. In the same way, as confidence declines and prices begin to slip, the speculator will start to buy—because the shares are cheaper and therefore are a bargain. The erratic prices shown in Fig. 52 are smoothed out as shown in Fig. 53.

The result of the speculators' activities is that prices have neither risen so high nor sunk so low as they would have done otherwise, and the investors therefore gain less in a boom, and lose less in a slump. The most important thing for the small investor is not to lose his money, so in fact the moderating action of the speculators safeguards the public interest.

(12) Sorting out the Transactions—the Fortnightly Account

With about 14,500 bargains every day, worth about £150 million, it is not surprising that a very confused picture exists before many days have gone by. Think again about Mrs. A's shares sold by her broker to the jobber mentioned on page 205, but this time, more realistically, they are bought and sold many times.

Mrs. Smith has given 500 shares to her broker, who has sold them to jobber B. Jobber B. resold them to broker C, who sold them to jobber D five minutes later. Jobber D sold them to broker E who, . . . etc. The shares are still with Mrs. A's broker, but they have been sold and resold hundreds of times. Sooner or later all these bargains must be settled. This is done on Account Day, which is the last day of the 'settlement period' that comes at the end of each Account Period.

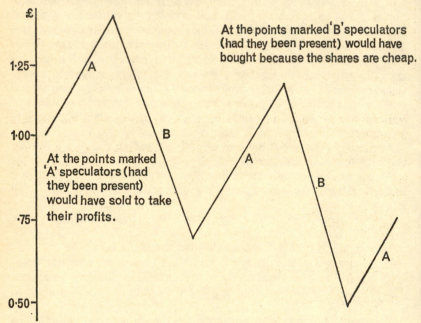

Violent movements in the shares of Jollyjourney Motors Ltd.

At the points marked 'B' speculators (had they been present) would have bought because the shares are cheap.

At the points marked 'A' speculators (had they been present) would have sold to take their profits.

Fig. 52. A market without speculators

The Stock Exchange year is normally made up of 25 **'Accounts'**, most of which last a fortnight. Two or three of these periods are extended to three weeks because public holidays (Christmas, Easter, etc.) interfere with the usual working of the market. By the end of the Account a very confused situation exists as to who owns which shares. Most of the shares dealt in are bought for settlement on Account Day, which means that payment will be made and the shares delivered to their new owner at the end of the accounting period. Some securities are 'brought for cash',

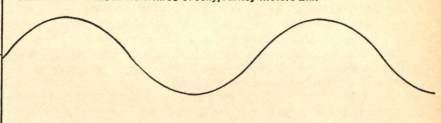

Since the speculators sell in booms and buy in slumps their activities reduce the erratic price movements to the benefit of the private investor.

Gentle fluctuations in the shares of Jollyjourney Motors Ltd.

Fig. 53. A market where speculators are at work, smoothing out the 'booms' and 'slumps'

which means payment to be made by cheque on the day after the bargain was struck.

At the end of a fortnightly Account, bargains cease for that period and a new dealing period commences at once. The oustanding transactions of the period just ended are cleared up in the 'settlement period', which is the next seven working days. These days are known as

Day 1: Contango Day
Day 2: Making-up Day
Day 3: Ticket Day
Day 4: ⎫
Day 5: ⎬ intermediate days
Day 6: ⎭
Day 7: Account Day

Contango Day and Making-up Day are the days when speculators can make arrangements to carry bargains over to the next accounting period. Jobbers or brokers who have been speculating and find that they are unable to fulfil their bargains may be either 'bulls' or 'bears'. The optimistic bulls have bought shares hoping to sell at a profit. The time has come to honour their bargains. They must pay up, or sell the shares to realize the money. If they feel very optimistic that further appreciation of the shares will take place in the next fortnight, they will be unwilling to sell the shares. An arrangement is made so that each bull can sell his shares at a fixed price and immediately buy them back again at the same price for the next Account.

Really he has borrowed the money for the next fortnight, and for this service pays a sum of money called a **contango** for the use of the cash provided by the dealer who 'took in' the shares for him. If all is well the appreciation of the shares in the next two weeks will leave him with a profit which will repay him for his trouble and the risk involved.

Meanwhile the pessimistic bears who were expecting prices to fall have sold shares (which they never really possessed), because they thought prices would fall and they could buy the shares before delivery date arrived at a cheaper price than that at which they had dealt. If they have been disappointed they now have the problem of delivering shares they do not possess. They will have to buy shares quickly, or borrow them for a fortnight. If there are bulls about anxious to sell, the bears may be able to buy; if not they will have to borrow shares and pay a charge called **backwardation** for the privilege.

On Ticket Day the buying brokers pass to the selling brokers the names of the eventual purchasers so that transfers may be arranged. When these transfers have been completed (on the intermediate days) the payments are made and the stock delivered on the seventh working day, which is the Tuesday of the second week after the Account closed. Meanwhile dealing has been pursued just as furiously as ever for the new Account, which will itself come to an end on the following Friday.

The whole settlement procedure is at present under discussion and may result, in the near future, in revised procedures and a slight change in the names of the days.

(13) What Service does the Stock Exchange render to the Investor?

(*a*) It enables the investor who wishes to buy stocks or shares to secure them at a 'fair' market price, i.e. the price that is generally believed to be the proper value of that share on that day.

(*b*) It enable the investor who wishes to have money instead of shares to sell his share at a 'fair' price for that share on that day.

(*c*) It protects the investor from sharp practices and unscrupulous operators by establishing a code of conduct which ensures fair play between the public and the operators on the market. It does not hesitate to discipline those who use its facilities and fail to follow its code.

(*d*) It rigorously scrutinizes companies which apply for a 'quotation'. Before their shares can be bought and sold on the Exchange, the Council will check that the assets and profits represent a worthwhile investment, and that its directors and officials are not undesirable people.

(*e*) It runs its own compensation fund, contributed by the members, so that where a firm is unable to honour its bargains and is 'hammered', the clients of the defaulting firm are protected.

(14) What Service does the Stock Exchange render the General Public?

(*a*) Without knowing it, nearly every member of the public is an investor through the institutional investors such as pension funds, trade unions, insurance companies, and building societies. As such the general public benefit in the same way as investors shown in Section 13 above.

(*b*) The Stock Exchange promotes the general prosperity of the nation, by providing the market which tempts us all to save, confident in the knowledge that savings invested in a government or industrial stock can be reclaimed at very short notice, if needed, by selling on the Exchange. Houses, factories, hospitals, and schools are built with these savings to promote the prosperity of all. Every year on average £2,000 million is collected in this way. The companies whose shares are dealt with on the Stock Exchange control over 80 per cent of all Britain's industry and commerce and employ the bulk of the population.

(*c*) Government activity of many sorts depend upon funds raised by the sale of securities. These funds would not be available if the Stock Exchange did not provide the market for the securities purchased. The nationalized industries and the great welfare activities of Government departments would be seriously impaired if these funds were not provided. Over £23,000 million pounds worth of Government and local government stock is marketed through the Stock Exchange in Great Britain alone.

(*d*) The private citizen is vitally affected by the activities of the Stock Exchange. Not only does his employment, housing, insurance, social welfare, and entertainment almost entirely depend upon funds made available through the stock market, but also the cheapness and abundance of the goods and services depends upon the large-scale enterprises which produce them, as explained in Chapter 1 on Production. Without large-scale industry, goods would be less plentiful and more expensive; so our standard of living is drastically affected by what jobbers and brokers do on the floor of 'the House'.

(*e*) Valuations have to be placed upon the assets of both private persons and firms at certain times. For instance at death the estate of the dead person has to be valued for tax purposes and in order to share up the inheritance as laid down in the will of the deceased person. With businesses it is often necessary to value the assets, for instance when the business changes hands. On these occasions a problem of valuation affecting shares owned by the deceased person, or by the business concerned, may have to be solved by using the Stock Exchange prices on the day of death, or the day of transfer of ownership.

(15) A Glossary of Stock-Exchange Terms

ACCOUNT—The period during which dealings take place, before a reckoning is made and securities are transferred for payment to their new owner. There are usually 23 fortnightly Accounts and two three-weekly Accounts.

BACKWARDATION—A charge made to a 'bear' for the use of shares to enable him to escape from his unsatisfactory position, by carrying his debts for shares he is unable to buy at present over to the next Account.

BANK RATE—The rate formerly charged by the Bank of England on loans to the discount market. It controlled all other rates of interest charged by banks throughout the country (see *Minimum Lending Rate*).

BEAR—A speculator who, believing share prices will fall in the near future, sells shares with the idea of buying them back more cheaply.

BEARER SECURITIES—Securities that can be transferred by mere delivery—without a transfer form being made out or the transfer being registered by the company that issued the shares.

BLUE CHIPS—High-class industrial shares of great reliability.

BOND—A security issued by a government, nationalized corporation or a company, which carries a fixed rate of interest to the holder. Company bonds are called *Debentures*.

BONUS ISSUE—An extra share issued to existing shareholders to capitalize reserves which have been built up over the years. It does not mean the shareholder is better off, but the capital structure is regularized.

BROKER—A member of the Stock Exchange who acts as an agent, buying and selling for his clients.

BULL—Someone who believes prices will rise and rushes in to buy shares with a view to selling them again at a higher price.

CALL OPTION—An option to buy shares at a future date at an agreed price, whatever happens to the market.

CAPITAL—The total of the financial resources of a company.

CAPITAL RESERVES—Reserves created by some extraordinary activity of a company, the most common types are profits prior to incorporation, premiums on Preference Shares, premiums on Debentures, and reserves created by revaluation of property.

CAPITALIZATION—The process of changing reserves into capital by a *bonus issue* (q.v.). When a company has built up reserves by a careful dividend policy, or has created capital reserves by revaluing assets at a higher figure, the reserves may or may not be available for distribution as a dividend in future years. If this is impossible, because the reserves have not been retained in cash form but have been used to buy more fixed assets, bonus shares are used to capitalize the reserves and recognize formally that the reserves concerned are no longer available as possible dividend. It should be noted that a bonus issue does *not* increase the value of the shareholder's holding.

COMMISSION—The reward earned by brokers for acting as agents in the purchase or sale of shares. The scale is fixed by the Stock Exchange Council.

CONTANGO—The amount paid by bulls who wish to carry the purchase of shares over to the next Account because the rise they hoped for has not materialized.

CUM DIV.—Literally, 'together with dividend'. Shares which are sold along with the dividend due on them are said to be *Cum Div*. Part of the purchase price will be an element of compensation for the dividend due to the previous holder of the shares, which will now be enjoyed by the buyer.

DAILY LIST—A list issued officially by the Stock Exchange showing quotations for about 9,500 stocks and other securities valued at over £120,000 million.

DEBENTURE—A fixed-interest bond issued by a company.

DEFERRED SHARES—also called FOUNDER'S SHARES—These are shares issued to the original creator of a firm who sells out to a company. To agree to be paid partly in these shares is a sign that the vendor has confidence in the business he is selling, since he agrees to defer any dividend due to him until the other shareholders have had a reasonable dividend—say 8 per cent. The deferred shareholders may then be entitled to all or a substantial part of the remaining profit the exact terms being set out in the memorandum or articles of association.

DIFFERENTIAL OPPORTUNITY—This is the result of poor communications between markets. Supposing the broker knew that the price of a share in Glasgow was less than in London, he could acquire them for his client more reasonably by buying there, and taking advantage of the opportunity offered him by the difference in price. Within the British Isles communications are so good that differential opportunities rarely occur. These activities are often called *arbitrage* activities.

DIRECTOR—A member of the governing board of a company whose duties and powers are laid down in the Companies Acts of 1948 and 1967.

DIVIDEND—That portion of a company's profits or revenue reserves which the directors recommend and the Annual General Meeting approves as the sum to be distributed to the shareholders. It is usually expressed as a percentage of the nominal value of the shares.

EQUITY—The name given to the ordinary capital of a company, since every share gets an *equal* division of the profit. In common language, Equities have come to be thought of as 'risk' shares, since they also carry the losses if the company goes through bad times. Timid investors should not buy Equity shares.

EX DIV.—(see also *Cum Div.*) When shares are sold *Ex Div.* the purchaser will not receive the dividend, which will be enjoyed by the previous owner. The situation arises three weeks before dividend date, when a public announcement is made that for dividend purposes transfers will cease. This gives the company secretary's staff a chance to prepare dividend warrants. The shares will adjust in value on the Stock Exchange, because part of the purchase price previously has been payment for the dividend the seller will now receive. After the announcement the price falls to a fair one taking into account that the purchaser will now effectively *lose* 21 days' interest on his money.

FOUNDER'S SHARES—See *Deferred Shares.*

GILT-EDGED—The securities issued by the British Government, the State-owned companies, and the Commonwealth Governments. Absolute security is supposed to attach to gilt-edged securities, but in the last 25 years erosion of the investment has occurred owing to inflation. The £100 repaid when the security is redeemed may not be as valuable as the £100 contributed by the investor at the start of the transaction.

'THE HOUSE'—The Stock Exchange itself.

INVESTMENT TRUSTS—A type of institutional investor. These firms specialize in balanced portfolios of shares designed to give reasonable yields with maximum safety. They are of particular benefit to investors who have not sufficient expert experience of the Stock Market themselves.

ISSUING HOUSE—A banking house specializing in launching new issues.

JOBBERS—Are 'stallholders' in the market, buying shares from, and selling shares to, brokers acting on behalf of the public. They may have no contact with the public, but deal only with brokers, or one another.

MARKET—Sometimes used for the whole floor of 'the House' but also for a particular section of it, e.g. Property market, etc. The market is often described as 'bullish', 'bearish', 'patchy', 'easier', 'brighter'.

MARKET PRICE—The price at which shares actually changed hands. For valuation purposes 'average market price' on a certain day is often used, since a day's bargaining may vary in market price throughout the day.

MINIMUM LENDING RATE—The rate of interest charged by the Bank of England for discounting first class bills of exchange. It replaced Bank Rate in October, 1972. It is found by rounding up the previous Friday's Treasury Bill rate to the nearest $\frac{1}{4}$ per cent, and then adding $\frac{1}{2}$ per cent. (e.g. Treasury Bill rate 10·71—minimum lending rate 10·75 + 0·5 = 11·25 per cent).

NOMINAL PRICE—The par value of a share given to it on its issuing day. This nominal value is retained throughout the life of the share but its actual value varies with the supply and demand, and the extent to which profits have been ploughed back since the share was issued.

OFFER FOR SALE—An announcement by an issuing house of shares for sale. It contains the same information as a Prospectus (see page 24), but usually refers to a smaller company.

OPTION—See *Call Option* and *Put Option*.

ORDINARY SHARES—See *Equity*.

PAR VALUE—The nominal value of a share. If a share is 'at par' it means that its market price is the same as its nominal value.

PLACING—A system of issuing shares by asking institutional investors to buy up the extra issue. It is cheaper than the usual way of issuing shares and is often helpful to the institutional investors who are glad to purchase shares in reliable businesses.

PORTFOLIO—A collection of securities by one investor or institution.

PREFERENCE SHARES—Shares with a prior right over Ordinary Shares to receive a dividend up to a certain fixed figure.

PREMIUM—Money paid in excess of the par value of a newly issued share for the privilege of entering a well established firm. Also used at any time to describe a share which is available at a price higher than the par value.

PRICE/EARNING RATIO—(often called P/E RATIO)—The ratio of the price paid for a share to the profits of the firm after paying Corporation Tax and prior charges (i.e. preference-share dividend). It calculates for the investor the true return on his investment, but it may not all be returned to him as dividend. This will depend on the directors' policy. Reserves will be enjoyed as capital appreciation.

PUT OPTION—An option to sell shares at a future date at an agreed price, whatever happens to the market.

QUOTATION—The price range, fixed by the Market each day, within which the Market is prepared to deal on that day. The Quotation is published in *The Stock Exchange Daily Official List*. In order to obtain a Quotation for its securities a Company must make application to The Stock Exchange Council, through a member firm, and comply with the requirements contained in the booklet *Admission of Securities to Quotation* issued by authority of the Committee of the Federation of Stock Exchanges in Great Britain and Ireland.

REVENUE RESERVES—Reserves created by ploughing back profits into the business. They may be either *Special Reserves* for particular purposes, e.g. Plant-replacement Reserve, or *General Reserves* whose main purpose is the equalization of dividends as between good and bad years.

RIGHTS ISSUE—These are new shares offered to an existing shareholder at a more favourable price than they will be offered to the general public. For instance, if a £1 share is to be sold at a premium at £1·50, the existing shareholders would be given a right to buy them at £1. If the shareholder wishes to do so he may sell his right for 0·50 through his broker, after filling in the renunciation-of-rights section on the letter of allotment.

SHARE CERTIFICATE—The legal document issued to a shareholder certifying ownership of a part of the company concerned.

STAG—A speculator who applies for shares in a new issue with the intention of selling them at once on the Stock Exchange should they be over-subscribed and therefore in strong demand.

TAKE-OVER BID—An offer addressed to the shareholders of a company by an individual or firm to buy their shares at a named price above the present market price with a view to securing control of the company.

TAKE-OVER CODE—A code of conduct drawn up by the City Working Party on Take-overs and Mergers, a body representative of the various elements in the City interested in the securities industry, at the suggestion of the Bank of England. In consultation with the City Working Party, the Panel on Take-overs and Mergers (with a full-time executive staff) has been set up to supervise the code, and ensure that its general principles are understood, and its rules, and even the spirit behind the rules, observed.

TENDERS—A way of selling shares to the highest bidder. In some new issues the interested public are invited to put in a tender for the shares they require. Suppose a £1 share is on offer. The application form would include the phrase 'I wish to purchase . . . shares at a price of . . .'. A shareholder who is very keen to secure the shares might insert the price he is prepared to go to, say £1·15. If the directors accept this offer he

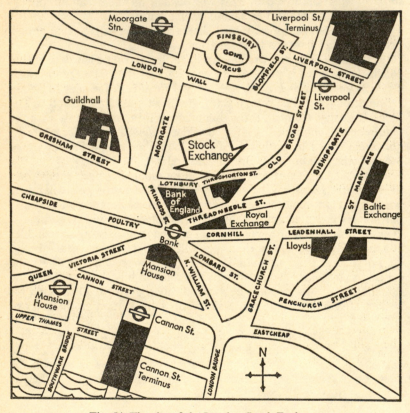

Fig. 54. The site of the London Stock Exchange

will pay the price he suggested. It is a way of reducing stag activities; the profits do not go to the stag but to the company as a premium on shares.

TIMES COVERED—A term used to denote how many times the dividend actually paid out to shareholders was covered by the net profits earned. The rest is retained as reserves.

TURN—The jobber's 'turn' is the profit margin he hopes to earn. It is the difference between his 'bid' price and his 'offer' price, although of course his prices are changing with supply and demand.

UNDERWRITERS—Men who, for a consideration, insure the issue of new shares by agreeing to buy what the public does not buy. Under the Companies Acts any Issuing House whose issue does not reach a certain minimum level must return the funds collected to the applicants. The minimum set is the amount required to ensure a successful start upon the proposed project. To avoid this disappointment directors underwrite the issue so that they are sure to be able to start the project.

UNIT TRUSTS—Like investment trusts, these institutions offer participation in a balanced portfolio to members of the public who are not themselves willing to run the risks entailed in buying and selling shares. By buying 'units' at quite small values, say £0·25, the small investor subscribes his funds into a pool which the unit-trust managers then employ to purchase a balanced portfolio of shares. The return to the investor comes partly in dividends, and partly in the appreciation of his units should he decide to sell them for cash.

YIELD—The true return to an investor on his investment. Consider a £1 share bought at par and on which a dividend of 5 per cent is declared. The yield is 5 per cent. Suppose it was bought for £3, i.e. at a great premium. The dividend of 5 per cent is really only 1⅔ per cent on the actual sum invested. The rule for calculating yields is

$$\frac{\text{par value}}{\text{market price}} \times \text{rate of dividend per cent.}$$

(16) How to see the Stock Exchange at Work

For anyone who can possibly do so, it is a good idea to visit the Stock Exchange in London. The visitors' gallery is at No. 8 Throgmorton Street, and is open from Monday to Friday from 10 a.m. to 3.15 p.m. Admission is free. Guides are in attendance and colour films are shown at regular intervals. Parties of up to 30 can reserve seats by writing to the Public Relations Officer, The Stock Exchange, London, E.C.2. A full visit takes about three-quarters of an hour.

(17) A Page to Test You on the Stock Exchange

Answer	Question
—	1. What is the Stock Exchange?
1. It is the market where existing shares are bought and sold.	2. Who would normally deal with the issue of new shares?
2. The Issuing Houses. These are specialists—often merchant bankers—who underwrite the issues.	3. What type of market is the Stock Exchange?
3. A highly organized market: only specialists may buy and sell: the general public are not admitted.	4. What are these specialists called?
4. Jobbers and brokers.	5. Describe the life of a jobber.
5. (a) He specializes in one class of share, e.g. oils. (b) He stays in the exchange. (c) He quotes prices for his shares like 'Standard Oil, 2·30½/2·32¾ (the lower price is his buying price, the higher one is his selling price).	6. What does the broker do?
6. (a) He meets the general public who have shares to buy and sell. (b) He goes into the Exchange and asks the jobber for a price. When he finds a suitable jobber he buys (or sells) shares on behalf of his clients.	7. Is there ever a time when no one is buying and selling?
7. Never, because: (a) Fate knocks on someone's door every day, forcing him to sell shares to raise the money he needs. (b) institutional investors (e.g. building societies and insurance companies) are always buying and selling. (c) speculators are busy, buying when others sell and selling when others buy.	8. What are the three classes of speculator?
8. Bulls, Bears, and Stags.	9. What do they do?
9. (a) Bulls buy in hopes of a rise. (b) Bears sell in hopes of a fall. (c) Stags buy new shares in hopes of an allotment which they can sell at a profit.	10. How long does business continue before everyone settles up?
10. An 'Account' lasts 10 business days.	11. What happens then?
11. A new Account starts at once, but seven working days are allowed to settle up the old one.	12. What are the seven days?
12. (i) Contango day (ii) Making-up day (iii) Ticket day (iv–vi) Intermediate days (vii) Settlement day	13. How many did you answer correctly? Go over the list again.

(18) The Stock Exchange

1. 'The function of the Stock Exchange is to provide a market place where shareholders wishing to dispose of shares may contact investors wishing to buy them, through the activities of agents called brokers, and market traders known as jobbers.' Explain.

2. 'The Stock Exchange is a highly organized market.' Explain what this means, and why the Stock Exchange is best operated in this way.

3. 'Markets yesterday were generally strong except for oils and industrials which declined slightly with the bad news from the Middle East.' Explain.

4. 'Without the Stock Exchange the working man would probably be unemployed, and would lack even the security which unemployment pay brings him in bad times.' Explain how the prosperity of a working man who does not himself invest could be affected by the dealings on the Stock Exchange.

5. What is a broker? How does he earn his living?

6. 'The Stock Exchange does not supply firms with new capital, only with new shareholders when existing shareholders wish to have money instead.' Explain.

7. Write short notes about four of the following: (*a*) The stockbroker; (*b*) A contract note; (*c*) Gilt-edged securities; (*d*) Blue chips; (*e*) Contango; (*f*) 'Bulls'; (*g*) 'Bears'; (*h*) 'Stags'.

8. What part does the speculator play on the Stock Exchange?

9. Describe the work of the London Stock Exchange and discuss its importance to industry and the government.

(Associated Examining Board)

10. 'The Company's Ordinary Shares were quoted on the London Stock Exchange yesterday at 197–198½' What is the meaning of these two prices? Explain how these figures are of interest to (*a*) existing shareholders (*b*) prospective shareholders (*c*) the Company's directors.

(R.S.A.—Adapted)

CHAPTER SEVENTEEN

INSURANCE

(1) The Purpose of Insurance

The purpose of insurance is to provide a sum of money in compensation for any damage that has been suffered as a result of running the risk that we insured against. Every policy of insurance defines the risk that is being insured against, and if that risk causes a loss the person insured will receive compensation to **indemnify him for the loss.** The meaning of this phrase will be made clear later in this chapter.

(2) The Nature of Insurance—the 'Pooling' of Risks

A 'pool' is a collection of money contributed by interested parties for a particular purpose. With a football pool, for example, the participants put a contribution into a central pool of money. They then try to guess something quite extraordinary, for example which eight teams will draw their matches next Saturday. Very often nobody guesses correctly, and the one who guesses nearest to the correct answer collects all the money in the pool, apart from the portions taken by the Government for taxation and by the management for the expenses of running the pool. A football pool therefore has the basic plan shown in Fig.55(a).

The difference with insurance is that it is not the lucky person who takes all, but the unlucky person or persons who take enough to enable them to recover from the unkind blow that fate has dealt them. This is much better than a football pool. A football pool is a gamble; a surrender of part of our assets in the wild hope that good fortune will smile upon us. Insurance is a much wiser and more sensible activity. It is a surrender of a tiny portion of our assets in order that a pool of money shall be created. From this pool, if we suffer the risk insured against, compensation will be paid to restore us to our previous good condition. We shall never win a fortune, we all know this is unlikely anyway, but we shall be sure that whatever standard of living we have achieved will continue for years to come. With life assurance the man who insures his own life so that his wife and children are provided for should he die, is not gambling upon his own death. He does not wish to win the money in the pool; he hopes to lead a normal healthy life, and the feeling of security he gets from knowing his family is covered by a Family Protection Policy will help him enjoy life all the more.

226

Everyone interested contributes
to the pool

£75,000

**The lucky
person wins**

Fig. 55 (a). How a football pool works

Everyone interested contributes
to the pool

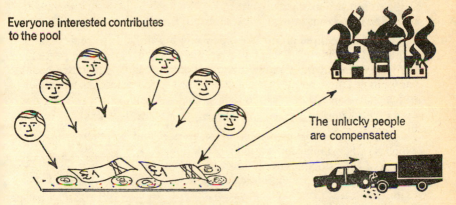

**The unlucky people
are compensated**

Fig. 55 (b). How an insurance pool works

(3) An Early Insurance Act

The preamble to an Act of Parliament of 1601 included the phrase

*By means of which policies of assurance. . . . the loss lighteth rather
easily upon many, than heavily upon few.*

This phrase explains rather well the basic idea of insurance, which is
that losses shall be shared more evenly among the whole population,
rather than be suffered by just the odd unfortunate person. The word
'population' here can mean just those who are interested, or it can mean
every person in the country, as for instance in Britain with its National
Insurance Scheme. Whichever meaning it has, we must be clear that the
losses that are suffered are real enough. The family whose house is
burnt down have suffered a loss, but if they were fully insured against fire
it may cost them only a small premium. Enough money will be provided

from the pool to restore them to their previous condition in a rebuilt house, or similar accommodation elsewhere.

It is worth returning to the phrase from the Act of 1601. It says so exactly, in its old-fashioned way, what happens when a heavy loss suffered by one person becomes only a tiny loss, because his partners in the insurance scheme have helped him bear the blows of a cruel and un-kind fate—*the loss lighteth rather easily upon many than heavily upon few.*

(4) How the 'Insurance Pool' works

The successful conduct of an insurance-pool system depends for success on three main points.

(*a*) The contributions to the pool must be adequate to pay the claims made by those who suffer a loss.

(*b*) The pool itself must be looked after carefully and wisely invested, so that it grows bigger year by year.

(*c*) The just claims must be paid promptly and in full.

Each of these three points is easy to say, but difficult to achieve, and a full understanding of what is involved in each point is important. Before looking at the detailed arrangements made by insurance companies to put these points into effect, we must first consider the principles which control all insurance activities.

(5) The Principles and Doctrines of Insurance

There are three main principles of insurance, and a famous doctrine which is rather similar to a basic principle.

Two of the principles apply to every contract of insurance. They are the principles of **Insurable Interest,** and *Uberrima Fides* or **Utmost Good Faith.** The third principle, **Indemnity,** applies to all contracts of insurance except personal accident and life assurance. It has two corollaries, **Contribution** and **Subrogation.** Finally, the doctrine is called the Doctrine of **Proximate Cause.**

Let us take a careful look at each of these principles.

Principle No. 1—Insurable Interest

Everyone who has an insurable interest in something is entitled to insure it against any risks that may occur. To have an insurable interest we must be in danger of suffering some loss or incurring some liability should the thing concerned be destroyed or damaged in any way. If we shall not suffer loss or incur some liability then we may not insure; if we do we shall waste our premium because under no circumstances will we be allowed to receive money from the pool.

It is therefore perfectly all right to insure my own house, furniture motor car, jewellery, barns, cattle, etc. because I will suffer loss should they be destroyed, damaged or stolen. I can insure my own life, or my wife's life, or even the life of the man who manages my business. It would be quite wrong to insure someone else's house, furniture, motor car, jewellery, etc. because I have no real interest in it, and will suffer no loss if it is damaged or stolen. I cannot insure Farmer Jones' haystack and claim money if it is burned down. If this were allowed I might just be tempted to help it burn down. Of course very few people do commit crimes, but if crime of this sort were encouraged, even if only by a small amount, it would be very unpleasant for the victims. It is therefore 'against public policy' to permit people to insure without an insurable interest.

Principle No. 2—Uberrima Fides, or Utmost Good Faith

When a contract is made it is presumed that people will deal honestly with one another, but it is also deemed that neither party will be a fool. You are therefore expected in the eyes of the law to ask sensible questions when entering into a contract. The law says *caveat emptor*, let the buyer beware. If I want an oak dining suite and I agree to buy a suite of furniture for £60, the law will not allow me to back out of the agreement, if the furniture turns out to be made of walnut. I should have inquired about which wood it was made from before I placed a firm order. The rule therefore for simple contracts is *caveat emptor*, let the buyer beware.

With insurance contracts the rules are more strict. *Uberrimae Fidei*, 'of utmost good faith' is the rule with these contracts. The person wishing to be insured must be absolutely open in his dealings with the insurance company, because in deciding what is a fair premium to charge, the insurance company will depend absolutely on the truth of the facts given by the applicant. For instance, if I reply to the question 'How old are you?' that I am 25 years old when in fact I am 45 years old, this would make a great difference to the premium in certain policies. Life assurance is very cheap to a 25-year-old, and much more expensive to a 45-year-old. We shall see later that a Proposal Form filled up by an applicant for insurance is really a set of questions designed to discover the full facts. On the basis of these facts a fair premium is decided. Incorrect answers to any question render the policy voidable at the election of the aggrieved party, so that the insurance company need not pay out compensation, although they will usually refund the premium.

The requirement to show the 'utmost good faith' is strict. Supposing I am asked in the proposal form, 'Is your father living?' It so happens that he is, but he is on his death-bed and in fact dies later the same day. It would be a breach of 'utmost' good faith not to reveal this material fact even though I was telling the truth when I wrote 'yes' in answer to the question.

These first two principles apply to all contracts of insurance. You may insure only if you have an insurable interest, and you must show the utmost good faith in all your dealings with the insurance company.

Principle No. 3—Indemnity, with Contribution and Subrogation

The contract of insurance is one of indemnity, except in the case of life assurance and personal-accident insurance. In everyday use the word 'indemnify' means to restore someone to the position that he was in immediately before the event concerned took place. For instance, an employer undertakes to indemnify his employee if the employee is put to expense of any sort on behalf of the employer's business. If I pay out fares, or postage for my employer he will refund the money to me.

Indemnity in insurance is the same, in that a person suffering a loss after insuring against it will be indemnified for the amount of the loss. He will be restored as near as possible to the condition that he was in immediately before the loss occurred. Indemnity never restores us to a better position than we were in before, if it did people might feel tempted to make the loss occur. Therefore any depreciation in value suffered by the property since it was purchased new, must be taken into account.

Example. A motor vehicle which originally cost £600 is wrecked in an accident two years after purchase. From the current list published by the motor traders, the insurance company can see that the vehicle is now worth only £350. This sum will therefore be complete compensation.

A Story of Indemnity. The insurance companies themselves have used the example of a man who knocks over someone's beer in a crowded public house to illustrate indemnity. Suppose I knocked over someone's glass of beer, from which he had already taken a generous swig, in a public house. I would of course apologize profusely, and insist on buying him another pint. In other words I would more than make up for the damage, and would restore him to a better position than he was in before. The insurance company would not be generous in this way. It would make the most careful inquiries as to how much had been drunk already, and would replace the exact quantity spilled. It is no function of the insurers to pay out more from the pool than is necessary; to do so would offend against the principle of indemnity.

The Principle of Indemnity and Life Assurance

The principle of indemnity cannot apply in a straightforward way to life assurance, for no sum of money can equate the loss of life. Similarly in personal accident cases the loss of a limb cannot be measured accurately in terms of money. All that these policies can do is to provide a sum of money, called *the benefit payment*, as compensation.

Even so the principle does have some influence. Life assurance premiums are roughly related to the way of life of the person concerned, for he must be able to afford the premiums, and weekly benefits for loss of earnings after an accident are not allowed to exceed the normal earnings of the insured.

The first corollary of Indemnity—Contribution

Suppose I insure myself against fire for £1000 and suffer a loss by fire of the insured goods for that amount. I shall be indemnified for the loss and receive £1000 out of the pool. Suppose I insure against the loss with two or three companies, would it be fair for me to claim from each company the sum of £1000? Clearly it would not, for I would be restored to a better position that I was in before. This would be against public policy, for it might encourage me to cause the loss to happen, so that my condition improves.

Such double insurance is unlikely today, and the insured might even be suspected of fraudulent intent. A more usual case would be where two policies overlapped, as for example where a burglary policy and an all-risks policy exist covering the same goods. The companies concerned will contribute to the loss proportionately, the exact division depending upon the terms of the original policies. To discover whether they should pay in full, or only contribute, every claim form asks the insured 'Is any other company interested in the goods which are the subject of this claim?' An honest answer to this question lets the insurance company know their true position.

The second corollary of Indemnity—Subrogation

If the principle of indemnity says that I must be restored to the condition I was in before I suffered the loss, it would be wrong for me to accept an agreed sum in compensation and then continue to have any other rights as well. A few examples will illustrate this.

Example 1. My car is wrecked in an accident. I agree to accept £400 in settlement of my claim. The wreck is worth £35 when sold to the breaker's yard for use as spare parts. If I received this £35 as well as the £400 I would be getting more than the true indemnity for my loss. The insurance company therefore steps into my shoes as owner of the wreck, and the £35 returns to the pool. The word 'subrogate' means 'to step into the place of', or 'to find a substitute for'. One could say that when they pay out the claim the insurance company inherits all the rights of the person accepting settlement of the claim. This means that they also inherit the right to sue other parties in the accident for any share of the loss which their negligence may have caused.

Example 2. A celebrated American racehorse which had won many classic races broke his leg on a Californian track. The owner had insured the horse for $250,000 with a British insurance firm, who had taken the precaution of sending a representative to the track. The owner was about to give the veterinary surgeon permission to destroy the animal when the insurance representative declared his interest. He would not permit the animal to be destroyed, and soon the rare sight of a horse with a leg in plaster could be seen in the stables where the insurance company were trying to cure the animal. They paid out the claim for the racehorse and although he never raced again he was put to stud and had many fine descendants. The insurance company eventually recovered from breeding fees more than the sum paid out, and restored to the 'pool' all its losses. Subrogation had taken place in the nick of time to prevent the destruction of the animal.

The Doctrine of Proximate Cause

This rule says that if we insure against a certain eventuality we are entitled to compensation only if that eventuality is the immediate (or proximate) cause of the loss. If the immediate cause is some other peril, which has been especially excepted by the insurance policy, then no claim arises. For instance, if I insure my house against fire and a petrol tanker runs into it and causes a blaze, the chain of events leads to a fire (an insured peril) and I may claim. Suppose the policy excludes fires caused by road accidents—because the house is situated at the bottom of a hill on the way to an oil refinery. The excepted peril is clearly the proximate cause of the loss, fire following naturally as a consequence of the accident, and no claim arises.

EXERCISES SET 18

(6) Basic Principles of Insurance

1. Choose the correct word from the list on the right to fill the gaps in the following sentences:

(*a*) A person who insures a motor vehicle must have an insurable . . . in it.

(*b*) The sums contributed to an insurance pool are called . . .

(*c*) Payment for losses suffered is called . . .

(*d*) Insurance contracts must be made with both parties showing the . . . good faith.

(*e*) To restore a person to his original position before he suffered a loss is to . . . him.

(*f*) The sum payable on a life policy is called the . . .

(*g*) An insurance company which pays out a claim then . . . the rights of the insured party.

(*h*) If two policies cover the same loss each company will . . . towards it.

(*i*) Public policy is aimed at reducing or preventing . . .

(*j*) By means of which policies of insurance the loss lighteth rather easily upon many than . . . upon few.

premiums
indemnify
subrogates
interest
utmost
benefit
contribute
compensation
heavily
crimes

2. Are you sure you understand the following points? If not re-read the section that refers to them.

(*a*) How insurance enables people to share risks.

(*b*) The principle of utmost good faith.

(*c*) The difference between *caveat emptor* and *uberrimae fidei*.

(*d*) The successful conduct of an insurance pool.

(*e*) What insurable interest means.

(*f*) The difference between a cause of a loss and the proximate cause of a loss.

3. Write down the letters *a–j* on your paper and then write against these letters either 'yes' or 'no' to the questions below. Has Andrew Ryder any insurable interest in:

(*a*) His motor vehicle, a recent Ford model?

(*b*) His house, a semi-detached near London?

(*c*) His partner's life in the Newtown Motel Co. Ltd?

(*d*) His chef's house, which is situated in the motel grounds and included in the motel mortgage?

(*e*) His aunt's life? She contributes towards the school fees of his three children.

(*f*) The life of the President of the Chamber of Trade, of which Ryder is a member?

(*g*) The honesty of the Treasurer of his golf club? Ryder is the Chairman of the Club Committee.

(*h*) A piece of property adjacent to the motel he hopes to buy next year?

(*i*) The jewellery he gave his wife last Christmas?

(*j*) The yacht owned by the motel's best customer?

4. (*a*) Make a list of the risks most likely to be run by an ordinary householder who owns the property he lives in.

(*b*) Now add any risks beside those in (*a*) which might be run by the same man if he owned a plastics factory employing 30 men situated within 50 yards of the banks of the River Thames.

5. College students in a class decide to insure themselves against the loss of textbooks during the year. The principal of the college tells them that an average of ten books worth £1·50 each are lost by each class in a year. There are 25 students. They appoint a class member to hold the pool of money.

(*a*) How much should each student put into the pool?

(*b*) If only six books are in fact lost, total value £12·50, how much should each student receive as an unused surplus at the end of the year?

(*c*) If Arthur Brown lost three of the books costing £1·60, £1·20 and £0·75, how much did he reduce his losses by joining the insurance pool?

6. What is the general idea of insurance? How does this benefit:

(*a*) the insured person;

(*b*) the insurance agent;

(*c*) the company giving the insurance?

7. What do you understand by the expression 'the pooling of risks'? Is it true that a trader may be relieved of all risks by paying others to undertake to indemnify him? (*R.S.A.*)

8. What are the principles of insurance? Explain why each of these principles is important.

9. Two motor vehicles are wrecked in a crash. Each driver is given complete indemnity. Explain who has lost as a result of this accident.

10. Mr. Jones wishes to insure his life. Suggest six reasons which might make Mr. Jones a poor risk as far as the insurance company is concerned.

(7) A Page to test you on Basic Principles of Insurance

Answers	Questions
—	1. What is the nature of insurance?
1. It is the pooling of risks.	2. Why do we insure?
2. To secure the right to claim compensation for loss suffered due to the insured peril.	3. *By means of which policies of insurance . . .* go on.
3. *The loss lighteth rather easily upon many than heavily upon few.*	4. What part does the insurance company play in insurance?
4. (*a*) It collects a fair premium for the risk involved and adds it to the pool. (*b*) It takes care of the pool and invests it wisely in a balanced portfolio. (*c*) It pays the just claims.	5. What principles and doctrines underlie insurance?
5. (*a*) Insurable interest (*b*) Utmost good faith (*c*) Indemnity with 　(i) Contribution 　(ii) Subrogation (*d*) The doctrine of Proximate Cause.	6. Insurable interest says we may insure only things in which we have an interest, which will lead to our suffering a loss if anything happens to them. What does utmost good faith mean?
6. It means that when we fill up a proposal form we must answer the questions with strict honesty.	7. Why must we answer with strict honesty?
7. Because the insurance company relies absolutely on the truth of our statements when they fix the premium.	8. What is indemnity?
8. Indemnity is the restoration of the insured person who suffers a loss to the position he was in before the loss occurred—not to a better position.	9. Are Life Assurance contracts 'contracts of indemnity'
9. No—Because it is not possible to restore the dead to life.	10. What does the insurance company do instead?
10. It gives a lump sum, called the benefit, to the widow or orphans.	11. What are the two corollaries of indemnity?
11. Contribution and Subrogation.	12. What is contribution?
12. Contribution is a situation that arises when two policies relate to the same loss. Each insurer contributes a proportion of the loss, so that the insured is restored to his indemnity position.	13. What is subrogation?
13. Here the insurance company subrogates (is substituted for) the insured, taking over all his rights.	14. What is the doctrine of proximate cause?
14. It is a doctrine which says that we can only be compensated out of the pool if our loss was caused directly by the risk we insured against.	15. How many did you answer correctly? Go over the list again.

PROPOSAL FORM
for
THEATRICAL ENTERTAINMENTS, FLOWER SHOWS AND SIMILAR EVENTS

1. Name of Person, Committee or Authority in whose favour insurance is required ...   .

2. Address   ...   .

3. (*a*) Date of event   ...   .
   (*b*) Number of days involved (allow for setting up and dismantling) ...   .
   (*c*) Full particulars of the event including where it is to be held   ...   .
   (*d*) Anticipated attendance ...   .

4. Are any grandstands, marquees or street decorations to be erected ?...   ...   .
   If so—(*a*) Will these be approved by the Local Authority?   ...   .
   (*b*) What will be the capacity of the grandstands or marquees?   ...   .
   (*c*) By whom will they be erected?   ...   ...

5. Is there to be a car park ?   ...   .
   If so—(*a*) What will be the maximum capacity?   ...
   (*b*) Will any charge be made?   ...   ...
   (*c*) Will tickets be issued?   ...   .
   (If so please attach a specimen) ...   ...
   (*d*) Will any notices be displayed disclaiming liability? ...   .
   (If so please attach wording) ...   ...

6. Will adequate precautions be taken to protect the public from any coconut shies, dart throwing, rifle shooting or similar side shows?   ...   .

7. Is there to be a display of fireworks?   ...   ...
   If so—(*a*) Will this be operated by independent contractors?   ...   .
   (*b*) What precautions to avoid injury will be taken?   ...   .

8. Please state—
   (*a*) Limit of Indemnity required ...   .
   (*b*) Whether insurance is required against liability arising out of:
   (i) Damage to property by fire and explosion ...   .
   (ii) Personal injury caused by fireworks ...
   (iii) Car park for which a charge is made ...

I desire to effect insurance as above with the .... Insurance Co. Ltd., in the Company's usual form of policy for such risks on the warranty that the above statements herewith are true and complete and that nothing materially affecting the risk has been concealed.

Date........................... Signature...

(8) **How an Insurance Policy is Brought into Effect**

The first thing to do when we wish to insure against any risk is to state clearly what the risk is, and to provide information which will enable the insurance company to assess the probability of the risk occurring. This is most easily done by filling up a standard **Proposal Form** which will be supplied by the company; if the risk is of a very unusual nature such a standard form may not be available and a written slip of paper will be used instead. Page 235 shows a typical proposal form; in this case for liability to members of the public who may suffer an accident of some sort at a fête, garden party, etc.

Insurable and Non-Insurable Risks

Not all risks are insurable. Insurance depends upon the calculation of probabilities. The probability that an event will occur is estimated by the *underwriter*. In Life Assurance statisticians called *actuaries* are experts in the statistical analysis of probabilities in the mortality, sickness and retirement fields. Statistical records available over a very long period enable them to calculate the chances of any particular applicant, say a bus driver, suffering from a disability, or dying before the policy matures. The premium is then fixed at such a figure that the insurance company will be able to meet the obligations it has assumed.

Some risks are not susceptible to insurance, because there are no records on which to make calculations. I cannot insure against the risk that I shall prove to be a fool in business, for there are no records of my success or failure to help the actuaries.

All the questions in the proposal from shown above affect the calculations of the probability of someone being hurt. For instance in Question 3:

(*a*) The date of the event. Some days are busier than others. A garden fête on Tuesday will not attract many people, for they will be at work. A garden fête on Saturday will attract a large crowd, with consequently greater chances that someone will be hurt.

(*b*) Number of days involved. If it goes on for only one day the risks will be smaller than if it is to run over a complete week.

(*c*) Full particulars of the event. If it is a 'Donkey Derby' the risks will be less than if it is a sports-car meeting or an air-display. The actuaries need to know what type of event is being staged before they can fix the premium.

(*d*) The anticipated attendance. It will make a great deal of difference to the chances of someone being hurt if the attendance is large. Not only will the numbers available to be hurt be greater, but the chances of collisions will be greater too. This applies especially in car parks, or on terraced stands.

Under the heading of insurable risks come such risks as fire, burglary, storm and tempest, marine disasters, and motor vehicle and aviation accidents. Non-insurable risks include such items as the chances that the goods a businessman has bought will cease to be fashionable before he has sold them, or the chances that a slump will develop so that his business proves unprofitable.

Fixing the Premium

On the basis of the answers given to the questions in the proposal form the underwriters will decide a fair premium for the policy that the proposer wishes to take out. It should be noted that one part of the proposal form is a declaration signed by the proposer to the effect that he warrants the truth of the statements made. This warranty reinforces his **common-law duty** to show the utmost good faith with a **contractual duty** to have told the truth in every particular. This contractual duty is even more strict than the common-law duty, since **any inaccuracy** makes the contract voidable, whether or not it relates to a material fact. A material fact is defined as one which will influence an underwriter in entering into, or fixing the premium for, a contract of insurance. This declaration is the basis of the contract of insurance. It is incorporated in the **offer** of the Insurance Company to insure the proposer for a certain sum of money called a premium. The person desiring insurance can **accept** this offer by paying the premium, whereupon the insurance commences, and a **policy** will be issued giving a full account of what has been agreed.

(9) **Taking care of the 'Pool'**

The pool of resources from which compensation is to be paid must be large enough to meet all possible eventualities, and the insurance companies therefore maintain adequate 'catastrophe reserves'. These reserves are invested as carefully as possible. Some idea of the scale of these activities can be seen from the following figures which show the total sums invested in various types of security and the percentage of total funds invested in each. It is an excellent example of a 'balanced portfolio' referred to on page 210.

The grand total of £22,849 million represents an enormous reserve from which claims can be paid. A high proportion of this sum is for life-assurance cover, which will be paid out to widows and orphans when death occurs. The rest is for general insurance activities, fire, marine, and accident policies. Clearly the skill of the investors in the service of the insurance companies is of the utmost importance to the policy holders and the shareholders of the companies.

The Insurance Companies as Institutional Investors

A slight diversion here is well worth while to take a quick look at the importance of the insurance companies as **institutional investors**. Inves-

Table 8. The Insurance Pool (£ millions)

Total Investments 1973	£m	%
Mortgages	3,205	14·1
British Government Authority Securities	3,165	13·9
Foreign and Commonwealth Government Provincial and Municipal Stocks	1,386	6·2
Debentures, Loan Stocks, Preference and Guaranteed Stocks and Shares	3,679	16·2
Ordinary Stocks and Shares	6,600	28·9
Real Property and Ground Rents	3,365	12·6
Other Investments	1,449	8·1
TOTAL	22,849	100·0

tors are people who save part of their incomes and lend the savings to firms who are in need of capital. The money invested is used by the firms, either in primary, secondary, or tertiary production. It is converted into fixed assets of every kind, which are then used to produce more and more consumer goods. In short this is the capitalist system of production. Whether you live in a Communist, Socialist, or Capitalist society the use of the invested funds is the same. The difference between these systems is purely one of ownership.

An institutional investor is an organization which collects savings from people and invests the savings in the same way as the private investor. The banks are an obvious example of institutional investors, but it is probably true to say that the insurance companies are at least equal in importance to the banks. This is particularly so today, because a change in the distribution of wealth since the Second World War has put more and more wealth into the hands of the poorer sections of our population. Heavy taxation of the rich has reduced the share of investment they are able to make, yet it has not put vast fortunes at the disposal of the poor. The increase in wealth has been so distributed that it has meant only a small increase for each family, and much of the increase is in better pension schemes, welfare facilities, etc. In other words personal and social insurance has played a large part in the increased standard of living of the mass of the people. The industrial life societies, with their countrywide network of agents, have been entrusted by many ordinary people with the small savings they can now afford, in the form of insurance and assurance policies. One of these companies alone is believed to collect about £1 million every week from small policy holders. This represents a very valuable contribution to the capital requirements of industrialists, transport and shipping firms, farmers, forestry and other extractive industries, and wholesale and retail traders.

It may fairly be said that through the medium of the insurance companies we have become a property-owning democracy.

By taking care of the 'pool', investing it wisely in a balanced portfolio, keeping away from any involvement in the industries themselves and concentrating on safe investments yielding a reasonable return the insurance companies have increased the reserves available to the insured members of the general public in times of distress or natural disaster.

(10) Paying out the Just Claims

If an insured person suffers a loss as a result of the peril against which he has insured he is entitled to be indemnified for the loss. The correct procedure is to make a claim on an appropriate claim form. This form must as usual be completed with the utmost good faith, and will then be considered by the insurance company. The following points will enter into their considerations:

(*a*) Was the insured peril the proximate cause of the loss? If so liability exists; if not the claim does not justify payment from the pool of an indemnity sum.

(*b*) Even if the claim appears at first sight to be justified, are there any breaches of the conditions of the policy? For instance in a motor-accident policy there is usually a clause that the vehicle must be regularly serviced, the tyres must be in good condition, etc. If I wreck my vehicle after skidding owing to the bad state of the tyres my claim will probably fail.

(*c*) If the claim is justified, what is the correct amount which will indemnify the applicant? Many claimants do not understand indemnity and ask for the replacement price of the goods destroyed. We have already seen that the true indemnity figure takes account of depreciation and may be considerably less than the replacement price of a new item.

When a 'fair' valuation has been agreed the insurance company pays the agreed sum. If this is large they may find it necessary to borrow from their bankers or even to sell some of their investments in order to realize the money to pay the claim. When the liner *Andrea Doria* sank, British insurance firms paid £4 million within a few days.

(11) The Types of Insurance

The four main branches of insurance are:

(*a*) Marine Insurance
(*b*) Fire Insurance
(*c*) Life Assurance
(*d*) Accident Insurance

There is no real difference between the words 'insurance' and 'assurance', but in Britain it has become customary to use the word assurance when referring to life policies. The events being insured in life assurance will assuredly happen—for we all die, whereas in all other insurances we do not necessarily ever suffer a loss. This seems to be the reason for the word 'assured' in connection with life policies.

(12) Marine Insurance

Ever since 1575, when a Chamber of Assurances was set up in the Royal Exchange of the City of London, there has been a recognized centre for the registration of marine-insurance policies. Registration is evidence of the terms of the contract and is helpful in settling disputes. The 1601 Act already referred to set up a Court of Arbitration to settle disputes over policies.

The main sections of marine insurance are hull, cargo, freight, and shipowner's liability.

(*a*) *Hull.* The hull of the vessel, which includes the machinery, can be covered against damage or total loss by storm, stranding, fire, collision, or other perils of the sea. Insurance begins from the laying of the keel, when the insurable interest lies with the shipbuilder. After passing into the hands of the buyer, the insurable interest lies with the shipowner from then on. Some policies are **time policies**, lasting usually for 12 months, or they may be **voyage policies** lasting from port of departure to port of arrival without a specific time being agreed.

(*b*) *Cargo.* The insurance of cargo is absolutely vital in the import and export trade, since the question of payment for the goods hinges around the existence of a reliable insurance policy. This is explained in detail on page 128, and the reader is urged to investigate this aspect of cargo insurance thoroughly. The main point is that the existence of an insurance policy in conjunction with a Bill of Lading means that whoever purchases the goods by purchasing the Bill of Lading also subrogates (inherits the rights to) the insurance claim that may arise if the goods are lost at sea. He therefore buys with confidence, since his purchase is completely secure. Without the insurance policy no one would be prepared to pay for the goods until they had arrived safely.

Cargo policies refer to the movement of goods exported from or imported to a country. At some point the insurable interest will pass from the seller to the buyer, according to the contract of sale. Usually this will be either an F.O.B. contract (Free on Board—the seller to deliver the goods on board the carrying vessel) or a C.I.F. contract (Cost, Insurance, Freight—the seller to deliver the goods to the port of destination).

Cargo policies cover all risks including war and strike risks, and are based on the value placed on them by the seller—this means the ordinary invoice price. The holder usually has the right to claim, since, except in rare instances, the property in the cargo vests with the holder of the Bill of Lading, to which the policy and invoice are attached. It follows that for the whole of the time the marine policy is in effect the cargo is the property of the holder of the Bill of Lading.

Floating policies are a variation of cargo policies. They give cover for a specified sum, say £1 million, and eliminate the necessity of insuring each cargo separately. For instance a cross-Channel ferry would be greatly inconvenienced if underwriting insurance had to be negotiated for every trip. The master simply notifies the value of the cargo before sailing on each voyage, and this is set against the floating policy. As soon as the sums already covered approach the total value of the policy the premium will be renewed to extend the cover for a further period.

Open-cover agreements are sometimes made by which an underwriter agrees automatically to cover any consignment notified to him up to a certain limit at a pre-arranged rate for a particular vessel on a particular voyage. Policies are issued after shipments are notified.

(c) *Freight.* The word 'freight' is often used as a synonym for cargo, but it has a different meaning in insurance. Here the word means the charge for carrying cargo. A shipowner often gets the freight in advance, but since he is not legally entitled to it until the cargo is safely delivered, he may face an action for recovery of the freight should the cargo be lost overboard. If it is not recoverable because of a special clause in the contract of carriage it will form part of the insured value of the cargo. If it is payable on delivery, it will be a matter for the shipowner to insure against possible loss of freight. It follows that in nearly every case there is some party with an insurable interest in the freight. Underwriters are prepared to cover this risk of loss of freight, just as in fire insurance they are prepared to cover not only the risk of a fire itself, but the risk of loss of profits while a building is out of use after the fire. Since 'freight' is the reward for carrying, it is the income of the carrier.

(d) *Shipowners' liabilities.* These are very numerous: not only cargo, passengers, and crew but other vessels, fixed installations such as piers and wharves, and even beaches are liable to be damaged by the actions of ships and ships' masters. After the *Torrey Canyon* disaster near Land's End, a bond of £3 million was required from the owners to cover claims for detergent used, and loss of business suffered by the authorities and businessmen involved in clearing the beaches of oil from the tanker. These eventualities represent a further heavy burden placed upon shipowners. Insurance relieves them of these risks, and enables them more confidently to go about their business on the high seas.

(13) Fire Insurance

Fire insurance began a few years after the Great Fire of London (1666) when a speculative builder Nicolas Barbon started the Fire Office in 1680. By 1805 there were 11 fire offices in London and over

30 in the British Isles. They ran their own fire brigades and issued fire marks to be affixed to the walls of buildings to mark them as being insured by a particular company. Brigades sometimes refused to put out a fire on properties which were not insured, but sat around to be ready if the flames spread to properties bearing their fire marks. Later a good deal of co-operation developed and eventually the fire-brigades became part of the public service.

By the start of the twentieth century the need for household policies covering a wider range of risks began to be appreciated. By the 1920s policies covering not only fire but storm and tempest, burst pipes, impacts, explosions, and burglary were introduced. In more recent years aircraft damage, collapse of television aerials, and householders' liabilities to the public have been added.

One feature of this type of insurance is the influence it has exerted over the years on public policy. The whole question of safety in buildings is continuously under review. Lower premiums are offered to firms and householders who take more sophisticated precautions such as installing sprinkler devices. Even the layout of towns and housing projects to leave adequate fire gaps and escapes on high buildings are affected by the activities of the insurance lobby, who have the public interest as well as their own interests at heart.

The chief types of policy issued by the fire offices are:

(*a*) Fire insurance on domestic and business premises, and their contents.

(*b*) Consequential Loss insurance. (This type of policy ensures that a firm continues to receive reasonable payments in lieu of profits while rebuilding is going on. Otherwise the business may lose all connection with its customers, and be unable to pay fixed charges such as rates and mortgage repayments which still continue even when the premises have been destroyed.)

(*c*) Special perils. Many of these are now covered in the normal householder's policies, but flooding is a special peril which is sometimes not covered by these policies.

(*d*) Household policies. These have already been described above.

(14) Life Assurance

Life assurance on a long-term basis became possible after Edmund Halley, the famous Astronomer Royal, published his mortality tables in 1693. Based on an investigation into man's expectation of life, the tables opened the way to predicting probable future mortalities. Previous to this, life assurance had only been conducted on a short-term basis. The earliest policies were designed to provide ransom money for sailors captured off the Barbary coast by the Barbary pirates. In 1705 an Amicable Society for a Perpetual Assurance Office was formed which collected contributions from members who wished to provide for their dependents. At the end of each year the funds available were shared among the dependents of members who had died during the year. The sum provided therefore was not steady, but depended upon (*a*) the sums collected, and (*b*) the number of members who died.

Industrial Life policies developed in the middle of the nineteenth century as a form of life assurance which would appeal to the industrial classes. It provided small benefits for very tiny premiums. 'Penny Death' policies were quite normal. For a penny a week a sum could be assured which would cover funeral expenses, and even a tombstone. It is perhaps no accident that these policies developed immediately after the Poor Law Amendment Act had created the workhouse system. Fear of that ultimate disgrace, to be buried by the parish in a pauper's grave, drove even the very poor to pay their insurance money to the insurance agent who called weekly and became in many ways a friend and legal and financial adviser to his poor and often illiterate customers. Today the Industrial Life Offices, through their countrywide network of agents, still have their finger on the nation's pulse, though now the benefits are less gruesomely necessary and the weekly savings may be pounds rather than pence.

Life assurance is primarily designed to cover the death or retirement of the insured. It is therefore often a provision for dependents. The possible benefits are:

(*a*) A lump-sum benefit at death. This may be considerable or may only be enough to cover funeral expenses.

(*b*) An income benefit commencing at death and lasting the widow for her life, or until re-marriage, or until the children reach a certain age.

(*c*) The provision of a pension in old age.

(*d*) The repayment of a mortgage on a house, so that the widow and dependents are sure of ownership of the property on the death of the mortgagor. As property values have risen in recent years, it has become more difficult for a widow to keep up the payments herself on the property. Many building societies now insist that mortgages must be backed by life assurance. It is distressing for a Society to have to evict a family because repayments are no longer being made, at a time when they have recently suffered the loss of their bread-winner.

The chief types of policy are:

(*a*) *Whole life policies*, payable at death; the premiums being payable either throughout life or to some agreed age, usually 60 years of age.

(*b*) *Endowment policies*. Here the sum agreed is payable at the end of a given number of years, or at death if this occurs sooner. It is a popular form of long-term saving, carrying with it the benefit of insurance cover during the time of the saving. 'With-profits' policies return not only the sum assured, but profits actually made on the savings, which have been invested by the company. Usually 90 per cent of the profits made are returned to the policy holder.

(*c*) *Family income policies.* In this type of policy it is arranged that if death occurs during the period stated in the contract the benefit will be paid not in one lump sum but by a series of regular repayments, terminating with a final sum at the end of a period. This is very suitable for a man with a young family, since it covers his widow and dependents with a certain minimum income at once in the event of his death. This income will continue until the end of the period agreed, which is usually arranged to cover the time before the children are able to support themselves.

(*d*) *Mortgage-security policies.* These have been referred to above.

(*e*) *Group life policies.* These are very convenient to small employers who cannot afford a pensions department to manage investments for pension purposes. The policies can be taken out to cover an agreed sum on each member of the group. An employee who leaves the firm can usually arrange to commute his benefits to a personal insurance cover on terms suitable to his age and pocket.

(*f*) *Unit-linked policies.* These policies are issued with a minimum of investigation into the life being insured. They are issued in conjunction with an Investment Trust, about 93 per cent of the monthly sum invested being used to purchase units in the trust. The other 7 per cent is used for insurance cover. Income tax advantages and capital gains on the units invested make this type of policy attractive to persons paying income tax at the standard rate.

(15) Accident Insurance

The term 'Accident Insurance' has come to mean any kind of insurance not covered by marine insurance, fire insurance, or life assurance. It became clear as the Industrial Revolution developed that accidents were an inevitable accompaniment to progress. The transport revolution, which accompanied industrial progress, filled first the canals, then the railways, and finally the roads with such a volume of restless traffic as our ancestors would never have deemed possible. Technology invaded every industry; mining, manufacturing, and commerce itself became increasingly mechanized.

The four types of accident insurance covered are: insurance of liability; insurance of property; personal accident insurance; and insurance of interest.

(*a*) *Insurance of liability.* The largest volume of accident business covers this kind of liability. Employer's liability for accidents at work, liability of the organizers of public functions for accidents occurring to the public in the course of the event, and above all the liability of motor-vehicle owners for accidents involving third parties, are the chief policies offered.

In any contract there are two principals to the contract, who may be termed the **First Party** and the **Second Party**. In insurance contracts these are the insured and the insurers. **Third Parties** are any other persons affected by the contract, for example passengers, pedestrians, cyclists, etc. The Road Traffic Act 1930 made it compulsory to have Third Party insurance, i.e. for motorists to protect themselves against liability for death of, or bodily injury to, members of the public. Third parties are therefore nearly always covered by the motorist's insurance policy. In those cases where an uninsured driver, or one whose policy is defective because of some breach of 'utmost good faith', causes injury, a Central Fund administered by the Motor Insurers' Bureau now provides compensation. A driver who has 'Fully Comprehensive' cover will also receive compensation if he is injured, or if his vehicle is damaged. Because of the high degree of risk when young persons are driving, many insurance companies will not give 'Fully Comprehensive' cover to persons under the age of 25.

(*b*) *Insurance of property.* Policies of this sort cover a wide range of risks. Many of these risks are covered by the Householders' Policies discussed under Fire Insurance. Others are the insurance of shop windows, insurance of herds and flocks against disease, insurance against vandalism, etc. Another type of policy is the 'all-risks' policy which offers cover against very wide possibilities. In one recent case a family returned home from holiday to find that a group of vandals had moved in during their absence and had completely wrecked their home. Unfortunately this was not included in their householder's policy, although a separate policy was available for a small extra premium.

(*c*) *Personal accident insurance.* These policies cover the insured in respect of death, total or partial disablement, loss of limbs, hospital expenses, etc. They may also cover parties or groups of people, e.g. club members on an outing, or sports club players who may be hurt. Short-term policies cover railway or aircraft journeys, and may often be purchased from machines in the concourses of airports or at railway termini. The sums covered by these policies are quite considerable, which emphasizes the rarity of aircraft accidents. A Canadian company once ran the slogan 'When did you last hear of someone getting kicked to death by a donkey?' It so happened that deaths in aircraft crashes and deaths by donkey kicks had occurred that year in Canada with equal frequency, 59 deaths by each. Aircraft accidents are common, but they are not as common as all that.

(*d*) *Insurance of Interest.* Very often interested parties in some event may find themselves open to criticism of their actions which may involve financial compensation. There are many examples; for instance a member of a club committee may authorize some payment which is outside the rules. Professional persons may be held liable for incorrect professional advice given to clients. An executor of a will may pay out the moneys involved and then find a genuine beneficiary who demands compensation. All these contingencies can be insured against. The commonest of the **Fidelity Guarantees** are the **Commercial Fidelity Guarantees** taken out by firms upon employees. These Fidelity Bonds restore moneys embezzled by the employee; but it should be noted that usually the firm is only reimbursed after the employee has been charged in the courts. There has to be a deterrent or this type of crime would increase, and that would be 'against public policy'.

EXERCISES SET 19

(16) More Questions about Insurance

1. Mr. Jones tells his son Paul, aged 17, that the insurance company has raised his premium from £17·50 to £25·50 now that Paul has started to drive. They have also notified that while Paul is driving the first £50 of each and every claim will be payable by Mr. Jones. Explain what all these matters mean, and why the insurance company has taken these actions.

2. Suggest what actions a wise driver would take to ensure that after an accident he was in full possession of the facts to make a claim on the insurance company.

3. 'Women drivers,' said the Chairman of the Insurance Company, 'are the *best* drivers in the motor-insurance field. They rarely take their cars out at busy times.' What are the implications of this statement?

4. Explain the following terms: (*a*) proposal form; (*b*) contractual duty to answer questions accurately; (*c*) premium; (*d*) insurable risks.

5. Imagine you are designing a proposal form for insurance against burglary. Suggest ten questions that would need to appear on the form.

6. 'Underwriters determine the probability that a particular risk will occur.' Explain this statement in detail, referring in your answer to (*a*) motor accidents, (*b*) lightning damage.

7. What is an institutional investor? Why are insurance companies particularly active in this field? What aims do they pursue when investing their funds?

8. Abel Driver has an accident, and the consequent repairs to his car cost £136·50. He has a Comprehensive Policy which costs him £32·50 per year, and one of the clauses says that he will pay the first £15 of any claim. How much has he saved by joining the insurance pool? He started only this year.

9. Tom Jenkins is insured for fire under his Householder's Policy, and his wife's jewellery is insured separately under an all-risks cover, with a different company. A fire which destroys his house and all the contents leads to a claim. How will this claim be met?

10. What are the main types of insurance? Explain how the principles of Insurable Interest and Utmost Good Faith affect policies on any *one* type of insurance.

11. What is a Consequential Loss Policy? Explain why it is desirable to take out such a policy.

12. 'Everyone should take out some insurance, few people can afford to take out every policy that is available.' Which do you consider are the most important policies for (*a*) a householder, (*b*) a shipowner, to take out?

(17) **The British Insurance Market**

Like all markets, the Insurance Market is a place where buyers and sellers are in contact with one another, either directly, or indirectly, to fix prices. The British Insurance Market is very large, and reaches out not only to every household in Britain but to every country in the world. The explanation lies in the absolute reliability of the market: Lloyd's, in particular, has an international reputation second to none. Despite the growth in many countries of an insurance market to cater for local populations, re-insurance through London as a 'hedge' against possible heavy claims is a normal practice, so that some of the benefit of this business still flows to Britain.

London is the largest insurance market in the world. Besides 250 British and Commonwealth firms there are 6,000 Lloyd's underwriters and 130 foreign companies with London offices. Business is more than £3,000 million per annum, and about £250 million annually is earned towards the British balance of payments.

Who are the Buyers of Insurance?

They are the general public of the United Kingdom and the whole world. They may be acting personally to protect themselves and their families. They may be acting in a corporate way, as a member of a firm, a Limited Company, a Council or Committee. They will be insuring against any eventuality which will involve them in loss, or liability to others.

Who are the Sellers of Insurance?

They are individuals or institutions who earn their living in this way. The individuals are Lloyd's underwriters, who engage as principals in the sale of insurance cover. Lloyd's Corporation does not itself transact insurance business. The institutions are as follows:

(*a*) Composite offices which offer more than one type of insurance (marine, fire, life, and accident). They are proprietary offices; i.e. they have shareholders and are often set up as Limited Companies.

(*b*) Industrial Life Offices, or Home Service Offices, who also offer most types of insurance cover but cater especially through their home-service agents for the small insured paying by weekly contributions.

(*c*) The Mutual Life Offices. These offer life assurance to members, in other words they do not have shareholders. The policyholders own the company.

(*d*) The Proprietary Life Offices. These offices offer life assurance to the public, but the policy holders are not members and do not own the company.

(*e*) The Mutual Insurance Offices. These offices offer insurance to members who have mutual interests, catering for firms in particular industries or trades.

Who Brings Buyers and Sellers Together?

Except for Lloyd's, a person wishing to insure may approach the insurance company directly, and many direct inquiries result from advertisements in magazines, trade journals, and the Press. Insurance is so

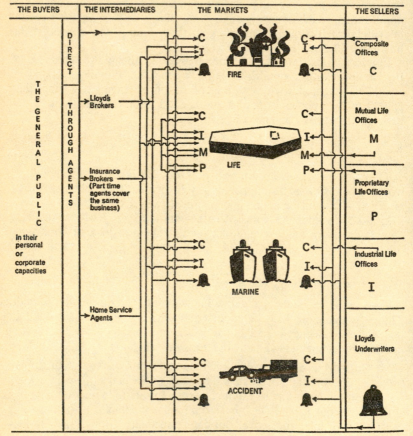

Fig. 56. The British Insurance Market

important, particularly to householders, motorists, and employers, that a network of agents is available to arrange policies for the public. The chief types are:

(*a*) Lloyd's brokers, whose function is explained later.

(*b*) Insurance brokers, who establish businesses as private enterprises earning commission on policies arranged with major companies and societies.

(*c*) Home-service agents, who are employees of the Industrial Life Offices, and call on clients weekly to collect their subscriptions.

(*d*) Part-time agents, who arrange insurance as a side-line to another profession, perhaps accountancy, hire-purchase finance, or the law.

The functions of the brokers and agents are shown in Fig. 56.

We will now look more closely at a very famous part of the British Insurance Market—Lloyd's of London.

(18) Lloyd's of London

Lloyd's is a market, of international standing, where individuals known as **underwriters** accept insurance. These underwriters have been elected 'Underwriting Members of Lloyd's' by a special voting process which involves meeting strict financial and other standards set by the Corporation of Lloyd's. This Corporation owns the premises and oversees the market. It also collects shipping and other information from all over the world. It does not itself transact insurance, which is entirely a matter for individual underwriters. The most succinct definition of Lloyd's was once given by a famous caller named Farrant. A caller is the red-robed presidential figure who sits in the rostrum beneath the Lutine Bell and calls brokers who are wanted by colleagues in the 'room' or on the telephone. Farrant said 'Individually we are underwriters, collectively we are Lloyd's'.

The History of Lloyd's. In the year 1688 a coffee house in Tower Street near the Tower of London, was owned by a man called Edward Lloyd. Being so near the River Thames, his customers included ships' masters, provision merchants, and bankers with a maritime interest. In those days there was no organized insurance market, and people wishing to insure went from house to house and shop to shop asking businessmen to cover their risks to whatever extent they could afford. On the chance of finding several such people at one call, those in search of insurance began to call at Lloyd's to inquire if anyone was interested. Lloyd began to provide paper and pens for the convenience of customers and gradually the sale of insurance became more important than the sale of coffee.

After Lloyd's death in 1713 the business continued, eventually becoming a private club whose members owned and controlled the premises and restricted entry to those interested in shipping and insurance. The Lloyd's Act of 1871 finally established Lloyd's as a Corporation, run by a committee elected by the members.

The underwriters, even in the modern premises in Lime Street, have 'boxes' around the floor which are reminiscent of the traditional coffee-house settle. These boxes give a certain amount of privacy to underwriters discussing risks with brokers.

Underwriters and Brokers

Lloyd's is a highly organized market, i.e. only experts may deal in the market; the general public are not allowed in except as visitors. The two classes of expert are the underwriters who sell insurance, of whom there are over 6,000, and the brokers who represent the general public wishing to buy insurance. There are about 230 firms of Lloyd's brokers approved by the Corporation who are free to enter the market on behalf of the public and discuss risks with the underwriters. The general public would find it quite impossible to locate in a reasonable time the 'best buy' for any particular risk, since Lloyd's is traditionally run without any separation into particular markets. The only division is that the main floor is used for marine, accident, and aviation risks, while non-marine risks of other sorts are dealt with on the gallery floor surrounding the main Underwriting Room.

Functions and Activities of the Lloyd's Broker

The broker's task is to find someone to insure his client's marine or other risk at the most reasonable price. When approached by a member of the public seeking insurance, the broker discusses the risk involved and writes a 'slip'. This 'slip' of paper now bears a concise statement of the risk involved with all the relevant details. A marine-risk 'slip' might state the value of the cargo being shipped, the name of the vessel, its destination, date of sailing, etc.

The broker now goes into Lloyd's and discusses the 'slip' with various underwriters in order to discover what terms they will offer. Each will quote him a premium for that particular risk and he is then able to select the most favourable price for his client. He returns to this underwriter and asks him to 'write a line' on the slip. This first line is called a 'lead' and states the amount of insurance the underwriter is prepared to take, at what premium. It is initialled by the underwriter. It might be £15,000 at £1·50 per £1,000. The broker is now in a good position to complete the transaction. He goes with the slip to other underwriters and persuades them to accept the same premium, and when he has collected enough insurance to cover the whole risk a policy is prepared and signed in the Lloyd's Policy Signing Office. This policy is a valid contract of insurance and goes to the broker, who forwards it to his client.

Lloyd's brokers are not restricted to dealing with underwriters, and if they think they can get better terms with equal security they are free to approach the Composite Offices, or the Industrial Offices.

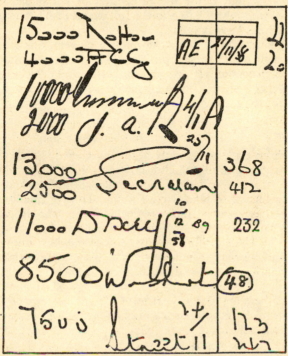

Fig. 57. A section of a broker's slip, showing portions of the risk taken by various underwriters

The Election of Underwriters

Underwriters are elected under strict rules designed to ensure absolute integrity on the part of all members. They must be nominated by a member, and supported by five other members, and then be elected unanimously by ballot.

Other rules for underwriters are as follows:

(*a*) They must transact business with unlimited liability.

(*b*) They must satisfy the Committee of their financial standing.

(*c*) Members wishing to accept both marine and non-marine business must provide security varying according to the volume of business to be transacted, of not less than £15,000.

(*d*) They must set aside an initial substantial sum as a Premium Trust Fund Deposit. All premiums must be paid into this Trust Fund and profits cannot be withdrawn unless this basic deposit is still intact.

(*e*) They must take out a guarantee policy each year with other under-writers, based on the premium income, and must also contribute to a Central Fund designed to protect insured parties from any fear of de-falcation. This fund is for the protection of the public not of the underwriter, who is still liable to the full extent of his personal wealth for any liabilities he may incur.

(*f*) They must submit to a strict audit each year, designed to detect any weakness in their financial positions. This audit sets reserves at such a level as to give an ample margin of security, and takes no account of the underwriter's private fortune which continues to exist as a further safeguard for the insured.

Syndicates

Although an underwriter acts purely as an individual, the insured values of cargoes and other liabilities are so great that it would be impossible to arrange insurance if individuals had to be asked personally for their agreement to take part of a risk. To save time therefore the underwriters are grouped into syndicates which take up considerably larger shares of a 'risk' than individuals could manage. These shares are agreed by the Underwriting Agents, whose presence during working hours enables the whole syndicate to carry a share of the risk. There are about 138 marine, 76 non-marine, 26 aviation, and 32 motor syndicates. Lloyd's does not insure lives in the normal way of life-assurance com-panies, but there are seven short-term life syndicates who handle life risks for particular events, such as holiday travel or business journeys, the maximum term being seven years.

The Lutine Bell

The Lutine Bell is mounted over the caller's rostrum in the Under-writing Room. It was salvaged from a vessel, H.M.S. *Lutine*, which sank in a storm off Terschelling in 1799, with a cargo of gold bullion valued at £1,400,000. A number of salvage attempts have been made but most of the cargo still lies at the bottom of the sea.

The use of the bell to signal news about overdue vessels has declined in this age of rapid communications, and it is now rung mainly for ceremonial occasions. One stroke is sounded for bad news and two strokes, a slightly more cheerful sound, for good news.

Exercises Set 20

(19) **The British Insurance Market**

1. What is the difference between an industrial life-insurance company and a composite office? What sort of insurance business do they transact?

2. 'We have,' said the Chairman of the Insurance Company, 'about a million pounds of premiums coming in every Friday.' What sort of insurance company was that, and what would they do with the money?

3. Describe the general features of the British Insurance Market and the types of insurance policy offered.

4. 'Lloyd's began as a coffee house and finished as a highly organized market.' Explain what Lloyd's is and how it functions.

5. 'The broker told me that in discussing my slip with the underwriter, the underwriter had told him that the ship I intended to send my goods on was reported a casualty that morning.' Explain.

6. 'Individually we are underwriters, collectively we are Lloyd's.' What is meant by this statement?

(20) The Importance of Insurance to the British Economy

Insurance confers benefits on the insured, who are freed from a great deal of worry. It also has very important effects upon the economy of the country. Some of the main effects are listed below:

(*a*) By removing uncertainty from business life, so far as it is possible to do, insurance releases the energies of businessmen who would otherwise hesitate to go ahead with risky projects. The result is a higher level of business activity, and consequently a higher standard of living and fuller employment. Even people who are not themselves insured benefit from the added opportunities thus given to them.

(*b*) By collecting regular sums from large numbers of people, the insurance companies help the whole nation to save, and savings means investment. The funds made available to insurance companies are used to provide the capital needed to develop industry and technology.

It is important that, as a nation, we should invest in new technological advances as they are introduced. We have a tendency to lag behind our competitors in this respect. We also have to some extent a tendency to enjoy a higher standard of living (a higher rate of consumption) than we should do in view of our present difficulties. This is called living on one's capital. The millionaire's son who comes into a fortune and fritters it away is living on his capital. If as a nation we wish to enjoy a higher standard of living we must invest in the new, more productive, machinery and equipment that produces wealth more rapidly. By assisting us to save and investing the savings the insurance companies help the whole nation to become more prosperous.

(*c*) One of Britain's major problems is the balance-of-payments position. As a nation that has long ago used up most of its natural resources we are forced to import much of our needs for manufacturing industries. We export in exchange a wide variety of manufactured goods, but these goods are usually insufficient to pay for the imports. There is therefore usually an adverse **balance of trade**. We hope to make up the deficit by earning money on services, or what are called 'invisible items'. Insurance is one of these invisibles. In 1973 insurance earned for the United Kingdom about £372 million in foreign exchange. This is a very important contribution to the balance-of-payments position.

Exercises Set 21

(21) Examination Questions on Insurance

1. Insurance against losses at sea is generally effected at Lloyd's. Describe Lloyd's and outline the procedure for taking out a policy against the loss of a ship and its cargo.

(*R.S.A.*)

2. Write short explanations of the following terms: (*a*) the principle of indemnity; (*b*) shipowner's liability; (*c*) third party, fire and theft; (*d*) fidelity guarantee.

(*O.N.C.*)

3. The proposal form is the basis of the contract of insurance which must be undertaken in the 'utmost good faith'. Comment on the validity of this statement, with special reference to Mr. R. A. Jones' application to the Worldwide Insurance Co. for cover against fire damage to his premises up to £10,000.

(*R.S.A.*)

4. What do you understand by the expression 'the pooling of risks'? Is it true that a trader may be relieved of all risks by paying others to undertake to indemnify him?

(*R.S.A.*)

5. How would you account for the extensive use made of insurance facilities in commercial transactions? In the insurance of merchandise for dispatch to foreign countries, what important factors affect the cost of the insurance?

(*Associated Examining Board*)

6. Why are insurance companies an essential part of the structure of modern commerce? Illustrate your answer by describing *three* of the services these companies provide for firms producing goods for the home and overseas markets.

(*R.S.A.*)

7. Describe briefly the principal risks against which a large wholesale company might insure. State how these insurances are effected.

(*University of London*)

8. Mr. A. B. Smith will lose £100 if August Bank Holiday is a wet day. The X Y Insurance Company offers him a policy to cover this possible loss in return for a premium of £20. How has this premium figure been fixed, and what will Mr. Smith have to consider carefully before he accepts or rejects it?

(*R.S.A.*)

9. (*a*) Explain briefly the meaning of the following terms used in insurance: insurable interest; cover note; indemnity; 'utmost good faith'.

(*b*) Name four risks a house owner might insure himself against.

(*East Anglian Examination Board*)

10. What is an insurance broker and what services does he offer?
(East Anglian Examination Board)

11. Why is insurance essential to modern industry and commerce? Describe *three* of the business risks against which a firm would normally insure, and say how the insurance companies would ascertain the premium to be charged for covering each of the risks.
(R.S.A.)

12. In what ways do British insurance companies help (*a*) the individual business and (*b*) the economy as a whole?
(University of London)

13. (*a*) What is meant by an insurable interest? Illustrate.
(*b*) What kind of risks are not insurable? Illustrate.
(University of London)

14. Give an account of the basic principles which must be observed if insurance is to work satisfactorily and say what risks you would insure against if you were the owner of a small shop.
(East Anglian Examination Board)

15. Describe the risks of loss facing a British exporter of manufactured goods and explain how these risks may be covered by insurance.
(R.S.A.)

CHAPTER EIGHTEEN

TRANSPORT

(1) The Position of Transport in the Pattern of Commerce

If specialized production is how advanced societies create the utilities they need to satisfy their 'wants', some way must be devised to bring to the market-place the surpluses created by each specialist.

The function of transport is to move goods and passengers geographically. It is part of tertiary production, satisfying 'wants' by making goods available and by giving service to those who need, for family, business, or recreational reasons, to travel in their day-to-day affairs.

It also enables a fuller use to be made of the division of labour, because transport increases the size of a market and therefore permits a higher degree of specialization to be employed. An improved transport system makes possible an increase in the scale of production so that the wealth of the whole nation increases.

(2) The Elements of Transport

The four elements of transport are (a) the way, (b) the unit of carriage, (c) the motive power unit, and (d) the terminal.

(a) *The way*. Natural ways are cheap and free, and have no maintenance costs unless we try to improve them artificially. The sea, the air, the rivers, and footpaths and bridleways are all natural ways. Being natural they are subject to the whims of nature, and this often requires that they be improved artificially. Rivers are subject to controls to prevent flooding in wet periods and insufficient flow in dry periods. They are dredged to maintain a channel and locks are built to improve navigation in the upper reaches. Bridlepaths are made up and turned into roads. Highways and motorways, canals, railways, tramways, tunnels, and monorails are similarly constructed. Clearly these are not 'free' like the sea or the atmosphere, but for historical reasons some of the costs may be borne socially rather than privately. If the costs are borne by the ratepayer and taxpayer we may have what is an apparently free way because no actual charge is made to the user. If the way is privately built the owner usually has sole use of it. He then charges for its use by other persons, to recoup his capital expense.

(b) *The unit of carriage*. Whatever we call it, some vehicle or craft must be used in transport. The efficiency of the mode of transport depends to some extent on the flexibility and adaptability of the unit of carriage used. Road vehicles are more adaptable than railway rolling stock because they are not entirely tied to the way: aircraft and ships are even less tightly bound by the way on which they travel.

Even a pipeline can be considered as a unit of carriage. It is not very adaptable in its behaviour: we cannot expect it to carry gas until noon, milk from noon till 3 p.m., and petrol from 3 p.m. to midnight. In choosing our method of transport the adaptability of the unit of carriage will be a major consideration.

(c) *The motive power unit.* Every vehicle must be driven, and the choice of a propulsion unit depends upon the strength of the vehicle, the speed required, the available fuel, and other factors. Today the steam engine, the first great prime mover, has been largely replaced by the petrol engine, the jet engine, the diesel engine, and the electric motor.

(d) *The terminal.* Nearly every journey involves junctions where we can transfer from one form of transport to another. A port is usually regarded as a terminal for ships, but in fact it is also a terminal for trains, roads, pipelines, and aircraft. In planning efficient transport systems, commercial firms and transport authorities must view the interchange of facilities as being part of a unified whole. Congestion in terminals in the past has spelt the death of a transport system, as it did when the congestion on the canals led to the growth of railways.

(3) Sea Transport

Types of vessel include the following:

Passenger liners have several decks, a great many portholes (one to each outer cabin) and aerial masts; the derricks which are seen only when the liner is actually in dock, are dismantled on putting to sea. Liners carry mail and express cargo besides passengers. They sail to major ports like New York, Cape Town, and Durban, and on the Australian run. Since they keep regular timetables they are at a disadvantage as far as cargo is concerned, having to take what is ready by sailing time. They cannot wait about if cargo is delayed for any reason.

Passenger cargo liners are chiefly concerned with cargo to and from the major ports of the world, but where passenger traffic is too slight to require a passenger liner. They have a few cabins for such passengers as are available, and consequently their superstructure is reduced, the number of portholes fewer, and the major part of the hull is taken up with the holds of the vessel.

Tramps are pure cargo ships which travel anywhere in the world to earn a living. Like a tramp they have no steady home. A typical journey might be as follows:

(a) Cargo of motor vehicles and engineering parts for South Africa.
(b) Across to India for a cargo of cotton goods for Australia.
(c) From Australia with wheat to China.

(*d*) From China to Japan with iron-ore.

(*e*) Japan to West Africa with manufactured goods and electrical engineering equipment.

(*f*) Home to the United Kingdom with cocoa and palm-oil.

Bulk carriers

A ship built for a particular type of cargo, e.g. iron ore, is often called a bulk carrier. The emphasis these days is on larger and larger bulk carriers, because the cost per ton of cargo carried is greatly reduced.

Oil tankers. In the last forty years the tanker has become the commonest ship on the high seas, and a wide variety of them is available. The largest are the v.l.c.c.'s (very large crude carriers) which operate from the oil-producing countries of the Middle East, Nigeria, Venezuela, etc., to the refineries of Europe, North America and Japan. L.N.G. carriers are special refrigerated tankers for liquefied natural gas, while L.P.G. carriers carry liquefied petroleum gas. Clean product carriers, often quite tiny (1000–5000 tons), carry refined products from oil refineries, chemical works, etc. Bulk transport of liquid products is cheap and convenient. In former times oil, for example, was moved in barrels, which had to be lifted on and off the ship by cranes.

Roll-on Roll-off Ferries. There are great advantages in sending goods by road on long-haul journeys. The roll-on roll-off ship enables lorries and cars to drive onto the ship to cross from one land mass to another. Even the transport of cars from continent to continent is economical by this method (i.e. from Japan to Europe).

Lash Ships. Lash stands for *l*ighter *a*board *sh*ip. These huge ships carry barges from river mouth to river mouth, collecting loaded barges at (say) the mouth of the Mississippi and releasing them to journey from Rotterdam up the Rhine to Germany, or up the Thames to inland wharves.

The Importance of Shipping

Britain is an island inhabited by over 50 million people. We could not possibly grow sufficient food to feed our vast population ourselves, and we have insufficient supplies of most raw materials. We therefore need to import food and raw materials of every kind. In order to pay for these we must export all sorts of finished goods and services. These quantities of goods can be moved only by sea, for air transport is too expensive for heavy goods. Shipping is our most important link with foreign parts, and on it depends the prosperity of our people.

Reference is often made to *Liner Conferences*. The conference system is a way of protecting the liner trade from unfair competition from tramp shipping at times when there is excess capacity in the tramp market. If liners are to provide regular services calling at scheduled ports and leaving at stated times irrespective of the cargo position, they must be assured of reasonable freight rates. Tramp freight rates fluctuate with supply and demand, but liner freight rates are held steady. At times when tramp rates are high the liners carry at their steady rates. When tramp rates are low there is a temptation for liner customers to transfer their cargoes to the cheaper tramps. If this happens the liners will suffer losses and may be driven out of business. To encourage regular support from traders, the conference system offers rebates which can be enjoyed only if the trader can prove that his goods have on every occasion in the previous trading period travelled by the conference liners. This conference 'tie' permits a trader to ship his goods by any line that is a member of the Shipping Conference. These liners charge similar freights, but it is unfair to regard them as price-fixing 'rings' since they have in no way a monopoly of shipping, which is international in character and highly competitive. The International Chamber of Commerce, which represents the liners' customers, itself approves the conference system because of the security and reliability of service that the liner owners give to businessmen.

Terminals for Ships

Passengers and cargo have to have access to ships. The terminal is the port, where ships can be serviced, provided with all their requirements before the voyage, and take on passengers and cargo.

Requirements of a Good Port

(a) *Deep water*. This may be permanent deep water or, if it is tidal water, the water in the dock must be kept in by lock gates when the tide goes out. Southampton is a port with a natural advantage; it gets four tides a day.

(b) *Shelter*. This may be in a natural bay or harbour, or it may be provided by the banks of a river. If these are not available groynes must be built.

(c) *A clear channel*. This may mean dredging, or blasting rocks out of the way, or marking the deep water with buoys and lights. It will certainly be necessary to avoid blocking the channel with sunken ships. Pilots who know the way into the harbour are given sole charge of vessels entering and leaving.

(d) *Supplies* of coal, oil, water, food, and electricity for ships calling at the port. When a ship arrives it will need to re-fuel and replenish its stores of water and food. While its engines are not working it may need to use the shore supply of electricity.

(e) *Wharves*, cranes, floating cranes, and barges are needed to help unload the ship, and turn it round quickly. A vessel is wasted in port—its function is to sail the seas. A labour force of dockers and stevedores is needed to carry out the work of loading and unloading.

(f) *Good communications*—roads and railways, perhaps canals, to bring in the new cargo and take away the imported goods. Boat trains, air services, and other services for passengers arriving and departing.

(g) *Government offices* for customs control, emigration, immigration.

licensing, quarantine centres, police and security establishments, public health and sanitation.

(*h*) *Commercial premises*—warehouses, bonded warehouses, refrigerator stores, grain elevators, forwarding depots for packaging exports, insurance offices.

(*i*) *Dry docks*, repair yards, workshops, dis-infestation equipment and maintenance centres.

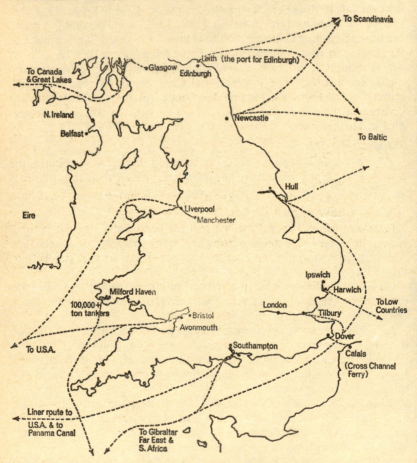

Fig. 58. The chief ports of the British Isles

(4) The Chief Ports of the British Isles

The map above shows the ports of the British Isles, and the shipping lanes which terminate in them. The importance of any port depends to some extent on its position and the industries and populations it caters for.

London is the largest 'mouth' in the British Isles. It used to be the largest in Europe, but the growth of the Common Market countries has enabled Rotterdam to claim this privilege because of its direct links with the German hinterland up the River Rhine.

It is estimated that two-thirds of all the wealth of industrial Europe is concentrated in the golden triangle that includes Birmingham, Paris, and the Ruhr. Here are grouped the three great conurbations of Europe, the Midlands and South-East of Britain, the French and Benelux industrial areas, and the German Ruhr. Since great manufacturing countries always trade with one another, the Port of London Authority is well placed to handle this expanding European trade, as well as the traditional trade with Australia, New Zealand, the Mediterranean and the Near East.

Tilbury, the 'outport' of London at one time, has now been developed as a major container port. Far enough down river to accommodate large ships, it has been chosen as Britain's major container terminal. The facilities which have come into use are some of the most advanced in the world. Six container berths with Paceco–Vickers container cranes, straddle carriers, and other handling equipment provide rapid turn-round for container ships. The two British container consortia, O.C.L. (Overseas Containers Limited) and A.C.T. (Associated Container Transport) use Tilbury for their Australia service. Roll-on roll-off ferries have started to use Tilbury as the U.K. port at which their ships call. There is a common-user berth and also two pre-packaged timber berths for the handling of wood products, manned by a permanent crew of skilled dockers who have set up new handling records with their side-loader fork-lift trucks. Just outside the container port in the main river a new grain terminal has been completed which can turn round large bulk carriers in two days. Land has been reserved for the erection of modern mills and grain-processing plants and also for three more deep-draught riverside berths.

Liverpool is the third seaport of the British Isles, controlling about 29 per cent of the trade. Its rise to power began with the cotton and tobacco trade about 250 years ago, but its continued growth is due to the general industrialization of the Midlands and the dense populations it serves. The docks are the largest in the world and the port is controlled by the Mersey Docks and Harbour Co. *Manchester*, *via* the ship canal, takes some of Liverpool's trade.

Hull, the convenient port for the industrial cities of the West Riding, is another important British port. It handles a large fish trade, woollen imports from Australia, wheat, and a wide variety of general cargo.

Southampton, the second port of the British Isles, has a large passenger trade with cruise ships taking a larger share of this business in recent years. It has become an important container port too, adding this type of packaged cargo to its traditional high speed cargoes of refrigerated meat, fruit and vegetables.

Glasgow grew to importance when the New World was opened up in the sixteenth century, handling in particular the tobacco trade. Later, the fortunate discovery in the Glasgow area of coal and iron ore led to the growth of heavy industries and a large export trade. Recently the Clyde Port Authority has been designated as Britain's first M.I.D.A. (Maritime Industrial Development Area). Its deep water makes it ideal for bulk carriers unloading directly into huge refineries, steel works, chemical plants, etc., which are being constructed in the estuary.

The Forth Port Authority, which includes *Leith and Grangemouth* is the port authority for East Scotland. It handles cargoes from Scandinavia, the Baltic and the Low Countries.

Bristol, a port that once gave its name to the British sailor's idea of efficiency 'ship-shape and Bristol fashion', has declined because it is too shallow for modern shipping. Instead the port of Avonmouth was built nearer to the sea by the Bristol authorities. This matter of shallow water is worth mentioning with regard to the new super-tankers, of 200,000 tons or more, the biggest ships in the world. Few British ports can adequately cater for these giants. One special tanker terminal has been constructed at Milford Haven in South Wales.

Another new development affects Canvey Island in Essex. Here the only base in the British Isles for 'methane carriers' has been built. These are new types of refrigerator ships which carry liquefied natural gas from the Sahara, at very low temperatures. The liquid methane, when allowed to warm slightly, turns back into its gaseous form and can be used in ordinary gas pipelines. Britain has 20 per cent of the world methane fleet.

Other ports. Several small ports have demonstrated since the Second World War that the smaller terminal has much to offer the carrier. They make up in personal relationships and ease of decision for the lack of large-scale facilities. Outstanding among the small ports are Felixstowe, which developed a container berth before the bigger ports had realized the revolution that was to come over shipping, Immingham, strategically placed for the Common Market and Baltic trades, and Shoreham, on the South Coast.

(5) Advantages and Disadvantages of Sea Transport

(*a*) The 'way' is free, and gives access to most parts of the world.

(*b*) Buoyancy of the water makes the effective weight zero. Hence sea transport is very suitable for heavy goods.

(*c*) Small power is needed to drive a vessel, so that large vessels are practicable and economies can be achieved.

(*d*) Because weight is not important, ships can be massive enough to be strong.

(*e*) Transport by sea is relatively slow, so that passengers are easily lost to airlines when speed is important.

(*f*) Ports are expensive and delays not uncommon.

(*g*) The possibility of deterioriation of cargo is great because sea water is corrosive, and also liable to affect the quality and flavour of cargoes.

(*h*) Pilfering of cargoes is not uncommon, though 'containerization' is doing much to reduce this.

(6) Rail Transport

For a century the railways were supreme in inland carriage, both for goods and passengers. Today there is hardly a country in the world where the railways do not lose money. In Britain the railways were nationalized in 1947, and a complete overhaul of the railway system has replaced steam power with electric or disel-electric rolling stock. High degrees of efficiency have been achieved on particular trunk routes, yet the overall system is still losing money.

(7) Advantages and Disadvantages of Rail Transport

(*a*) Rail traffic is fast when actually moving, for it has a private way which is kept clear. It follows that if goods are to go a long way, rail transport is probably best. The economic limit seems to be about 200 miles. Below that limit the disadvantages of rail traffic make road transport more economic.

(*b*) It is economical in the use of labour, one driver and guard can take 60 carriages or trucks. Compared with road transport, where long-distance lorries carrying only 32 tons often have a crew of three, the advantage is clearly with the train.

(*c*) Railway transport is dominated by the 'terminal' problem, for heavy capital costs preclude running a line to every customer's door. Goods must therefore be loaded and unloaded at terminals to complete their journey by road vehicle. Fig. 59 shows one of the latest container-handling devices for effecting this type of changeover.

Even though sophisticated handling equipment is now available to load and unload trains, delay seems inevitable and demarcation disputes between groups of workers are common.

(*d*) Because of the nature of the way, a breakdown, strike, or go-slow movement holds up all traffic behind so that its effects are cumulative, building up an enormous backlog of goods which may include perishables, live-stock, etc.

(*e*) Rail transport is impersonal, so that pilfering, delay, and negligent behaviour are difficult to locate and remedy. The consignors and owners of goods are powerless themselves to expedite the handling of goods. One Wiltshire firm sending daily supplies of packaged perishable foodstuffs to South Coast towns found it could not get its packing cases back in less than an average of three weeks. This may not have

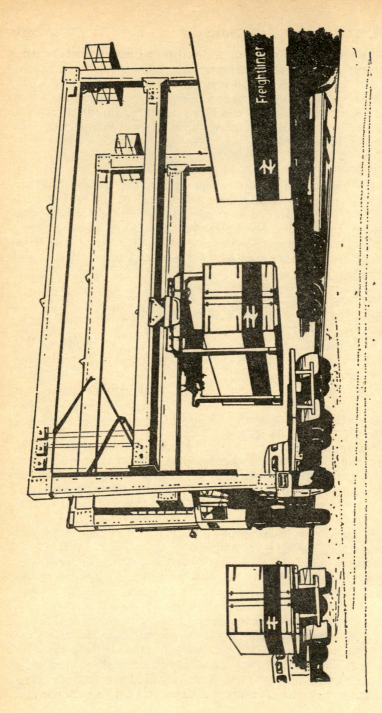

Fig. 59. Transferring containers from rail to road haulage

been any fault of the railway, the fault may have lain with the retailers, but the impersonal nature of the service operated against the supplier and forced him to invest in much larger numbers of containers than would have been necessary otherwise.

(*f*) Traffic density presents a problem to railways, which operate ideally when the train is full. Highly concentrated traffic is the best. Even very dense traffic at very high speeds can be safely operated with modern equipment. The Inter-City trains run by British Rail commonly reach speeds of 100 miles per hour.

The Beeching Report on the Railways

Continuing heavy losses on the railway network led the Government to appoint one of Britain's leading businessmen, Dr. Beeching, to head a full scale inquiry into the railway organization. His report made drastic suggestions for ending the deficit. They included the following:

(*a*) Reducing the rail network itself from 17,000 miles to 8,000 miles, eliminating in the process many rural passenger services, suburban services, stopping passenger trains, and country stations.

(*b*) Concentrating on the profitable, long-distance, dense traffic routes, chiefly London–North, London–Midlands, London–West–South Wales, and Glasgow–Manchester–Bristol lines. Nearly all of these were carrying 1,000 tons per day in each direction; some were carrying almost 2,000 tons.

(*c*) Uneconomic freight trains were to be replaced by **liner trains** running at regular times with a limited number of stopping points. By having fewer but larger depots increased efficiency could be obtained, but at some loss of convenience to the customer.

In fact, for political reasons, the full Beeching scheme was never introduced and Dr. Beeching himself left the railways. The Ministry of Transport has instead set the lower limit of the railway system at 11,000 miles, and the Transport Act of 1968 has implemented a modified scheme. The effect of the Beeching Report has still been very great.

Freightliners—The Railway Container Service

In March, 1963 the Beeching Report 'The Re-shaping of British Railways' proposed that freightliner trains be introduced. They were to use road and rail transport for door-to-door delivery of 'containerized' goods, the change-over from road to rail being effected by completely mechanical means at special rail terminals.

By 1970 the scheme had developed to the point where a national freight grid had been established between 29 freightliner terminals in main industrial and commercial centres. Four of these are in London, at King's Cross, York Way, Stratford, and Willesden. Others are at Glasgow, Manchester, Liverpool, Aberdeen, Birmingham, Cardiff, Edinburgh,

Hull, Leeds, Newcastle, Sheffield, Stockton, Belfast, Dublin, Felixstowe, Harwich, Nottingham, Southampton, Swansea and Tilbury.

All these terminals have now passed into the control of the National Freight Corporation, which under the 1968 Transport Act assumed responsibility for integrating road and rail transport. About £20 million had been spent on the freightliner system by the time the National Freight Corporation took over, through a company called Freightliners Ltd.

(8) Road Transport

Road transport has great advantages over inland rail and waterways, now that petrol, diesel, and jet engines have furnished a variety of cheap motive powers. The chief advantages are as follows:

(*a*) Intermediate terminal handling is eliminated by door-to-door delivery. The operator's terminal is under his personal direction and control, designed to do what he requires. Delivery is made direct to the consignee's premises, and if these premises are not equipped to handle the goods being delivered this can often be overcome by appliances actually on the vehicle.

(*b*) Road vehicles are extremely flexible, and computerized route charts can now be prepared which give the most direct, or most economic, route to be followed.

(*c*) Although slower than rail freight when in actual transit, the slow speed is more than made up by the elimination of transhipment, the directness of the journey and the personal control of the entire movement. Two-way radios even enable drivers to report their exact positions so that they can be called to assist other drivers or to pick up new loads.

(*d*) Specialized vehicles of great variety have been produced by the road-vehicle manufacturers. They include specialized vehicles for bulk haulage, containers, packaged timber and other loads.

(*e*) Low capital requirements are a feature of the industry, which permits a new entrant to start with a single vehicle. True, he has to face a licensing problem with certain kinds of vehicle, but many new operators do secure licences especially since the industry is continually expanding.

(*f*) The 'way' is at present still free, if one ignores vehicle taxation. Proposals that electronic devices should be fitted to vehicles to charge them for use of busy roads have not yet been implemented.

(9) Road Transport—A Growth Industry

There are 200,000 miles of roadway in Great Britain, of which about 9,000 miles are trunk roads, 80,000 miles are classified roads, nearly 1,000 miles are motorways and the rest are minor roads.

The following statistics from the official *Monthly Digest of Statistics* demonstrate the growth of the road-transport industry:

Vehicles Licensed

1960	9,384,000
1971	15,505,000

Volume of Goods Carried

1952	19,000 million ton-miles
1968	44,000 million ton-miles

Percentage Change in Goods Traffic

	1958	1968
Road	100	146
Rail	100	85

The comparison with rail figures is particularly interesting. In 1968 the railways carried 14,700 million ton-miles of goods. The roads carried three times as much as this. Nearly all the railways goods were bulk haulage. If we took *all* the general merchandise off the railways and sent it by road, it would increase road haulage by only 5 per cent, and at present it is growing by about 5 per cent per annum anyway.

Motorways, Bridges, and Tunnels

If road transport is growing by 5 per cent per annum, congestion of the present roads is inevitable, and an expanding road network is crucial to progress. The motorway is the answer to some of the problems, giving fast journeys between towns. A start on the motorway network in Britain was made in 1958, and considerable progress has been achieved already in linking the main areas of the country. By 1972 Britain had about 1,000 miles of motorway, compared with Germany's 3,000 miles, Italy's 1,500 miles and France's 1,200 miles.

The dilemma of transport is revived by these modern highways, for while the cost is borne socially the benefits in cheaper running costs and faster journeys are enjoyed by the individual families and firms who use the motorway. Tolls have been suggested as a way of reducing the social costs of these projects, but vehicle taxation is still the favourite method of paying for motorways. Some idea of the constructional engineering involved can be seen from the artists' drawing of the Almondsbury four-level road linkage shown in Fig. 60.

The effect of motorways on the location of industry and the availability of labour is considerable. Country towns which once had an unemployment problem, and where emigration to the cities has been the solution for two centuries, suddenly find that land values are soaring as

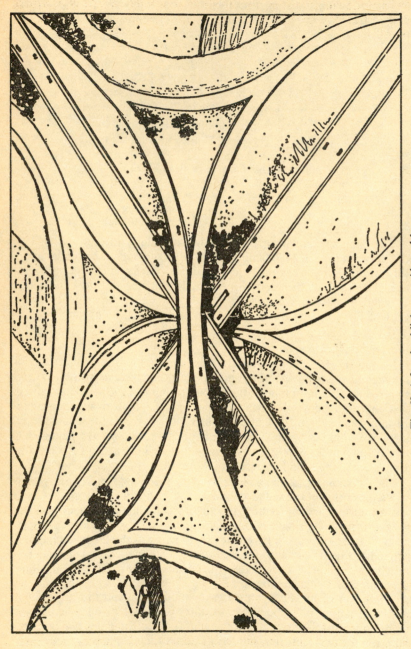

Fig. 60. A four-level link-up at Almondsbury

access to the motorway makes the town a desirable site for industry of every sort. Workers begin to travel in from farther afield to take employment.

Bridges and tunnels are essential if motorways are to take direct routes across river estuaries, and some splendid work has been done since the War in bridging the Firth of Forth and the Bristol Channel. The drawings of the Severn Bridge, and its position in the motorway network to South Wales (Figs. 61 and 62) illustrate the grandeur and utility of such engineering feats.

The Dartford–Purfleet tunnel is a similar link across the Thames Estuary. It is proposed to duplicate it shortly, so that two one-way tunnels are available. It is being paid for, like the bridges mentioned above, by tolls charged to users. By giving direct access to Kent and Essex from the other side of the river it is promoting the prosperity of both counties.

Use of Containers in Transport

Container services were started as early as 1928 by the four British main-line railway companies, but they have recently become firmly established in road, rail, and sea transport. A wide range of off-the-peg containers is now available in a variety of materials, and, while standardization of size is important, containers suitable to the personal needs of most private users can be obtained.

The basic advantages of containers are low freight charges and door-to-door security. Where individual parcels, cartons, or crates are sent by a carrier the work involved in loading and unloading many small items makes for expensive use of labour. If a shipper or distributor is moving large enough consignments to fill a container he can load it himself, either by stacking goods on one another or by making use of the shelving and partitioning systems devised by the designers. The container is then sealed, and moved as one unit with the advanced lifting equipment available. It is impossible to tell what is in it, which is a deterrent to thieves, and without lifting tackle it is impossible to spirit the whole consignment away. Freight charges, insurance, and losses due to minor pilfering are reduced.

Container design is important, and handling presents problems. If sea-going containers are to be piled six high, which is not uncommon, the containers must be strong enough to take the weight. This usually requires a steel framework, but steel is corrosive. Stainless steel is better, but is more costly, and stainless-steel framework with aluminium panels is a useful compromise. Bottom-lift handling devices reduce the need for strength in the container. Top-lift handling devices rely on the container itself to support the weight and place considerable strain upon it. It appears that current freightliner rates are working out about 25–30 per cent cheaper than ordinary freight charges, and therefore consider-

Fig. 61. An artist's impression of the Severn Bridge

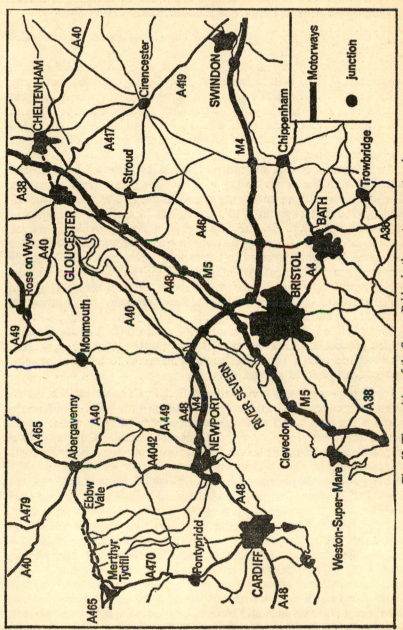

Fig. 62. The position of the Severn Bridge in the motorway network

able advantages are offered to commercial firms. By 1973 60 per cent of all Japanese–European cargo was containerized.

(10) Solving the Inland Transport Problem—Integrated or Co-ordinated Services?

Since the Transport Act of 1947 first set up a nationalized system, inland transport in Britain has been bedevilled by politics. For many years we were in the position of operating a system which had just become law, but was about to be modified by the next Government. The discussion revolved around whether we should have an integrated transport system or a number of co-ordinated services each of which was a separate organization.

An integrated system of transport would be operated by a central authority with the power to say who should operate certain services. It would clearly be an enormous organization, and experience has already shown that a system of this size suffers from the diseconomies of large-scale operation. On the other hand, it does provide an overall body to control the opposing factions in transport and ensure that the vast sums of capital invested in transport systems, much of it socially provided, are wisely spent. An integrated service will be governed by the basic precept that what is needed is a cheap, efficient transport system which provides consumers with goods and services at the minimum personal and social cost.

Three White Papers issued in late 1967 outlined the Labour Government's proposals, which were put into effect by the 1968 Transport Act. This Act has been a very effective Act and seems to have the support now of both political parties.

(*a*) *Transport of freight.* A National Freight Corporation was set up as an independent body, directly responsible to the Minister of Transport for the integration of freight services previously provided by the British Railways Board and the Transport Holding Company. It is responsible for all public-sector freight traffic moving wholly by road, or originating by road and moving partly by rail, leaving British Rail in charge of freight originated by rail—which is mainly bulk cargo. The Transport Holding Company handed over to the National Freight Corporation all its general and specialist road-haulage and shipping services, and the National Freight Corporation also took from the Railways Board their freightliner, freight sundries and road cartage services.

Road licences were drastically altered. Directly the Bill became law, all vehicles less than 30 cwt. were freed from licence requirements. This meant almost a million tons of capacity became available to carry small loads. Road transport is particularly suitable for small loads over short distances. Larger vehicles still have to be licensed, but licences are now issued only if a firm has properly qualified staff and an adequate financial structure. The new licences, which have been called vehicle operators' licences, are issued to operators, not vehicles. This gives an advantage to large firms.

(*b*) *Railway policy*. Here the chief effect of the Bill has been to reduce accumulated capital debt which previously represented a serious expense to the industry. Over £1,200 million of debt has been cancelled, reducing the railways' debt to only £300 million. Fuller use of railway workshops and vehicle-maintenance departments is being made by permitting these organizations to compete with private companies in the sale, manufacture, and repair of a wide range of goods. The official view here is that it is ridiculous to have these expensive assets, which have been provided at public expense, under-utilized.

In 1974–5 the Government provided very large sums to assist the transfer of goods from road to rail to subsidise uneconomic but socially desirable lines.

(*c*) *Passenger transport*. The solution here has been to set up local Passenger Transport Authorities (P.T.A.'s) to integrate and develop passenger services by bus and rail. A national bus company has been set up to take over the bus services previously run by the Transport Holding Company, and with power to acquire voluntarily other undertakings.

(11) Air Transport

The transport of goods and passengers by air is the greatest transport achievement of the post-war era. The great advantage of air transport is its speed, and for this reason it is particularly suitable for the transport of passengers. Shipping lines that once were prosperous, with full bookings on the New York, South Africa, and Australia runs, have had to turn to cruises and the emigrant trade to earn a living. However, air transport is expensive, since aeroplanes are sophisticated technical products. Design, operation, and maintenance are all costly, and the actual pay load is small. Even the giant air-buses now in service carry only a few hundred passengers.

The use of aircraft as freighters has been slower to develop because the advantages of air freighting have been less obvious. Only when Air Canada began to publish its market research on air-freight costs did the world wake up to the fact that air freighting was a practicable and economically advantageous method of transport for many industrial and commercial enterprises. Previously it had been thought that it was advantageous only for perishable commodities or small packets of high value, or for freight (particularly cars) directly related to passengers. Even so, the cheapest place for cargo is on the passenger aircraft.

(12) The Economic Viability of Air Freighting

The essential point concerning the transport of goods by air is that the actual cost of the air-freight ticket is less important than the *overall* cost of moving the goods from their present position to their destination. The overall cost includes many other expenses besides the actual carriage charge, some of these are listed below.

(*a*) *The cost of packing.* Packaging can be very expensive for a sea voyage, where inclement weather may damage the goods, salt air may taint produce, humidity may rust metals, etc. With air freighting most packaging is quite unnecessary. Modern aircraft fly above the clouds,

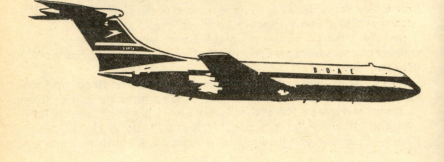

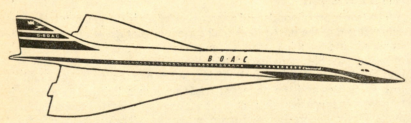

Fig. 63. Sophisticated technical products

nowhere near the sea, and apart from possible effects of cold, the goods in transit are unlikely to come into contact with 'weather'.

(*b*) *Factory condition* can be preserved. In many trades goods are finished at the factory and sent to the consumer in first-class condition: dresses and suits are pressed; motor bikes are tuned; bicycles are assembled for delivery. The need to pack and ship goods destroys this sort of activity, which has to be done at the destination, with high costs of establishing depots, employing and training skilled labour, etc. With air freight, special racks installed in the aircraft enable goods to be moved in factory condition, with just a light polythene sheet over them.

(*c*) *Insurance costs* are lower by air. Aircraft risks are high, but the duration of the journey is so short that for any given transit the risks are much smaller than by surface vehicle.

(*d*) *The saving of time* may prevent losses by idle factories or over-stocked warehouses. One case on which Air Canada reported concerned a leading German hosiery-making firm which ordered 230 machines from Pennyslvania. The air-freight charge was £80 per unit, six times more than the cost of dispatch by sea. The machines were installed ten days ahead of schedule as a result, and turned out 207,999 pairs of hose in the ten days. This was more than enough to yield a handsome profit on the venture. Another firm flew in its raw materials and components from suppliers daily, so that there was no need to warehouse or stockpile these goods. Its savings in warehouse space alone permitted an extension of plant layout to achieve economies of large scale, which more than off-set the high cost of air freight.

(*e*) *Where goods are fashionable*, they sell best on the crest of the wave. One manufacturer of wallpaper filled a charter aircraft with rolls showing a popular recording group and followed them around America selling at fancy prices.

These are some of the aspects which, when taken into account, make air freighting an extremely useful solution to man's transport problems.

(13) Other Transportation Systems

Hovercraft. Hovercraft operate on a cushion of air which is pumped under the vehicle and kept in by a skirt of heavy material. They are particularly effective over water, where they enable much higher speeds to be achieved than by the conventional ship. There is no water resistance worth speaking of, and a cross-channel ferry is now operating from a base at Pegwell Bay near Dover, carrying vehicles and passengers at about 80 knots. The hovercraft is particularly advantageous in estuaries where its ability to ignore sandbanks and shallow water means it can operate by more direct routes. The use of longer skirts, possibly up to 12 feet deep will improve the ability of these craft to negotiate the larger waves.

A second use for hover skirts has been found in moving heavy loads over bridges which are not strong enough to carry the load. By fitting a temporary skirt to lorries carrying heavy loads of this type the weight can be spread evenly over the surface of the bridge, reducing the weight which is usually borne by the axle assemblies, and enabling the load to cross without damage to the bridge.

Pipelines are increasing in importance for the transportation of natural gas and oil fuels from the ports to inland depots. While the capital cost is great, the savings on motor-vehicle costs for comparable movements by road, quite apart from the social costs of congested highways, make this form of transport both economical and socially desirable. Pipelines cannot however compete with tanker costs, especially giant tankers on long hauls. Pipelines are also being used for the transport of solids carried in slurry form.

Monorails are a form of transport that offer quick passenger and goods services along overhead routes, erected on concrete pillars along the highways. The carrying units are small but make up for this by frequency of service, and high speed. Although not practicable for long routes they have advantages in solving local transport problems, especially the connection of airports with city centres.

(For readers with a special interest in transport, *Transport and Distribution Made Simple* gives a fuller account of modern transport methods.)

EXERCISES SET 22

(14) Transport

1. Motor vehicles are delivered by the manufacturers to their customers all over the country. Discuss the alternative forms of transport of such vehicles from a factory in Birmingham to various destinations in Great Britain, and indicate what factors are most likely to influence the manufacturer's choice.

(*R.S.A.*)

2. It has been stated that there has been a failure to build up the facilities of ports to keep pace with the impressive advances in merchant-ship design and performance during the past ten years. Discuss sea transport, bearing in mind the above statement.

(*R.S.A.*)

3. What are the advantages and disadvantages of the liner-train system? Candidates may wish to use the following headings in their answers: (*a*) why introduced; (*b*) liner-train routes and timings; (*c*) speed of delivery; (*d*) effect on cost; (*e*) possible advantages.

(*University of London*)

4. Discuss the relative advantages and disadvantages of air and sea transport for Britain's overseas trade.

5. What factors make container traffic suitable for the dispatch of consignments of radio sets from Britain to Australia?

6. 'Bulk carriers seem to be getting larger year by year, and the ports must be prepared to accommodate them.' Discuss the advantages of bulk carriers and the problems they present to ports.

7. Why have passengers taken to the air so readily, while freight is much less easily persuaded into the sky?

8. Write a few lines each about the implications of transport by: (*a*) air car ferry; (*b*) hovercraft; (*c*) 'roll-on roll-off' ferries; (*d*) charter flights.

9. 'Insurance companies regard aircraft as high-risk methods of transport.' . . . 'One of the advantages of sending goods by air is that insurance is usually cheaper than for goods sent the same distance by sea.' Discuss the apparent contradiction in these two statements.

10. Why has Tilbury been chosen for the container berths of the Port of London Authority?

11. What facilities and equipment must be available to enable a modern commercial port to function efficiently?

(*University of London*)

12. Compare rail transport and canal transport for the movement of freight,

explaining how a business would decide whether to use the one or the other for a particular consignment.

(University of London)

13. What matters need to be considered in assessing the type of transport to be used when goods are to be sent from point A to point B? Illustrate your answer by referring to two very dissimilar commodities.

(University of London)

14. Air freight charges are usually much higher than the charges for sending goods by sea. Explain the reasons why, in spite of this, a businessman may decide to send goods to an overseas market by air rather than by sea.

(East Anglian Examination Board)

15. What do you consider to be the chief advantages of pipelines over road haulage for the transport of fuel oils. Are there any disadvantages?

CHAPTER NINETEEN

COMMUNICATIONS

(1) Introduction

Businessmen must be able to communicate with one another if they are to contract for the purchase and sale of goods. The finance of these transactions and the instructions for delivery and distribution must be arranged through agents and employees. Knowledge of what is going on in markets is essential to fix prices, while the activities of governments, politicians, and competitors may bring a need to modify actions already started or expedite arrangements that are under consideration. In order to make the intricate decisions of modern life, a network of communication services must be available at all times. The President of the United States has his 'hot line' to Moscow, the discount houses ring just as frantically to borrow half a million pounds before they are 'forced into the Bank'.

Many of these services are handled by Government departments, for secrecy is essential at certain times, and the sovereign body in most countries keeps communications within its personal control. One of the main landmarks in London is the Post Office Tower, which dominates the Tottenham Court Road area. The Post Office is the chief link in the multitude of connections and communications made daily by businessmen. About 30 million telegrams, 5,000 million telephone calls and 12,000 million letters are handled annually. The Post Office Corporation has over 400,000 employees.

(2) The Services of the Post Office

A full account of the many and varied services offered by the Post Office is available in the *Post Office Guide*, which is published annually in July, and is brought up to date by monthly amendments. Every reader is recommended to obtain a copy and study the services for himself. It is impossible to give more than a brief outline here, since the *Guide* has over 600 pages.

Inland post. The most important service is the ordinary post, which for a few pence delivers a letter anywhere in the British Isles within a day or two of posting. Besides letters the service carries postcards, printed papers and parcels, samples, newspapers, special packages for the blind, and many other specialized items.

Business-reply post. On application a licence will be issued to cover this service, for either postcards or folded advertisements. Members of the public who wish to make inquiries about an advertiser's product do so free of charge. The postage is charged to the licensee, 0·00½ extra being charged on each.

Franking (*postage-meter*) *machines.* On application a licence will be issued to use these machines which are available from Roneo Ltd, and Pitney Bowes Ltd. On application to a specified post-office they are set with the sum prepaid, usually about £100. Letters need not be stamped, but are franked by the meter and daily records must be kept of the amount spent.

Poste restante facilities for the convenience of commercial and other travellers are available at most main post offices.

Private boxes and bags which enable firms to collect mail at convenient times are available at £20 per annum for letters and a further £20 for parcels.

Railex. This is a service available to the public, which enables an unregistered packet to be delivered by messenger, to the appropriate railway station for dispatch to its destination, where it will be collected and taken to the post office for delivery by messenger. The charge is £1 and the weight limit is 1 lb.

Recorded delivery. For a small charge plus normal postage, the delivery of a letter or packet will be recorded so that proof of delivery is available. This is useful for legal documents, certificates, etc.

Registered letters. Most readers will be familiar with these; the compensation payable is up to £500 (charge £0·35).

Telegraphic addresses. For a charge of £3 per year a firm receiving many telegrams may register a two-word telegraphic address, e.g. 'TOOTHBRUSH NOTTINGHAM', 'EVERYTHING LONDON'. These are the telegraphic addresses of Boots' Nottingham headquarters, and of Harrods, the Knightsbridge department store.

Telegrams are less important now than formerly, but about 30 million inland and overseas telegrams are handled each year. At the start of the century about 100 million were handled annually. The reduction is due to the growth of the telephone service, and the Telex.

Telephone services. There are in the United Kingdom roughly eight million telephone subscribers, about 90 per cent of whom dial their numbers on the Subscriber Trunk Dialling system. There are still some manually operated exchanges but these will gradually be reduced.

By means of the Continental and International Exchanges in London it is possible to communicate with Europe, Canada and the United States, Honolulu, and Australasia.

Radio and television. Also travelling over the cables of the Post Office network go messages which end up as radio and television programmes. These are also transmitted by satellite. Although satellite communications are still in their infancy millions of people throughout the world are now able to enjoy spectacles such as the World Cup football matches in their own homes at the instant they happen. While not wishing to minimize such miracles, the greatest importance of the satellite system may eventually prove to be the multi-channel telephone circuits it makes available to put businessmen in touch with one another around the world.

Telex services. Telex services provide a direct link between subscribers and other users all over the world. Messages typed at the sender's end will be transmitted to the receiving machine at the other end, where they are printed out for the addressee. Coded messages to preserve privacy are possible, and as the message automatically switches on the receiver in the addressee's office, messages can be sent at any hour of the day or night.

(3) Future Developments in the Communications Field

Progress in communications is extremely rapid, and its impact upon routine operations can be considerable. Post Office engineers are already considering the possibility of reading electricity and gas meters over the telephone wires automatically without the present need for meter readers to call at houses. The possibility of feeding television programme signals into houses over the same wires as the telephone (without interrupting either when the other is in use) is another distinct possibility. The same circuits may be used to signal fires or burglaries on the premises. The ingenuity of the telecommunications engineer seems boundless.

(4) The Position of Advertising in Commerce

One important aspect of communications is advertising. Without advertising a mass-production free-enterprise system could not function, for the mass-market can only be secured and maintained by advertising. Unlike the village trader of former days, whose products were ordered after personal recommendation, the businessman today has to produce in anticipation of demand. Advertising alone can create this demand. Critics of the free-enterprise system deplore advertising, but not all of it is bad.

There are two kinds of advertising, **informative advertising** and **persuasive advertising.** Informative advertising makes clear the availability of the product, its uses and advantages, its price, quality, and terms of sale. There can be no serious objection to informative advertising. In a specialist world we are all too busy to investigate products for ourselves. The variety of our lives is enhanced by being informed about products which otherwise would escape our attention.

Persuasive advertising does not just inform, it uses subtle techniques to persuade, and even delude, the public into buying. At best it is unnecessary. It may be misleading, wasteful, and even harmful, if it makes anti-social behaviour appear desirable. The critics are certainly right when they condemn repetitive advertising on television of branded detergents, each of which is supposed to be better than the next. The Monopolies Commission has reported that it finds such advertising against the public interest and has recommended a 40 per cent cut in advertising in this field.

The main fields of advertising are television, radio, the daily press, weekly and monthly magazines and journals, and postal advertising. The latter is aimed at particular groups of interested individuals. Many organizations charge a fee for the use of their membership lists for mailing purposes. The best lists are those built up over the years from satisfied customers. Nurserymen such as those referred to on page 283 circularize former customers as a matter of course with their annual catalogue of roses, shrubs and plants.

EXERCISES SET 23

(5) Communications

1. Discuss the services offered by the Post Office to businessmen.

2. Write a short account of (*a*) the telephone S.T.D. system, and (*b*) the telex system.

3. (*a*) Describe briefly and compare in respect of speed and convenience, the following services provided by the Post Office for the transmission of commercial information: express services, railway letters, telegrams.

(*b*) Give at least two examples of losses that poor services might cause to a business. (*University of London*)

4. 'If communications improve, transport will be more efficient.' How can improved communications increase the efficiency of a transport department?

5. What is the Post Office Guide? Describe two services in the postal field which would enable a businessman to increase the market for his goods.

6. What is a satellite-tracking station? How does it enable television programmes to be received across the world?

7. 'Communications were once dependant upon man; later upon the horse: today they are instantaneous.' Explain how this improvement benefits the ordinary public by its impact upon commerce.

8. What do you understand by: (*a*) a franked envelope; (*b*) a reply-paid postcard; (*c*) Railex services; and (*d*) a telegraphic address?

CHAPTER TWENTY

THE DOCUMENTS USED IN BUSINESS

(1) Business Transactions

The word 'transaction' implies a transfer of goods or services from one person to another. Any type of business deal, however simple or complicated, is a transaction. Millions of transactions take place every day. Where the transaction involves the provision of goods or services in return for immediate payment it is called a **cash transaction.** Where payment is delayed until a later date it is called a **credit transaction.** There is therefore a dual nature to all transactions:

(*a*) The commodity, or service, is supplied.
(*b*) Payment is made for it.

The time interval between the happening of event (*a*) and event (*b*) is termed the period of credit, and varies from no time at all in the case of a cash transaction to years in the case of hire-purchase transactions.

The usual arrangement between firms who are doing regular business with one another is that accounts are settled monthly, so that the normal transaction is one of limited credit, goods or services required during one month being settled in the first few days of the next month. In order to keep a record of these transactions every transaction must have an original document, which can be recorded in the books of account.

The most important documents are: (*a*) Orders: (*b*) Invoices; (*c*) Debit Notes; (*d*) Credit Notes; (*e*) Statements; (*f*) Receipts; (*g*) Petty Cash Vouchers; (*h*) Cheques; (*i*) Bills of Lading; and (*j*) Bills of Exchange.

(2) The Order

An order may be merely in the form of a letter, but may be prepared on a specially printed form issued by the supplier. This is to make it convenient for his stores department to prepare the order, since the goods are usually arranged in the warehouse in the same sequence as on the order form.

Such orders can be extremely complicated, listing hundreds of items, and it is impossible to reproduce one here. Where the customer is unlikely to want more than half a dozen items a simpler type of order is used which permits the customer to write in what is required; but the order form is printed so that the supplier can make clear what his terms

ORDER FORM

To WILLIK BROS. LTD.

Rearsby, Leicester LE7 8YQ

Telephone SYSTON 3936/7

Name in Block Letters please

....

Address..

....

Tel. No. ....

When filling in this order form, please do not give any plant names but only use the CORRECT CODE AND PRICE.

AMOUNT ENCLOSED

	£	P
Banknotes or Cash		
Gift Tokens		
Cheque/Giro		
Postal Orders		
Money Orders		
TOTAL		

Quantity	CODE	£	p	Quantity	CODE	£	p
					Brought forward		

| | CARRIAGE AND PACKING (see below) | | | | | | |

CARRIAGE AND PACKING

The following scale applies to all orders, except those which are collected from our Nurseries, on which no extra charge is made.

For orders up to 1·50 please add 0·15
  ,, ,, ,, 3·00 ,, ,, 0·25
  ,, ,, over 3·00 ,, ,, 0·30

PLEASE SEND ME A COPY OF WILLIK GARDENING GUIDE.

I enclose Postal Order/Cheque/Stamps for FIVE PENCE (0·05)

Name...

Address..

(BLOCK LETTERS PLEASE)

PAGE 24

We shall be pleased to send a copy of this Catalogue to friends or relatives if you will fill in their name and address below :—

Name...
Address..

Name...
Address..

Name...
Address..

Name...
Address..

Name...
Address..

Fig. 64. A nurseryman's order form

of business, carriage, etc. are. The layout of the form may also help his accounts department in recording the many small orders received. Fig. 64 shows such an order form, well laid out to assist the accounts staff and with sensible advertisement material designed to extend the supplier's market.

(3) The Invoice

Definition: an invoice is a business document which is made out whenever one person sells goods to another. It can be used in the courts of law as evidence of a contract for the sale of goods. It is made out by the person selling the goods, and in large businesses it may have as many as five copies printed on paper of different colours.

Fig. 65 shows the usual form of invoice in use in large firms. It must have the following information:

(*a*) Names and addresses of both the interested parties to the sale.

(*b*) The date of the sale.

(*c*) An exact description of the goods, with quantity and unit price, and details of the trade discount (if any) given. (This invoice is not one for goods to be re-sold, so no trade discount appears.)

(*d*) The terms on which the goods are sold, i.e. the discount that may be taken and the credit period allowed. The words 'Terms Net' means no discount is allowed. The words 'Prompt Settlement' means no credit period is allowed.

Many firms write 'E. & O. E.' on the bottom of the invoice. These letters mean 'Errors and Omissions Excepted'. If an error or omission has been made, the firm selling the goods may put it right.

Value Added Tax. With the introduction of V.A.T. on April 1st, 1973, it became necessary for suppliers to include on all invoices likely to be used as 'tax invoices' a statement of the V.A.T. charge for the supply described on the invoice. The invoice may then be used by the supplier as proof of 'output tax' and by his customer as proof of 'input tax'. An explanation of these terms and of the new tax may be found on pages 323–8.

What Happens to the Four Copies?

Top copy: this is sent by post or by hand to the person buying the goods, and he uses it to enter in his Purchase Day Book. He then keeps the invoice as his copy of the contract of sale.

Second copy: this is usually the Sales Day Book copy, which is kept by the seller, entered in his Sales Day Book, and then filed to be kept as his copy of the contract of sale.

Third and fourth copies: these are sent together to the Stores Department of the seller, where the storekeeper takes the goods out of the store. The third copy, often called the **Delivery Note,** is given to the carman to take with him in cases where goods are being delivered to the buyer's warehouse. He presents it with the parcel of goods and gets a signature on it to prove that the goods arrived safely. This copy is then taken back by the carman to the storekeeper and is filed in the stores department after being entered in the Stores Record Book. The fourth copy is wrapped up in the parcel before it is given to the carman. It is often called the **Advice Note** and it enables the buyer's storekeeper to check the contents of the parcel and record in his Stores Record Book the stores that have just arrived.

Other copies. Where a set of invoices has more than four copies, they will usually include: (*a*) a representative's copy which is sent to the commercial traveller handling the order; (*b*) a traffic planning copy for the transport department; (*c*) a consignee's copy for the actual con-

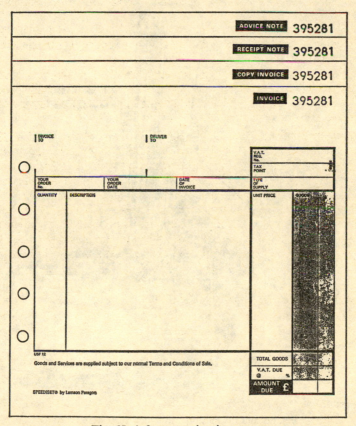

Fig. 65. A four-copy invoice system

signee, as distinct from the Head Office of the buyer's firm; (*d*) a costing copy for the Costing Department.

How Long do we Keep an Invoice?

Usually for six years. Under the Limitation Act of 1939 an action in the courts on a simple contract cannot begin more than six years after the contract was made. If we keep our invoices for six years the chance of the invoice being needed as legal evidence disappears. Many firms get rid of their old invoices by shredding them into packing material.

(4) Cash Discounts and Trade Discounts

There are two kinds of discount in business, Cash Discount and Trade Discount.

Cash Discount is given to debtors who pay promptly for their goods

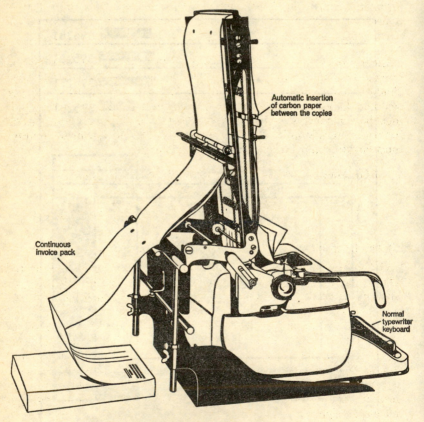

Automatic insertion
of carbon paper
between the copies

Continuous
invoice pack

Normal
typewriter
keyboard

Fig. 66. and the machine on which they were typed

when the time for payment arrives. It is a great inconvenience to a businessman to have debtors who are slow in settling their accounts, because it means that his capital is being used by someone else. To encourage prompt payment a cash discount is offered. Naturally this means a smaller profit than he would otherwise earn, but it may be cheaper to give this discount than to allow debts to accumulate and perhaps suffer bad debts.

Trade Discount is quite different. It is a reduction in the catalogue price of an article, given by the wholesaler or manufacturer to the retailer, to enable him to make a profit.

Take the example of a manufacturer of bicycles. He produces leaflets about his particular brand of bicycle explaining the merits of the machine. The price is either printed on this literature or on a separate price list supplied on request, but the important point is that he, and everyone else, thinks of this particular machine as the £28·50 model. When invoicing a supply of machines the simple way to invoice them is to list them at the catalogue price. The invoice might therefore read:

6 'Mercury' bicycles, 26-inch frame @ £28·50 = £171·00

Clearly the retailer cannot sell these at the catalogue price if he has bought them at the catalogue price. The manufacturer therefore deducts Trade Discount at an agreed rate, usually somewhere between 10 per cent and 45 per cent of the catalogue price. If these figures seem high, it must be remembered that durable goods of this sort may remain in stock for some considerable time before being sold, and the profit margin must be fairly large on such slow-moving items.

6 'Mercury' bicycles 26-inch frame @ £28·50 = £171·00
Less Trade Discount 25% =   £42·75
————
£128·25
————

(5) The Debit Note—A Document Very Like an Invoice

Definition: a Debit Note is a document which is made out by the seller whenever the purchaser has been undercharged on an invoice, or when he wishes to make some charge on a debtor which increases the latter's debt.

Suppose that an invoice has been sent to a purchaser of a typewriter value £100, but by mistake the typist has typed £10 as the purchase price. Clearly the seller will want to correct this undercharge, but another invoice would not be appropriate since no 'goods' are being delivered. A debit note for £90 treated exactly like an invoice and put through the Day Books in exactly the same way as an invoice will put this matter right.

In the same way, charges for carriage or insurance, which are not known at the time the invoice was made out, can be charged to the debtor by means of a Debit Note.

(6) The Credit Note—the Document for Returns

We must expect in the course of business that some customers will return goods for valid reasons. For example, the purchaser may hold that the goods are unsatisfactory for some reason such as wrong colour, wrong size, not up to sample, not up to specification, imperfectly finished, damaged in transit, etc. Additionally provision has to be made for the return of goods sent on approval. A purchaser is not entitled to return something just because he has changed his mind about having it, but occasionally it may be necessary to oblige a client by accepting this type of return. In all these circumstances the document used is the **Credit Note.**

Definition: a Credit Note is a business document made out whenever one person returns goods to another. It is usually printed in red, to distinguish it from an invoice. Like an invoice, it is made out by the seller of the goods, who is now receiving them back again. Usually there are only two copies.

The credit note should show: (*a*) the names and addresses of both parties to the transaction; (*b*) an exact description of the goods being returned; and (*c*) the unit price, the number and the total value of the goods returned.

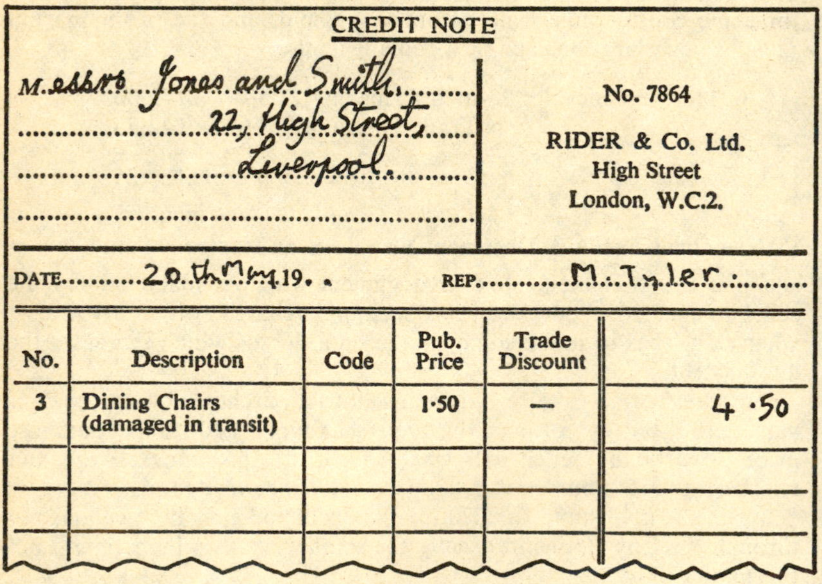

CREDIT NOTE

Messrs Jones and Smith, 22, High Street, Liverpool

No. 7864

RIDER & Co. Ltd.
High Street
London, W.C.2.

DATE 20th May 19..   REP M. Tyler.

No.	Description	Code	Pub. Price	Trade Discount	
3	Dining Chairs (damaged in transit)		1·50	—	4·50

Fig. 67. A Credit Note—the original document for returns

Other Reasons for Sending a Credit Note

(*a*) Sometimes goods that are unsatisfactory for some reason are not returned because of the inconvenience and cost. A piece of furniture that has been damaged by rain in transport may only need repolishing. The purchaser may be perfectly prepared to have this repolishing carried out by one of his own employees, provided the seller will make him an allowance to cover the cost. This will be done by sending a credit note for the agreed amount.

(*b*) We saw on page 287 that when an undercharge is made on an invoice a document called a *debit note* was sent to increase the original invoice to the proper figure. Invoice typists can make errors which result in overcharges instead of undercharges. Supposing the typewriter valued at £100 was invoiced at £1,000. Clearly a credit note for £900 will be required to correct the overcharge.

Credit notes may therefore be sent for three reasons:

(*a*) To credit a debtor with returns.
(*b*) To credit a debtor with an allowance.
(*c*) To credit a debtor to correct an overcharge.

What Happens to the Two Copies?

Usually credit notes are made out in duplicate. The top copy is sent to the purchaser who has returned the goods, and is recorded in his Purchases Returns Book. The duplicate is kept by the seller and is recorded in his Sales Returns Book.

(7) Original Documents for the Settlement of Accounts

(*a*) The Statement

Fig. 68 below shows a simple statement. It is a business document

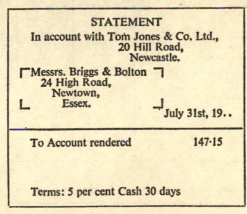

Fig. 68. A simple statement

which a firm sends out at the end of the month to all its debtors, reminding them what they owe for the purchases they have made during the past month. The phrase *'To account rendered'* is used to save the trouble of listing the various invoices, debit notes, credit notes, and receipts which have been sent to them during the month.

Mechanized Statements

Many firms today are using mechanized forms of book-keeping. There are several mechanized systems. The example shown in Fig. 69 does not just contain the words *'To account rendered'* but instead sets out details of all payments by the debtor and of goods sent to him and items returned by him. This is because under mechanized book-keeping the statement is typed automatically as the other entries are made during the month. It therefore is ready to be sent out as soon as the end of the month comes, and no extra labour is involved.

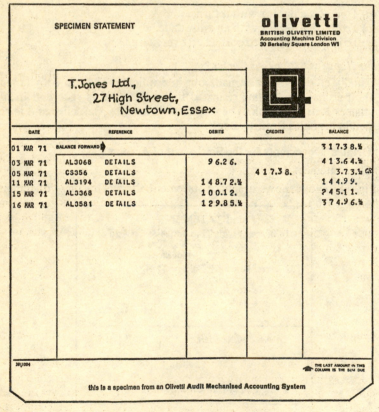

Fig. 69. A mechanized statement

What Happens to the Statements We Send Out?

The debtor who receives our statement first checks it against his book-keeping records. If it is correct he then uses it as a covering document for his cheque, which he draws up and sends with the covering statement to our accounts department. If he is entitled to deduct 5 per cent cash discount, he will write on the statement 'Less 5 per cent Cash Discount', deduct it, and send us the cheque to cover the net amount.

What Happens to the Statements We Receive?

The same process as above, because we are now the debtor and it is up to us to pay our debt after deducting Cash Discount if entitled to do so.

(*b*) The Receipt

A receipt is a business document which is given to a debtor when he pays a debt; as proof of payment. It should be made out at once on receiving the payment and be either given, or sent through the post, to the debtor. As already explained in the section on cheques (see page 155) the law has been changed in Great Britain by the Cheques Act, 1957 so that receipts are no longer necessary (though they may be demanded) when payments are made by cheque. The cheque itself acts like a receipt when cleared by the paying banker, but it is not a receipt, in that it does not acknowledge that a particular debt has been paid.

(*c*) The Petty Cash Voucher

Every transaction to be recorded in the books of account needs an original document, and in the case of petty cash items the document concerned is the Petty Cash Voucher. 'To vouch' is to certify the honesty of something, and the Petty Cash Voucher certifies the honesty of the petty-cash disbursement made. Petty Cash Vouchers may be receipts obtained from someone outside the business or may be an internal voucher. The former are preferable since they give the employee less opportunity for dishonesty. Even then one cannot always be certain. If the office boy is sent to buy a ball of string he is expected to produce a bill for it. Any shopkeeper will provide one on request when a purchase is made. In this way a check can be kept of the money actually spent.

Even so, fraudulent conspiracies are not uncommon, as any newspaper will show. Every week one reads in the police reports about such minor cases. A van driver who has been told to buy petrol and to ask for a receipt when he buys it, may bribe the garage employee for a receipt showing a quantity greater than that really issued and paid for. When he shows the false receipt and is reimbursed from the petty cash, the driver is cheating his employer. This sort of practice can easily be detected if regular checks are made of the mileage per gallon. The low-mileage-per-gallon vehicle which is as new as other vehicles but unaccountably uses more petrol may have a dishonest driver.

Petty Cash Vouchers may be very small both in value and in physical size. Bus tickets, for example, are proof of money spent and are therefore valid as vouchers; such tickets may be stuck in books, or on larger sheets of paper. Where it is impossible to produce a voucher from outside the business—for instance when letters are posted—it is usual to provide an internal voucher, signed by the manager or some person in authority, to vouch for the expense.

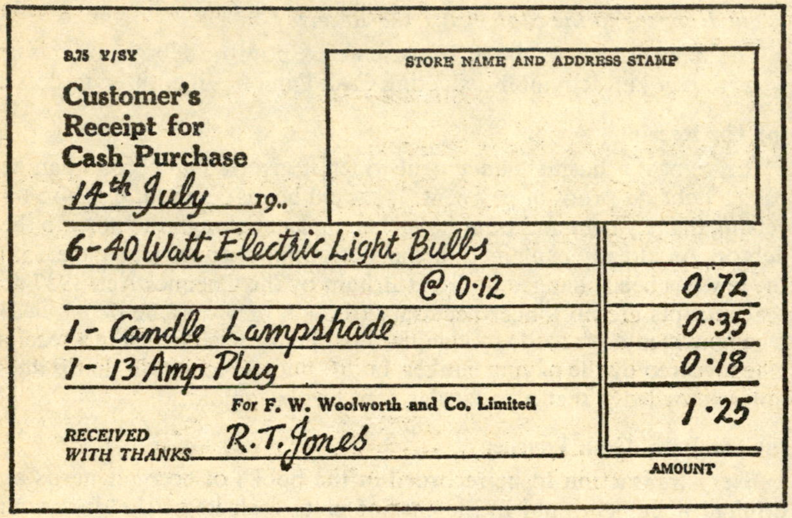
8.75 Y/SY

Customer's Receipt for Cash Purchase

14th July 19..

STORE NAME AND ADDRESS STAMP

	AMOUNT
6-40 Watt Electric Light Bulbs @ 0·12	0·72
1- Candle Lampshade	0·35
1- 13 Amp Plug	0·18
	1·25

For F. W. Woolworth and Co. Limited

RECEIVED WITH THANKS R.T. Jones

Fig. 70. An 'External' Petty Cash Voucher

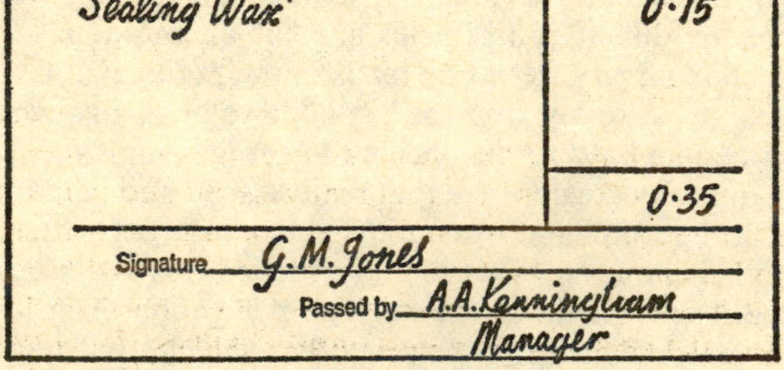
Petty Cash Voucher

Folio PCV27

Date May 15th 19..

For what required	AMOUNT
Methylated spirit	0·20
Sealing Wax	0·15
	0·35

Signature G.M. Jones

Passed by A.A. Kenningham Manager

Fig. 71. An 'Internal' Petty Cash Voucher

These vouchers are numbered, and the numbers are recorded in the petty-cash voucher column in the Petty Cash Book. They are then filed away in numerical order, so that if required the auditors may inspect them.

(8) Other Documents

Cheques are dealt with fully in the chapter on Banking, see page 156.

Bills of Exchange are dealt with on pages 128 and 130.

Bills of Lading are dealt with in the section on Export Documentation see page 136.

EXERCISES SET 24

(9) The Documents Used in Business

1. What is an invoice? Draw up a typical invoice for the sale of goods by a wholesaler to a retailer, which shows three items of electrical goods.

2. Define 'cash discount' and 'trade discount'. Draw up an invoice showing the purchase from R. Jones, 20 Hill St., Bradford, of 2 rolls of woollen cloth at £38·50 per roll, with 20 per cent trade discount. The purchaser is R. Lawson, 25 Lower Meadow Road, Rainbridge, Essex.

3. On March 17th, 19.., J. M. Lindley & Co. Ltd of Wellington Mills, Stoke, invoice to their customers, E. G. Brown of Main Street, Holbury, the following items:

> 12 dozen white cups DF23 @ 0·45 per dozen;
> 12 dozen white saucers DG23 @ 0·35 per dozen;
> 10 only teasets (18 piece) AHM @ 1·25 per set;
> 6 only teasets (21 piece) BKC @ 2·25 per set;

The whole invoice was subject to a trade discount of 30 per cent.

When the goods arrived on March 19th, Brown found that one of the 18-piece teasets was badly damaged, and Lindley & Co. agreed to make an allowance to Brown of the purchase price of the damaged teaset.

There were no other transactions between the two firms. On April 1st, 19.., the Statement of Account received by Brown contained the following words— 'Terms: $2\frac{1}{2}\%$ 10 days, net one month.'

(*a*) Draft a copy of the invoice priced and totalled.

(*b*) Draft a copy of the document granting the allowance to Brown.

(*c*) Draft the Statement of Account received on April 1st, by Brown.

(*d*) Draft in suitable form a cheque drawn on the Southern Bank Ltd., sent to Lindley on April 6th.

(R.S.A.—Adapted)

4. Define 'debit note' and 'credit note.' Under what circumstances would each be sent to a trader in the ironmongery trade, by a wholesale supplier?

5. What is the essential difference between a cash transaction and a credit transaction? Enumerate the documents which would pass between the wholesaler and a retailer from the time the latter orders goods on credit from the former, until the account is settled. Explain the functions of the documents.

(University of London)

6. Describe a routine business transaction involving the supply of goods, the return of part of the goods, and the payment for the order, explaining the documents that would be used.

7. Explain the following terms and say how they may all arise from one transaction: cash discount, trade discount, credit note, debit note, statement.

(*University of London*)

8. (*a*) The London Paintworks Co. Ltd. of Industrial Estate, London, E.12, have supplied The General Paint Co. Ltd., Main Street, Chelmsford, with the following goods:

> 1 doz. 1 gallon tins of White Paint.
> 2 doz. 4 oz Paint Dyes.
> ½ doz. 1 pint tins of Varnish.
> 3 doz. 4 inch Paint Brushes.

Make out an invoice to The General Paint Co. for these goods, inserting all the necessary names, addresses and descriptions and calculate the costs of the individual items and also the total cost.

For the information you need to do this, refer to the Price List shown below.

LONDON PAINTWORKS CO. LTD.
INDUSTRIAL ESTATE
LONDON E.12

PRICE LIST

Goods	Size	Recommended Retail Price
		£
White Paint	1 gallon	2·06 per tin
Paint Dyes	4 oz.	0·16 per tube
Varnish	1 pint	0·55 per tin
Paint Brushes	4 inches	0·43 each
Trade Discount 20%		

(*b*) Explain how (i) an overcharge and (ii) an undercharge on an invoice may be corrected.

(*c*) What is the difference between an invoice and a pro-forma invoice?

(*d*) Explain the terms E. & O.E. and Cash Discount.

(*e*) In what way can an invoice serve as a record?

(*East Anglian Examination Board—Adapted*)

CHAPTER TWENTY-ONE

SETTLING INDEBTEDNESS BETWEEN BUSINESSMEN

(1) Introduction

When businessmen enter into a transaction they will eventually have to settle the matter by payment in some form or other. Many of the methods of payment have already been described, and the reader is referred to the pages where they can be found. Remember that transactions in business involve two ideas:

(*a*) The provision of some useful commodity or service by one party.
(*b*) The payment for the commodity or service by the recipient.

If the payment occurs simultaneously, as when I buy something in a shop for cash, it is called a **cash transaction.** If there is a time-lag before the payment occurs we have a **credit transaction.** Credit transactions are the usual thing between firms who deal regularly with one another, payment being made at the end of the month. Hire-purchase credit transactions may be spread over longer periods.

(2) Payment in Legal Tender

Coins of the realm and bank-notes are legal tender, that is to say they must be accepted by citizens of the state concerned as payment for debts owed to them. Britain has now completed the complicated changeover to a decimal system of coinage. Any debt may be settled by payment in notes, which are legal tender up to any amount. Coins are not legal tender up to any amount, for it would be unfair to give people huge bags of coins. Decimal bronze coins are legal tender up to 20 pence only. Cupro-nickel coins (often mistakenly called 'silver') are legal tender up to £5, but the seven-sided 50p coins are legal tender up to £10.

(3) Payments through the Banking System

The chief methods, all of which have been discussed in earlier chapters, are:

(*a*) The cheque system (page 154).
(*b*) The credit-transfer system (page 158).
(*c*) Standing orders (page 158).
(*d*) Banker's drafts (page 166).

(4) **Payments through the Post Office System**

(*a*) Payment for items less than five new pence may be made in postage stamps.

(*b*) *Postal orders* are sold at values ranging from 5 new pence to £10. A small charge called 'poundage' is made varying from one to eight new pence. The payee's name should be filled in on the order and the name of the Post Office where it is to be cashed. If it is crossed by the sender it cannot be cashed, but must be paid into a bank account. It can still be passed on to another person and be banked by him.

The counterfoil is used (i) to make claims if the Postal Order is lost; but these will not be honoured if it has already been cashed, (ii) to enable the purchaser to get his money back—even if the name of a payee has been filled in. To do this he presents both halves.

A Postal Order is not negotiable, but it may be passed on, and cashed through a bank.

(*c*) *Money orders*. Money orders are no longer issued for sending by ordinary post, but telegraphic money orders are still available. These enable the sender to pay money over the counter of a Post Office, and send a telegram to the payee telling him to collect the money from his local Post Office. To prevent fraudulent collection of the money the payee has to name the person who is sending him the money. This service is most useful in emergencies. For example, a child on holiday with a school party who loses his pocket money could have a further supply telegraphed to him. A certificate of issue is given to the sender of a money order as proof of payment.

(*d*) *The National Giro system*. The United Kingdom National Giro has recently been introduced, although many other countries have used Giro systems for many years. The explanation is that Giros are more suitable for countries which lack a sophisticated banking system, and even in Britain the vast majority of those recruited to Giro have proved to be from the non-banking sector of the community. The Giro system is particularly useful to firms such as mail-order houses, whose home agents (mostly housewives from the non-banking section of the community) are now able to pay their weekly payments in to their local post offices for the credit of the mail-order house's account.

The services are mainly *transfers* from one account to another, *deposits* into an account by either the account holder or his debtors, and *cash payments* at the post office either to the account holder himself (a withdrawal) or to other people by means of a Giro cheque.

The system is based on an advanced computerized organization at Bootle in Lancashire. The system offers limited overdraft facilities, but interest is not paid on sums deposited. *Standing-Order* facilities are available for people who wish to pay regular sums towards mortgages, hire purchase, etc. It is also now possible, through a system called

A.D.T. (*Automatic Debit Transfer*) to claim payment for irregular sums of money. A standing order must be the same amount, payable each month, whereas an A.D.T. payment can vary. For example gas, electricity, and telephone bills can be automatically deducted from a customer's account so long as he has given permission for this to be done, and the company billing him allows a sufficient time between sending the bill and claiming payment so that a customer who wishes to object to the bill has time to do so.

Wages can be paid direct to the customer's account, so that payroll costs are cut and security risks avoided. However, as one critic pointed out, this may merely transfer the pay queue from the factory to the post office and the payroll bandit to a different site for his attacks.

Giro has not made a big impact on banking but it appears to be a useful addition to the pattern of institutions used by businessmen to settle their indebtedness.

Cash-on-delivery services. C.O.D. services are a way of securing payment for goods when the consignee is not known well enough to be given credit by the consignor. The consignor fills up a form at the post office stating the value of the goods, called the 'Trade Charge'. This sum of money will be collected by the postman on delivery, and if it is not forthcoming he will retain the packet and return it to the post office. The addressee can then collect the parcel from the post office on payment of the Trade Charge, which will be remitted by Money Order to the consignor. If not collected by the consignee in a reasonable time the packet will be returned to the consignor. The charge varies with the amount of the Trade Charge, up to about £0·25 for a £50 trade charge.

(5) Settling Overseas Payments

These have already been largely dealt with, but the following points are worth revising:

Cash with order—This is very safe from the seller's point of view but disadvantageous to the buyer as his capital is expended without any return until the goods arrive—possibly 3 months later.

Sight draft terms—This is really a foreign sight Bill of Exchange. The goods are sent to their destination, but the documents of title are sent to the buyer's bank on condition that they are not released until the buyer has paid the sight draft sent with them. On payment the buyer receives the documents and can claim the goods. This is a 'D/P transaction' (documents against payment).

Term drafts—If credit is to be given the buyer, the seller will use the same procedure but the documents will be released against the acceptance only by the buyer. This is a 'D/A transaction '(documents against acceptance) and gives the buyer the usual advantages of a Bill of Exchange, i.e. time to sell the goods, before he has to honour the bill.

Letters of credit—(see page 130)
Irrevocable letters of credit—(see page 130)
Confirmed letters of credit—(see page 130)

Direct remittances are possible between exporters and importers where perfect trust exists.

Consignment transactions. These are exports on 'agency' terms, the property in the goods remaining vested in the principal, who receives from his agent a monthly 'account sales' for the 'gross proceeds' less charges, commission and *del credere* commission.

EXERCISES SET 25

(6) Settling Indebtedness between Businessmen

1. In what ways may a businessman pay for the goods he receives from a wholesaler?

2. A wholesaler supplies goods 'payable C.O.D. unless credit previously arranged with this office.' What do 'C.O.D.' and 'credit' mean in this sentence. Are there any risks in collecting payments C.O.D.?

3. What is a 'Giro' system? Explain with reference to both Bank Giros and Post Office Giros.

4. Tom is away from home and his wallet is stolen. How may his brother, who receives a telephone call for help, send him funds so that they arrive the same day?

5. What different facilities for making payments do the commercial banks provide? Compare them with those provided by the Post Office.

(*University of London*)

CHAPTER TWENTY-TWO

GUIDE-LINES IN RUNNING A BUSINESS

(1) Introduction

There are a number of guide-lines which enable the businessman to conduct his affairs efficiently and profitably. An understanding of these guide-lines calls for some knowledge of accounts. (Readers who are not familiar with elementary accounts would do well to read the companion volume to this book—*Book-keeping Made Simple*.) For the benefit of readers who seek a nodding acquaintance with these matters, here are some quick definitions of terms often used in business, and a short explanation of their relevance in controlling a firm.

(2) Capital

Capital is the store of accumulated wealth contributed to the firm by its proprietor: it is the *net worth* of the business to the owner. The Balance Sheet below (Fig. 72) illustrates the position. The business of M. Erasmus is worth £38,500, but some of these assets have been obtained with other people's money. The creditors really own £6,000 of the assets, and the bank owns another £10,000 of them. This leaves M. Erasmus with a capital (net worth) of £22,500.

M. ERASMUS

BALANCE SHEET

(as at December 31st, 19..)

CAPITAL			FIXED ASSETS		
At Start	24,000		Premises	7,400	
Add Net Profit 4,500			Plant and		
			machinery	14,000	
Less Drawings 6,000			Motor vehicles	3,800	
	—1,500				
					25,200
		22,500			
LONG-TERM					
LIABILITIES			CURRENT ASSETS		
Bank Loan		10,000	Stock	8,898	
			Debtors	3,704	
CURRENT			Bank moneys	650	
LIABILITIES			Cash in hand	48	
Creditors		6,000			
					13,300
		£38,500			£38,500

Fig. 72. The Balance Sheet of a business

299

(3) Fixed Capital

Fixed capital is capital tied up in **fixed assets.** Fixed assets are assets purchased for use in the business on a permanent basis, e.g. land and buildings, plant and machinery, furniture and fittings, and motor vehicles. Another fixed asset is 'goodwill'; this is the kind feelings of customers towards the business, and though it is intangible and difficult to measure, one has to pay good money for it when one purchases a going concern, so it is an asset like anything else. In Fig. 72 M. Erasmus's fixed capital is £25,200.

(4) Working Capital, and Working-Capital Ratio

Working capital is the capital available for working the business, over and above the fixed capital. When we have bought fixed assets, we still need further capital to run the business; we need raw materials to make up into finished goods, stock to sell to our customers and money to pay wages and working expenses. The working-capital figure is found by the formula:

Current Assets − Current Liabilities = Net Working Capital.

In Fig. 72, M. Erasmus's working capital is therefore

$$\begin{array}{r} 13{,}300 \\ -\ 6{,}000 \\ \hline £7{,}300 \\ \hline \end{array}$$

A firm should never allow itself to run short of working capital. This is a very common reason for failure in business. If we allow our firm to buy too many fixed assets (called **over-capitalization**), we are forced to borrow from the bank to find our working capital, and this will cost us 2 per cent more than the minimum lending rate, say 12 or 13 per cent. Consequently the bank is creaming off most of our profits, and in fairly competitive trades this may leave us unable to earn a fair reward. A wise investor never buys shares in a firm that is short of working capital.

What is reasonably safe working capital? It is generally agreed that 1 : 1 is a minimum ratio of current assets to current liabilities. This is known as the working-capital ratio.

$$Working\text{-}Capital\ Ratio = \frac{Current\ Assets}{Current\ Liabilities}$$

and in this case come to

$$\frac{13{,}300}{6{,}000} = 2\cdot2\ \text{times}$$

This is perfectly satisfactory.

(5) Liquid Capital and Liquid-Capital Ratio

The term 'liquid' in business means 'in cash form'. The liquid capital is that portion of the assets that are available as cash, or near cash. In the balance sheet of Fig. 72 it is £4,402, the total of cash, bank moneys and debtors.

Once again a firm should never get too short of liquid assets. The guiding figure now is the liquid-capital ratio.

$$Liquid\text{-}Capital\ Ratio = \frac{Current\ Assets\ -\ Stock}{Current\ Liabilities}$$

$$= \frac{4,402}{6,000} = 0 \cdot 73\ times$$

This is very interesting because it shows how weak this firm is as far as liquid assets are concerned. Most of its current assets are stock, and if his creditors pressed Erasmus for payment he would be unable to pay.

(6) Appraising a Balance Sheet

The reader should now be able to appraise a Balance Sheet and ask himself whether the owner of the firm is well placed financially or not. If he is not well placed the owner is said to be **'overtrading'**, and the wise investor or bank manager will hesitate to lend him any funds without good security.

(7) The Turnover of a Business

Whenever a business is bought or sold one of the important things to be taken into account in fixing the price to be paid by the purchaser is the turnover figure, or **Net Turnover.** The word 'turnover' refers to the sales of the business. As we often find that some of the goods we sell are returned to us, we must deduct the 'Sales Returns' from the 'Sales' figure to find the Net Turnover.

Why is turnover so important? Naturally it reflects the 'busyness' of the business. If a business has only a small turnover it offers poor prospects to the would-be purchaser, so that he will not pay a high price for it. Some businessmen specialize in curing the ills of bad businesses; they take over a firm cheaply because it has a poor turnover, improve it and restore to it good heart, and then sell it at a much higher price since it now offers a new owner a good prospect of profitability. This profitability is best brought out as a percentage figure, and there are two possible ratios: the Gross-Profit Percentage and the Net-Profit Percentage.

(8) Gross-Profit Percentage

Gross Profit is the difference between the cost price and the selling price of the goods sold. The 'Sales' figure referred to above (Net Turnover) is the selling price. If we calculate the cost of the sales (i.e. the cost

302 Commerce Made Simple

price + expenses of handling) we can quickly discover the Gross Profit. Let us imagine a case where

$$
\begin{array}{ll}
\text{Net Turnover (Sales)} = \text{£20,000} \\
\text{Cost of Sales} \quad\quad = \text{£19,000} \\
\hline
\text{Gross Profit} \quad\quad\quad \underline{\text{£1,000}}
\end{array}
$$

This appears to be a substantial profit figure, but we must remember that the overheads of the business have still to be paid out of this gross profit. We shall probably finish up with a loss by the time all the overheads have been paid.

If we work the figure out as a percentage we have:

$$
\text{Gross-Profit Percentage} = \frac{Gross\,Profit}{Turnover} \times 100
$$

$$
= \frac{1,000}{20,000} \times 100
$$

$$
= 5\%
$$

This is a very poor Gross-Profit Percentage. If we had put our money into a Building Society we would safely earn about 8 per cent interest. We are having all the worry and trouble of the business, we haven't even paid the overheads, and all we get is 5 per cent return on the sales.

Clearly it is not worth it, we should sell the business and try something else. Most businesses need at least 20–40 per cent Gross-Profit Percentage to be worthwhile.

The Gross-Profit Percentage also tells us very accurately a great deal about any business we are considering. This is because the Gross-Profit Percentage should remain constant from year to year. A firm that normally makes 20 per cent Gross Profit should immediately hold an investigation if the percentage drops, say to 18 per cent.

What Can be Wrong When the Gross Profit Percentage Falls?

Remember, year by year, the Gross-Profit Percentage should be constant. If we find that it has fallen we should look out for one of the following possible explanations:

(*a*) The manager, or the staff, are embezzling the cash takings. This will reduce the sales figure, and the profits will fall. The cash is being diverted into the manager's or someone else's pocket. What can we do about it? We can query the matter with the manager. (Letting him know we are watching the situation may be enough.) If it appears unlikely that he is responsible, we can watch the assistants. Who has the luxurious handbag or the expensive new clothes? How does she do it on her money?

(*b*) Perhaps someone is stealing the stock. One of the good things about stock-taking is that it discovers losses of stock. A low stock figure means a high cost-of-sales figure and a lower Gross Profit. Who takes the stock home? Two pounds of sugar and a quarter of tea every night for a year makes quite a big hole in the stock. A very common practice of dishonest shop assistants is to help their friends to free goods. A packet of cigarettes to each boy friend soon causes a drop in the Gross-Profit Percentage.

(*c*) If neither (*a*) nor (*b*) is the cause, stock might be getting lost in other ways. For instance, breakages due to clumsiness in the crockery department transfer some of the stock to the dustbin. Bad buying of perishables has the same effect—we throw away the tomatoes that go bad, the cheese that gets stale, the cakes that go dry. If we don't actually throw them away we have to sell them cheaply and that still means the profit on them is lost.

(*d*) Another type of bad buying, in the clothing and footwear trades especially, concerns the out-of-touch buyer who is behind the times and buys lines that have to be reduced in 'Clearance Sales' because we can't get rid of them in any other way. We have to keep our fashion buyers young in heart or their work will adversely affect the Gross-Profit Percentage.

(e) A quite legitimate explanation for the falling Gross-Profit Percentage may be that the cost of goods to us has risen and we have been slow to pass this on to the public. It may be because we have poor control in our pricing department, or because competition from more efficient traders prevents us from raising prices. Sometimes governments regulate prices by law, and force the trader to accept lower profits margins. A government tax may be levied which, because of the demand in our particular market, we are unable to pass on and must suffer ourselves. The astute businessman will at least be ready with his plans to recoup these losses as soon as the law, or the market situation, changes.

(*f*) The 'expense' items in the cost of sales may be the cause of the trouble. Is the manager taking on more staff than he needs? Perhaps the lighting and heating bill has risen violently. Is it a hard winter? If it is, there is nothing we can do about it. If it is not, perhaps the staff have brought in electrical appliances without our knowledge and are producing hot buttered toast with our electricity. In this case we will order the bright fellow who thought of the idea to take his toaster home again.

What Can Cause a Rise in Gross-Profit Percentage?

If the types of inefficiency described in the last section cause a fall in Gross-Profit Percentage, then an improved efficiency in these directions will cause a rise in Gross Profit Percentage. Honesty over the cash takings will keep the cash-sales figure up, and hence the Gross-Profit Percentage will improve. A manager who takes over and at once detects sharp practice by assistants with cash takings or stock, will similarly improve the percentage. If he improves the buying, or eliminates breakages, or is quick to pass on increased prices to the customer, he will keep up the Gross-Profit Percentage.

What action should we take in this event? Clearly we should reward him. That is what a bonus is all about; it is a reward for efficiency in the line of duty.

(9) Net-Profit Percentage

The Net Profit is the clear profit made when we have paid all the expenses of the business, i.e. the overheads. This leaves us with a residue of profit which belongs to the proprietor. If we work the figure out as a percentage we have:

$$Net\text{-}Profit\ Percentage = \frac{Net\ Profit}{Turnover} \times 100$$

Suppose that in our earlier example where we had a Gross Profit of £1,000, the overheads had been £500. The Net Profit would have been £500 and

$$Net\text{-}Profit\ Percentage = \frac{500}{20,000} \times 100$$
$$= 2\tfrac{1}{2}\%$$

Clearly this is a very low profit figure and it is really not worth while being in business at all.

Once again we would expect the Net-Profit Percentage to be constant, i.e. to remain roughly the same from year to year, provided that we always prepare our Profit and Loss Account in the same way. It follows that any significant change in Net-Profit Percentage, say 2 per cent or more, should be investigated to discover the cause.

Suppose that last year the Net-Profit Percentage was 16·5 per cent and this year it has fallen to 13 per cent. This is a significant fall and we must find the reason.

What Can Have Caused a Fall in the Net-Profit Percentage?

If the Gross-Profit Percentage is steady, but the Net-Profit Percentage has fallen, the fault must lie in the expenses that make up the overhead. We should examine each expense item carefully, working out an Expense/Turnover ratio for the current year and the previous year. This is quite simple and involves a calculation:

$$\frac{Expense}{Turnover} \times 100$$

So for salaries it would be:

$$\frac{Salaries}{Turnover} \times 100$$

By comparing the expense ratio with the similar figure for the previous year we may discover some increase in expense. Perhaps the manager has taken on more staff than are really necessary. Perhaps the advertising has been excessive, or an increased advertising budget did not yield proportionately higher sales. Perhaps insurance rates have risen, and have not been passed on to the consumer in higher prices.

When we discover the cause of the fall in Net-Profit Percentage we must take the necessary action to correct the profitability of the business. This means we must reduce the expenses that are soaring. If such action is impossible, we must pass the increased cost on to the final consumer.

Interim Accounts

Some firms find the annual check-up on Gross-Profit Percentage and Net-Profit Percentage too long a period to wait before correcting undesirable trends. The quicker we can discover adverse variations, the quicker we can take steps to put them right. For this reason many firms prepare interim Accounts, say at three-monthly intervals. A quick check every three months on Gross- and Net-Profit Percentages keeps management and staff informed of the dynamic trends of the business.

(10) Rate of Turnover, or Rate of Stock Turnover

We have already defined turnover as the net sales of a business, i.e. *sales less returns*. Another figure that can easily be confused with turnover is the **Rate of Turnover,** sometimes called the **Rate of Stock Turnover.** This is not at all the same thing as turnover, but it is a most important concept which every reader should understand.

We say that stock has 'turned over' when it has been sold and replaced with new stock. If we want to double our profits, one way is to double the rate of stock turnover.

The rate of stock turnover is always expressed as a number. To say that 'the rate of stock turn is six' means that the stock turns over six times a year. Is this a good rate of stock turn? Or is it poor? We can't possibly say until we know the product we are discussing. If a grocer turned over his stock of eggs six times a year, they would be in stock for an average of two months each—so they could hardly qualify as new-laid eggs by the time they were consumed. On the other hand, grand pianos tend to be a slow-moving line and do not deteriorate if kept in stock for two months or more. Some classes of goods are very 'perishable'; newspapers, for example, must be turned over every day if they are to be sold at all.

Calculating the Rate of Stock Turnover

The formula for calculating Rate of Stock Turnover is

$$\text{either} \quad \text{Rate of Stock Turn} = \frac{Cost\ of\ Stock\ Sold}{Average\ Stock\ at\ Cost\ Price} \quad (1)$$

$$\text{or} \quad \text{Rate of Stock Turn} = \frac{Net\ Turnover}{Average\ Stock\ at\ Selling\ Price} \quad (2)$$

both formulae give the same answer.

Using Formula 1. If we find the average stock, and divide this into the amount of stock sold *at cost price*, we will discover how often the stock turns over each year.

The average stock is found by taking opening stock + closing stock and dividing by 2. If quarterly stock figures are available we can add up the four quarterly figures and divide by 4.

$$\text{Suppose we find the cost of stock sold} = £13,000$$
$$\text{and the average stock} = £1,725$$

We have:

$$\text{Rate of Stock Turn} = \frac{13,000}{1,725}$$

$$= \frac{520}{69}$$

$$= 7 \cdot 5 \text{ times per year}$$

Whether this is a good rate of stock turnover we cannot say, but it means that goods are in stock for roughly seven weeks on average. For some classes of goods this might be a good rate of stock turn. For fresh fish or spring flowers, it would hardly do.

(11) The Return on Capital Invested

Finally, the figure that really matters in the end to any businessman is his **return on capital invested.**

It is found by the formula:

$$\text{Return on Capital Invested} = \frac{Net\ Profit \times 100}{Capital\ at\ start\ of\ the\ year}$$

Referring back to the Balance Sheet of Fig. 72 we have as follows: The capital invested by Erasmus on January 1st was £24,000. This earned him £4,500 in profits.

$$\text{Return on Capital Invested} = \frac{4,500}{24,000} \times 100$$

$$= 18 \cdot 75 \%$$

This was a very satisfactory return. If Erasmus had invested in the ordinary type of savings account he would scarcely have got more than 6 per cent. It was certainly worth his while being in business.

(12) A Page to Test You on Capital and Statistical Control Figures

Answer	Question
—	1. What is capital?
1. Capital is accumulated wealth which is being used in a business.	2. What is fixed capital?
2. It is capital tied up in fixed assets which are used in the business and permanently increase its profit-making capacity.	3. What forms does it take?
3. (a) Land and buildings (b) Fixtures and fittings (c) Plant and machinery (d) Motor vehicles (e) Intangible assets (which are very fixed).	4. What is the Gross Profit?
4. It is the 'over-all' profit on trading, i.e. Turnover *less* Cost of Sales.	5. What is the Net Profit?
5. It is the clear profit, i.e. Gross Profit *less* Overheads.	6. What is the Gross-Profit Percentage?
6. $\dfrac{\text{Gross Profit}}{\text{Turnover}} \times 100$	7. Why is it important?
7. It should be constant from year to year, therefore it reveals inefficiency.	8. What sort of inefficiency?
8. Any inefficiency on (a) buying, (b) stocktaking, (c) theft of stock, (d) theft of money, (e) Expense items.	9. What do you do if Gross-Profit Percentage falls?
9. Investigate all these items but especially the manager.	10. What is Net-Profit Percentage?
10. $\dfrac{\text{Net Profit}}{\text{Turnover}} \times 100$	11. Why is it found?
11. It checks up on the efficiency of the office: like Gross Profit Percentage it should be a constant.	12. What sort of inefficiency is checked up on by this percentage?
12. Too much office expenditure on: (a) Salaries (too many pretty girls about); (b) Light and Heat (too cosy an atmosphere); (c) Advertising (it is worthwhile only if it brings extra sales).	13. What percentage helps us to decide whether our money is wisely invested?
13. Net-Profit Percentage on capital invested. i.e. $\dfrac{\text{Net Profit} \times 100}{\text{Capital Invested}}$	14. What is Rate of Turnover?
14. It is the number of times our stock turns over every year. Nothing to do with Turnover.	15. How do we calculate Rate of Turnover?
15. $\dfrac{\text{Cost of Sales}}{\text{Average Stock}}$	16. What is the significance of Rate of Turnover?
16. If we can increase the rate of turnover, we can increase our profits.	17. How many did you answer correctly? Go over the list again.

(13) Statistical Control Figures

1. The Multiple Shop Company Ltd. has four branches, each selling the same classes of goods in very similar areas. The following results are achieved:

Branch	Monthly Turnover	Gross Profit	Selling Expenses	Net Profit
	£	£	£	
Grays	1,650	480	230	?
Tilbury	2,380	920	350	?
S. Ockendon	850	240	180	?
W. Thurrock	1,710	450	220	?

Find the Gross-Profit Percentage for each branch.
Find the Net-Profit Percentage for each branch.
Hence conclude: (*a*) which branch is making the best efforts; (*b*) which branch is making the worst efforts.
Give some reasons why they might be successful or unsuccessful in each case.

2. (*a*) What is the Gross Profit of a business?
 (*b*) List the information you would need to find the Gross Profit and explain how you would calculate it.
 (*c*) What is the turnover of a business?
 (*d*) If the turnover of the ABC Company for 19 . . was £50,000, the average value of stock at cost £4,000 and the sales mark up was 25 per cent above cost, calculate the rate of turnover.

3. Fill in the missing parts of the following table.

	Opening Stock	Closing Stock	Average Stock	Mark-Up	Rate of Turn-over	Gross Profit	Sales Figure
Mr. Brown	£2,000	£3,000	?	10%	20	?	?
Mr. Green	£4,000	£6,000	?	20%	5	?	?

Now calculate the Gross-Profit Percentage and the Net-Profit Percentage, bearing in mind that general administration expenses are Mr. Brown £2,500, Mr. Green £2,000.

4. Mr. Black and Mr. White are two retailers. The following details relate to their trading over the past 12 months:

	Average stock at cost	Mark-up	Rate of turnover
Mr. Black	£2,500	10%	12
Mr. White	£8,000	25%	2

Work out the Gross Profit of each retailer. Suggest methods by which greater gross profits could be achieved by each retailer.

(*University of London*)

5. A trader carries an average stock valued at cost price of £2,000 and turns this over five times per year. If he marks his stock up by 25 per cent on cost price, what is his Gross Profit for the year?

6. A trader carries an average stock valued at cost price of £6,250 and turns this over four times a year. If his mark-up is 20 per cent on cost, and his overheads came to £2,800, what is the Net Profit for the year?

7. A retailer carries an average stock valued at cost price of £600. His rate of stock turn is 150, his average profit is 10 per cent on cost, and his overheads and running expenses came to £6,500. What is his Net Profit for the year?

8. During 19.. Harper made a Gross Profit of 20 per cent on sales. His total turnover was £42,000. His Net Profit was $12\frac{1}{2}$ per cent on turnover, and his rate of stock turn was 6.

During the next year Harper estimates that he can increase his rate of stock turn to 10, while carrying the same average stock, if he reduces his prices by 10 per cent, and this should also bring him a reduction in expenses of $2\frac{1}{2}$ per cent on turnover.
Calculate:

(*a*) Gross Profit for 19..
(*b*) Net Profit for 19..
(*c*) Expenses for 19..

and then calculate, to the nearest £1, for the following year:

(*d*) His estimated Sales
(*e*) His estimated Gross Profit
(*f*) His estimated Expenses
(*g*) His estimates Net Profit.

Would it be worth his while to carry out this policy?

(*University of London*)

9. (*a*) What are (i) the assets of a company,
(ii) the liabilities of a company?
(*b*) What is the purpose of a balance sheet?
(*c*) Explain the difference between fixed and current assets.
(*d*) Explain the difference between Gross and Net Profit.
(*e*) A retailer has fixed assets of £10,000 and a stock of £6,000 which is turned over three times a year. A Gross Profit of 20 per cent on sales is made and his expenses are £1,500 for the year. Find the percentage of his Net Profit to his capital.

(*East Anglian Examination Board*)

10. The following details relate to J. B.'s business for the year ended December 31st, 19..:

Sales	£33,984
Sales Returns and Allowances	£380
Stock (January 1st, 19..) valued at cost price	£1,378
Stock (December 31st, 19..) valued at cost price	£1,814
Gross Profit for the year	£8,068

Calculate:

(*a*) The turnover for the year
(*b*) The cost of goods sold during the year
(*c*) The amount of purchases for the year
(*d*) The rate of turnover of stock for the year
(*e*) The percentage of Gross Profit to turnover (to the nearest whole number).

CHAPTER TWENTY-THREE

THE WORK OF GOVERNMENT DEPARTMENTS
IN COMMERCE

(1) Introduction

From the point of view of commerce, Government departments are involved in four types of work:

(*a*) Activities that must be performed by the State.

(*b*) Activities that have been found, for one reason or another to be carried out best by the State, even though businessmen have done them in the past and could no doubt do them still if they were allowed to.

(*c*) Activities to help businessmen in their ordinary business affairs.

(*d*) Activities to maintain prosperity and economic welfare in the widest meaning of these words.

All these activities are called the 'Public Sector' of the economy, to distinguish them from the 'Private Sector' run by ordinary businessmen for their private profit.

(2) Duties that Must be Performed by the State

Among these duties are the defence of the nation from foreign enemies and the protection of citizens from the criminal acts of other citizens. The Army, Navy, Air Force, Police and Prison Services are part of our social framework. We rarely realize their importance until the bombs start dropping, or the burglars arrive, or there is a spectacular accident. Education is a service which must be provided out of public funds if the majority of children are to receive its benefits. Of course there are private schools, but the charges are too high for most parents who have several children. Public-health departments are a similarly necessary but non-profit-making activity.

(3) Duties that are Performed by the State, even though Businessmen could Undertake Them

In the United Kingdom for a variety of reasons, many enterprises have been nationalized. Some of these reasons were frankly political. Other reasons were economic; the enterprises concerned were too run-down to be conducted efficiently by their private owners. These bodies may be nationalized enterprises or autonomous authorities. They are set up as public corporations. It is impossible to look closely at all such enterprises for each has its own special features, but to give the reader some idea of how they evolved the Port of London Authority is described briefly below.

A Typical Public Corporation—The Port of London Authority

The Public Corporation is a solution to the problem presented by an accumulation of vested interests, many of which offer facilities that are run down and inappropriate to modern times. The Port of London is taken as an example of the procedure used to solve such problems.

History of the Port of London

From Elizabethan times onwards private wharves developed along the banks of the Thames, especially as the trade with the Baltic and with the West Indies developed. In 1799 the West India merchants asked Parliament to pass a private Act setting up a company to build a dock on the Isle of Dogs. The West India Dock opened in 1802. In quick succession there followed the London Dock (1805), the East India Dock (1806), the Surrey Commercial Docks (1807 onwards) and later came St. Katherine's Dock (1828), the Royal Victoria Dock (1855), the Millwall Dock (1868), the Royal Albert Dock (1880), and Tilbury Dock (1886).

All these dock companies gradually became very run-down because of competition with one another, and because the owners were reluctant to invest capital in carrying out necessary improvements. At the same time, any suggestion to modernize the river installations met serious opposition from these vested interests. The solution to this complex problem has been achieved through three main stages.

Stage I: Finding out the True Situation

The usual procedure when such an unsatisfactory state of affairs develops is for Parliament to appoint a Royal Commission to inquire into the whole complex situation, discover just how bad the real circumstances are and invite suggestions from all the interested parties as to the solution of the problems involved. In 1900 such a commission was appointed to investigate the situation in the docks, and after two years it reported in favour of creating a new Port of London Authority to take over and administer the property, the river itself, and the powers and obligations of all the companies concerned.

This sort of rearrangement is less drastic than it sounds because the only people capable of managing a port are the people who already have experience of the river and its installations. What the setting up of such a corporation really does is to shake up the whole industry, precipitate the retirement of older men who dislike the change that is to come about, and replace the individual firms with a larger, more competent organization armed with all the necessary powers. These powers are granted by an enabling Act of Parliament.

Stage II: An Act to Empower all Necessary Action

The 1908 Port of London Act created a **body corporate** (The Port of London Authority) to administer, preserve, and improve the Port of London. It was to have 28 members, 10 to be appointed and 18 to be elected. The Chairman and Vice-Chairman were to be chosen by the Board, possibly from outside the industry, bringing the membership to 30 in all. The 18 elected members were to be chosen by the 'registered voters'. A registered voter was any person or firm who had paid dues in the previous 12 months. Elections were held every three years.

The tasks of the Authority on takeover were as follows:

(*a*) To compensate the previous owners on some fair basis, usually by the issue of suitable gilt-edged stock, in this case Port of London Stock.

(*b*) To take over the assets and begin the task of streamlining the organization and bringing the standard of the service up to what was desirable.

(*c*) To set up a career basis at all levels to supply the labour and management forces for the future. This gives secure employment to officials who therefore have every reason to stay with the Authority and serve it devotedly.

(*d*) To plan and oversee the long-term future of the service, envisage developments in technology, and prepare for them; provide the service at 'reasonable cost', bearing in mind the need to make provision for future developments and to cover the interest on the stock issued.

By these measures the industry is restored to good heart, the services are raised to an adequate level and, by reviewing the activities of the Authority at regular intervals, Parliament can ensure that they are kept adequate. The Authority's constitution was, for example, modified to reduce the number of members of the Board in 1967.

Stage III: Controlling the Public Authority

Day-to-day parliamentary control by the 'Question Time' procedure of the House of Commons is deemed to be undesirable for public corporations, which must be run like commercial enterprises if they are to be economically viable. Parliamentary control is achieved by the following methods:

(*a*) The Authority is under the general control of a particular Cabinet Minister, who presents to Parliament an Annual Report prepared by the Corporation. This gives Parliament an opportunity to discuss the Authority's work, if it deems it necessary.

(*b*) Annual Accounts are included in the report, which are investigated by the Public Accounts Committee; any major sources of complaint are referred back to the corporation for an explanation.

(*c*) Periodic re-enactment of the Authority's powers as and when necessary. In the case of the Port of London, this has in fact been done recently, and the Port of London Act, 1968 is now the appropriate statute. The 1968 Act has changed some of the arrangements, giving extended powers and different powers from those deemed appropriate 60 years ago. The Act constitutes a thorough review of the whole of the work of the Authority, and although it is impossible to go into the details here, any reader who is interested to know the powers and duties of a body of this type is strongly recommended to obtain a copy and study the Act for himself.

(4) Activities to help Businessmen in their Ordinary Business Affairs

Some of these activities have already been described, for instance the work of the Department of Trade in assisting exporters (page 134), and the work of the Export Credit Guarantees Department in helping the finance of foreign trade (page 131). The multitude of activities performed by government departments is so great that there is no space to describe them all, only a few are shown below. The recent preference for large ministries controlling major aspects of our way of life has given way to smaller departments with clearly defined responsibilities.

(*a*) *The Department of Industry*, led by the Secretary of State for Industry, is responsible for general industrial policy and for regional policies designed to encourage industry in declining areas and restricting it in overcrowded regions. It controls two nationalized industries (the British Steel Corporation and the Post Office Corporation), while its influence in a whole range of industries—paper making, chemicals, textiles, vehicle building, aerospace, shipbuilding, etc.—is growing. It also provides statistical and accounting services for its own purposes and for the Departments of Trade and Prices and Consumer Protection.

(*b*) *The Department of Trade.* The work of this Department is described fully on page 315.

(*c*) *The Department of Prices and Consumer Protection.* This Department, under its Secretary of State, controls policy on prices and consumer affairs. The Secretary has appointed a Director General of Fair Trading, who is about to begin the major task of reviewing unfair practices and recommending measures to eliminate them.

(*d*) *The Department of the Environment*, led by the Secretary for the Environment, has wide powers to control the environment in which our people live. It embraces three ministries, the *Ministry for Local Government and Development*, the *Ministry for Housing and Construction* and the *Ministry for Transport Industries*. Businessmen are affected by controls to promote business efficiency without harmful effects on the countryside, atmosphere, water and drainage systems, etc.

(*e*) *The Foreign and Commonwealth Office* exercises control over international aspects of trade and aid. The Foreign Office has traditional functions as a representative of, and mediator for, British citizens in all activities abroad.

(*f*) *The Ministry of Health* is in charge of pharmaceuticals, radiographic paper, and surgical and hospital equipment.

(5) Functions of the Department of Trade

Since we cannot expect to know all about every government department we will pick the Department of Trade as a good example. The Board of Trade began in 1786, under the President of the Board of Trade, a title still preserved today. Its traditional functions are now carried on by the Department of Trade under the Secretary of State for Trade. Here are some of the main functions:

(*a*) *Overseas trade.* Its British Overseas Trade Board assists British businessmen to deal abroad. It has representatives on all the main international committees, e.g. G.A.T.T. (General Agreement on Tariffs and Trade), and E.E.C. (European Economic Community) Committees; has trade commissioners in many foreign countries; it decides what tariffs shall be put on foreign goods entering Britain. It negotiates with foreign governments when disputes arise. It is in charge of shipping and civil aviation, because of their importance to overseas trade.

(*b*) *Home trade.* It is the liaison between businessmen and the Government—meeting them to hear their point of view, through their big organizations such as the Confederation of British Industries. It regulates the legal framework within which industrial and commercial enterprises operate.

(*c*) *British Overseas Trade Board.* The Board directs export promotion work advised by members drawn from commerce, industry and the Civil Service.

(*d*) It is in charge of all Acts of Parliament concerning business life, e.g. Company Acts, Partnership Acts, patent rights, trade marks, and the Bankruptcy Acts.

(*e*) It is in charge of all short-term Acts of Parliament affecting trade, e.g. Control Orders, licences to trade, H.P. controls, etc.

(*f*) *Miscellaneous functions:*

(i) It controls the Export Credits Guarantee Department (see page 131).

(ii) It has a Solicitor's Department which prosecutes company directors who publish false prospectuses, etc.

(iii) The department spends a great deal of money both in supplying information to the public and collecting information for the Government.

(iv) It deals with Parliamentary business. The department has to answer questions and keep Members of Parliament informed.

(6) Activities to Maintain Prosperity and Economic Welfare

As soon as we try to understand the general influences at work in Government departments to maintain the economy in good heart, we come up against the fact that policies influence not only what is done, but the way in which things are done. Furthermore, Britain has gone through a very rapid change in fields of responsibility since 1964, and these changes are still proceeding.

First, a Department of Economic Affairs was set up to co-ordinate the long-term planning of economic policy, leaving the Treasury still charged with the short-term control of the economy and responsibility for the balance of payments. Later, it became clear that the most vexing question of all in the economy was that of incomes policy, since our whole standard of living, and our ability to export hinged around the rewards paid to the nation's citizens. To deal with this very difficult problem a separate Department of Employment and Productivity was set up in 1968. Then these departments were themselves replaced by the super-departments set up by the Conservative Government elected in 1970. These super-departments were to some extent disbanded in 1974 (see page 314).

(7) Controlling the Economy in the Short Term—the Financial, Fiscal, and Monetary Aspects

The Treasury assumes responsibility for the short-term control of the economy. It has three weapons to use.

First it can use **financial measures** to influence the economy. Finance involves the provision of capital for business enterprises, and the Treasury can do much to make it easy, or difficult, for businessmen to find the capital they need. An easy credit policy, and a low rate of interest, will encourage businessmen to go ahead with new projects. A 'credit squeeze' will have the opposite effect. If businessmen refuse to expand even though finance is available, the Government can go ahead itself with new government projects, road building, school building, space programmes, the construction of atomic power plants and so on.

The second set of weapons are **fiscal measures**. *Fiscus* is the Latin for purse, and the public purse is filled by the taxation system. Heavy taxation will remove money from the pockets of the people, making it impossible for them to buy the things they had been planning to buy. A reduction in taxation will encourage people to spend money, and will lead to increased business activity. Of course it all depends on what the Goverment does with the taxes it collects: if the purpose of heavy taxation is to damp down business activity, the Government will not spend the money, but will freeze it.

Taxes are imposed in the **Budget** (see below). To budget for a surplus is to tax the people heavily and not spend the money, but keep it unused. To budget for a deficit is to tax the people lightly, keep Government spending at a high rate and hence finish up with a deficit, i.e. an increased National Debt. This leave the people free to spend their money, and unemployment falls as business activity increases.

Budget Day is held on a Tuesday early in April each year, unless a time of unusual crisis develops. It is the day on which the Chancellor of the Exchequer presents to Parliament the Government's plans for raising the money needed in the coming year—the fiscal programme. The House of Commons sits as the 'Committee for Ways and Means'. This is a committee of the whole house, and the chamber is usually packed. The chairman of the committee takes over from the Speaker, and in an atmosphere of keen interest the fiscal proposals are announced in the course of a general review of the economic state of the nation.

When prices stay steady, wages stay steady. Unfortunately as prosperity rises it reaches a point where the unemployed now being taken into employment (and unemployed here refers to physical as well as human resources) are less efficient than the earlier ones. It is at this point that the prices begin to rise, for extra money is being paid out as incomes and extra goods are not being made, so that the price of goods must rise. This leads to a spiral of rising prices and rising wages which is called a 'cost-push' inflation, prices are being forced up by wage demands which increase the cost of the goods so that more wage demands are immediately put in. The task of the Treasury is to control the economy just before full employment is reached to try to prevent inflation. If it cannot do so it must use legislation (legal measures) to compel price and wage controls. These have had limited success. (See page 322.)

The Balance-of-Payments Problem

Britain is sometimes faced with a balance-of-payments problem. It arises because our densely populated island has few natural resources left. Apart from coal, oil, gas, salt, chalk, some poor-quality iron ore, and agricultural products, we are unable to supply industry with its requirements. We must import large quantities of food, minerals, fuel oil, fibres, fats, and timber. In exchange we sell large quantities of manufactured goods. This balancing of imports and exports is a permanent problem to the Government. Since it is fundamental to the balance-of-payments problem, the Treasury keeps the balance of imports and exports constantly under review. The 1973 figures (on a Balance of Payments basis) were:

	£m
Imports	13,810
Exports and Re-exports	11,435
Visible Balance of Trade	—2,375

This was a very large adverse balance.

These items are often called 'visibles' since we can actually see the goods moving in and out of the country. The *Visible-Trade Balance* is almost always an adverse one, and we should be permanently in debt to other countries were it not for the **invisible items** which are a second source of foreign earnings.

The Main Kinds of Invisible Earnings

The Central Statistical Office lists invisibles under eight main headings: (*a*) Government military spending; (*b*) Government non-military spending; (*c*) shipping earnings; (*d*) civil aviation; (*e*) travel; (*f*) other services, which includes banking and insurance; (*g*) interest, profits and dividends; and (*h*) private transfers.

Britain's surplus on invisible earnings arises partly from our traditional skills and services in the commercial field, particularly in banking and finance, where we provide more valuable services to foreigners than we receive from them. It also arises from our overseas holdings of property and business enterprises which yield us returns in interest, dividends, and profits, which are greater than comparable sums paid out by us to overseas investors in this country.

Table 9. Invisible Debits and Invisible Credits 1964–73
£ million

	1964	1965	1966	1967	1968	1969	1970	1971	1972	1973
Debits (Outgoings)										
Government payments	477	493	512	500	507	504	536	586	636	933
Shipping	724	728	716	780	895	914	1,437	1,672	1,705	2,185
Civil aviation	116	134	150	172	206	246	279	309	346	420
Travel	261	290	297	274	271	324	382	439	527	674
Other services	291	320	345	366	432	490	508	547	615	726
Interest, profits and dividends	495	557	579	601	777	841	889	970	1,176	1,457
Private transfers	154	167	183	201	257	253	226	228	288	409
Total	2,518	2,689	2,782	2,894	3,345	3,572	4,257	4,751	5,293	6,804
Credits (Incomings)										
Government Receipts	45	46	42	36	45	46	51	59	72	143
Shipping	685	724	716	796	955	959	1,361	1,615	1,656	2,110
Civil aviation	143	162	180	199	235	287	316	354	410	481
Travel	190	193	219	236	282	359	432	489	550	680
Other services	558	590	648	755	897	1,010	1,207	1,332	1,476	1,708
Interest, profits and dividends	890	999	959	969	1,094	1,292	1,414	1,495	1,689	2,552
Private transfers	131	135	134	143	161	176	192	215	231	295
Total	2,642	2,849	2,898	3,134	3,669	4,129	4,973	5,559	6,084	7,969
Net Favourable Balance	124	160	116	240	324	557	716	808	791	1,165

A comparison of the invisible debits (outgoings) and credits (incomings) shown in Table 9 reveals that we have had a deficit on government payments every year, and a surplus on 'Other Services' every year. When these figures are related to the balance-of-trade figures we are

VISITORS TO BRITAIN, 1973
(There were 7·7 million visitors)

1973: where 7,724,000 visitors came from;
number of visits (000 visits)

Rest of World
528

Other
Sterling
731

Other
Western
Europe
778

U.S.A.
1576

Canada
483

France
866

Other
E.E.C.
1927

Germany
F.R.
835

Total money spent: £682 m

Rest of World, £m
71

Other
sterling
128

Other
Western
Europe
76

Other
E.E.C.
109

U.S.A.
158

Canada
48

France
42

Germany
F.R. 50

Fig. 73. Invisible earnings—travel

able to discover the balance of payments for the current year. Taking the two sets of 1973 figures we have

	£m	Exports	Imports
Balance of Trade	−2,375	(11,435	13,810)
Balance of Invisibles	+1,165	(7,969	6,804)
Balance on Current Account	−1,210		

Capital Items in the Balance of Payments

British Government summaries of the balance-of-payments figures have traditionally been divided into current-account items and capital-account items. Current-account items are items which are settled and cleared up fairly quickly, usually in less than one year. Capital-account items are items which take much longer to complete, and generally involve investment by Britain overseas, or investment by foreigners in this country. A full understanding of what is involved in capital movements is not really relevant to a study of commerce; it belongs more to the field of economics. One aspect of it is relevant though. This is the final effect of the total balance of payments on the world scene. If we always have a favourable balance of payments we become what is known as a creditor nation, because the other countries of the world owe us balances which they probably cannot pay out of their reserves. In effect they borrow from us, and will pay us interest in years to come for the sums borrowed. If we always have an adverse balance of payments we become a debtor nation, owing large sums of money to overseas creditors.

In order to maintain world stability it is necessary that the creditor nations, generally speaking the advanced industrial nations, help the underdeveloped nations to achieve prosperity by developing their own natural wealth and skills. This is done by lending them capital and giving aid of various sorts. It is not possible for international trade to continue unless it is mutually advantageous to the nations trading with one another, and this is not so when one half of the transaction is being conducted by a poor nation. Poor people cannot buy our goods, any more than human beings who 'want' things can satisfy their wants unless they have the purchasing power to demand goods. 'Want' is not the same as 'demand'.

The Balance of Payments figures over the last decade reveal wide fluctuations in Britain's earnings and requirements of foreign exchange. They range from huge deficits in 1967 and 1973 to huge surpluses in 1971. A full account of the measures Governments may take to overcome financial problems in the Balance of Payments field is inappropriate to the present volume. Readers wishing to pursue their studies in this field are advised to read the companion volumes *Economics Made Simple* and *Applied Economics Made Simple*.

(8) **Planning the Long-term Prosperity of the Nation**

The last aspect of Government activity affecting Commerce is the responsibility governments assume for the management of prosperity. Representatives of all parties agree that only the government can arrange that levels of employment are maintained properly. Some debate between parties does arise as to the most appropriate measures to achieve full employment without producing Balance of Payments difficulties.

The Department of Economic Affairs was set up in 1965 to take responsibility for planning the long-term prosperity of the nation. Its activities were changed in 1968, when some of its functions were taken over by a new department, the Department of Employment and Productivity. The Department of Economic Affairs assumed responsibility for the implementation of Government policy in the real-resources fields. These particularly involved the changeover from home consumption (both public and private) to exports, import saving, and investment. The aim was to achieve a Balance of Payments by importing less and exporting more. To export more we had to reduce the market price of our goods. This we must do by investing in more modern equipment to raise productivity.

The Department of Employment and Productivity had been set up to deal specifically with the problem of the inflationary spiral, where wages force up prices and prices force up wages. It is true that wages are not the only rewards paid to citizens (rents, interest, and profits are also involved), but they are the most important rewards, taking about 80 per cent of the National Income. Because of the high propensity to consume of working people, who spend a high proportion of all the income they receive, wage increases have an immediate effect upon demand. If a section of the working people, because of their strong union organization, can force increases in wages from employers they can only enjoy their extra share of the nation's wealth at the expense of other people, particularly those on fixed incomes, the pensioners and unorganized workers. This is so because the higher wages force up prices, so that those on fixed incomes are worse off than before.

To resolve this unfairness, the Government had tied wage increases to productivity. If productivity rose, the extra wealth created could be given as extra wages. The extra wages paid would not force up the prices of goods.

In 1970 the Conservative Government decided to change the system again by forming two super ministries to control the major affairs of the nation.

The new super-ministries attacked the problem of inflation in a slightly different way. By encouraging a more competitive atmosphere in industry they attempted to achieve higher productivity by the self-interested efforts of people who were less severely taxed, and therefore had more incentive to raise output. The result was a considerable improvement in productivity, but at some cost. The division of the nation into two groups, a large prosperous group and a smaller group who faced some degree of serious unemployment, was an unfortunate side effect of the new competitive atmosphere.

In December 1972 the Government took firm measures to re-impose an incomes policy. There was for a short period (Phase 1) a complete wages and other incomes freeze. Later this was changed (Phase 2) to a cautious increase of incomes in line with over-all productivity. This period ended in November 1973 as we moved into Phase 3, a further limited rise in incomes. The Phase 3 arrangements led to a confrontation with the miners, and a general election which produced a minority Labour Government in March 1974. This minority Labour Government was re-elected—again without a very clear lead in the House of Commons—in the Autumn of 1974. It faces a major problem in solving a serious inflationary situation without a statutory incomes policy. It is attempting to do this by a 'social compact' (or contract) which attempts to limit wage increases to the increase in national output. This presents considerable difficulties and businessmen have to play their part if the policy is to succeed.

EXERCISES SET 27

(9) The Work of Government Departments in Commerce

1. Discuss the services provided by the Ministry of Trade to businessmen.
2. How does the Ministry of Trade influence (*a*) the conduct of limited companies, and (*b*) the Export Trade?
3. How are nationalized industries controlled by Parliament?
4. Discuss the case for and against operating the Postal Services as a Public Corporation.
5. What is a natural monopoly? Why should a natural monopoly be run as a State undertaking? Refer in your answer to (*a*) railways and (*b*) the gas industry.
6. What are the functions of the Treasury?
7. Explain the terms (*a*) fiscal measures and (*b*) inflation. How many fiscal measures control inflation?
8. Write short notes (5–8 lines each) on: (*a*) Visible trade; (*b*) Invisibles; (*c*) The trade gap; and (*d*) The Balance of Payments.
9. Write short notes on: (*a*) The Department of the Environment; (*b*) The Department of Trade and Industry.
10. What is the purpose of encouraging industry to settle in a 'depressed area'?

APPENDIX

VALUE ADDED TAX

(1) What is Value Added Tax?

On 1st April, 1973, a new taxation system was introduced in the United Kingdom, replacing two other forms of taxation, purchase tax and selective employment tax, which were abolished on that date. The new tax is designed partly to bring the United Kingdom taxation system into closer alignment with Common Market systems, but it has also spread taxation over a wider range of consumer products, making taxation fairer than before. The disadvantage of the new tax system is that it requires about 1,500,000 businesses, many of them quite small, to keep VAT records. This means that VAT routines have become part of office practice for every firm in the country.

The principle of VAT is that tax is levied on the value added to goods at every stage as they pass from the natural raw material stage to the finished product, and then onwards to the final consumer. Every middleman along the way buys goods and uses services which have already had some tax levied upon them. When he in turn sells goods or provides services, he levies tax on the price he charges his customers. The amount he is liable to pay over to Customs is the difference between his 'output tax' levied on customers and the 'input tax' levied upon him by his suppliers. It is directly related to the value he has added.

Imagine an oak tree cut down in a farmer's field, taken to a sawmill and cut into planks, sold to a manufacturer and turned into 500 coffee tables eventually retailed at £11 each including tax. The following list of values added, etc., might be calculated. Tax has been levied at 10 per cent (see Table 10 overleaf).

The effect of the tax is that the final consumers pay a total price of £5,500, of which £5,000 is the true value of the coffee tables they bought and £500 is tax. This £500 will be accounted for as shown in the tax payable column of Table 10.

(2) Office Activities made Necessary by Value Added Tax

A businessman must perform the following activities to comply with the regulations for the new tax:

(*a*) Complete and send off to the Customs and Excise authorities a registration form VAT 1, which registers the business as a 'Taxable Person'.

(*b*) Record his outputs. These are the charges for goods and services which he makes to his customers, and to which he adds the tax payable to the customer. This enables him to calculate his **output tax** for any tax period.

(*c*) Record his inputs. These are the charges made to him by his suppliers of goods and services. The tax charged to him by these suppliers is called his **input tax.**

Table 10.   Calculations—Value Added Tax

Business	Cost Price free of tax	Sale Price free of tax	Value added	Final charge to customer (incl. 10% tax)	Input tax	Output tax	Tax payable
	£	£	£	£	£	£	£
1. Farmer	0	200 (tree trunk)	200	220	0	20	20
2. Sawmill Co.	200	500 (sawn planks)	300	550	20	50	30
3. Furniture manufacturer	500	3,000 (coffee tables)	2,500	3,300	50	300	250
4. Retailer	3,000	5,000	2,000	5,500	300	500	200

(*d*) Complete his VAT return (Form VAT 100) at intervals, and account for the tax due.

(*e*) Keep records and accounts that are adequate for these purposes.

An explanation of these items in greater detail is given below:

Registration Form VAT 1

Every one carrying on a business after 1 October 1972, whose taxable outputs (i.e. charges for goods and services supplied to customers) are likely to exceed £5,000 per annum must complete a form VAT 1. This makes the individual, firm or company a 'taxable person' under the regulations. He is then required to act virtually as the collecting agent of the Customs and Excise, charging his customers tax on goods and services supplied, and remitting it (less any tax he is entitled to recoup on inputs) to the department. A person whose business is so small that the turnover is not more than £5,000 need not be registered, and all his output will be exempt. He does not charge his customers tax but is not entitled to deduct the tax he pays on goods and services received. He is therefore very much like a consumer, paying tax on all goods and services he receives.

Output Records and the Rate of Tax

Every 'taxable person' must keep records of the goods and services he supplies to his customers, and must add to the charges made the correct rate of tax. Tax was originally chargeable at 10 per cent but is now charged at 8 per cent (the standard rate) and $12\frac{1}{2}$ per cent on certain 'luxury' items such as petrol, television sets, hi-fi, furs, jewellery, etc. Certain goods and services are taxable, but at the zero rate. These include food, water, books and newspapers, items for the blind, fuel and power, building work, export services, transport and drugs supplied on prescriptions. It might seem pointless to say an item is taxable and then tax it at the zero rate, but in fact this enables a businessman who is not charging his customers tax on his outputs to reclaim the tax on his inputs, which he has paid to suppliers.

There is a class of **exempt goods and services** which are not taxed at all. These include the leasing of land and buildings, insurance, banking, finance, postal services, and lotteries. The suppliers of these services do not need to register or keep records, but they are unable to claim back any tax paid on inputs.

The final effect of keeping 'output records' is that the businessman is able to calculate the total tax which he has added to his customers' statements, and which he must account for to the Customs and Excise authorities.

Input Records

A taxable person who is collecting tax from his customers as in (*b*) above, does not have to pay the full amount over to the Customs and Excise. He is entitled to deduct from the sums collected as 'output tax', the total sums paid to his own suppliers. These are revealed by keeping 'input records' which show the value of goods and services supplied to him by other firms, and the tax that these firms have charged him—his 'input tax'.

The Tax Return (Form VAT 100)

The taxable person must render a return of the tax outputs and inputs of his business and pay tax every three months. The three monthly intervals are known as 'tax periods' and the return and any tax due must be sent in within one month of the end of the tax period. A special tax period of only one month is allowed where a taxable person feels sure that his 'tax inputs' will exceed his 'tax outputs' in the usual course of events. For example, a small grocer selling zero-rated goods might be entitled to regular refunds of tax from the Customs and Excise. It would be hard on such small businessmen if they had to wait for three months to recover tax paid on inputs.

A typical extract from the return might look like this:

Output tax for period		£26,323·10
Tax on imported goods		£974·40
Underpaid tax from previous period		£196·70
Total tax due		£27, 494·20
Less		
Input tax for period	£23,649·60	
Tax overpaid previously	None	
		£23,649·60
Net tax payable		£3,844·60

Where the input tax exceeded the output tax the difference between the two figures would be 'Net tax refundable by Customs and Excise' and not 'Net tax payable'.

Accounting Records

The designers of business systems have had to devise improved rulings for documents and account books to suit the new system. These rulings may be obtained from these specialist firms, and the reader is urged to consult his supplier for appropriate rulings. The example given in Fig. 74 is reprinted by kind permission of Her Majesty's Customs and Excise.

(3) VAT Calculations

In 1974 the Chancellor of the Exchequer reduced the rate of VAT from 10 per cent to 8 per cent. This is not an easy figure to calculate but in these days of cheap electronic calculators most businessmen find little difficulty. For the benefit of students the following sample calculations may be helpful.

(1) *To add 8 per cent VAT—Output prices*

Take the desired selling price, say £12

$$8\% \text{ of } £12 = \frac{8}{100} \times £12 = £\frac{96}{100} = £0·96$$

∴ Selling price with tax = £12·96

(2) *To reduce a selling price to the net of tax price.*

This calculation is used when the businessman knows the total sales including VAT for the day, and wishes to calculate the VAT element and the net-of-tax sales figure.

Suppose daily takings are £274·50. This includes 8 per cent VAT,

| A. Wholesaler Ltd. | | | | INVOICE NO. 3654 | | |
| 22 North Road, London N12 4NA | | | | DATE 4 May 1985 | | |

VAT Registration No. 912 3456 78

To: Messrs General Electrical Retailers Ltd., 12 High Street, Newtown

Delivery Note No. G497

Tax Point 4 May 1985

Consignee: General Electrical Retailers Ltd., NEWTOWN

	Terms $2\frac{1}{2}$% for 7 days settlements, otherwise strictly net					
Quantity	Description and Price	Cost	Total	VAT† Rate	Amounts of VAT at rate	
					Standard	Higher
		£	£		£	£
4	Radios SW139 at £15	60.00				
4	Grillers G176 at £20	80.00				
2	Toasters M126 at £15	30.00				
			170.00	$12\frac{1}{2}$%	——	20.72*
4	Electric Drills B197 at £6	24.00				
2	Electric Saws S43 at £20	40.00				
6	Table Lamps T321 at £10	60.00				
			124.00	8%	9.66*	——
	Delivery charges (strictly net)	4.00	4.00	8%	0.32	
	Total Goods		298.00		9.98	20.72
	Total VAT		30.70			
SALE	Total		328.70			

Notes:

† Alternatively if the rates of tax are shown above the columns headed 'Standard' and 'Higher' a special 'VAT Rate' column need not be used.

*Calculated on the discounted price.

Fig. 74. A Tax Invoice

VAT Calculations (*continued*)

so it is 108 per cent of the net-of-tax takings figure. The VAT element is therefore

$$\frac{8}{108} \times £274{\cdot}50 = \frac{2}{27} \times £274{\cdot}50 = \frac{£549{\cdot}00}{27} = £20{\cdot}33$$

$\therefore$ Sales net of tax = £274·50 − £20·33 = £254·17

Check. To check the correctness of this calculation, take the

Sales net of tax figure =   £254·17
Add 8% (= 8 × 2·5417) =   20·3336
_____

This gives the 'daily takings'   £274·5036

(3) *To find the VAT on inputs from suppliers*

Take the price charged by the supplier—say £40. Since this includes 8 per cent VAT it is 108 per cent of the true price. The VAT element in the price is therefore

$$\frac{8}{108} \text{ of } £40 = \frac{2}{27} \text{ of } £40$$

$$= \frac{£80}{27} = £27\overline{)80·00}^{\;2·963}$$

$$= £2·96$$

EXERCISES SET 28

(4) Value Added Tax

1. Rule up an invoice similar to the one on page 327. The supplier is R. Montague Ltd., 24 High Rd., Sleighton, Suffolk. The customer is R. Jones, 14 Hill Road, Bemfleet, Essex. The date is today's date. Terms Net. Enter the following items on the invoice:

200 large folders @ £1·50 each. VAT rate 8%
500 small folders @ £0·75 each. VAT rate 8%
20 books (*How to Run a Small Business*) @ £0·50. VAT rate zero.

2. A shopkeeper's takings (all his goods being charged to consumers with VAT at 8 per cent) were as follows: Monday £89·50, Tuesday £46·60, Wednesday £15·45, Thursday £86·60, Friday £176·70, Saturday £195·45. Calculate: (*a*) his total takings; (*b*) his output tax; (*c*) his net-of-tax takings.

3. A small businessman is supplied with goods valued at £780 in a given tax period. This figure is increased by 8 per cent VAT. His sales during the same period totalled £1,760, according to his till rolls, and this figure included VAT at 8 per cent charged to customers. Calculate the tax payable to Customs and Excise.

4. A grocer only deals in goods charged at the zero rate, but pays VAT on many items supplied to him. During the tax period (July–September, 19..) he pays tax on goods supplied to him worth £4,800, net of tax. What sum will pass between the Grocer and the Customs and Excise in respect of this transaction and who will pay whom? VAT rate 8 per cent.

5. A professional man is told by the Customs and Excise authorities that his profession is exempt from VAT. What are the likely effects of this upon him? In your answer mention the following matters: (*a*) Charges to be made for VAT to his customers; (*b*) registration on form VAT 1; (*c*) charges made to him by his suppliers.

INDEX